ISTANBUL

By Lale Surmen Aran & Tankut Aran

CONTENTS

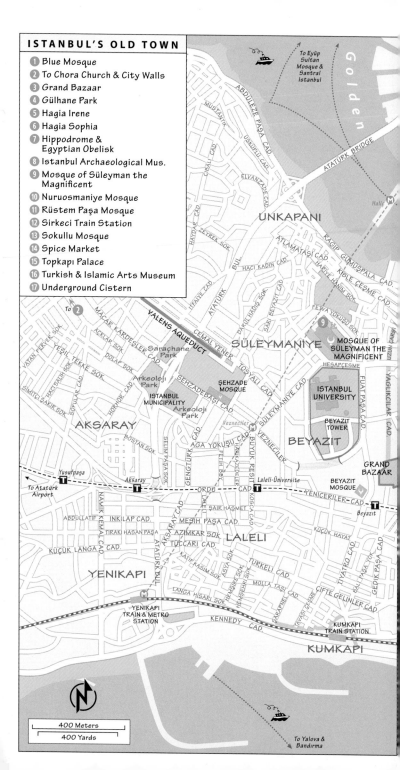

ISTANBUL'S OLD TOWN

1. Blue Mosque
2. To Chora Church & City Walls
3. Grand Bazaar
4. Gülhane Park
5. Hagia Irene
6. Hagia Sophia
7. Hippodrome & Egyptian Obelisk
8. Istanbul Archaeological Mus.
9. Mosque of Süleyman the Magnificent
10. Nuruosmaniye Mosque
11. Rüstem Paşa Mosque
12. Sirkeci Train Station
13. Sokullu Mosque
14. Spice Market
15. Topkapı Palace
16. Turkish & Islamic Arts Museum
17. Underground Cistern

400 Meters
400 Yards

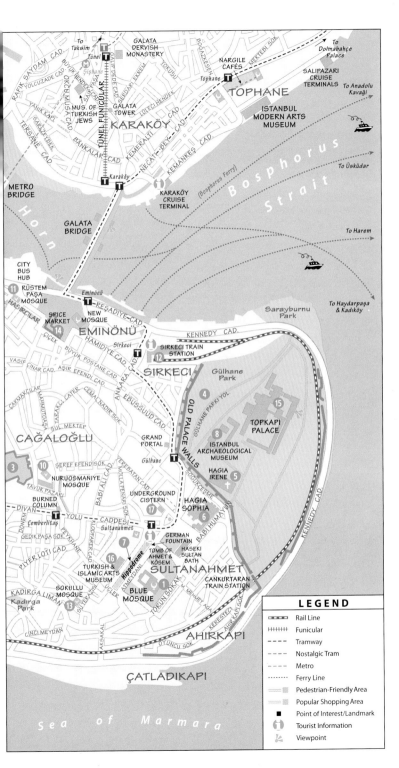

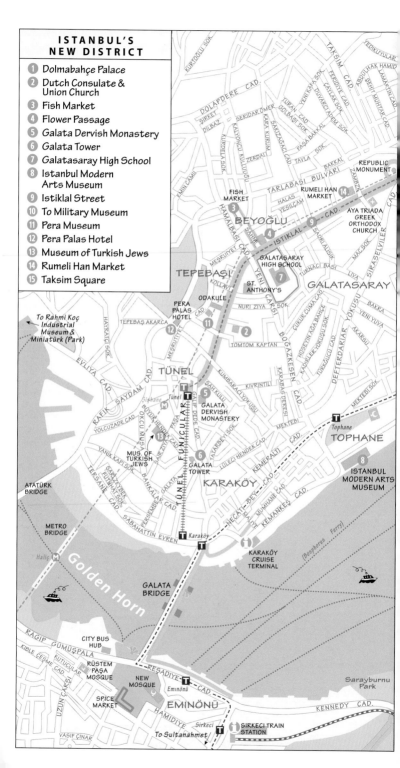

ISTANBUL'S NEW DISTRICT

1. Dolmabahçe Palace
2. Dutch Consulate & Union Church
3. Fish Market
4. Flower Passage
5. Galata Dervish Monastery
6. Galata Tower
7. Galatasaray High School
8. Istanbul Modern Arts Museum
9. Istiklal Street
10. To Military Museum
11. Pera Museum
12. Pera Palas Hotel
13. Museum of Turkish Jews
14. Rumeli Han Market
15. Taksim Square

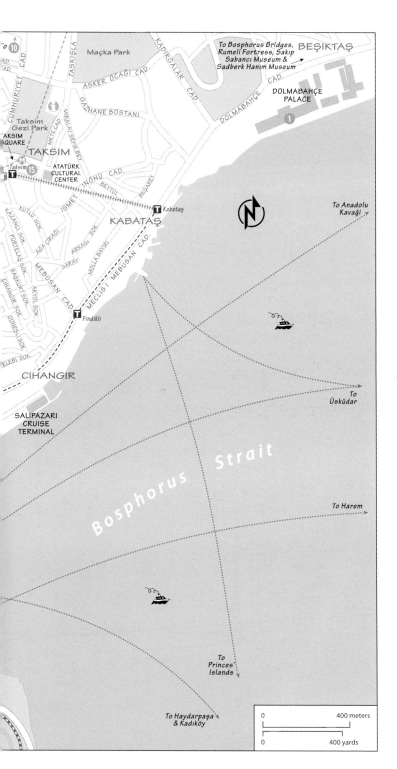

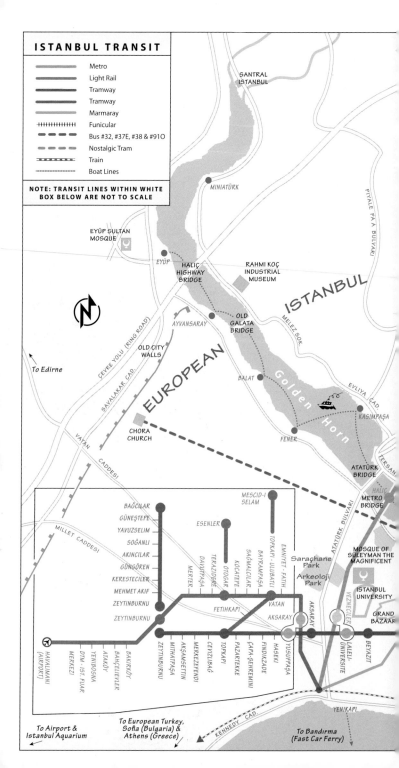

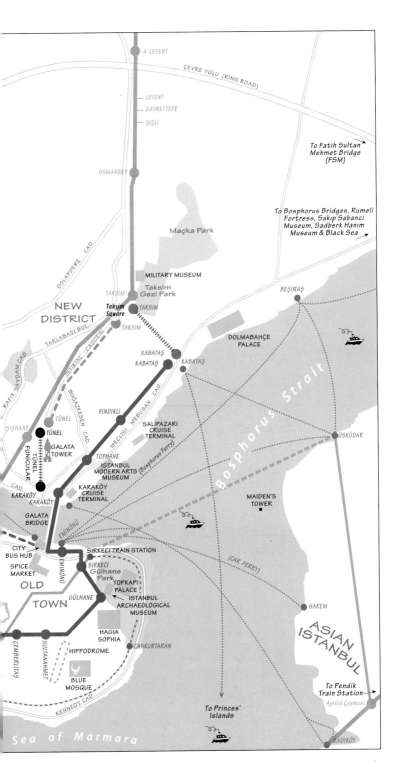

Spice Market in Old Town

The Bosphorus Strait / Süleyman Mosque

Traditional Turkish tea

Grand Bazaar vendor

Topkapı Palace

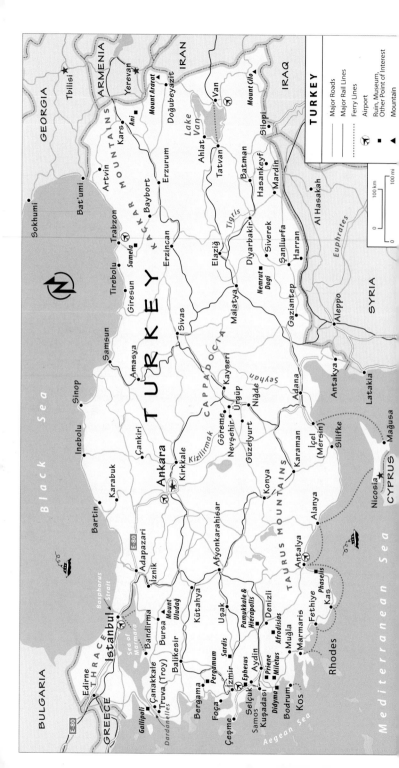

ISTANBUL

INTRODUCTION

Walk in the footsteps of Roman emperors and Ottoman sultans. Explore some of the world's greatest monuments, their names etched in history: Hagia Sophia, the Blue Mosque, Topkapı Palace. Bargain-hunt your way through a twisted warren of lanes in the Grand Bazaar—the world's oldest shopping mall—pausing to sip tea with a merchant. Set sail on the Golden Horn, and take in a spine-tingling skyline bristling with minarets. Inhale the apple-flavored smoke from a water pipe as you listen to the strains of exotic music. And enjoy meeting some of the planet's friendliest people, whether you're chatting with a fisherman on a bustling bridge, haggling for a carpet, learning about Islam from a peace-loving Muslim, or playing backgammon with a grizzled old Turk.

Istanbul is one of the world's great cities, period. For millennia, this point where Europe meets Asia has been the crossroads of civilization. Few places on earth have seen more history than this sprawling metropolis on the Bosphorus. Once called Byzantium, then Constantinople, Istanbul boasts the opulent trappings of an epic past—from the Byzantine emperors and the Ottoman sultans of distant ages, to the modern Republic-builders and "Eurocrats" of our own time. And, as the biggest city of a moderate Muslim nation, Istanbul also offers the inquisitive traveler a unique opportunity to grapple with the rich and inspiring Islamic faith: Hear the eerie wail of the call to prayer echo across the rooftops, poke into a neighborhood mosque, and watch a dervish whirl in prayer.

Turkey has long been the most exciting and inviting cultural detour from Europe. With their membership in NATO and "guest workers" spread across Europe, the Turks are more Western-facing and welcoming than ever. Now's the time to visit.

INTRODUCTION

Map Legend

∠ Viewpoint	✈ Airport	) (Tunnel
↑ Entrance	Ⓣ Taxi Stand	Pedestrian Zone
❶ Tourist Info	▯ Tram Stop	------ Railway
ᴡᴄ Restroom	Ⓑ Bus Stop	.... Ferry/Boat Route
ᴍ Castle	ᴘ Parking	├—┼—┤ Tram
⌂ Church	)⟮ Mtn. Pass	⊞⊞⊞ Stairs
☒ Mosque	Park	∙ ∙ ∙ ∙ ∙ Walk/Tour Route
▪ Statue/Point of Interest		------ Trail

Use this legend to help you navigate the maps in this book.

ABOUT THIS BOOK

Rick Steves Istanbul is a personal tour guide in your pocket. Better yet, it's actually two tour guides in your pocket: The authors of this book are Lale Surmen Aran and Tankut Aran, who have been guiding Rick Steves' tours in Turkey for more than a decade. As Turkish natives and residents of Istanbul, Lale and Tankut give you an insightful, knowledgeable look at this exciting and complex destination. While Rick is not a co-author, he is committed to the quality of this book and has personally visited nearly every recommended sight.

In this book, you'll find the following chapters:

Orientation to Istanbul has specifics on public transportation, helpful hints, local tour options, easy-to-read maps, and tourist information. The "Planning Your Time" section suggests a schedule for how to best use your limited time.

Sights in Istanbul describes the top attractions and includes their cost and hours.

Experiences in Istanbul prepares you to dive into Turkish culture, whether visiting a mosque or a Turkish bath, sipping Turkish coffee, trying a water pipe *(nargile)*, or playing backgammon.

The **Self-Guided Walks** and **Tours** cover Istanbul's most intriguing neighborhoods and sights: the historic core of the city, Hagia Sophia, Topkapı Palace, the Istanbul Archaeological Museum, the Turkish and Islamic Arts Museum, the back streets of the Old Town, the Grand Bazaar, the Mosque of Süleyman the Magnificent, the Golden Horn, the New District, the Chora Church, and the City Walls. And to help you see more than Istanbul, we've narrated a cruise along the Bosphorus Strait.

Sleeping in Istanbul describes our favorite accommodations, from good-value deals to cushy splurges.

Eating in Istanbul serves up a buffet of options, from inexpensive kebab stops to elegant seafood restaurants.

INTRODUCTION

Key to This Book

Updates

This book is updated regularly, but things change—especially in Istanbul. For the latest, visit www.ricksteves.com/update.

Abbreviations and Times

We use the following symbols and abbreviations in this book:

Sights are rated:

▲▲▲	**Don't miss**
▲▲	**Try hard to see**
▲	**Worthwhile if you can make it**
No rating	**Worth knowing about**

Tourist information offices are abbreviated as **TI,** and bathrooms are **WC**s. To categorize accommodations, we use a **Sleep Code** (described on page 303).

Like Turkey, this book uses the **24-hour clock.** It's the same through 12:00 noon, then keeps going: 13:00, 14:00, and so on. For anything over 12, subtract 12 and add p.m. (14:00 is 2:00 p.m.).

When giving **opening times,** we include both peak season and off-season hours if they differ. So, if a museum is listed as "May-Oct daily 9:00-16:00," it should be open from 9 a.m. until 4 p.m. from the first day of May until the last day of October (but expect exceptions).

A symbol in a sight listing means that the sight is described in greater detail elsewhere—either with its own self-guided tour, or as part of a self-guided walk.

For **transit** or **tour departures,** we first list the frequency, then the duration. So, a train connection listed as "2/hour, 1.5 hours" departs twice each hour and the journey lasts an hour and a half.

Shopping in Istanbul gives you tips for shopping painlessly and enjoyably, without letting it overwhelm your vacation or ruin your budget. Read up on Istanbul's great marketplaces, where you can find textiles, tiles, ceramics, jewelry, and (of course) carpets.

Entertainment in Istanbul is your guide to events, low-key evening fun, and lively nightlife.

Istanbul Connections lays the groundwork for your smooth arrival and departure (with detailed information on Atatürk Airport and Istanbul's train stations).

The **Turkish History and Culture** chapter introduces you to some of the key people and events in this nation's complicated past, making your sightseeing more meaningful. The language tips and glossary of terms will come in handy.

The **Understanding Islam** chapter covers the basics of one of the world's most widely practiced religions.

Practicalities is a traveler's tool kit, with our best advice about money, sightseeing, sleeping, eating, and staying connected.

The **appendix** has the nuts-and-bolts: useful phone numbers and websites, a holidays and festival list, recommended books and films, a climate chart, a handy packing checklist, and Turkish survival phrases.

Browse through this book and select your favorite sights. Then have a great trip! Traveling like a temporary local, you'll enjoy the absolute most of every mile, minute, and dollar. As you visit places we know and love, we're happy that you'll be meeting our favorite Turkish people.

Planning

This section will help you get started planning your trip—with advice on trip costs, when to go, and what you should know before you take off.

TRAVEL SMART

Your trip to Istanbul is like a complex play—it's easier to follow and really appreciate on a second viewing. While no one does the same trip twice to gain that advantage, reading this book in its entirety before your trip accomplishes much the same thing.

Design an itinerary that enables you to visit sights at the best possible times. Note festivals, holidays, specifics on sights, and days when sights are closed. If you have only a few days for Istanbul, keep in mind that most of the city's museums are closed on Monday, and the Grand Bazaar is closed on Sunday. For a daily look at what's open, see the "Daily Reminder" sidebar in the Orientation to Istanbul chapter. To connect the dots smoothly, read the tips in the Practicalities chapter on taking trams, subways, ferries, and buses. Designing a smart trip is a fun, doable, and worthwhile challenge.

Make your itinerary a mix of intense and relaxed stretches. Every trip—and every traveler—needs slack time (laundry, picnics, people-watching, and so on). Pace yourself. Assume you will return.

Even with the best-planned itinerary, you'll need to be flexible. Update your plans as you travel. Get online or call ahead to double-check tourist information, learn the latest on sights (special events, tour schedules, and so on), book tickets and

tours, make reservations, reconfirm hotels, and research transportation connections.

Enjoy the friendliness of the Turkish people. Connect with the culture. Set up your own quest for the best mosque, kebab, or Turkish coffee. Slow down and be open to unexpected experiences. Ask questions—most locals are eager to point you in their idea of the right direction. Keep a notepad in your pocket for noting directions, organizing your thoughts, and confirming prices. Wear your money belt, learn the currency, and figure out how to estimate prices in dollars. Those who expect to travel smart, do.

TRIP COSTS

Five components make up your trip costs: airfare, surface transportation, room and board, sightseeing and entertainment, and shopping and miscellany.

Airfare: A basic round-trip flight from the US to Istanbul can cost, on average, $1,000-2,000 total, depending on where you fly from and when (cheaper in winter). If Istanbul is part of a longer trip, consider saving time and money by flying into one city and out of another; for instance, into Istanbul and out of Athens. Overall, Kayak.com is the best place to start searching for flights on a combination of mainstream and budget carriers.

Surface Transportation: You'll spend most of your time in Istanbul doing your sightseeing on foot, because distances between most attractions are short. You can reach far-flung sights with Istanbul's affordable trams, light rail, funicular, Metro, ferries, and buses. Allow $15-20 per person per week for public transportation (each individual trip costs a little more than a dollar). It's cheap to treat yourself to a cab—$10-20 will cover the cost of connecting virtually any two sights listed in this book. From Atatürk International Airport (code: IST), a taxi ride to your hotel in the Old Town or New District will total about $15-25 (some hotels offer free airport transfers if you stay three nights). From Sabiha Gökçen Airport (code: SAW) on the Asian side of Istanbul, a taxi ride to Old Town or the Taksim area will cost around $40.

Room and Board: You can thrive in Istanbul on $135 a day per person for room and board. This allows $15 for lunch, $25 for dinner, and $95 for lodging (based on two people splitting the cost of a $190 double room that includes breakfast). Students and tightwads can enjoy Istanbul for as little as $60 a day ($30 for a bed, $30 for meals and snacks).

Sightseeing and Entertainment: Some attractions, such as mosques and markets, are free. At museums and sights, fees range from $5 to $20. Figure an average of $10 per major sight (Hagia Sophia-$10; Topkapı Palace-$10, or $15 to also see the Harem) and $3-7 for minor ones. Concerts can run as low as $15; for less than

Merhaba (Hello) from Rick Steves

I love Istanbul. When I was in my 20s, I finished six or seven trips in a row with a visit here. I didn't plan to...it was just the subcon-scious cherry on top of every Euro-pean adventure. And since before the first Gulf War, my company has been taking tour groups to Istanbul, turn-ing people on to one of this planet's most exciting cities. Today, a visit to Istanbul is more important than ever: It's a city that's 99 percent Muslim, and still welcoming to outsiders and eager to connect with the West. I am personally committed to the notion that without visiting a place such as  Istanbul, we cannot hope to understand the dynamics of a faith and a region that will be in our headlines for the foreseeable fu-ture.

In short, Istanbul is an essential destination that certainly merits a top-notch guidebook. And, selfishly, I'd love to write that guidebook. But you deserve the expertise of locals to guide you through this rich, complex, and fast-changing metropolis.

I've worked with this book's authors, Lale Surmen Aran and Tankut Aran, for more than a decade as tour guides. I believe they know their hometown better than any non-Turk ever could. And, after a lifetime of tour guiding, they relate well to Americans and understand their needs and concerns. They know how to present their city in a way that's inspiring rather than tiring.

$30, you can see dervishes whirl. An overall average of $40 a day works for most people. Don't skimp here. After all, this category is the driving force behind your trip—you came to sightsee, enjoy, and experience Istanbul.

Shopping and Miscellany: Figure $1-2 per ice-cream cone, coffee, and soft drink. Shopping can vary in cost from nearly noth-ing to a small fortune. Good budget travelers find that this category has little to do with assembling a trip full of lifelong memories.

WHEN TO GO

Istanbul has a moderate climate year-round. It is generally hot and humid from mid-July to mid-August, and it can snow during Janu-ary and February. The peak-season months (with the best weather) are from mid-April to June and September to October. During the off-season, you can generally find better deals and smaller crowds, the weather is usually good, and all the sights are open. Weather conditions can change throughout the day—especially in spring and fall—but extremes are rare. Summer temperatures generally

A while ago, Lale and Tankut told me of their powerful desire to share Istanbul with more Americans than can squeeze into their tour buses. I knew they were right. And so, you hold in your hands the first "Rick Steves" book that I didn't actually author. It was a big step for me, and not one I took lightly—I know that people who enjoy my guidebooks have high expectations. But because of Lale and Tankut's fine work and deep knowledge, I was confident they would do a good job of writing a book that would be an invaluable tool for my traveling readers. They did and it is.

Before the first edition was printed, Cameron Hewitt (co-author of my *Eastern Europe, Croatia & Slovenia,* and *Budapest* guidebooks) traveled to Istanbul from our office with Lale and Tan's work and shaped it to my readers' unique needs. And for the next edition, I spent a busy week in Istanbul, giving the guidebook a thorough shakedown and visiting nearly every covered sight.

I came home from that trip thankful for Lale and Tankut's passion for sharing their city with our readers, appreciative of Cameron's expert editing, satisfied that we have produced the best book available on Istanbul, and newly enthused about what is one of the world's most vibrant and fascinating cultural capitals.

I hope this guidebook helps you have the time of your life exploring Istanbul.

Happy travels,

range from 65 to 85 degrees Fahrenheit (42-60 degrees in winter). Temperatures below freezing and above 90 degrees make headlines. For more information, refer to the climate chart in the appendix; for daily weather throughout Turkey, go to www.meteor.gov.tr.

Keep in mind that prices in Istanbul are higher during festivals and holidays such as Easter, Christmas, and New Year's. On holidays, you'll see lots of vacationing Europeans, mostly from Spain, Italy, and France.

KNOW BEFORE YOU GO

Check this list of things to arrange while you're still at home.

You need a **passport** and a **visa,** but no shots, to travel in Turkey. You must buy your visa before you enter Turkey (online or at an embassy or consulate; see page 387). You may be denied entry into certain European countries if your passport is due to expire within three months of your ticketed date of return. Get it renewed if you'll be cutting it close. It can take up to six weeks to get or

Rick Steves Audio Europe

The **Rick Steves Audio Europe app** makes it easy to download audio content to enhance your trip. This includes Rick's audio tours of many of Europe's top destinations, as well as a far-reaching library of insightful travel interviews from my public radio show with experts from around the globe—including many of the places in this book. The app and all of its content are entirely free. You can download Rick Steves Audio Europe via Apple's App Store, Google Play, or the Amazon Appstore. For more information, see www.ricksteves.com/audioeurope.

renew a passport (for more on passports, see www.travel.state.gov). You are required to have proof of identity with you at all times in Istanbul, and may be asked to show your passport when entering sights or using a credit card. Pack a photocopy of your passport in your luggage in case the original is lost or stolen.

Book rooms well in advance, if you'll be traveling during peak season (mid-April-June and Sept-Oct) or any major holidays or festivals (see page 424).

Call your **debit- and credit-card companies** to let them know the countries you'll be visiting, to ask about fees, request your PIN code (it will be mailed to you), and more. See page 389 for details.

Do your homework if you want to buy **travel insurance.** Compare the cost of the insurance to the cost of your potential loss. Also, check whether your existing insurance (health, homeowners, or renters) covers you and your possessions overseas. For more tips, see www.ricksteves.com/insurance.

If you plan to hire a **local guide,** reserve ahead by email. Popular guides can get booked up.

If you're bringing a **mobile device,** consider signing up for an international plan for cheaper calls, texts, and data (see page 412). Download any apps you might want to use on the road, such as translators, maps, transit schedules, and **Rick Steves Audio Europe** (see sidebar, above).

Traveling as a Temporary Local

We travel all the way to Turkey to enjoy differences—to become temporary locals. You'll experience frustrations. Certain truths that we find "God-given" or "self-evident," such as cold beer, ice in drinks, bottomless cups of coffee, "the customer is king," and bigger being better, are suddenly not so true. One of the benefits

How Was Your Trip?

Were your travels fun, smooth, and meaningful? If you'd like to share your tips, concerns, and discoveries, please fill out the survey at www.ricksteves.com/feedback. To check out readers' hotel and restaurant reviews—or leave one yourself—visit our travel forum at www.ricksteves.com/travel-forum. We value your feedback. Thanks in advance.

of travel is the eye-opening realization that there are logical, civil, and even better alternatives. A willingness to go local ensures that you'll enjoy a full dose of Turkish hospitality.

The Turkish people (and most Europeans) generally like Americans. But if there is a negative aspect to the Turks' image of Americans, it's that we are loud, wasteful, ethnocentric, too informal (which can seem disrespectful), and a bit naive.

While the Turks look bemusedly at some Yankee excesses—and worriedly at others—they nearly always afford individual travelers all the warmth they deserve.

Judging from all the happy feedback we receive from travelers who have used this book, it's safe to assume you'll enjoy a great, affordable vacation—with the finesse of an independent, experienced traveler.

Thanks, and happy travels!

Rick Steves

Back Door Travel Philosophy

From *Rick Steves Europe Through the Back Door*

Travel is intensified living—maximum thrills per minute and one of the last great sources of legal adventure. Travel is freedom. It's recess, and we need it.

Experiencing the real Europe requires catching it by surprise, going casual..."through the Back Door."

Affording travel is a matter of priorities. (Make do with the old car.) You can eat and sleep—simply, safely, and comfortably—anywhere in Europe for $100 a day plus transportation costs. In many ways, spending more money only builds a thicker wall between you and what you traveled so far to see. Europe is a cultural carnival, and time after time, you'll find that its best acts are free and the best seats are the cheap ones.

A tight budget forces you to travel close to the ground, meeting and communicating with the people. Never sacrifice sleep, nutrition, safety, or cleanliness to save money. Simply enjoy the local-style alternatives to expensive hotels and restaurants.

Connecting with people carbonates your experience. Extroverts have more fun. If your trip is low on magic moments, kick yourself and make things happen. If you don't enjoy a place, maybe you don't know enough about it. Seek the truth. Recognize tourist traps. Give a culture the benefit of your open mind. See things as different, but not better or worse. Any culture has plenty to share. When an opportunity presents itself, make it a habit to say "yes."

Of course, travel, like the world, is a series of hills and valleys. Be fanatically positive and militantly optimistic. If something's not to your liking, change your liking.

Travel can make you a happier American, as well as a citizen of the world. Our Earth is home to seven billion equally precious people. It's humbling to travel and find that people don't have the "American Dream"—they have their own dreams. Europeans like us, but with all due respect, they wouldn't trade passports.

Thoughtful travel engages us with the world. It reminds us what is truly important. By broadening perspectives, travel teaches new ways to measure quality of life.

Globe-trotting destroys ethnocentricity, helping us understand and appreciate other cultures. Rather than fear the diversity on this planet, celebrate it. Among your most prized souvenirs will be the strands of different cultures you choose to knit into your own character. The world is a cultural yarn shop, and Back Door travelers are weaving the ultimate tapestry. Join in!

ORIENTATION TO ISTANBUL

Istanbul is the crossroads of civilizations, where Europe meets Asia, and where West meets East. Truly one of the world's great historic cities, Istanbul was once called Constantinople, named for the fourth-century Roman Emperor Constantine the Great. Over the centuries, the city has been the capital of two grand empires. The Byzantine Empire was born here in the fourth century A.D. and lasted until the 15th century, when the Ottoman Empire took over, ruling through the end of World War I. Even though Turkey isn't actually governed from Istanbul (Ankara, in the east, is the official capital), the city remains the historical, cultural, and financial center of the country.

ISTANBUL: A VERBAL MAP

Istanbul, with almost 15 million people, sprawls over an enormous area on both banks of the **Bosphorus Strait** (Boğaziçi). The

Bosphorus runs north to south (from the Black Sea to the Sea of Marmara) through the middle of Istanbul, splitting the city in half and causing it to straddle two continents: Asia and Europe. Asian Istanbul (east of the Bosphorus) is mostly residential, while European Istanbul (west of the Bosphorus) is densely urban and contains virtually all of the city's main attractions. Two suspension bridges—the Bosphorus Bridge and the Fatih Sultan Mehmet Bridge—span the Bosphorus Strait, connecting the two halves, and a third should open in 2016. A rail tunnel now connects the two sides, and a second tunnel is

under construction for cars and trucks. Public ferries also link the banks, carrying millions of commuters each day.

A tapering inlet of the Bosphorus, called the **Golden Horn** (Haliç), runs roughly east to west, slicing through the middle of European Istanbul.

South of the Golden Horn is a peninsula known as the **Old Town**—the 3,000-year-old historical core of the city, surrounded by fragments of the original Byzantine wall. Near the tip of the Old Town peninsula is a compact and welcoming district called Sultanahmet, home to many of the city's most famous sights (Hagia Sophia, Blue Mosque, Topkapı Palace) and its highest concentration of hotels.

North of the Golden Horn is the modern, westward-looking, European-feeling **New District** (called "Pera" or "Beyoğlu" by locals), centered on Taksim Square and bisected by the main pedestrian drag called İstiklal Caddesi (which we'll refer to as İstiklal Street). The New District offers some interesting sights, good hotels and restaurants, and a 21st-century contrast to the Old Town.

Unlike many other European cities, Istanbul doesn't branch out from a main Town Hall or central square. In many parts of town, you may get lost if you're searching for a predictable, European-style square. (The Turkish word for "square"—*meydanı*—actually means something more like "area.") Instead, Istanbul is a cobbled-together collection of various landmarks and patches of land, all interconnected by twisty alleys. Sightseeing this decentralized, seemingly disorganized city can be intimidating for first-time visitors. But even though the city is an enormous metropolis, the tourist's Istanbul is compact and walkable, and an impressive public-transportation network efficiently connects the major sightseeing zones.

ORIENTATION

PLANNING YOUR TIME

Istanbul demands a minimum of two days, but we'd suggest at least four days to do it justice. Even with a week, you'd find yourself running out of time trying to tackle everything the city has to offer.

Istanbul in Two Days

On the morning of Day One, focus on the Sultanahmet district in the center of the Old Town. Take our self-guided Historic Core of Istanbul Walk to get your bearings, visiting Hagia Sophia, the Underground Cistern, and the Blue Mosque. With additional time, tour Topkapı Palace (time-consuming sultans' complex a short walk away) or the Turkish and Islamic Arts Museum (small collection in the heart of Sultanahmet).

On Day Two, follow the self-guided Old Town Back Streets Walk—including tours of the Grand Bazaar, Mosque of Süleyman the Magnificent, and Spice Market. You'll finish near the Galata Bridge, where you can end your day with the self-guided Golden Horn Walk.

Day Three

If you haven't done so already, tour Topkapı Palace and the nearby Istanbul Archaeological Museum. Or, if you're museumed out, consider Day Four's New District activities.

Day Four

Devote this day to the New District, following our self-guided walk (including the Pera Museum and Galata Tower). Then, take a taxi to the Chora Church to see its sumptuous Byzantine mosaics, and consider following the self-guided City Walls and Neighborhoods Walk, which starts nearby. Or, if you'd rather stay in the New District, choose from a range of other sights:

Dolmabahçe Palace, Military Museum, Quincentennial Museum of Turkish Jews, or Istanbul Modern Arts Museum.

Day Five

Go to Asia. Set sail on the Bosphorus Strait, spending a full day going up to the Asian fishing village of Anadolu Kavağı, then returning to the Old Town.

Istanbul in a Week

More time gives you more options, from some of the smaller museums to quintessential Istanbul experiences, such as getting scrubbed in a Turkish bath, watching Whirling Dervishes spin themselves into a trance, or lazily smoking a water pipe *(nargile)* filled with apple tobacco.

Istanbul Overview

TOURIST INFORMATION

Istanbul's state-run tourist offices, abbreviated as **TI** in this book (and marked with an *i* sign in Istanbul), are often not the best sources of information. They suffer from long lines, offer little or no information, and usually have only colorful promotional booklets, brochures, and maps. The only reason to visit one is to pick up the good, free city map. The TI staff, many of whom are not fluent in English, will try to help you with your requests, likely with mixed results.

Tourist Offices

If you must visit a tourist office, here are some handy locations. The first two are in the Old Town, the third and fourth are in the New District, and the last two are at the airports (all have sporadic hours; generally daily 9:00-17:00):

• In the **Sultanahmet** neighborhood, in the center of the Old Town (Divan Yolu Caddesi 3, at the bottom of the square called the Hippodrome, next to the tram tracks, tel. 0212/518-8754).

• At the **Sirkeci** train station, near the Golden Horn in the Old Town's Eminönü district (by the station entrance, in the left corner next to a ticket booth, tel. 0212/511-5888).

• Near **Taksim Square** in the New District (Mete Caddesi 6, a short walk from the square, tel. 0212/233-0592).

• At **Karaköy,** the cruise ship port, located where the Golden Horn and Bosphorus meet—rarely open (Kemankeş Caddesi, inside the passenger terminal, tel. 0212/249-5776).

• At **Atatürk Airport,** Istanbul's main airport, nine miles outside the city center (at the International Arrivals desk inside the terminal, tel. 0212/465-3151).

Daily Reminder

Open Every Day: Hagia Sophia, the Underground Cistern, Bosphorus cruise boats, Galata Tower, Miniatürk, and most Turkish baths welcome tourists daily. Mosques are open daily, but close to tourists five times each day, when worshippers come to pray. The closure lasts from about 30 minutes before the service begins until after it ends (services last 15-30 minutes). Specific prayer times change daily and are listed in local newspapers, or you can ask your hotelier. For tips on visiting a mosque, see page 62.

Sunday: The Grand Bazaar is closed. The Rahmi Koç Industrial Museum stays open until 19:00 (April-Sept).

Monday: Most of Istanbul's museums are closed today, including those operated by the Ministry of Culture—such as the Istanbul Archaeological Museum and the Turkish and Islamic Arts Museum. The Dolmabahçe Palace, Galata Dervish Monastery, Military Museum, Istanbul Modern Arts Museum, Pera Museum, Sakıp Sabancı Museum, and Rahmi Koç Industrial Museum are also closed. Topkapı Palace and Hagia Sophia are open.

Tuesday: Topkapı Palace, Hagia Irene, and the Military Museum are closed.

Wednesday: Closed sights include the Chora Church, Rumeli Fortress, and Sadberk Hanım Museum. The Sakıp Sabancı Museum is free today and open until 20:00. Because Topkapı Palace is closed on Tuesday, it may be especially crowded first thing this morning.

Thursday: All sights are open except for Dolmabahçe Palace. The Istanbul Modern Arts Museum is open until 20:00.

Friday: The Blue Mosque is closed until the end of the Friday noon service. All other mosques are closed during this important service, and very crowded before and after.

Saturday: Everything is open except the Quincentennial Museum of Turkish Jews. The Rahmi Koç Industrial Museum is open until 19:00 (April-Sept).

Ramadan: During the Muslim holy month (June 6-July 4 in 2016, May 27-June 24 in 2017), a big, convivial, multigenerational festival breaks out each evening at sunset (ask for time locally). The Hippodrome square is most convenient for most visitors. There's hardly a tourist in sight as the fun builds, the sun sets, the call to prayer rings out, people eat, and the party starts. For more information, see page 64.

Religious Holidays: The Grand Bazaar and the Spice Market are closed during religious festivals. Museum hours are also readjusted for the first day of religious holidays: Most museums are closed in the morning, and a few close the entire day.

ORIENTATION

Istanbul Essentials

English	Turkish	Pronounced
Blue Mosque	Sultanahmet Camii	sool-tah-nah-meht jah-mee
Bosphorus Strait	Boğaziçi	boh-ahz-ee-chee
Burned Column (and major tram stop)	Çemberlitaş	chehm-behr-lee-tahsh
Chora Church	Kariye Müzesi	kah-ree-yeh mew-zeh-see
Divan Yolu (main street in Old Town)	Divan Yolu	dee-vahn yoh-loo
Galata Bridge	Galata Köprüsü	gah-lah-tah kohp-rew-sew
Galata Dervish Monastery	Galata Mevlevihanesi	gah-lah-tah mehv-leh-vee-hah-neh-see
Galata Tower	Galata Kulesi	gah-lah-tah koo-leh-see
Golden Horn (inlet between Old Town and New District)	Haliç	hah-leech
Grand Bazaar	Kapalı Çarşı	kah-pah-luh chahr-shuh
Gülhane Park	Gülhane Parkı	gewl-hah-neh pahr-kuh
Hagia Sophia (church-and-mosque museum)	Aya Sofya	eye-ah soh-fee-yah

• At **Sabiha Gökçen Airport**, the city's alternate airport on the Asian side (at the International Arrivals terminal, tel. 0216/588-8794).

More Resources

For current information on cultural activities, entertainment options, shopping ideas, and classy restaurants, pick up *The Guide*, a magazine published every two months and written by Turks and expats (10 TL). You can find it at bigger newspaper stands and major bookstores on İstiklal Street in the New District.

The English edition of the monthly *Time Out Istanbul* magazine lists sights, hotels, restaurants, nightclubs, and more (6 TL, sold at most Istanbul newsstands, www.timeoutistanbul.com).

Hürriyet is one of the popular daily national papers. Its online English version, called the Hürriyet Daily News, makes for good

Hippodrome (ancient chariot race track)	*Hipodrom*	hee-poh-drohm
Historic Core of the Old Town	*Sultanahmet*	sool-tah-nah-meht
İstiklal Street (main street in New District)	*İstiklal Caddesi*	ees-teek-lahl jahd-deh-see
Mosque of Süleyman the Magnificent	*Süleymaniye Camii*	sew-lay-mah-nee-yeh jah-mee
New District	*Pera, Beyoğlu*	peh-rah, bay-yoh-loo
Rüstem Paşa Mosque	*Rüstem Paşa Camii*	rew-stehm pah-shah jah-mee
Sirkeci Train Station	*Sirkeci Tren Garı*	seer-keh-jee trehn gah-ruh
Spice Market	*Mısır Çarşışı*	muh-suhr chahr-shuh-shuh
Süleymaniye Neighborhood	*Süleymaniye*	sew-lay-mah-nee-yeh
Taksim Square (heart of New District)	*Taksim Meydanı*	tahk-seem may-dah-nuh
Topkapı Palace	*Topkapı Sarayı*	tohp-kah-puh sah-rah-yuh
Tünel (old-fashioned funicular in New District)	*Tünel*	tew-nehl
Underground Cistern	*Yerebatan Sarayı*	yeh-reh-bah-tahn sah-rah-yuh

pre-trip reading, with its local and often anti-government perspective on headline news (www.hurriyetdailynews.com).

ARRIVAL IN ISTANBUL

For a rundown of Istanbul's train stations and airports, see the Istanbul Connections chapter.

HELPFUL HINTS
Health Concerns

Don't Drink the Water: Drinking Istanbul's tap water can make you sick. While some hardy travelers do brush their teeth with tap water (being careful not to swallow), it's safer to brush your teeth with bottled water. Avoid getting tap water in your mouth while showering, shaving, and so on. Any bottled or canned drinks are fine. Most restaurants sell cheap little plastic cups of safe water with peel-off tops. Tea and coffee are usually made with bottled or filtered water. At better restaurants, produce is washed with safe, filtered water. At cheaper restaurants, choose cooked food instead of raw.

Dealing with Diarrhea: No matter how careful you are, you might get a touch of "Istanbul intestines." Don't panic, revise your diet, and take it easy for 24 hours. For a day or so, eat very bland food (bread, rice, applesauce, boiled potatoes, clear soup, toast, weak tea). Keep telling yourself that tomorrow you'll feel much better, because you probably will. If loose stools persist, drink lots of water to replenish lost liquids. Don't take anti-diarrheal medications if you have blood in your stools or a fever greater than 101°F (38°C)—you need a doctor's exam and antibiotics. A child (especially an infant) who suffers a prolonged case of diarrhea also needs prompt medical attention.

Pharmacies: Pharmacies (*eczane;* edge-zah-neh) are generally open Monday through Saturday (9:00-19:00) and closed Sunday. In every neighborhood, one pharmacy stays open late and on holidays for emergencies. These *nöbetçi eczane* (noh-bet-chee edge-zah-neh; "pharmacy on duty") are generally within walking distance or a short cab ride from wherever you are. Just ask your hotelier for help. Or, if you're on your own, the location of the nearest *nöbetçi eczane* is posted by the entrance to any pharmacy. When interpreting signs, note these translations: *bu gece* (tonight), *Pazar* (Sunday), and *gün/günü* (day). As in the rest of Europe, dates are listed day first, then month (e.g., 06/04 is April 6).

Medical Problems: Istanbul's hospitals *(hastane)* usually have 24-hour emergency care centers (*acil servis;* "emergency service"), but are short on English-speaking personnel. Unless you need to be rushed to the nearest hospital, go to a private facility with English-speaking staff. The **American Hospital** in the New District is a good option (Valikonağı Caddesi, Güzelbahçe Sokak 20, Nişantaşı, tel. 444-3777—dial ext. 9 for English, then 1 for ambulance services). **Med-line** has medical assistance and ambulance service (tel. 444-1212). The **International Hospital** is close to the airport (Istanbul Caddesi 82, Yeşilköy, tel. 0212/468-4444; for an ambulance call 444-9724).

Street Smarts

Theft Alert: In Turkey, travelers are rarely mugged, but often pickpocketed. Thieves thrive on fresh-off-the-plane tourists. Try to keep a low profile. You'll be better off without your best clothes, expensive-looking gear, and fancy jewelry or watches. Be careful on all public transportation and in crowds. Watch for distraction tactics such as dropped coins, "accidental" spills, kids who seem to be fighting for no reason, and locals who ask you for directions.

If you're out late, avoid dark back streets or any place with dim lighting and minimal pedestrian activity. Ignore anyone who asks if you need help or a cab ride into the city. Wear a money belt, be smart with your bags, sling your daypack across your front, and keep change in buttoned or front pockets. Carry a photocopy of your passport and plane ticket in your luggage or money belt in case the original is lost or stolen. Especially valuable items are more secure left in your hotel room (and in a hotel safe, if available) rather than with you on the streets.

Advice for Women: Modesty is valued in this culture; it's best to cover your shoulders and knees, and avoid form-fitting clothes. Carry a scarf to cover your head while inside mosques as a sign of respect.

Buses and trams are very crowded, and some contact is unavoidable. But if someone tries to touch you in a deliberate way, be clear about your disapproval. Push him away and say in a loud voice, "*Çek elini*" (check eh-lee-nee; Take your hands off me).

Advice for Men: Men should consider wearing lightweight pants instead of shorts, as Turkish men generally don't sport shorts beyond the beach. When visiting mosques, it is respectful to wear clothing that covers your knees and shoulders.

Street Safety: Be extremely cautious crossing streets that lack traffic lights. Look both ways, since many streets are one-way, and be careful of seemingly quiet bus, tram, or taxi lanes. Don't assume you have the right-of-way, even in a crosswalk. When crossing a street, keep your pace constant and don't stop suddenly. Drivers calculate your speed and won't hit you, provided you don't alter your route and pace. (Don't expect them to stop for you; they probably won't.)

Although it's technically illegal, cars park on sidewalks, especially in the Old Town. These parked cars, as well as free-standing merchandise kiosks or makeshift stands, can make sidewalks difficult to navigate. Try to stay by the side of the road, and pay attention to passing cars.

Finding Addresses: When you're trying to locate a particular place, you may notice several different elements in the address. Sometimes it's as straightforward as a street name (usually with *Caddesi*—"street," or *Sokak*—"alley"), followed by a number, such as Akbıyık Caddesi 21. The address is sometimes preceded by the name of a larger street that's nearby (such as İstiklal Caddesi, Meşelik Sokak 10) to help you or your cabbie find the general location (İstiklal Caddesi) before searching

ORIENTATION

Gay- and Lesbian-Friendly Istanbul

Istanbul has a significant gay population that you'll find mainly in the neighborhoods of the New District. The gay population is hip, follows trends, and likes to hang out at classy (but not necessarily upscale) places. Several gay-friendly restaurants, cafés, clubs, and hotels are on or close to İstiklal Street and Taksim Square. You can hardly go wrong if you go to the heart of the Cihangir neighborhood (near Taksim Square and İstiklal Street) to hang out in a café. While some of these places focus on attracting gay customers, others are gay-friendly but serve a mixed clientele.

For restaurants in the New District, try **Bilsak 5. Kat** ("Bilsak 5th Floor"), the trendy **House Café** chain, or **Münferit.** Beyond the New District, **Kahvealtı** and **Mama** are two good places (all are listed in the Eating in Istanbul chapter). A classy, predominantly gay dance club is **Love Dance Point** (see page 357).

Good choices for accommodations include **Noble House Galata** (near the Galata Tower) and **House Apartments** (with modern apartments in four locations; see the end of the Sleeping in Istanbul chapter).

Lale and Tan, the authors of this book, can also refer travelers to gay-friendly tour guides and services (for contact information, see "Tours in Istanbul" at the end of this chapter; www.srmtravel.com).

for a tiny alley (Meşelik Sokak 10). And sometimes the address is followed by the name of the neighborhood it's in; for example: Şifahane Sokak 6, Süleymaniye.

Aggressive Sales Pitches: As you walk through the Old Town, you'll constantly be approached by people who greet you enthusiastically, ask if you need help, ask you where you're from, and then tell you about their cousin who just happens to live in your hometown. Before long, what began as a friendly conversation devolves into a greedy sales pitch. These salesmen—who prey on Americans' gregariousness and desire to respond politely to a friendly greeting—are irritating and can waste a lot of your valuable sightseeing time. While not dangerous, the salesmen can be particularly aggressive, or even intimidating, to single women. Just smile and say, "No, thank you!" without breaking stride...then ignore the escalating attempts to grab your attention (or elbow) as you walk past. For more on dealing with salesmen, see page 196.

Public WCs: You'll generally pay 1-2 TL to use a public WC. The İstanbulKart (see page 27) is valid in some public WCs. Carry toilet paper or tissues with you, since some WCs are poorly supplied. Use the WCs in museums (likely free and better than public WCs), or walk into any sidewalk café or American fast-food joint as if you own the place and find the WC in the back (if you find your way barred by a passcode lock, ask permission or make a small purchase).

In the heart of the Old Town, plumbing isn't always up to modern standards. Rather than flush away soiled toilet paper, locals dispose of it in a designated trash can next to the toilet. It's culturally sensitive—and sometimes essential plumbing-wise—for visitors to do the same (especially if there's a sign requesting this).

Western-style toilets are the norm nowadays, but don't be surprised if you run across an "Oriental toilet," also known as a "Turkish toilet." This squat-and-aim system is basically a porcelain hole in the ground flanked by platforms for your feet. If this seems outrageous to you, spend your squatting time pondering the fact that those of us who need a throne to sit on are in the minority; most humans sit on their haunches and nothing more.

Services

US Consulate: In case of an emergency, call for 24-hour assistance (tel. 0212/335-9000, recorded info tel. 0212/335-9200). American citizen services are available in person on a walk-in basis (Mon-Fri 7:45-16:30, closed Sat-Sun and on Turkish and American holidays, İstinye Mahallesi, Üç Şehitler Sokak 2, Istinye, roughly a 30-minute cab ride from downtown Istanbul via the Bosphorus coastal road, http://istanbul.usconsulate.gov).

Baggage Storage: Easy-to-use, computerized lockers are available in both terminals at Atatürk Airport and at the Sirkeci train station (fees vary depending on the size of your items). To store your luggage near Taksim Square, use **Bagaj,** behind the French Consulate (10 TL/day for the first item, 5 TL/day for each additional item, Şehit Muhtar Mah, Utarit Sok 4A, tel. 0212/243-1743, www.bagaj.co). Another option is getting help from your hotelier; if you're leaving Istanbul and returning later, ask your hotel staff if they can store some baggage for you.

English-Language Church: Christian services are held in English every Sunday at the **Dutch Chapel** (Union Church of Istanbul, just off İstiklal Street by the Dutch Consulate at #393, contemporary service at 9:30, traditional worship at 11:00, tel. 0212/244-5212, www.unionchurchofistanbul.org).

Updates to This Book: For the latest, see www.ricksteves.com/update.

Getting Around Istanbul

Even though Istanbul is a huge city, most of its tourist areas are easily walkable. You'll likely need public transportation only to connect sightseeing zones (for example, going from the Old Town to the New District across the Golden Horn). Istanbul has an impressively slick, modern, and user-friendly network of trams, funiculars, and Metro lines. Once you learn the system, it seems custom-made for tourists—the stops are located within a short walking distance of major attractions. Taxis, buses, and ferries round out your transportation options.

On religious festival days—when public transit may be free or discounted—buses and trams can be loaded with locals visiting their families and heading out to parks, fairs, and theaters. Streets are crowded—it's a great time for people-watching.

BY TAXI

Taxis are generally an efficient, affordable way to get around town (3.20-TL drop fee, then roughly 2 TL/kilometer; no nighttime tariff). Figure about 15-25 TL for a longer trip within the Old Town or New District (such as from Sultanahmet to the Chora Church), or about 45-65 TL between Atatürk Airport and a hotel in European Istanbul.

Taxi Tips: Scams are on the rise in Istanbul. Use only official taxis. These are painted yellow, with their license plate number, name, and home-office phone number displayed on the front doors.

If a taxi's top light is on, it's available—just wave it down. Drivers usually flash their lights when they see you waiting by the side of the road to indicate that they'll pick you up. Taxis can take up to four passengers. If you have difficulty hailing a cab off the street, ask someone where you can find a taxi stand. You can also call a taxi company, usually for no extra charge. Hotels, restaurants, museums, and even shopkeepers almost always have the phone number of a nearby taxi company—just ask.

All cabs have electronic meters and cabbies should use them. As long as the meter is on, the only way you can be cheated is if the driver takes a needlessly long route. Never go for an off-meter deal, because you'll always pay more than if you'd used the meter. To ask for the meter to be turned on, use the phrase *"taksi metre lütfen"* (tahk-see meh-treh lewt-fehn; meter, please).

ORIENTATION

Turkish Do's and Don'ts

Turkey gives Western visitors a refreshing dose of culture shock. Here are a few of the finer points to consider when interacting with your Turkish hosts:

- Don't signal to someone with your hands or your fingers, except when you're hailing a cab or trying to get your waiter's attention. In any other situation, it's considered rude.
- Don't get too close to people as you talk. Allow for plenty of personal space (an arm's length is fine). Especially when talking to someone of the opposite sex, keep your distance and don't touch them as you talk.
- Be careful with gestures: A "thumbs up" is—and means—OK. But putting your thumb between your index and middle finger and making a fist is equivalent to showing your middle finger in the US. (And you always thought Grandma was "stealing your nose.") Making a circle with your thumb and index finger while twisting your hand is a homophobic insult.
- Be aware of Turkish body language for "yes" and "no." A Turk nods her head down to say yes. She shakes it back and forth to say no, like Westerners do. But she might also say no by tilting her head back. Learn the Turkish words for "yes" (*evet*; eh-veht) and "no" (*hayır*; hah-yur) to confirm.
- If you're offered food or a gift, either keep it for yourself or politely decline. Turkish people love to share what they have, but what they offer to you is for you alone. If you invite others to share the food, you may put your Turkish friend in a difficult position (they may not have more to share). If you don't want the food or gift, don't wave it away. Do as the Turks do: Either put your right hand on your heart and say, "Thank you" (*teşekkür ederim*; teh-shehk-koor eh-deh-reem), or if it's food, pat your abdomen to indicate that you're full.
- Don't blow your nose at the dining table—either leave the table, or turn to face the other way. And afterward, don't shake hands right away. (Come to think of it, that's a rule everyone could use.)

The cabbie may claim you have to pay bogus extra charges; for example, if he claims that you owe him a 5-TL "luggage charge" for a 15-TL ride, politely refuse and pay what's on the meter.

Some cab drivers use a sleight-of-hand trick with bill denominations. For example, they'll take your 50-TL bill, then insist you gave them only a 5-TL bill (while showing you a 5-TL bill they have ready and handy for this scam). If you need to pay your fare with a big bill, announce the bill's denomination as you give it to the cabbie.

Tipping: Although some cabbies are con artists, many are honest and deserve a tip. To tip, simply round up the bill (generally 1-2 TL; for exceptional service, you could add a few liras more). If you need a receipt, ask: *"Fiş, lütfen"* (fish lewt-fehn; receipt, please).

BY PUBLIC TRANSPORTATION

Istanbul's transit is convenient and inexpensive. Tram, light rail, funicular, and Metro lines intersect at central locations, and they

all use the same cards and passes (in theory at least—see the sidebar on page 26). Refer to the color map of the transit system at the beginning of this book; note that some routes may be extended before your visit (see timetables and maps at www.istanbul-ulasim.com.tr/en).

Tram

The seemingly made-for-tourists *tramvay* (trahm-vay) cuts a boomerang-shaped swath through the core of Istanbul's Old Town, then crosses the Golden Horn to the New District, where it continues along the Bosphorus. Destinations are posted on the outside of the tram—just hop on the one heading in the direction you want to go. Key tram stops include (from south to north):

• **Beyazıt** and **Çemberlitaş:** Flanking the Grand Bazaar in the Old Town.

• **Sultanahmet:** Dead-center in the Old Town, near Hagia Sophia, the Blue Mosque, the Hippodrome, and most recommended hotels and restaurants.

• **Gülhane:** At the side entrance to the Topkapı Palace grounds, near the Istanbul Archaeological Museum.

• **Sirkeci:** Sirkeci train station, near the Golden Horn and several Bosphorus ferry terminals.

• **Eminönü:** On the Golden Horn in the Old Town, near the Spice Market, Galata Bridge, and additional Bosphorus ferry terminals.

• **Karaköy:** In the New District (directly across Galata Bridge from the Old Town), near the Galata Tower and Tünel train up to İstiklal Street.

• **Tophane:** Near Istanbul Modern Arts Museum.

• **Kabataş:** End of the line in the New District, next to the funicular up to Taksim Square (described later) and a few blocks from Dolmabahçe Palace.

There's also the **Nostalgic Tram** that runs up and down İstiklal Street, through the middle of the New District. For details, see the New District Walk chapter.

Light Rail

West of the Grand Bazaar in the Old Town (at the Yusufpaşa stop), the tram connects to the *hafif raylı sistem* (hah-feef rahy-luh sees-tehm; light-rail system), which stretches west and south. While few sights are on this light-rail line, it's handy for reaching the city's main bus terminal (Otogar) and Atatürk Airport (the stop called Havalimanı, at the end of the line). This tram-and-light-rail connection to the bus terminal or airport—while a hassle with a lot of luggage—is cheap (8 TL to the airport from the Old Town; 12 TL from the New District), costing much less than a cab or airport shuttle. For more information on the bus terminal and airport, see the Istanbul Connections chapter.

Funiculars

An easy one-stop, two-minute underground *füniküler* connects Taksim Square (and İstiklal Street) in the New District with the Kabataş tram stop along the Bosphorus below. At Kabataş, the tram and funicular stations are side by side; to find the funicular station from Taksim Square, look for the combined funicular/ Metro entrance at the center of the square, right across from the Marmara Hotel, and follow *Kabataş-Füniküler* signs.

A second underground funicular, called **Tünel**, connects the Galata Bridge on the Golden Horn with İstiklal Street on the hill above. This late-19th-century funicular is as historic as it is convenient. For details, see page 243.

Metro

The underground Metro line 2—generally not useful for tourists—begins at Yenikapı, stops at Taksim Square, and then heads north into the business and residential Levent district. On the Asian side,

ORIENTATION

Paying for Public Transportation

Istanbul's public transportation is fairly easy to use, with one caveat: The city is constantly tinkering with the ticketing system, so the following information may change by the time you visit. For the latest, check the Istanbul public transportation website at www.istanbul-ulasim.com.tr/en or www.ricksteves.com/update.

There are three types of tickets: tokens, disposable cards (for one to 10 rides, rarely available), and a rechargeable pass (best for longer visits). You can buy these at most major bus, tram, light rail, Metro, and ferry stops (note that *arızalıdır* means out of order). You must buy your ticket or pass before you board. None of these options covers Bosphorus cruise boats.

Tokens: The simplest way to go is a 4-TL single-ride token (*jeton*; zheh-tohn). You can buy tokens at ticket booths or at vending machines (*jetonmatik*; zheh-tohn-mah-teek). The machines are easy to use and accept both bills (5-20 TL) and coins (5-50 Kr and 1 TL). To buy one token, insert money into the machine and press

the green button on the right. To buy several tokens, insert money, hit the dark-blue button to select the number you want, and press the green button to confirm. Collect your tokens and change from the slot at the bottom.

Note that tokens for rail and ferry services are different and not interchangeable. Tokens are not accepted on buses; to ride a bus you'll need either a card or pass.

Single or Multiple-Ride Cards: These nonrechargeable electronic cards should, in theory, cover all forms of public transit. However, since they're still fairly new to Istanbul, you may find that some forms of transit have switched to electronic cards, while others still use tokens, and some use both. A single-ride card costs 4 TL; multiple-ride

Metro line 4 links the Kadıköy ferry terminal to a stop near the suburban train station—Pendik—which is Istanbul's temporary rail hub for the rest of Turkey. To find a Metro entrance, look for the big *M* signs.

Marmaray Rail

The Marmaray (pronounced mahr-mah-rahy), the new underground (and underwater) rail system provides by far the fastest

cards offer lower fares (2-ride card-7 TL, 3 rides-10 TL, 5 rides-15 TL, 10 rides-30 TL). You can buy these cards from ticket booths at major bus, tram, light rail, Metro, and ferry stops (not available through vending machines).

İstanbulKart Pass: If you're staying more than a few days and plan to use public transport frequently, consider the

İstanbulKart. This credit-card-size pass is embedded with a computer chip and is re-chargeable. There's a nonre-fundable 6-TL charge to buy the card, then each ride costs 2.15 TL (a deal compared to a 4-TL token or single-ride card). Transfers within a two-hour window are even cheaper, at about 1 TL per ride (up to five transfers; you must wait at least 15 minutes between the start of your first ride and your transfer; no time limit between additional transfers). The pass works on all forms of transit, including double-decker buses that cross the Bosphorus (4.30 TL with pass) and ferries to the islands (3.85 TL with pass).

İstanbulKart passes are available at ticket booths and news-stands; to reload the card you can also use a vending machine or visit a tobacco shop near the central stops. To reload at vending machines, use coins, bills, or credit or debit cards—do not use large bills, as machines do not give change and will load that entire amount onto the card.

To use the İstanbulKart, hold it over the card reader as you go through the turnstile (on the top, just below the LCD screen). The screen will show your remaining balance. For more informa-tion about the İstanbulKart, call 0212/444-1871 or visit http://istanbulkart.iett.gov.tr/en.

If you're traveling outside the main tourist areas, it's a good idea to have a transit pass or extra tokens and cards on hand in case you find yourself at a stop without a working ticket vending machine.

ORIENTATION

connection between the two banks of the Bosphorus. Trains run between Kazlıçeşme (just outside of the Old Town) and Ayrılık Çeşmesi (close to Kadıköy in Asia; switch to the Metro here to get to Kadıköy). For visitors, the most convenient stop to begin the journey to Asian Istanbul is Sirkeci (accessible from within the train station).

ORIENTATION

Buses

Although the bus system was designed for commuters, it can work as a last resort for tourists (but avoid buses during the busy morning and evening rush hours). It can be difficult to tell where you're going and where to transfer or get off. Bus numbers on a particular route are clearly marked on signs at the stops (bus info at www.iett.gov.tr/en). The bus is mostly useful for getting to the Chora Church (see Chora Church Tour chapter) and to the sights along the Bosphorus, including the Sakıp Sabancı Museum, Sadberk Hanım Museum, and Rumeli Fortress (bus #25E from Kabataş; all described in the Sights in Istanbul chapter).

To ride a bus, you need to have either a single- or multiple-ride card or a transit pass (İstanbulKart), as bus drivers do not take cash or tokens. For more on how to get a card or a pass, see the sidebar.

BY FERRY AND SEABUS

In this city where millions of people sail across the Bosphorus to work each day, the ferry system had better work well...and it does. In fact, locals much prefer ferries to avoid heavy traffic on the bridges over the Bosphorus, especially during rush hour. Ferries are convenient and inexpensive—many cost as little as 4 TL one-way (2.15 TL with an İstanbulKart pass). Note that the Bosphorus cruise boats and ferries to the Princes' Islands cost more.

Seabuses (*deniz otobüsü;* deh-neez ow-toh-bew-sew) are a newer, faster alternative to Istanbul's increasingly congested roads. They're speedy and comfortable, but not as popular or as frequent as public ferries. The cost of a ticket varies depending on the destination.

The main ports for ferries and seabuses in European Istanbul are in the **Eminönü district** in the Old Town (by the Spice Market and Galata Bridge, near the mouth of the Golden Horn), **Karaköy** (across the Golden Horn from Eminönü, in the New District), and **Beşiktaş** on the Bosphorus. The major ports in Asian Istanbul are **Üsküdar** and **Kadıköy**. For more on these commuter ferry ports, see page 220.

Tours in Istanbul

Note that tour companies and local guides often list prices in dollars or euros. This is partly for convenience, but also to protect vendors against inflation.

Hop-on, Hop-off Bus Tours

Bigbus' narrated double-decker bus tours enable you to hop off at any stop, tour a sight, and then catch a later bus to your next destination—but departures are so infrequent that this isn't really practical. The tour amounts to a pricey two-hour ride in heavy traffic with useless, multilingual commentary. The Old Town's single tram line will take you to any of these sights without the hassle and for a lot less money. The bus does, however, take you along the entire old city wall (quite impressive and hard to see otherwise, unless you catch a glimpse on your way from the airport), and offers views from the top deck, making it a convenient and scenic place to munch a kebab or picnic. (Thanks to a convertible roof, this option still works in rainy or cold weather.) Pick up their brochure at most hotel lobbies or from their booth across from Hagia Sophia. The loop starts on the main street across from Hagia Sophia, but you can hop on at nearly any of the major sights along the route. Buses run year-round (€35, €25 online—can download e-ticket to mobile device; 3/hour April-Sept, 2/hour Oct-March, tickets valid for 24 hours; 0212/283-1396 http://eng.bigbustours.com).

Basic Boat Tours

Turyol offers short cruises on the Bosphorus for 12 TL per person. There's no narration, but you can follow the route using the first part of this book's Bosphorus Cruise chapter. Boats only go to the second bridge, so you won't see all of the Bosphorus. You don't need a reservation. Boats leave from the Golden Horn, right behind the Eminönü bus stop, across from the Spice Market (mid-June-mid-Sept Mon-Fri hourly 10:00-21:00, Sat every half hour 12:00-19:00, Sun hourly 11:00-18:45; fewer boats off-season, tel. 0212/527-9952, ask for Mr. İhsan).

Bosphorus and Black Sea Cruise

Guided cruises up the Bosphorus to the Black Sea are rare and can take most of the day. However, if you have the time and interest, **İBO** sails all the way to the sea. If it's warm, you can even swim in the Bosphorus. Cruises depart from Kabataş and stop at Ortaköy, Küçüksu Pavilion, and Rumeli Fortress. Lunch is served on board, and the swimming break (weather permitting) is at Poyrazköy Bay (north on the Bosphorus). The price includes admission to all sights and lunch (€79, €55 for kids ages 3-7, half-day cruise may be available, check website for details, tel. 0212/528-0475 or 0212/528-0476, www.ibocruise.com, owner İbrahim Şancı). For a self-guided cruise on a public ferry, see the Bosphorus Cruise chapter.

Local Guides

There are plenty of very good private guides in Istanbul. In Turkey, tour guides must be certified, and only travel agencies are authorized to make travel arrangements such as reserving minibuses or plane tickets. We have indicated which of the listed guides also run travel agencies so you know what they are permitted to arrange for

ORIENTATION

you. All of the guides and travel agencies listed here are certified with the appropriate authorities.

Lale and Tan, the co-authors of this book, own **SRM Travel,** which runs city tours, offers private guides, and helps develop custom itineraries for trips to Istanbul and the rest of Turkey. Mention this book to receive free travel consulting when you buy any travel service (half-day-from $235, full-day-from $265, tel. 0216/386-7623, www.srmtravel.com). Other recommended travel agents who also serve as guides include **Kağan** and **Lale Koşağan** of KSG Tours (half-day-€250, tel. 0216/343-4215, mobile 0532-234-2042, www.tourguidesinturkey.com, kosagan@yahoo.com) and **Attila Kılınç** (half-day-$150, full-day-$200, mobile 0532-294-7667, www.marmaratours.com, Attila@MarmaraTours.com).

The following certified tour guides have also served our readers well: **Nilay Türkeli** (half-day-$220, full-day-$250, mobile 0532-720-8679, nilayturkeli@gmail.com), **Nilüfer İris** (half-day-$225, full-day-$300, especially good with senior travelers, mobile 0532-244-1395, tel. 0212/273-1142, niluferiris@hotmail.com), **Pınar Çağlayan** (full-day-$250-$325, offers food tours, mobile 0538-315-5888, guidepinar@hotmail.com), and **Kürşat Taner Ünal** (half-day-$150, full-day-$225, mobile 0552-222-2022, ktanerunal@yahoo.com).

You can find a listing of other certified tour guides at www.turkishguides.org—switch to the English view, then use the language drop-down menu to search for English-speaking guides. It's best to use an official guide or travel agency—otherwise you might be left in the lurch without the tour or services you paid for...and no legal recourse for a refund.

Bus Tours Beyond Istanbul

If you want to see much more of Turkey without having to figure out the long-distance bus system, consider **Murti's,** a hop-on, hop-off bus designed for backpackers (6 itineraries ranging from €345 to €935, mention this book for a 10 percent discount, tel. 0212/529-7708, www.travelshopturkey.com/hop_on_hop_off_bus).

SIGHTS IN ISTANBUL

The sights listed in this chapter are arranged by neighborhood for handy sightseeing. When you see a 📖 in a listing, it means the sight is covered in much more depth in one of our walks or self-guided tours. This is why Istanbul's most important attractions get the least coverage in this chapter—we'll explore them later in the book. The Old Town's major sights have long been discovered, which is why this area gets approximately three million visitors every year. Yet Istanbul is so wonderfully rich that hidden gems known only to locals wait to be explored outside the main tourist zones.

If you're visiting Istanbul with children, check out the kid-friendly sights listed at the end of this chapter.

Renovations: Istanbul is one of the fastest-changing cities in Europe. Add to this the fluctuating agenda of the government and the wait-until-the-last-minute attitude of its officials, and even locals have a hard time keeping up. Renovation projects are announced late, and the information is often inaccurate. Expect changes during your visit—ask your hotelier or the TI for the latest news about the sights you're planning to visit.

Opening Hours: The ticket offices of the city's museums are in the process of being privatized. It's unclear what changes that could bring, but it may mean that opening times will differ from what we've listed here. If a sight is a must-see for you, check its hours in advance (on its website or at a TI), and visit well before the closing times listed here.

Museum Pass: The five-day Museum Pass Istanbul (currently 85 TL) covers Hagia Sophia, Topkapı Palace (including the Harem), Istanbul Archaeological Museum, Istanbul Mosaic Museum, Turkish and Islamic Arts Museum, Museum for the History of Science and Technology in Islam, Chora Church, Galata Mevlevi House Museum, Yıldız Palace, Rumeli Hisar Museum, and

Fethiye Museum. However, a new policy going into effect some-time in 2016 will institute a three-day pass (85 TL) covering the first six sights on this list, and a five-day pass (115 TL) that covers all of them. If you plan on visiting many or all of these sights, the Museum Pass will save you substantial money. And besides the price advantage, this pass allows you to bypass ticket lines to the city's most popular attractions—Hagia Sophia and Topkapı Palace (including the Harem). Each card can be used once at each covered museum. Validate it only when you're ready to tackle covered sights on consecutive days. The pass is sold at ticket offices and vending machines at participating sights (buy it at a less-crowded sight, not Hagia Sophia or Topkapı Palace).

Online Tickets: If you don't need a pass, individual tickets are available at www.muze.gov.tr/en for Hagia Sophia, Topkapı Palace and Harem, Istanbul Archaeological Museum, and Chora Church. These etickets allow you to skip the lines, but don't give you a price break. If you plan on visiting the first three sights, you'll save a little with the 85-TL Museum Pass. If you buy etickets, keep in mind that they cannot be canceled, refunded, or changed.

Going with a Guide: You can skip the line without buying tickets ahead of time if accompanied by an official tour guide. Just make sure your guide is registered with the appropriate authorities (see page 29).

In the Old Town

Istanbul's highest concentration of sights (and hotels) is in its Old Town, mostly in the Sultanahmet neighborhood.

IN THE SULTANAHMET AREA

Some of the following sights are linked by the 📖 Historic Core of Istanbul Walk chapter, which describes the Blue Mosque, the Hippodrome, and the Underground Cistern (Basilica Cistern) in greater detail.

▲▲▲Hagia Sophia (Aya Sofya)

It's been called the greatest house of worship in the Christian and Muslim worlds: Hagia Sophia (eye-ah soh-fee-yah), the Great Church of Constantinople. Built by the Byzantine Emperor Justinian in A.D. 537 on the grand-est scale possible, it was later converted into a mosque by the conquering Ottomans, and now serves as Istanbul's most impressive museum. Hagia Sophia remains the high point of Byz-antine architecture. Enjoy the Christian and

Islamic elements that meld peacefully under Hagia Sophia's soaring arches.

Cost and Hours: 30 TL, covers entire museum; daily 9:00-19:00, until 17:00 off-season, temporary exhibits and upper galleries close 30 minutes earlier, last entry one hour before closing, ongoing renovations may cause slow lines at the entry, in the heart of the Old Town at Sultanahmet Meydanı, tel. 0212/528-4500, www.ayasofyamuzesi.gov.tr.

See the Hagia Sophia Tour chapter.

▲▲▲Blue Mosque (Sultanahmet Camii)

Officially named for its patron, but nicknamed for the cool hues of the tiles that decorate its interior, the Blue Mosque was Sultan

Ahmet I's 17th-century answer to Hagia Sophia. Its six minarets rivaled the mosque in Mecca, and beautiful tiles from the İznik school fill the interior with exquisite floral motifs. The tombs of Ahmet I and his wife Kösem Sultan are nearby.

Cost and Hours: Free, generally open daily one hour after sunrise until one hour before sunset, closed to visitors five times a day for prayer and Friday morning, Sultanahmet Meydanı.

▲▲Underground Cistern (Yerebatan Sarayı)

Stroll through an underground rain forest of pillars in this vast, subterranean water reservoir (also known as the Basilica Cistern). Built in the sixth century A.D. to store water for a thirsty and fast-growing capital city, the 27-million-gallon-capacity cistern covers an area about the size of two football fields. Your visit to the dimly lit, cavernous chamber includes two stone Medusa heads recycled from earlier Roman structures. The cistern also hosts occasional concerts of traditional Turkish and classical Western music.

Cost and Hours: 20 TL, daily 9:00-18:30, until 17:30 off-season, Yerebatan Caddesi 1/3, Sultanahmet, tel. 0212/512-1570, http://yerebatan.com.

▲Hippodrome (Sultanahmet Meydanı)

This long, narrow, park-like square in the center of Istanbul's Old Town was once a Roman chariot racetrack. Today it's the front yard for many of Istanbul's most famous sights, including Hagia Sophia,

SIGHTS

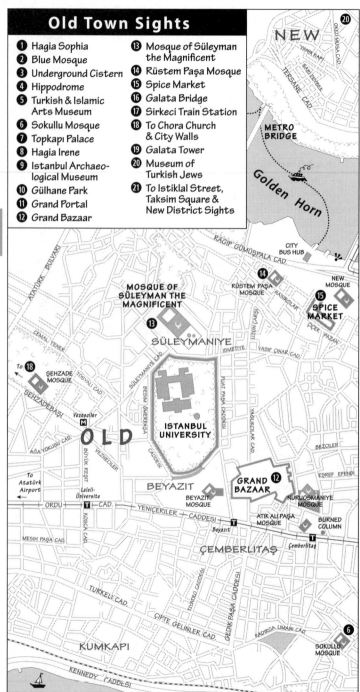

Old Town Sights

1. Hagia Sophia
2. Blue Mosque
3. Underground Cistern
4. Hippodrome
5. Turkish & Islamic Arts Museum
6. Sokullu Mosque
7. Topkapı Palace
8. Hagia Irene
9. Istanbul Archaeological Museum
10. Gülhane Park
11. Grand Portal
12. Grand Bazaar
13. Mosque of Süleyman the Magnificent
14. Rüstem Paşa Mosque
15. Spice Market
16. Galata Bridge
17. Sirkeci Train Station
18. To Chora Church & City Walls
19. Galata Tower
20. Museum of Turkish Jews
21. To Istiklal Street, Taksim Square & New District Sights

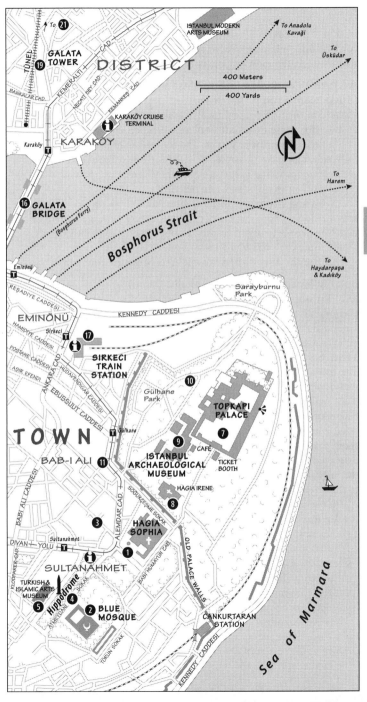

the Blue Mosque, and the İbrahim Paşa Palace (home to the Turkish and Islamic Arts Museum). Strolling the Hippodrome's length, you'll admire monuments that span the ages, including the Egyptian Obelisk, Column of Constantine, and German Fountain.

▲▲Turkish and Islamic Arts Museum
(Türk-İslam Eserleri Müzesi)

Housed in the former İbrahim Paşa Palace across from the Hippodrome, this museum's 40,000-piece collection covers the breadth of Islamic art over the centuries. The compact exhibit displays carefully selected, easy-to-appreciate works from the Selçuks to the Ottomans, including carpets, calligraphy, ceramics, glass, and art represented in wood, stone, and metal.

Cost and Hours: 20 TL, Tue-Sun 9:00-19:00, until 17:00 off-season, closed Mon, last entry one hour before closing, Sultanahmet Meydanı—across from the Hippodrome's Egyptian Obelisk, Sultanahmet, tel. 0212/518-1805, www.tiem.gov.tr.

📖 See the Turkish and Islamic Arts Museum Tour chapter.

Sokullu Mosque (Kardirga Sokullu Camii)

This 16th-century mosque, a few hundred yards from the Hippodrome, is more down-to-earth than the big showpiece mosques around Sultanahmet, but contains some notable decorations. The famous royal architect Sinan built the Sokullu Mosque for Grand Vizier Sokullu (for more on Sinan, see the sidebar on page 211). The mosque, a fine example of Sinan's mature work, is decorated with İznik tiles even older than those used in the Blue Mosque. But what makes the Sokullu Mosque unique are several gold-framed fragments of the Black Stone of Kaaba—priceless relics for Muslims, who believe that this stone descended from the heavens to show the Prophet Abraham where to build a temple. One piece is displayed above the mosque's main door, another is directly above the mihrab (prayer niche in the apse), and a third is on the entrance to the *mimber* (pulpit-like staircase).

Cost and Hours: Free, generally open daily one hour after sunrise until one hour before sunset, closed to visitors five times a day for prayer; imam may lock the door if there are no visitors, but he's usually nearby, so try waiting a few minutes; located at Şehit Mehmet Paşa Yokuşu 20-24, Sultanahmet.

Getting There: Leave the Hippodrome at its south end (past the Column of Constantine) and take the street called Şehit Mehmet Paşa Yokuşu to the right of the big building at the bottom of the square. Follow this road downhill, and after it makes a sharp right turn, continue on it another block. You'll see the mosque on the left, at the corner of the intersecting Su Terazisi Sokak. Walk a little farther and take the steps to the north to enter the courtyard.

TOPKAPI PALACE AND NEARBY

This walled zone, at the tip of the Old Town Peninsula, is a five-minute walk from the heart of the Sultanahmet district. On the sprawling grounds of the Topkapı Palace complex, you'll find the former residence of the sultans, one of Istanbul's top museums, and all the historical trappings of a once-thriving empire.

▲▲▲Topkapı Palace (Topkapı Sarayı)

For centuries, this was the palace where the great sultans hung their turbans. Built on the remains of ancient Byzantium, estab-

lished by Mehmet the Conqueror as an administrative headquarters, and turned into a home by Süleyman the Magnificent, Topkapı Palace's history reads like a who's who of Istanbul. Your wander through the many pavilions and courtyards includes a 16th-century kitchen, 10,000 pieces of fine Chinese porcelain, traditional weapons, royal robes, ceremonial thrones, and

Sultan Ahmet III's tulip garden. The Imperial Treasury is home to the famous jewel-encrusted Topkapı Dagger and the stunning 86-carat Spoonmaker's Diamond. Its Holy Relics exhibit—with some of the most important fragments of Islamic history anywhere—sends chills down even non-Muslims' spines. A separate ticket covers the cloistered rooms of the famous Harem, where the sultan's wives and concubines lived. Note that parts of the Treasury and the Harem will likely be under renovation during your visit, and other sections may close without prior notice.

Cost and Hours: Palace—30 TL, Wed-Mon 9:00-19:00, until 17:00 off-season, closed Tue, last entry one hour before closing, exhibits begin to close one hour earlier; Harem—15 TL, Wed-Mon 9:00-17:00, closed Tue; audioguide—15 TL for whole palace complex except the Harem, 10 TL for Harem; between the Golden Horn and Sea of Marmara in the Sultanahmet district, tel. 0212/512-0480, www.topkapisarayi.gov.tr.

📖 See the Topkapı Palace Tour chapter.

Hagia Irene (Aya İrini)

Near the Topkapı Palace, this was the patriarchal (main) church of Constantinople before Hagia Sophia. While the current structure was built by the Emperor Justinian in the sixth century, the original may have been built by Constantine. In the early days of the Eastern Roman Empire, this was the site of the Second Ecumenical Council in A.D. 381—which set the course for the future of the Orthodox Church.

Istanbul at a Glance

▲▲▲**Hagia Sophia** Constantinople's Great Church, later converted to an Ottoman mosque, and now a museum. **Hours:** Daily 9:00-19:00 in summer, until 17:00 off-season. See page 32.

▲▲▲**Blue Mosque** Ahmet I's response to Hagia Sophia, named for its brightly colored tiles. **Hours:** Generally open daily one hour after sunrise until one hour before sunset, closed to visitors five times a day for prayer and Friday morning. See page 33.

▲▲▲**Topkapı Palace** Storied residence of the sultans, with endless museum exhibits, astonishing artifacts, and the famous Harem. **Hours:** Palace—late March-late Oct Wed-Mon 9:00-19:00, until 17:00 off-season, closed Tue. Harem—Wed-Mon 9:00-17:00, closed Tue. See page 37.

▲▲▲**Grand Bazaar** World's oldest shopping mall, with more than 4,000 playfully pushy merchants. **Hours:** Mon-Sat 9:00-19:00, closed Sun and during religious holidays. See page 41.

▲▲▲**Mosque of Süleyman the Magnificent** The architect Sinan's 16th-century masterpiece, known for its serene interior and the tombs of Süleyman and his wife, Roxelana. **Hours:** Mosque—generally open daily from one hour after sunrise until one hour before sunset, closed to visitors five times a day for prayer. Mausoleums—daily 9:00-17:00, until 18:00 in summer. See page 42.

▲▲▲**Bosphorus Cruise** Public ferry ride on the Bosphorus Strait, offering a glimpse of untouristy Istanbul (and an Asian adventure). **Hours:** April-Oct at 10:35 and 13:35, additional departures may be added in peak season; Nov-March at 10:35 only. See page 44.

▲▲▲**İstiklal Street** Cosmopolitan pedestrian-only street in the New District, teeming with shops, eateries, and people. **Hours:** Always open. See page 47.

▲▲**Underground Cistern** Vast sixth-century subterranean water reservoir built with recycled Roman columns. **Hours:** Daily 9:00-18:30, until 17:30 off-season. See page 33.

▲▲**Turkish and Islamic Arts Museum** Carpets, calligraphy, ceramics, and other traditional arts on display at the former İbrahim Paşa Palace. **Hours:** Tue-Sun 9:00-19:00, until 17:00 off-season, closed Mon. See page 36.

▲▲**Istanbul Archaeological Museum** Complex covering Istanbul's ancient civilizations, including sumptuous tiles and highly decorated sarcophagi. **Hours:** Tue-Sun 9:00-19:00, until 17:00

off-season, closed Mon, parts of the museum will be closed until mid-2016. See page 40.

▲▲**Spice Market** Fragrant and colorful spices, dried fruit, and roasted nuts inside a 350-year-old market hall. **Hours:** Mon-Sat 8:00-19:30, until 19:00 off-season, Sun 9:30-18:00 year-round, closed during religious holidays. See page 42.

▲▲**Galata Bridge** Restaurant-lined bridge spanning the Golden Horn, bristling with fishermen's poles and offering sweeping views of the Old Town. **Hours:** Always open. See page 43.

▲▲**Chora Church** Modest church on the edge of the Old Town with some of the best Byzantine mosaics in captivity. **Hours:** Late March-late Oct Thu-Tue 9:00-19:00, until 16:30 off-season, closed Wed. See page 44.

▲▲**Galata Tower** 14th-century stone Genoese tower with the city's best views. **Hours:** Daily 9:00-20:00. See page 50.

▲**Hippodrome** Roman chariot racetrack-turned-square, linking Hagia Sophia and the Blue Mosque. **Hours:** Always open. See page 33.

▲**Gülhane Park** Former imperial rose garden, now a grassy park. **Hours:** Always open. See page 40.

▲**Rüstem Paşa Mosque** Small 16th-century mosque of Süleyman's Grand Vizier with extravagant tile decor. **Hours:** Generally open daily one hour after sunrise until one hour before sunset, closed to visitors five times a day for prayer. See page 42.

▲**Taksim Square** Gateway to the pedestrianized İstiklal Street, and heart of Istanbul's New District. **Hours:** Always open. See page 45.

▲**Pera Museum** Compact New District collection of world-class Oriental paintings, Anatolian weights and measures, and Kütahya tiles. **Hours:** Tue-Sat 10:00-19:00, Sun 12:00-18:00, closed Mon. See page 48.

▲**Galata Dervish Monastery** Meeting place for dervishes, who whirl here once a week. **Hours:** Tue-Sun 9:00-17:00, until 16:00 in winter, closed Mon; dervish services generally held on Sun at 17:00. See page 49.

▲**Dolmabahçe Palace** Opulent 19th-century European-style home of the sultans, accessible only by guided tour. **Hours:** Tours run late March-late Oct Tue-Wed and Fri-Sun 9:00-16:00, until 15:00 off-season, closed Mon and Thu. See page 52.

SIGHTS

Cost and Hours: 20 TL, Wed-Mon 9:00-19:00, until 17:00 off-season, closed Tue, last entry one hour before closing; between the Golden Horn and Sea of Marmara in the Sultanahmet district. For more on Hagia Irene, see page 114.

▲▲Istanbul Archaeological Museum (İstanbul Arkeoloji Müzesi)

In a city as richly layered with the remains of fallen civilizations as Istanbul, this museum is an essential stop. Although not as extensive as its more-established European counterparts (such as London's British Museum), the variety and quality of the Istanbul Archaeological Museum's collection rival any. The complex consists of three separate museums (all covered by the same ticket). The Museum of Archaeology houses a vast exhibit on the Greeks, Romans, and other early civilizations of the Near East. The star attraction here is the world-class collection of ancient sarcophagi, including the elaborately decorated and remarkably well-preserved Alexander Sarcophagus. Parts of the Museum of Archaeology will be closed until mid-2016 for restoration. The Museum of the Ancient Orient shows off striking fragments from the even-more-ancient civilizations of Mesopotamia and Anatolia (the Asian portion of modern-day Turkey, east of the Bosphorus Strait), such as the 13th-century B.C. Kadesh Treaty—the first written peace agreement in world history. And the Tiled Kiosk Museum sparkles with a staggering array of sumptuous ceramics and tiles.

Cost and Hours: 15 TL includes all three sections; Tue-Sun 9:00-19:00, until 17:00 off-season, closed Mon, last entry one hour before closing; Osman Hamdi Bey Yokuşu, Gülhane, Eminönü, tel. 0212/520-7740, www.istanbularkeoloji.gov.tr.

📖 See the Istanbul Archaeological Museum Tour chapter.

▲Gülhane Park

Originally Topkapı Palace's imperial garden, today it's Istanbul's oldest park and a welcoming swath of open green space within the bustling city. Located on the hillside below the palace, with terraces stretching to the shore below, Gülhane is a favorite weekend spot for locals. Come here to commune with Turks as they picnic with their families and enjoy a meander along the park's shady paths. On some summer weekends, the park hosts free concerts.

Grand Portal (Bab-ı Ali)

In the 19th century, this grand gate with its wavy roof and twin fountains was the entrance to the office of the Grand Vizier. The gate was called Bab-ı Ali because, historically, the word *bab* (door) was also used to refer to the authority of the state. Each Wednesday and Friday, commoners could enter here and tell their problems to public officials. It was here that all domestic and foreign affairs were discussed and presented to the sultan for a final decision. The surrounding neighborhood (also known as Bab-ı Ali) was the center of the Turkish news media for about 50 years (until the 1990s). Now it's a dull administrative district. But you can still find the historic gate just outside the old palace walls, near the Gülhane tram stop (see map on page 34).

WEST OF SULTANAHMET: FROM THE GRAND BAZAAR TO THE GOLDEN HORN

SIGHTS

Heading west from Sultanahmet, you enter an area that's more residential and less touristy, offering an opportunity to delve into the "real" Istanbul—rubbing elbows with locals at some of the city's best mosques and markets. While some attractions here—such as the Grand Bazaar—are tourist magnets, the lanes connecting them are filled mostly with residents. The following sights are linked by the ☐ Old Town Back Streets Walk chapter, which describes the Rüstem Paşa Mosque and Spice Market in greater detail.

▲▲▲Grand Bazaar (Kapalı Çarşı)

Shop till you drop at the world's oldest market venue. Although many of its stalls have been overtaken by souvenir shops, in many

ways Istanbul's unique Grand Bazaar remains much as it was centuries ago: enchanting and perplexing visitors with its mazelike network of more than 4,000 colorful shops, fragrant eateries, and insistent shopkeepers. Despite the tourists and the knickknacks, the heart of the Grand Bazaar still beats, giving the observant visitor a glimpse of the living Istanbul.

Cost and Hours: Free, Mon-Sat 9:00-19:00, closed Sun and during religious holidays, www.grandbazaaristanbul.org. It's across the parking lot from the Çemberlitaş tram stop, behind the Nuruosmaniye Mosque.

☐ See the Grand Bazaar Tour chapter.

▲▲▲Mosque of Süleyman the Magnificent (Süleymaniye Camii)

This soothing and restrained—but suitably magnificent—house of worship was built by the great 16th-century architect Sinan for his sultan Süleyman. Although less colorful than the Blue Mosque, this mosque rivals it in size, scope, and beauty. Enjoy the numerous courtyards and tranquil interior, decorated in pastel hues and stained glass. Out back are the elaborate tombs of Süleyman the Magnificent and his wife, Roxelana.

Cost and Hours: Mosque—free, generally open daily from one hour after sunrise until one hour before sunset, closed to visitors five times a day for prayer; mausoleums—free, daily 9:00-17:00, until 18:00 in summer. It's on Sıddık Sami Onar Caddesi, in the Süleymaniye district.

📖 See the Mosque of Süleyman the Magnificent Tour chapter.

▲Rüstem Paşa Mosque (Rüstem Paşa Camii)

This small 16th-century mosque, designed by the prolific and talented architect Sinan, was built to honor Süleyman the Magnificent's Grand Vizier, Rüstem Paşa. Elevated one story above street level in a bustling market zone, it has a facade studded with impressive İznik tiles—but the wall-to-wall decorations inside are even more breathtaking.

Cost and Hours: Free, generally open daily from one hour after sunrise until one hour before sunset, closed to visitors five times a day for prayer, on Hasırcılar Caddesi, Eminönü.

▲▲Spice Market (Mısır Carşışı)

This market was built about 350 years ago to promote the spice trade in Istanbul...and, aside from a few souvenir stands that have wriggled their way in, it still serves essentially the same purpose. Today the halls of the Spice Market are filled with equal numbers of locals and tourists. In addition to mounds of colorful spices (such as green henna and deep-red saffron), you can also get dried fruits (including apricots and figs), fresh roasted nuts, Turkish delight, supposed aphrodisiacs (Sultan's paste, or "Turkish Viagra"), imported caviar, and lots more.

Cost and Hours: Free to enter; Mon-Sat 8:00-19:30, until 19:00 off-season, Sun 9:30-18:00 year-round, closed during religious holidays. It's right on Cami Meydanı Sokak along the Golden Horn, at the Old Town end of the Galata Bridge, near the Eminönü tram stop.

Istanbul's Best Views

Galata Tower: The medieval, distinctively Italian tower offers visitors perhaps the best view of Istanbul, from the Golden Horn to the Bosphorus, over the rooftops of the European side and across to Asian Istanbul. Climb the little staircase behind the tower, take the elevator to the seventh-floor restaurant, and go to the observation terrace (see page 50).

Ferry Ride to Kadıköy: While riding from Galata Bridge to the Asian side of town, you can get great shots of the Old Town from a different perspective, as well as the skyline of the contemporary New District, the bustling Asian side, and out to the Sea of Marmara (one-way ride-4 TL, ferries available from Eminönü and Karaköy piers, at either end of Galata Bridge).

Istanbul Modern Arts Museum: From the restaurant of this museum at the Karaköy port, you can enjoy great views of the Old Town—if it's not blocked by a row of cruise ships anchored in the front (see page 51).

Mosque of Süleyman the Magnificent: The mosque's huge courtyard offers an outstanding view over centuries-old domes and chimneys, across to the New District and all the way to the mouth of the Golden Horn and the Bosphorus (see the Mosque of Süleyman the Magnificent Tour chapter).

Adamar Hotel: This recommended hotel's terrace, above the restaurant floor, has a spectacular view of the Hagia Sophia and Blue Mosque rising above the Old Town's core. The blue waters of the Bosphorus serve as a backdrop (Yerebatan Caddesi 37, Sultanahmet, tel. 0212/511-1936, www.adamarhotel.com).

Restaurants: Some of our recommended eateries have superb views, including Cankurtaran Sosyal Tesisleri, Mimar Sinan Café, Hamdi Restaurant, 360, and Bilsak 5. Kat (see the Eating in Istanbul chapter).

SIGHTS

ON THE GOLDEN HORN

The following sights are on the inlet called the Golden Horn, near the Spice Market. Known as Eminönü, this district is a major transit hub, where the tram, bus, seabus, and ferry systems link up—so it can be packed at rush hour. This area is covered by the 📖 Golden Horn Walk chapter.

▲▲Galata Bridge (Galata Köprüsü)

In 1994, this modern bridge replaced what had been the first and, for many years, only bridge spanning the Golden Horn. Now, lined with hundreds of fishermen dipping their hooks into the water below, the new Galata Bridge is an Istanbul fixture. A stroll across the Galata Bridge offers panoramic views of Istanbul's Old Town. Consider stopping for a drink or a meal at one of the many restaurants built into the bridge's lower level (tram stops: Eminönü on the Old Town end of the bridge, and Karaköy on the New District end).

▲▲▲Bosphorus Cruise

Between the Galata Bridge and the Sirkeci train station is the dock where you can catch a public ferry for a relaxing day-long cruise on the Bosphorus Strait. The round-trip ferry cruise goes by mansions, fortresses, and two intercontinental bridges before stopping for lunch at an Asian fishing village. As an alternative, take the ferry only to Sarıyer, then hop on a bus to access sights north of Istanbul.

Cost and Hours: 15 TL one-way, 25 TL round-trip, April-Oct at 10:35 and 13:35, additional departures may be added in peak season; Nov-March at 10:35 only. The public ferry leaves from the Bosphorus Cruise Pier in the Old Town's Eminönü district. Private cruises are also available nearby.

📖 See the Bosphorus Cruise chapter.

Sirkeci Train Station (Sirkeci Tren Garı)

This 19th-century example of European-Orientalism architecture was the terminus of the Orient Express. The famous train, which traveled from Paris through "exotic" Eastern Europe to Istanbul, was immortalized by Agatha Christie in her classic crime novel *Murder on the Orient Express*. Due to renovation work on the tracks, regular train operations at the station are suspended until late 2016. Though trains will again depart to Europe from here, the station is currently used mostly by local commuters. The modest Railway Museum inside the station is worth a look.

Cost and Hours: Railway Museum—free, Tue-Sat 9:00-12:30 & 13:00-17:00, closed Sun-Mon; near the ferry ports, tram stop: Sirkeci, tel. 0212/527-1201.

ON THE EDGE OF THE OLD TOWN
▲▲Chora Church (Kariye Müzesi)

This small but remarkable ancient church—now a museum—is packed full of some of the most impressive Byzantine mosaics anywhere (parts may be under renovation during your visit). Although it's tucked just inside the Old Town wall, far from the rest of Istanbul's sights, art lovers and history buffs find Chora Church to be worth the trip. Tilt back your head and squint at the thousands of tiny tiles artfully plastered on the ceilings and domes. Mosaics depict the birth, life, and death of Christ, as well as the Holy Family, saints, and other Christian figures. Vivid frescoes show the agony and the ecstasy of Judgment Day.

Cost and Hours: 15 TL, late March-late Oct Thu-Tue 9:00-

19:00, until 16:30 off-season, closed Wed, last entry one hour before closing, tel. 0212/631-9241, http://kariye.muze.gov.tr/en.

Getting There: The church is in the Edirnekapı district, west of downtown (20-25 TL taxi ride each way from Sultanahmet; bus #87 from Taksim Square (catch buses in underground tunnel under the square); bus #32, #37E, #38, or #910 from Eminönü; or tram to Topkapı stop and transfer to light rail, then ride 3 stops to Edirnekapı.

📖 See the Chora Church Tour chapter.

Walls of Constantinople

Originally built by Constantine, and expanded and fortified by Theodosius II in the fifth century, these walls are among the most extensive fortifications in history. The land walls stretched from the Golden Horn to the Sea of Marmara and were complemented by sea walls encircling the rest of the peninsula. Together the walls protected the city from invaders for more than 1,000 years. Many sections still survive.

Cost and Hours: Free and always open, although best viewed by day; located about four miles northwest of the historic core. The best way to see the Walls of Constantinople is to walk there after touring Chora Church (see previous listing).

📖 See the City Walls and Neighborhoods Walk chapter.

In the New District

The New District, across the Golden Horn from the Old Town, offers a modern, urban, and very European-flavored contrast to the historic creaks and quirks of the Old Town.

📖 The New District Walk chapter covers the best of these sights, which are listed roughly in the order you'll reach them going from Taksim Square toward the Golden Horn.

ON OR NEAR TAKSIM SQUARE

▲Taksim Square (Taksim Meydanı)

At the center of the New District is busy, vibrant Taksim Square. Taksim is the gateway to Istanbul's main pedestrian thoroughfare, İstiklal Street, with its historic buildings and colorful shops. This enormous square is also the New District's "Grand Central Station," connecting to the rest of the city by bus, Metro, funicular, and Nostalgic Tram.

Military Museum (Askeri Müze)

Organized with military precision, this museum is a scaled-up version of the Imperial Treasury's Armory collection at Topkapı Palace, focusing on the progress of Turkish military might. The collection itself—including imperial tents of Ottoman sultans and the

SIGHTS

New District Sights

200 Meters
200 Yards

BRITISH CONSULATE

SURP YERRORTUTYAN ARMENIAN ORTHODOX CHURCH

STADIUM

HAMALBAŞI CADDESI

BALIK SOK.

REFIK SAYDAM CADDESI

MEŞRUTIYET CAD.

SAHNE SOKAK

BEYOĞLU

BALO

TEPEBAŞI

PANAIA GREEK ORTHODOX CHURCH

KALLAVI

POST

PERA PALAS HOTEL **5**

ODAKULE

ST. ANTHONY'S ROMAN CATHOLIC CHURCH

TURNACIBAŞI SOKAK

CADDESI

ESKI ÇIÇEKÇI

YENI ÇARŞI CAD.

GALATASARAY HIGH SCHOOL

4

ARMENIAN CHURCH

MEŞRUTIYET CADDESI

BALYOZ

GÖNUL

NURU ZIYA SOKAK

WC

DUTCH CONSULATE

TÜNEL

AŞMALI MESCI

ISTIKLAL

POSTACILAR

UNION CHURCH

GALATASARAY

BOĞAZ KESEN CADDESI

To **M** Şişhane

T
Tünel

SANTA MARIA DRAPERIS LATIN CATHOLIC CHURCH

KAPTAN SOKAK

RUSSIAN CONSULATE

SOFYALI

KUMBARACI YOKUŞU

SWEDISH CONSULATE

TERRAE SOCLARE CHURCH

TÜNEL FUNICULARO

GALIP DEDE

KAHKULU

6

To **7**

---

sword of Süleyman the Magnificent—thrills military historians, but bores everyone else.

The Janissary Band, which puts on a one-hour performance at 15:00 each day the museum is open, can make it worth the trip (and is rated ▲). Also known as the Ottoman Military Band (Mehter Bandosu), the Janissary Band was the first of its kind, eventually prompting other European monarchs to create similar military bands of their own. The band's primary role was to lead the army into war, but in peacetime it also entertained the public with Turkish folk tunes. (Turkish-style rhythms were fashionable in 18th-century Europe, inspiring the likes of Mozart and Beethoven.) Today's costumed concerts still evoke the Golden Age of the Ottoman Empire, with all the regal pomp of ages past.

Cost and Hours: Museum—5 TL, Wed-Sun 9:00-16:30, closed Mon-Tue, last entry one hour before closing; Janissary Band concert—included in museum ticket, Wed-Sun at 15:00 at the Atatürk auditorium, no performances Mon-Tue; one-hour demonstration of traditional archery with visitor participation—Wed and Sat at 14:00; Harbiye district, tel. 0212/233-2720. You

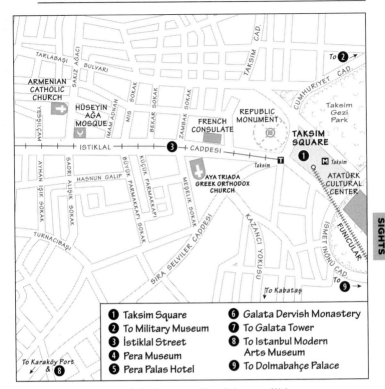

1 Taksim Square
2 To Military Museum
3 İstiklal Street
4 Pera Museum
5 Pera Palas Hotel
6 Galata Dervish Monastery
7 To Galata Tower
8 To Istanbul Modern Arts Museum
9 To Dolmabahçe Palace

can take photos of the Janissary Band, but you'll have to pay extra to photograph museum exhibits (10 TL for still cameras, 20 TL for video cameras).

Getting There: The Military Museum is a huge, walled complex at the end of Cumhuriyet Caddesi (joom-hoo-ree-yeht jah-deh-see), which is the main avenue leading north from Taksim Square into the trendy residential and business districts. You can walk there from Taksim Square in about 15 minutes (you'll see the museum on the right just before the avenue forks, past the multistory military club). Or take the Metro from Taksim one stop to Osmanbey, then backtrack a few blocks on Halaskargazi Caddesi to the museum (on your left, just as Halaskargazi runs into Cumhuriyet).

ON OR NEAR İSTIKLAL STREET
▲▲▲İstiklal Street (İstiklal Caddesi)
Linking Taksim Square with the Tünel district (and, below that, the Galata district), İstiklal Street is urban Istanbul's main pedestrian drag, passing through the most sophisticated part of town. The vibrant thoroughfare, whose name translates as "Independence Street," is lined with a lively mix of restaurants, cafés, shops, the-

aters, and art galleries. Visitors are enchanted by İstiklal Street's beautiful Art Nouveau facades and intrigued by the multicultural mix of tourists, international businesspeople, and locals who throng its elegant sidewalks.

▲Pera Museum (Pera Müzesi)

This museum beautifully displays its modest but interesting collection of historic weights and measures, Kütahya tiles, and Oriental paintings and portraits. It's housed in a renovated late-19th-century building typical of the once high-end Pera neighborhood.

Cost and Hours: 20 TL, Tue-Sat 10:00-19:00, Sun 12:00-18:00, closed Mon; museum's 4-TL audioguide, which covers only the paintings, is fast-moving and worthwhile; Meşrutiyet Caddesi 65, Tepebaşı, Beyoğlu, tel. 0212/334-9900.

Visiting the Museum: Floor 1 (one floor up from the lobby) displays centuries of **weights and measures** from the Anatolian peninsula. Circling clockwise, you'll watch the weights evolve more or less chronologically—from prehistoric times to the modern Republic—to suit an ever-more-sophisticated economy. Look for the weights shaped like fine statues.

Also on Floor 1 is a collection of **Kütahya tiles** (named after a city southeast of here). During the 18th and 19th centuries—the scope of this collection—İznik tiles were used by the Ottoman court, Çanakkale tiles were for the common folk, and Kütahya tiles were for both. This exhibit shows off pieces that Turks of that time bought to decorate their homes.

On Floor 2, you'll find the museum's most striking exhibit: one of the world's best collections of **Oriental paintings.** More than 300 canvases capture both royal pomp and everyday life during Ottoman times. Dating from the 17th to the 19th centuries, most of these were actually painted by visiting Europeans, who were mesmerized by the "mysteries of the Orient" they found here. Imagine a painter from buttoned-down Victorian England or Habsburg Austria traveling to this faraway land, with its pointy minarets, exotically scented spices, and seductive harems. Indeed, one of the themes of the exhibit is Ottoman women and harems, and the way their reputation became distorted through a European lens. The paintings are works of fancy, as the painters never set foot in a harem. (For the real story on harems, see the sidebar on page 132.) You'll also see works by the leading Turkish Oriental painter, Osman Hamdi. Find Hamdi's masterpiece, *The Tortoise Trainer.* The patience required to train slow-motion tortoises is a metaphor for the patience required to live life. Rounding out the collection is a who's who of royal portraits, depicting both Ottoman bigwigs (find the sultans you've been learning about) and foreign ambassadors wearing Ottoman clothing (to curry favor with the sultan).

Pera Palas Hotel

Agatha Christie fans will want to visit this hotel down the street from the Pera Museum (just past the multistory Hotel Pera Marmara), especially since this historic landmark has been extensively renovated.

By the late 19th century, the Orient Express train service from Western Europe had become all the rage (for more, see page 221). But Istanbul lacked a European-style hotel elegant enough to impress the posh passengers arriving on those trains. To satisfy the upper-crust demand, the company that operated the Orient Express built the top-of-the-top Pera Palas Hotel in 1892. Allied forces used the hotel as a base during the occupation of Istanbul at the end of World War I. In World War II, it was a hotbed of spies and counterspies. The hotel's guest book reads like a history lesson: Atatürk, Mata Hari, the Duke of Windsor, Yugoslav president Josip Broz Tito, Jackie Kennedy, and Agatha Christie (who stayed here several times in the 1920s and 1930s while writing *Murder on the Orient Express*).

Some of Atatürk's personal belongings and medals are displayed in Room 101 (free, but attendants expect a tip; open to visitors daily 10:00-11:00 & 15:00-16:00; Meşrutiyet Caddesi 52, tel. 0212/377-4000, www.jumeirah.com).

▲Galata Dervish Monastery (Galata Mevlevihanesi)

Recently reopened following a multiyear renovation, this *mevlevihane* (mehv-leh-vee-hah-neh) serves as one of the few meeting places left for dervishes in Istanbul. Poke into the modest courtyard and the surrounding religious buildings. The museum is dull, but the monastery is worth visiting on Sundays for the once-a-week dervish services conducted here (for details, see the Entertainment in Istanbul chapter).

Cost and Hours: Monastery museum—10 TL, Tue-Sun 9:00-17:00, until 16:00 in winter, closed Mon; dervish services—50 TL, generally held on Sun at 17:00 (possibly on some Sat); see page 352 for ticket information, Galip Dede Caddesi 15, tel. 0212/245-4141.

IN THE GALATA DISTRICT

The old-feeling neighborhood climbing up a hill from the Golden Horn into the New District, called Galata, has a seedier, less modern-European ambience than Taksim Square or İstiklal Street. Running up and down the hill under Galata is the old-fashioned subterranean funicular called Tünel (the entrance at the top of the hill is at the end of İstiklal Street; down below, it's near the Karaköy tram stop and Galata Bridge). You can visit these sights after finishing our New District Walk; they're listed in order from the top of the hill down to the waterfront.

▲▲Galata Tower (Galata Kulesi)

The most prominent feature of the New District skyline, the 205-foot-tall stone Galata Tower was built by the Genoese in the mid-14th century and has been used over the centuries as a fire

tower, a barracks, a dungeon, and even as a launch pad to test the possibility of human-powered flight.

In the Middle Ages, when Byzantines controlled the historic core of the city, this was the territory of Genoa (the Italian city once controlled much of the Mediterranean). This tower—sometimes called the "Genoese Tower"—was part of a mid-14th-century fortification. But, with a key location facing the Byzantine capital across the Golden Horn, the dramatic tower's purpose was likely as much to show off as to defend.

Today, the tower is a tourist attraction—offering visitors perhaps the best view of Istanbul. Climb the little staircase behind the tower, take the elevator to the seventh-floor restaurant, and go to the observation terrace.

As you enjoy the view, ponder the attention-grabbing story of a 17th-century aviation pioneer, Hezarfen Ahmet Çelebi. According to legend, Hezarfen Ahmet was so inspired by the drawings and models of Leonardo da Vinci that he built his own set of artificial wings, which allowed him to hang-glide a few miles from the top of this tower, across the Bosphorus, to Asian Istanbul.

Cost and Hours: 25 TL, daily 9:00-20:00, Büyük Hendek Sokak, tel. 0212/293-8180.

Quincentennial Museum of Turkish Jews (500 Yıl Vakfı Türk Musevileri Müzesi)

In 1492, King Ferdinand and Queen Isabel of Spain ordered their Sephardic Jewish population to accept the Christian faith, or leave and "dare not return." The Ottoman sultan Beyazıt Han was the only monarch of the time who extended an invitation to take in these refugees. Jewish people—many of whom can still trace their roots back to Spain—remain a vibrant part of Turkey's cultural mosaic. This museum, founded 500 years after the Spanish expulsion (hence the "quincentennial") and newly housed in the Neve

Shalom Synagogue, commemorates those first Sephardic Jews who found a new home here. The building was an early-19th-century synagogue built on the remains of a much-older synagogue; now it displays items donated by the local Jewish community. Particularly interesting are the ethnographic section, showing scenes from daily life, and a chair used in the Jewish circumcision rite.

Cost and Hours: 10 TL, Mon-Thu 10:00-16:00, Fri and Sun 10:00-14:00, closed Sat and during Jewish holidays; check website or call prior to visit since times and prices may change, Büyük Hendek Caddesi 61, tel. 0212/292-0386, www.muze500.com.

Getting There: The museum is located near the Şişhane Metro stop. From the Metro stop, walk downhill on the Yolcuzade İskender Caddesi and take the first left onto Büyük Hendek Caddesi. The entrance is on the small side street directly after the synagogue.

ALONG THE BOSPHORUS, BETWEEN GALATA AND BEŞIKTAŞ

This area, stretching north along the Bosphorus from the Galata Bridge, has been enjoying a wave of renovation, yet still retains the charm of its genteel past. We've listed these sights in the order you'll reach them coming from Galata.

Istanbul Modern Arts Museum (İstanbul Modern Sanat Müzesi)

The main museum in Istanbul dedicated to the works of contemporary Turkish artists, "Istanbul Modern" offers a look at Istanbul's current art scene and the upper crust of local society that it attracts. Located in a huge warehouse in the port area (often dwarfed by cruise ships moored at the adjacent wharf), the museum is a bright and user-friendly space. Here you can see the well-described art of a hundred Turkish painters from the 20th century on one floor, with temporary exhibits downstairs. The good but expensive museum cafeteria has an outdoor terrace with fine Old Town views (or a claustrophobic peek at the hull of a giant cruise ship, if one happens to be in port).

Cost and Hours: 10 TL, open Tue-Sun 10:00-18:00, Thu until 20:00, closed Mon, closed on January 1 and on the first day of religious festivals, Meclis-i Mebusan Caddesi, Liman İşletmeleri Sahası, Antrepo 4, tram stop: Tophane, tel. 0212/334-7300, www.istanbulmodern.org.

Getting There: It's in the Tophane neighborhood (close to Karaköy), at the dock behind Nusretiye Mosque, by the mouth of the Golden Horn. From the Old Town, take the tram to the second stop after the Galata Bridge (Tophane), walk a block farther past the Nusretiye Mosque, and take the alley to the right (toward the water) into an industrial parking lot. You'll see the big blocky gallery signposted to the right. Between the tram stop and the museum, along the waterfront side of the park that faces the tram tracks, check out the strip of cool lounges where young locals sprawl on big beanbag chairs playing backgammon, sipping tea, and sucking on water pipes.

▲Dolmabahçe Palace (Dolmabahçe Sarayı)

This palace was the last hurrah of the Ottoman Empire. By the late 19th century, the empire was called the "Sick Man of Europe," and other European emperors and kings derided its ineffective and backward-seeming sultan. In a last-ditch attempt to rejuvenate the declining image of his empire, Sultan Abdülmecit I built the ostentatious Dolmabahçe (dohl-mah-bah-cheh) Palace—with all the trappings of a European monarch's showpiece abode—to replace the unmistakably Oriental-feeling Topkapı Palace as the official residence of the sultan. It didn't work—instead, Dolmabahçe was the final residence of the long line of Ottoman sultans, falling empty when the royal family was sent into exile in 1922.

Two parts of the palace can be visited, and only with a tour—the Selamlık and the Harem. Visit the Harem only if you have time to spare—it's nothing compared to the Selamlık.

Cost and Hours: The palace is accessible only with a guided tour, which is available in English; 30 TL for Selamlık, 20 TL for Harem, 40 TL for both sections; 2-4/hour, one hour, late March-late Oct Tue-Wed and Fri-Sun 9:00-16:00, until 15:00 off-season, closed Mon and Thu; best to reserve ahead by calling 0212/327-2626, ask to be connected to an English-speaking agent. If you hear a recording in Turkish, just wait to be connected; reservation office hours Mon-Sat 9:00-17:45, closed Sun; Dolmabahçe Caddesi, Beşiktaş, tel. 0212/236-9000, www.millisaraylar.gov.tr.

Services: Just as you pass the ticket-taker, WCs are behind the wall to your right, and the baggage check is to your left. You can't take photos in the palace, but you can snap away in the gardens. A café and a bookstore are on the way to the exit, on the left.

Getting There: It's a few blocks from the Kabataş tram/funicular stop. From Taksim Square, take the funicular down to Kabataş; from the Old Town, take the tram to Kabataş. Once at Kabataş, walk along the water with the Bosphorus on your right. You'll pass a mosque (its unusual slender minarets have balconies that look like flowery Corinthian capitals), then a parking lot and a clock tower. The ticket office is to the left just before the palace's huge gates (wave at the statuesque honor guard—he's real).

Visiting the Palace: Dolmabahçe (meaning, roughly, "filled-in garden") sits on what was once a bay, on land long ago reclaimed from the Bosphorus. Built over a decade by an Ottoman-Armenian father-and-son team of architects, and completed in 1853, the palace is a fusion of styles—from Turkish-Ottoman elements to the frilly Rococo that was all the rage in Europe at the time. Its construction drained the already dwindling treasury, and the empire actually had to take a foreign loan to complete the palace. Today the building belongs to the Turkish Parliament, which uses it only for important occasions, such as the 2004 NATO summit.

After buying your ticket, you'll walk through the palace's well-manicured garden, past a small pool flanked by lion statues, and up the steps to the entrance. Before you line up inside for the tour, take a look at the magnificent ceremonial land gate on the palace wall to your left. When the palace was the sultan's home and seat of government, this was the door through which royal processions entered the palace grounds.

The decorations in the Selamlık section are alternately breathtaking and chintzy. Standouts include huge, hand-woven Turkish carpets; the sultan's alabaster bathroom; crystal everywhere (much of it Bohemian), including a Baccarat crystal staircase; and the Imperial Hall, built to accommodate up to 2,500 people. This room's dome is 118 feet high—you can't see it from outside—and the world's largest crystal chandelier hangs down from its center, weighing in at some four tons.

The Selamlık tour ends outside the throne room. Those continuing on to the Harem can stick with the guide; otherwise, take your time to enjoy the garden and the view of the Bosphorus.

A Quick Trip to Asia

While virtually all of Istanbul's "sights" are on the European side, the city itself spills over the Bosphorus into Asia. Of Istanbul's 15 million residents, more than a third (including this book's authors) live in Asian Istanbul, a.k.a. Anadolu Yakası (ah-nah-doh-loo yah-kah-suh, "the Anatolian side").

Getting to Kadıköy, in Asian Istanbul: You can take the new Marmaray train under the Bosphorus or, for a slower and more scenic intercontinental trip, ride the ferry from the Old Town. Catch the **Marmaray** inside Sirkeci train station and ride to Ayrılık Çeşmesi (second and last stop in Asia, 4 TL one-way with token, 2.15 TL with İstanbulKart), then switch to the Metro and ride one stop to Kadıköy (another 4 TL one-way fare with token, discount-

SIGHTS

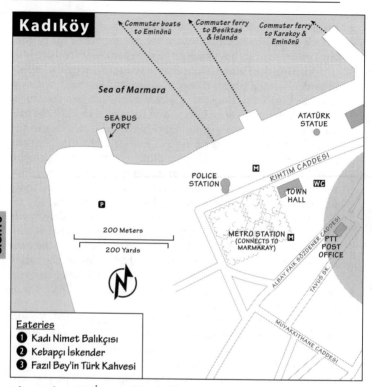

Kadıköy

Commuter boats to Eminönü

Commuter ferry to Beşiktaş & Islands

Commuter ferry to Karaköy & Eminönü

Sea of Marmara

SEA BUS PORT

ATATÜRK STATUE

POLICE STATION

M

RIHTIM CADDESI

WC

TOWN HALL

P

200 Meters

200 Yards

METRO STATION (CONNECTS TO MARMARAY)

M

ALBAY FAIK SÖZDENER CADDESI

PTT POST OFFICE

TAVUŞ SK.

MÜVAKKİTHANE CADDESI

N

Eateries
1 Kadı Nimet Balıkçısı
2 Kebapçı İskender
3 Fazıl Bey'in Türk Kahvesi

ed transfer with İstanbulKart). To travel by **boat,** catch the ferry to the Kadıköy dock from the Old Town side of the Golden Horn, near the Galata Bridge, at Eminönü (2/hour, 25-minute ride, 4 TL one-way with token, 2.15 TL with İstanbulKart). The boat ride is enjoyable—the views alone justify the trip.

Visiting Asian Kadıköy: There have long been small towns and villages in this area, but today Asian Istanbul consists mostly of modern sprawl. Development boomed here after the first bridge over the Bosphorus opened in 1974 (though regular ferry service started in the 1850s). While European Istanbul has its old quarters and traditional living, the residents of Asian Istanbul generally choose to live on the Asian side for its modern infrastructure, bigger houses and condos, and the efficiencies of modern life. The people of Asian Istanbul tend to be more progressive and secular than their counterparts across the strait (for example, you'll see fewer women wearing head scarves, and it's a voting stronghold for the modern Social Democrat party). Each day, millions of people commute across the Bosphorus (mostly on ferries) from their homes in Asia to their jobs in Europe.

Whether you take the train or the boat, head for **Kadıköy.** A historic town known in ancient times as Chalcedon, Kadıköy

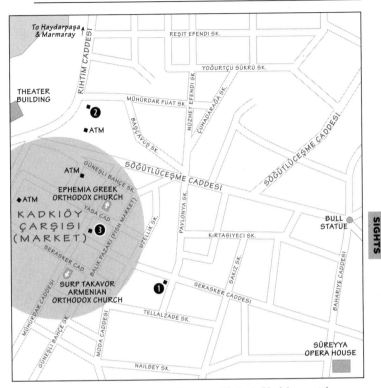

predates even the Byzantine Empire. Today's Kadıköy, with over a million people, is a modern commercial and residential district that grew up around the ferry landing.

Upon arrival in Kadıköy, you'll see that it's well-designed to deal with hordes of commuters. Trains and buses fan out from the ferry dock. Shops and restaurants fill the grid-planned commercial zone that stretches inland from the dock. Notice the shopping-mall ambience, youthful and Western energy of the crowds, and modern efficiency of the commerce.

If you've come by boat, step off the ferry dock and walk about 100 yards to the right to Kadıköy station (past the Atatürk statue at the center of the square). If you came via the Metro, you're already here. The Town Hall is right across from you, by the traffic light. Cross the street and walk straight (with the Town Hall on your right) by the side of the park, then cross a second street, which will put you in the market area.

Kadıköy Çarşısı (chahr-shuh-suh, market) is the historic core of the area—and it doesn't get more authentic than the surrounding neighborhood. Here in the market area, you can find everything from grocers and fishmongers to popular delis and specialty olive-oil stores. (Watch for a live goose, the mascot of shopkeepers, waddling around loose.) The streets are lined with boutiques, bookstores, fast-food kiosks, grocery stores, and cafés, bars, and restaurants (which begin bustling in the late afternoon). Busy as it is throughout the day, it gets even more crowded at rush hour—commuters pause here to enjoy a drink or meal with their friends, or to do some last-minute shopping. Shops start to close around 18:30 or 19:00, and eateries stay open until around 21:00 (places that serve alcohol stay open till midnight). After 21:00, the thriving crowd simply vanishes.

Elsewhere in Istanbul

These sights are scattered around the urban sprawl of Istanbul, and can easily be reached by taxi or bus. For locations, see the color "Istanbul Transit" map at the beginning of this book.

Rahmi Koç Industrial Museum (Rahmi Koç Müzesi)

This museum is located on the Golden Horn in a historic shipyard that once produced anchors and parts for Ottoman navy vessels. Inspired by the Henry Ford Museum in Michigan, Turkey's industrial giant, Rahmi Koç, started this museum in 1994 with his private collection, which is dedicated to the history of industry, transport, and communication. Today the collection has been expanded to include a vast number of metalworking tools, engines of all sizes and applications, scientific instruments, machinery, and vehicles including motorcycles, bicycles, a submarine, and a small train. What makes the Rahmi Koç special is its location—off the beaten path—and its optional but highly recommended Golden Horn cruise (offered only in summer) aboard a fully restored, 65-foot, 1936 tugboat powered by a steam engine. Most travelers to Istanbul don't get to see this part of the Golden Horn, let alone in an antique boat. Also of interest is an old olive-oil press. Triggered by a sensor, it starts to run the moment you enter the room. The Rahmi Koç isn't essential if your time in Istanbul is limited, but it's worth considering on a longer visit.

Cost and Hours: Museum—14 TL, submarine—7 TL, 20 percent discount with Museum Pass; Tue-Fri 10:00-17:00, Sat-Sun 10:00-19:00, until 18:00 off-season, closed Mon; 45-minute Golden Horn cruise—5 TL, June-Aug Sat-Sun at 13:00, 14:30, 16:00, and 17:30, check for weekday departure times, may also run in May and Sept—call to confirm; Hasköy Caddesi 5, tel. 0212/369-6600, www.rmk-museum.org.tr. The museum's Halat Restaurant serves great food.

Getting There: It's right on the Golden Horn in the Hasköy neighborhood. The easiest way to go is the Haliç Hattı ferry (4 TL one way, usually hourly, depart from the Eminönü pier on the

Golden Horn—west of the Galata Bridge and hidden behind the bus station, a huge jewelry store, and a large parking lot). Disembark at Hasköy, walk straight to the main road, turn left, and walk along the wall of the museum for about 50 yards to reach the entrance on the left. You can also go by bus: From the Old Town, take bus #47 (Eminönü-Alibeyköy) or #47E from Eminönü, next to the Galata Bridge. From Taksim Square, take bus #54HT (Taksim-Hasköy). Tell the driver that you want to get off at Hasköy (hahs-kohy), "Rahmi Koç Müzesi" (rah-mee koch mew-zeh-see). Alternately, a taxi ride from Eminönü should cost around 15 TL.

Miniatürk

This huge park, by the Golden Horn, has more than 100 scale models of Turkish monuments. The display is divided into three groups: monuments of Istanbul, the rest of Turkey, and elsewhere in the former Ottoman Empire. This wonderful, kid-friendly sight gives you a glimpse of the parts of Turkey you're not visiting. It's also a fun family scene, especially on sunny weekends. The Ottoman Mehter Band occasionally performs on Sundays at 16:00, playing music that once inspired Mozart; their costumes are colorful, their mustaches are big, and their drums are huge. Other kid-friendly highlights include a small pond with remote-control boats, a go-cart track, a mini train that tours the grounds, a maze, and a trampoline.

Within Miniatürk are two other, smaller museums: The Victory Museum tells the story of the War of Independence (after World War I, 1919-1922), while the tacky Crystal Museum displays laser carvings of monuments in crystal.

Cost and Hours: 10 TL, free for children under 8; daily 9:00-19:00, last entry one hour before closing; children's playground, İmrahor Caddesi, Borsa Durağı Mevkii, Halıcıoğlu, Sütlüce, tel. 0212/222-2882, www.miniaturk.com.tr.

Getting There: The park is located near the west end of Golden Horn. It's a 20-minute taxi ride from Taksim Square or Eminönü. By public transport, you can take bus #36T from Taksim or #47 or #47E from Eminönü.

Rumeli Fortress (Rumeli Hisarı)

This mighty fortress was built by the Ottoman Sultan Mehmet II in 1452, a year before his conquest of Constantinople. He was later given the title Fatih (fahtee; "Conqueror") after he succeeded in capturing the city.

Completed in a record time of 80

days at a strategic location up the Bosphorus from the Old Town, Rumeli stands across from an earlier, smaller fortress (the Anatolian Fortress of Sultan Beyazıt). With strategic views of both banks of the Bosphorus, the Rumeli Fortress was built—like its predecessor—to control the strait and to prevent any aid from reaching Constantinople while the city was under siege. It was renovated and turned into an open-air museum in the 1950s. Although the mosque that once stood at the castle's center is no longer there, you can see a section of its brick minaret.

The fortress alone isn't worth the trip. But if you're returning from a Bosphorus cruise, consider hopping off the boat at Sarıyer to see the fortress on your way back to town (this option is explained in the sidebar on page 294). If you have plenty of time, join the locals at the fortress for a leisurely morning and a late breakfast at a nearby café, such as the Hisar Café. The fortress can also be combined with a visit to the Sakıp Sabancı Museum and/or Sadberk Hanım Museum (both described next).

Cost and Hours: 10 TL, Thu-Tue 9:00-17:00, closed Wed; near the second bridge (FSM Bridge) up the Bosphorus, on the European shore at Yahya Kemal Caddesi 42; tel. 0212/263-5305.

Getting There: From the Old Town, take the tram to Kabataş, then take northbound bus #25E (Kabataş-Sarıyer). From Taksim Square in the New District, take the funicular to Kabataş, and then bus #25E; from Sarıyer (where you can disembark from the Bosphorus cruise), take southbound bus #25E (Sarıyer-Kabataş). Buses stop at Rumelihisarı, near the fortress.

Sakıp Sabancı Museum

This attractive private museum has two main collections: paintings and Ottoman calligraphy. The calligraphy collection is outstanding—one of the best and most extensive in the world. Temporary exhibits are usually well done and worthwhile.

The museum is located on the grounds of a waterfront mansion called Atlı Köşk ("Horse Mansion"). This glamorous property, with a wonderful view of the Bosphorus, was the residence of a giant of Turkish industry, Sakıp Sabancı. A philanthropist and an art admirer, he developed a significant collection of traditional artworks, which he donated to Sabancı University, along with this mansion, just before his death. The museum has a trendy outdoor restaurant, **Müzedechanga** (open in summer only), and a gift shop offering a fine selection of art and history books.

Cost and Hours: 20 TL, free on Wed, Tue-Sun 10:00-18:00, Wed until 20:00, closed Mon and on the first day of religious holidays, Sakıp Sabancı Caddesi 42, Emirgan, tel. 0212/277-2200, www.sakipsabancimuzesi.org.

Getting There: Follow the Rumeli Fortress directions (see previous listing), but instead get off the bus at the stop called Çınaraltı.

Sadberk Hanım Museum (Sadberk Hanım Müzesi)
Two 19th-century mansions overlooking the Bosphorus display separate exhibits dedicated to archaeology and art history. Their collections rival, and sometimes surpass, that of the Turkish and Islamic Arts Museum (except for the carpets).

Opened in the 1980s, this was one of the first private museums in the country. It's named for Sadberk Hanım, wife of über-businessman Vehbi Koç (father of Rahmi Koç, who founded the industrial museum described earlier). While not worth a dedicated trip if you're short on time, it works well when combined with the Sakıp Sabancı Museum and/or Rumeli Fortress (both described previously), or a Bosphorus cruise (disembark at Sarıyer—see page 281).

Cost and Hours: 7 TL, Thu-Tue 10:00-17:00, closed Wed, Piyasa Caddesi 27-29, Büyükdere, tel. 0212/242-3813 or 0212/242-3814. Photography is not allowed.

Getting There: Follow the directions in the Rumeli Fortress listing, get off the bus at the stop called Sefaret (seh-fah-reht), and walk south a few blocks along the coastal road.

Eyüp Sultan Mosque (Eyüp Sultan Camii)
This mosque attracts a conservative pilgrim crowd, making it one of the most interesting people-watching experiences in the city. You'll be surrounded by Turks who are humble in mood and attire, each looking for spiritual fulfillment. Ayyub El Ansari, called Eyüp Sultan by the Turks, was the Prophet Muhammad's standard-bearer and companion. He died outside the city walls during the siege of Constantinople by Muslim Arabs, and was buried where he fell. Centuries later, Sultan Mehmet the Conqueror built a mosque and mausoleum at the location of Eyüp's grave. Over the years, the mosque became an important religious center and destination for Muslim pilgrims. Throughout history, this is where new Ottoman sultans received their sword of sovereignty as they took the throne (comparable to being crowned). The complex you see today dates from the 1800s.

The Eyüp Sultan Mosque is crowded with locals at all times of the day. Crowds increase at prayer times—particularly on Fridays for the midday service—and for religious festivals. Year-round, especially from late spring to early fall, you'll see boys in fancy circumcision outfits, and newlyweds in their gowns and tuxedoes, here for a prayer. In the mausoleum, you'll see people praying in front of the tomb of Eyüp Sultan, as well as at the glass screen covering a supposed footprint of the Prophet Muhammad. There are no prayers to the dead in Islam, but it is a tradition to invoke

SIGHTS

the names of the deceased (such as Eyüp Sultan or Muhammad) to give prayers more weight with Allah.

Because this is a religious shrine, dress modestly, even if you're not going into the mosque—women should cover their hair with a scarf; men and women should cover their shoulders and knees.

Cost and Hours: Free, generally open daily from one hour after sunrise until one hour before sunset, closed to visitors five times a day for prayer.

Getting There: Its address is Camii Kebir Caddesi, Eyüp. From Eminönü in the Old Town, take bus #99 (Eminönü-Akşemseddin Mahiye) to the Eyüp Sultan stop. The bus may use an alternative stop, so ask the driver or another passenger where to get off. Other buses that will get you there include #36CE, #399B, and #399C. By taxi it's a quick 15-TL ride (consider a detour to see some of the old city walls along the way; see the ▢ City Walls and Neighborhoods Walk chapter).

For a fun and scenic alternative, take the Haliç ferry from Eminönü on the Golden Horn. The ferry port is just west of the south end of the Galata Bridge: With fishing boats on your right, walk past the bus stops, take the first right, and walk through the car park to Eminönü Haliç İskelesi. Get off the ferry at Eyüp, the sixth stop (ferry departs from Eminönü Mon-Fri at :50 past the hour from 7:45-16:45 and on the hour from 18:00-20:00, Sat-Sun 10:45-16:45 and 18:00-20:00, additional run Sun at 21:00; 35-minute ride; 4 TL, 2.15 TL with İstanbulKart).

Istanbul with Kids

Of the sights already described in this chapter, here are some kid-pleasers (depending on the ages of your children): the spooky Underground Cistern (page 33), Miniatürk (page 57), the Bosphorus Cruise (page 44), the bustling Grand Bazaar (page 41), the fragrant Spice Market (page 42, with a courtyard/square with pigeons), and the transportation-oriented Rahmi Koç Industrial Museum (page 56). A ride on the Nostalgic Tram down İstiklal Street is fun, too (page 223).

Here are a couple more sights worth considering:

Santral Istanbul

This industrial museum, formerly a power plant, is a popular destination for school groups. In the Museum of Energy, kids can explore the original turbine rooms, have fun in the Energy Play Zone, try interactive science experiences, generate energy, morph into batteries, and make magnetic sculptures. A highlight is the high-tech sound machine called the Reactable (made famous by the singer Björk). The Main Gallery houses contemporary art exhibits. Their art and technology workshops for kids may soon be offered in English; check during your visit.

Cost and Hours: Free; guided tour—25 TL, 15 TL for students, ID required for discount; daily 10:00-18:00, closed on the first day of religious holidays; reservations required for guided tour, Eski Silahtarağa Elektrik Santrali, Kazım Karabekir Caddesi 2, Eyüp, tel. 0212/311-7878, www.santralistanbul.org.

Getting There: A free shuttle bus runs between the museum and Atatürk Cultural Center at Taksim Square (see museum's website for hours; sometimes you may have to call for the shuttle). You can also take the Golden Horn ferry from Eminönü and get off at the Eyüp stop (see directions to Eyüp Sultan Mosque on page 59); from there, it's a short walk to the museum.

Istanbul Aquarium (Istanbul Akvaryum)

Located near Atatürk Airport, the aquarium is a scaled-down version of Sea World. With more than 1,500 species and 15,000 animals, the exhibits are organized by 16 different geographical locations, ranging from the Black Sea to the Pacific Ocean. Try to schedule your visit to overlap with the daily feeding at 15:00. Touch screens in both Turkish and English offer plenty of visuals and information, and two "5D" theaters (extra charge) add special weather effects to impact all your senses. The aquarium is set in a 20-acre rainforest with a mile-long trail.

Cost and Hours: 42 TL, kids age 2 and under-free, students and seniors—29 TL (ID required), family discounts, 5D movies—7 TL; daily 10:00-20:00, Şenlikköy Mahallesi Yeşilköy Halkalı Caddesi 93, Florya, tel. 0212/444-9744, www.istanbulakvaryum. com.

Getting There: You can take a taxi, or use the free round-trip shuttles that connect the aquarium with the Old Town (stopping by the ATMs in Sultanahmet Meydanı) and Taksim Square (stopping at Atatürk Cultural Center; both routes 4/day, every 2 hours starting at 10:15 or 10:30, check aquarium website for details and other stops).

EXPERIENCES IN ISTANBUL

Perhaps more than any city in Europe, Istanbul is a place to experience. Istanbul's best attractions aren't in its museums, but in its streets: coming across a gathering of Muslims washing their hands and feet at a fountain before they enter a mosque. Delicately sipping a cup of high-octane Turkish coffee, and taking a slow drag of sweet apple-flavored smoke from a traditional water pipe. Playing a spirited game of backgammon with a new friend at a teahouse, or getting a power massage in a Turkish bath. Learning to make Turkish cuisine—and eating it, too. This chapter is a how-to guide for these unforgettable Istanbul experiences.

▲▲▲VISITING A MOSQUE

Touring some of Istanbul's many mosques (*camii* in Turkish; pronounced jah-mee) offers Westerners an essential opportunity to better understand the Muslim faith. (For a primer, see the Understanding Islam chapter.) But, just as touring a Christian church comes with a certain protocol, the following guidelines should be observed when visiting a mosque.

When to Go

• Most mosques are open to worshippers from the first service in the morning (at sunrise) until the last service in the evening (at sunset). Tourists are generally allowed to enter during these daylight hours, except during the five daily services (explained on the next page). Specific "opening times" can vary greatly, but figure that most mosques are open to visitors from one hour after sunrise until about an hour before sunset.

• Because mosques are active places of worship, visitors are not allowed inside from about a half-hour before the service until the end of the service. (Services generally last 15-30 minutes.) If you are already inside, you may be asked to leave so as not to disturb the congregation.

• To avoid showing up at a mosque only to find that it's closed for worship, look up the daily service times in advance. The times generally change by a minute or two each day, and are listed in local newspapers: Look for *namaz vakitleri* (service hours) in a box at the top of the page (usually on the third page). Your hotelier can also find out for you.

• If you're visiting a mosque on Friday, avoid the midday service, which is more heavily attended than others, and longer, because it includes a sermon.

At the Mosque

• Both men and women should cover their knees and shoulders. Some major mosques (such as the Blue Mosque) loan sheets for this purpose.

• Women should also cover their hair with a scarf. This is appreciated as a sign of respect. Although scarves are available for loan, you might want to bring your own (easy to buy at a market) for hygienic reasons.

• Shoes must be removed before entering a mosque. If you'll enter and exit the mosque through different doors, borrow a plastic bag at the entrance to carry your shoes with you. Otherwise, leave them on the wooden rack by the entry door.

• Inside the mosque, a large area close to the apse (or mihrab) is often cordoned off and reserved for worshippers. Stay behind this line. Areas in the back of the mosque behind screens, or the upper-level galleries, are reserved for female worshippers.

• Amateur photography and videotaping are allowed inside a mosque. Be discreet, and ask for permission before photographing worshippers.

▲▲SIPPING TURKISH COFFEE

"Turkish coffee" refers not to a type of coffee, but to the way the coffee is prepared: The coffee grounds float freely in the brew, leaving behind a layer of "mud" at the bottom of the cup. But there's more to it than just coffee grounds and water.

Traditionally, coffee (*kahve;* kah-veh) is added to cold water in a copper pot. (Some use hot or lukewarm water to speed up the process, but you can taste the difference—Turks call this hasty version "dishwater.") The coffee-and-water mixture is stirred and slowly heated over medium heat. Just before the water boils, the pot is set aside and its contents are allowed to settle. Then the pot is put back

EXPERIENCES

Ramadan

Every year, devout Muslims keep the month-long observance of Ramadan—or *Ramazan* in Turkish. During Ramadan (June 6-July 4 in 2016, May 27-June 24 in 2017), Muslim people refrain from eating during daylight hours. This fasting is intended to turn the heart away from the world and toward God. By allowing people of all classes to feel hunger pangs, it also encourages generosity toward the less fortunate: For many Muslim families, Ramadan concludes with acts of charity and gift-giving.

Ramadan turns Istanbul's Old Town into a particularly colorful place—especially in the evenings, when locals pack the Hippodrome area. The happy, multigenerational partying that follows the breaking of the fast at sunset every night is one of the great travel experiences of the world...definitely not to be missed. After hours of fasting, people are ready for the first meal of the day as the sun goes down. Many rush home, while others stop for a quick bite at one of many temporary food stands. Restaurants that have been empty all day are suddenly marked by long lines stretching up the street.

On and near the Hippodrome, the city presents shadow pup-

on to boil. This time, half is poured into a cup, while the rest is reheated and then used to top off the drink. Turks joke that the last step is to put a horseshoe in it—if the horseshoe floats, you know it's good coffee.

Locals prefer Turkish coffee without sugar, but first-timers—even coffee-loving ones—often prefer to add sugar to make its powerful flavor a bit more palatable. In Turkey, the sugar is added while the coffee is being cooked, so you'll need to ask for it when you place your order: *az şekerli* (ahz sheh-kehr-lee) will get you a little sugar, *orta şekerli* (ohr-tah sheh-kehr-lee) is a medium scoop, and just *şekerli* (sheh-kehr-lee) roughly translates as "tons of sugar—I hate the taste of real coffee."

Because it's unfiltered, the coffee never completely dissolves. When drinking Turkish coffee, the trick is to gently agitate your cup time and

pet theaters, public concerts, and traditional folk dances. The Blue Mosque's interior courtyard turns into a huge market with religious books for sale. (If you're here during this time, study this scene in terms of a religion marketing itself, as Christian churches do back home. There are computer programs, trendy teen wear, and plenty of affordable literature.)

After going to bed late, be ready for traditional drummers to wake you up early. These drummers go from street to street in the Old Town a couple of hours before dawn, reminding people to get up and have a small bite to eat—or at least a glass of tea—before fasting resumes at sunrise. The drummers start practicing long before Ramadan, and some even sing a bit as they bang out their wake-up call. One musician who trains Ramadan drummers told us that he tries to teach them well so that he can "wake up to an acceptable rhythm."

During Ramadan, the minarets of many mosques are decorated with strings of lights and banners with Muslim sayings...not too different from Christmas lights and wreaths back home.

After Ramadan concludes, Turks celebrate a three-day religious festival, spend time with their families, and visit the graves of deceased family members. (The Grand Bazaar and Spice Market are closed in observance of the festival.) On these days, Istanbul has a festive atmosphere—its streets are packed with people who are off work, and its public transportation (often free at this time) is jammed with locals enjoying their time off.

time again to remix the grounds with the water. Otherwise you'll drink weak coffee, and wind up with a thick layer of grounds at the bottom when you're done.

The Best Coffee in Town

Şark Kahvesi is an Istanbul institution and a good place to sample Turkish coffee for the first time (Mon-Sat 9:00-18:30, closed Sun, in the Grand Bazaar at Yağlıkçılar Caddesi 134, tel. 0212/512-1144, www.sarkkahvesi.com).

Fes Café serves Turkish coffee (8-13 TL) with different aromas, such as coffee with mastic (the resinous Greek version) or with cardamom (the Arabic version), at two locations at the Grand Bazaar—one inside the bazaar (Mon-Sat 9:00-18:30, closed Sun, Halıcılar Caddesi 32) and the other outside the bazaar (Mon-Sat 9:00-19:00, closed Sun, Ali Baba Türbe Sokak 25/27, Nuruosmaniye, tel. 0212/526-3070, www.fescafe.com).

Kahve Dünyası, a national coffee chain, has premium-quality Turkish coffee (with or without mastic), as well as international coffees at reasonable prices (6-9 TL). Branches are spread around

Istanbul—a convenient location is near the Grand Bazaar (Mon-Sat 7:30-20:30, Sun 9:00-19:00, Nuru Osmaniye Caddesi 79, tel. 0212/527-3282, www.kahvedunyasi.com).

Café Grand Boulevard is actually a Turkish-style coffee shop, though the name sounds French. There's nothing grand about this place, except for the experience and location: the spacious atrium of a century-old historical passage on İstiklal Street, from which you can observe the bustle of an old-fashioned lingerie shop, a handmade-hat store, and an old book shop as you sip your beverage. You can try a variety of coffees and natural herbal infusions (a.k.a. teas), such as sage, linden, and rosehip (3-10 TL, daily 10:00-22:00, Hazzo Pulo Pasajı, Hangeçidi Sokak 116/3A, İstiklal Caddesi).

Reis Café has fine coffee (3--4 TL) and an authentically shabby atmosphere, with tiny stools and tables in the shade of a historic inn (Mon-Sat 6:00-20:00, closed Sun, Vezirhan Caddesi, Alibaba Türbe Sokak 13, Çemberlitaş).

Fazıl Bey'in Türk Kahvesi (Mr. Fazıl's Turkish Coffee), open since 1923, is a tiny coffee shop in Kadıköy's market area with a local clientele that keeps it busy every hour of the day. Its meticulous coffee preparation makes it one of the best in the business (Turkish coffee-5.50 TL, Turkish coffee with mastic—6.50 TL, daily 8:30-23:00, on the Asian side of the city at Serasker Caddesi 3, Kadıköy Çarşısı, tel. 0216/450-2870, see map on page 54).

Mandabatmaz is a tiny coffee shop in a characteristic narrow alley off busy İstiklal Street. The name translated literally means "water buffalo won't sink in," suggesting the rich thickness of the shop's coffee. The marble counter dominates the snug interior, leaving room for a few low coffee tables and stools; the outdoor seating is popular with locals (5-8 TL, daily 9:00-22:00, İstiklal Caddesi, Olivia Geçidi 1/A, www.mandabatmaz.com.tr).

▲▲SMOKING A WATER PIPE

Even non-smokers enjoy the Turkish tradition of *nargile* (nahr-ghee-leh)—also known as a "water pipe," "hookah," "hubbly-bubbly," "shisha," or "really big bong." Sucking on a *nargile* is all about the relaxing social ritual. And it's fun to lounge while you play with the pleasant-smelling smoke.

While similar instruments are happily—and usually illegally—used by marijuana enthusiasts back home, the water pipes you'll see in Istanbul are filled not with pot, but with low-nicotine tobacco leaves mixed with molasses and dried fruit or herbs (apple is the most common, but you'll also see cappuccino, strawberry, and other flavors). Because the fruit-infused tobacco contains zero to very little nicotine, it's not addictive and provides no buzz, but it's still fun to let the taste and rich aroma linger in your mouth. Even without much tobacco, you're still inhaling smoke, but it's filtered and cooled by the water before you inhale, allowing you to breathe it deeply. Tobacco enthusiasts can look for the strong, high-nicotine, and relatively rare *tömbeki* (tewm-beh-kee).

One of Turkey's oldest traditions, the water pipe originated in India before migrating to Anatolia (the Asian part of Turkey, east of the Bosphorus Strait). A *nargile* has a glass water jar at the bottom, called a *şişe* (shee-sheh). Attached to the top of the *şişe* is a long metal body with a little metal plate on top, where you place a container called a *lüle* (lew-leh). The tobacco goes in the *lüle*, with a piece of glowing coal (*mangir;* mahn-gheer) on top. A long, flexible hose (*marpuç;* mahr-pooch) is connected to the metal body. It has a wooden mouthpiece at the end, called an *ağızlık* (ah-uhz-luhk). When you inhale, the smoke fills the little container on top, moves down into the bottle, and makes the water bubble. Impurities are filtered out, and the smoke (as clean and cool as smoke can be) heads up the tube to your mouthpiece.

During the last century, as tobacco smokers switched to cigarettes, the *nargile* almost vanished. But over the last two decades, nostalgic Turks and curious tourists have revitalized the *nargile* tradition. You can order a water pipe in various coffee shops and trendy *nargile* cafés in the Old Town and New District (figure on paying roughly 10-15 TL per group). A *nargile* is shareable, and each person will get his or her own personal plastic mouthpiece to insert into the bigger wooden mouthpiece (sometimes these are free, sometimes you'll pay). After you take a drag, remove your personal mouthpiece and pass the hose to the next person. When you're done, keep your mouthpiece as a souvenir...or use it next time.

▲▲PLAYING BACKGAMMON

From the ancient Greeks to the Romans, to the teahouses of today, backgammon has been around for thousands of years. Walking the marble-paved streets of ancient sites in Turkey, such as Ephesus and Aphrodisias, you'll see backgammon boards carved on stones. The game was originally Persian, and Turks still call it by its Persian name, *tavla*.

As with checkers back home, most everyone in Turkey knows how to play backgammon. You'll often see people playing the game in coffee shops. If you're outgoing, challenging a local to a game can be a fun icebreaker.

EXPERIENCES

While a man can challenge anyone anywhere, it's considered inappropriate for a solo woman to challenge a man in a traditional coffee shop where most or all of the clientele is male. It's fine for a woman to challenge men if she's traveling with a group that includes men, or even on her own if she's in a mixed-gender coffee shop in modern areas of the city, such as the side alleys of İstiklal Street in the New District, the Ortaköy district on the Bosphorus, and the Kadıköy district on the Asian side.

Backgammon is a game of luck and skill, but it's not as drawn out or cerebral as chess. Turks tend to play the game very quickly, making each move instinctively rather than following a carefully plotted strategy. As you play, onlookers will gather and give you tips on how to win. Money is almost never involved. But to spice things up, players typically challenge one another for baklava, or the loser pays the bill (usually a few glasses of tea). Playing the game online with competitors from around the world is a recent trend in Turkey.

Because the game is of Persian origin, locals like to use the Persian (not Turkish) words for numbers. They'll be tickled and impressed if you do the same:

English	Persian	Pronounced
one	*yek*	yehk
two	*dü*	dew
three	*se*	seh
four	*cahar*	jah-hahr, or jahr for short
five	*beş*	behsh
six	*şeş*	shehsh

The dice are called *zar* (zahr) in Turkish, but their nickname is *kemik* (keh-meek)—literally "bone," since dice were originally made from bone. For luck, kiss the dice in your fist, and as you roll, say, *"Hadi kemik!"* (hah-dee keh-meek)—"Come on, dice!"

How to Play

There are two players, each with 15 checkers. The board has 24 triangle-shaped spaces, called "doors" (*kapı;* kah-puh), grouped into four sections of six triangles apiece: Each player has a "home board" (the quadrant closest to you on your right,

numbered starting with 1 on your right) and an "outer board" (on your left). You begin with all 30 checkers scattered around the board (two on each player's 24 door, five on each player's 13 door, three on each player's 8 door, and five on each player's 6 door). You're the winner if you bring all your checkers "home" and remove them from the board first.

After each player rolls a die to determine who goes first, you take turns rolling the dice and moving your checkers the appropriate number. You always move your checkers counterclockwise, toward your home board. A checker can only be moved to an "open" door (one that is occupied by no more than one opposing checker).

Each die indicates the number of doors for one move. The two moves can be combined into one longer move. For example, if you roll a 3 and a 6, you may move one checker three doors and a different checker six doors; or move a single checker three doors, then six more doors, for a total of nine (but only if the third or sixth door is open). If you roll a double, you can use each number twice—so if you roll double 3's, you have four separate moves of three doors each (which, as always, can be combined). You're required to make any moves that are possible; if you have to choose between two moves, you must make the larger one. If no move is possible (because of closed doors), your checkers stay put.

To make things more competitive, you can "hit" your opponent's checkers. Remember, if a door has only one checker on it, it's still considered open. If the opponent's checker lands on that door, the checker that was there first is "hit" and removed from play. Once your checker is taken off the board, you're required to enter it back into play on your opponent's home board. You can move a hit checker to an open door that corresponds to the number on one of your rolled dice. You can't use your roll to move any of your existing checkers until you bring back the hit one; if the doors corresponding to your roll are closed, you lose that turn. Once your checker re-enters the board, you can resume normal moves.

Ultimately, the goal of the game is to collect all of your checkers. First you need to move all 15 of your checkers to your home board. Then, when you roll the dice, you can collect a checker from a door with a number corresponding to each die. If the rolled number does not have a checker on it, you're still required to perform a move with that roll. If the roll is higher than any of your checkers' doors (for example, you roll a 6 but have no checkers on the six-door), you can remove the highest checker on your board. If one of your checkers is hit and removed from the board, you have to return it to your home board before you can continue collecting your checkers.

If you win the game, you get a point. If you collect all your checkers before your opponent gets all his checkers to his home board, your score doubles to two points (called *mars* in Turkish). Typically you play until one player reaches five points.

Good luck!

▲▲TAKING A TURKISH BATH

A visit to a *türk hamamı* (tewrk hah-mah-muh; Turkish bath) is perhaps the best way to rejuvenate your tired body while soaking in Turkish culture. It's not for everyone: Some of the baths—mostly those that cater to tourists—are mixed-sex, and the bathers are at least partially naked. Attendants touch your bare skin. The air inside is hot and humid, and you won't be able to keep any part of your body dry. Still, for most of those who've tried it, one visit isn't enough. For more on the history and practice of the Turkish bath, see the sidebar.

The Bath Procedure

The whole experience generally takes an hour and a half to two hours. It's useful to bring along a hairbrush, shampoo, clean underwear, flip-flops, a *kese* (keh-seh; a raw-silk mitten used to exfoliate dead skin), and a bottle of water.

While nudity is the norm at Turkish baths, it's not required: If being nude in front of strangers makes you uncomfortable, you can wear a bathing suit or your underwear. Most Turks prefer to keep a *peştemal* (pehsh-teh-mahl; a large piece of cotton fabric provided at the bath) wrapped around their bodies. Most baths have plastic slippers you can use. You can bring flip flops for hygiene, but don't forget that the soapy floor is slippery regardless.

Unless you bring your own *kese*, bath attendants will use the same *kese* on you that they've used on the last 20 people. *Keses* cost around 5 TL and make nice souvenirs (see page 342).

All of the sweating will likely dehydrate you; that's why it makes sense to bring a bottle of water. Leave your glasses in your locker, as the steam inside will fog them up. If you eat a huge meal or drink alcohol before going to a Turkish bath, you'll wish you hadn't.

As you enter the bath, you'll find yourself in a waiting chamber with sofas and maybe a decorative fountain. You'll be directed to a changing room or cabin and given a *peştemal* to wrap around your body. Lock your clothes and valuables in the changing room or a separate locker (the key stays around your wrist on an elastic band).

The central section of the bath is the hot, wet caldarium, or *sıcaklık* (suh-jahk-luhk). Marble basins are spaced at regular intervals along the walls. Sit next to a basin, adjust the water temperature to your liking (it should be as hot as you can stand), dip the provided metal bowl into the basin, and pour water on yourself.

The Turkish Bath

Going to a Turkish *hamam* (bath) on a regular basis is one of the region's oldest traditions. Baths are still popular in today's

Turkey, especially in the countryside. Ritual cleansing is an essential part of the Muslim religion and an important element of Turkish culture.

Turks brought the steam bath from Central Asia, blended it with the Roman bath culture they found here, and created the synthesis we call the Turkish bath. With no pools for soaking, Turkish-style baths instead use heat, steam, and humidity to stimulate perspiration, followed by a dousing with cool water and a vigorous massage.

The Turkish bath was introduced to Europe by the ever-encroaching Ottoman Empire. Europeans loved this exotic experience, especially painters of *turqueries* (fantastical representations of imagined Turkish culture), who used the baths as an excuse to paint frolicking naked girls.

Over time, baths became an integral part of everyday Turkish life. The *hamam* of the past was both health club and beauty parlor—like many spas in the US today. Rubdowns with a raw-silk mitten, herbal therapy, and oil massage became popular treatments.

Baths were also a place for social interaction. Two centuries ago, a woman could ask for a divorce if her husband failed to finance her twice-weekly bath visits. The baths were a place where Muslim women could socialize outside of their homes. Here they could look for a suitable bride for their sons or celebrate the birth of a new child. Meanwhile, men met at the baths to mark circumcisions, religious festivals...and for bachelor parties.

Turkish baths remain a part of the culture, especially in rural areas and in folk songs and proverbs. A common Turkish maxim about facing the consequences of one's actions goes, "He who enters a bath, sweats."

This will soften your skin and prepare it for exfoliation. Spend the next 20-25 minutes lazily pouring hot water over yourself to achieve maximum sweating and relaxation.

At the center of the chamber is a large marble slab. When it's your turn, an attendant will ask you to lie down on this slab. Men keep their *peştemal* on the entire time. Women wear their *peştemal* in co-ed baths, but generally remove it to lie on the slab in segregated facilities. (Again, women who are uncomfortable with nudity can keep on their *peştemal*, or wear a swimsuit.)

If you brought your own *kese*, this is the time to hand it over to the attendant for your scrub-down. Attendants often have a sense of humor, and they may toss you around on the slippery marble. Submit and go along for the ride. You may be amazed by what comes off as the attendant scrubs your skin. If you want the attendant to be gentle, say *"yavaş"* (yah-vahsh; "slow"). If overenthusiastic scrubbing causes this word to slip your mind, body language and "Ouch!" will suffice.

Then the attendant takes a piece of sponge or knitted wool, dips it into soapy water, bathes you with bubbles, and gives you a short, relaxing massage. (If you're a glutton for punishment, you can get what locals call the "bone-crunching massage.") After your massage, go back to the basin to wash your hair.

By the time you're finished, you're cleaner than you've ever been, and your skin is softer than a baby's. Take a towel from an attendant when you're ready to return to the waiting chamber. As you cool off for 10-15 minutes in the waiting chamber, you'll usually be offered tea. When you're relaxed and ready to confront the outside temperature, it's time to get dressed.

Choosing a Bath

Baths in the Old Town and New District have become quite touristy (in order to stay in business). On the upside, this means attendants are usually accustomed to the needs and expectations of international visitors. Don't worry—you're still getting an experience pretty close to an authentic Turkish bath.

If you're not comfortable with mixed-sex bathing, check the bath's policy before heading out. Since most Turks find mixed-sex bathing unacceptable, it's not hard to find single-sex baths. In segregated baths, only attendants of the same sex work on you. In co-ed baths, most attendants are male, serving both men and women.

It's also worth checking the price and asking what's included. In touristy baths, expect to pay 100-155 TL for the experience, plus a tip of about 25 TL for the otherwise poorly compensated attendants. (In some baths, it's the tip that motivates the overworked attendants—if the attendants just hang around without showing any interest in you, check with the supervisor and consider tipping before you start.)

Baths in the Old Town
Çemberlitaş Hamamı

This bath, designed by the famous architect Mimar Sinan in the late 16th century for the sultan's mother, is known for its fine architecture (segregated, daily 6:00-24:00, women's section opens at

7:30, credit cards accepted, next to Çemberlitaş tram stop, across from Burned Column, Vezirhan Caddesi 8, tel. 0212/522-7974, www.cemberlitashamami.com).

Another of Sinan's creations, the **Süleymaniye Hamamı** baths were built to be part of a larger mosque complex (co-ed—only couples and families with children ages 4 and up are admitted, daily 10:00-21:00, right next to Mosque of Süleyman the Magnificent, Mimar Sinan Caddesi 20, tel. 0212/519-5569 or 0212/520-3410, www.suleymaniyehamami.com.tr).

Cağaloğlu Hamamı is one of the more attractive historic baths in Istanbul (segregated, daily 8:00-22:00, halfway between Underground Cistern and Grand Bazaar, Prof. Kazım İsmail Gürkan Caddesi 24, tel. 0212/522-2424, www.cagalogluhamami.com.tr).

The historic **Ayasofya (Hürrem Sultan)** bath—commissioned by Süleyman the Magnificent's wife Roxelana and built by Sinan—was recently restored to its original purpose. At the very heart of the Old Town, between Hagia Sophia and the Blue Mosque, everything is fit for royalty, spotlessly clean, and well-kept. All of the attendants have been formally trained and are paid accordingly. The luxury is reflected in the prices (segregated, reservations required; packages from €85-170; €105 Keyf-i Hamam package covers the expected services, requires a tip, and takes about an hour—but you can stay afterward to enjoy the facility as long as you want; daily 8:00-23:00, last entry at 21:30, Aya Sofya Meydanı 2, Sultanahmet, tel. 0212/517-3535, www.ayasofyahamami.com).

Baths in the New District

Only recently discovered by travelers, **Büyük Hamam** is the most "local" bath of the bunch. Though the staff is not yet accustomed to serving tourists, they're helpful and make an effort. Enjoy the beautiful surroundings—built by Sinan—for a far more reasonable price than the other baths listed here. Women should take along their own bath accessories, as this place only provides men the necessary supplies, like a towel and a *peştemal*—though upon request, they'll borrow these from the men's section (segregated, men's section daily 5:30-22:30, women's section daily 8:30-19:00, Büyük Cami yanı, Potinciler Sokak 22, men's section tel. 0212/253-4229, women's section tel. 0212/256-9835). It's located in the Kasımpaşa (kah-suhm-pah-shah) neighborhood, near the Kasımpaşa Mosque, at the edge of the New District. Even though it's not far from İstiklal Street and the Old Town, you'll need to take a cab to get here.

The nicely restored **Galatasaray Hamamı** baths have a local clientele (segregated, men's section daily 7:00-22:00, women's section daily 8:00-20:00; Museum Pass provides 20 percent discount; a block off İstiklal Street at Turnacibasi Sokak 24, general info and men's section tel. 0212/252-4242, women's section tel. 0212/249-4342, www.galatasarayhamami.com).

Kılıç Ali Paşa Hamamı is on the Golden Horn and close to historic shipyards—it was built to serve the Ottoman navy in the 16th century. The bath's creator and namesake, Kılıç Ali Paşa, was grand admiral of the Ottoman fleet (he appears in Cervantes' *Don Quixote* as the character Uchali). Well-trained staff welcome you with a cup of traditional chilled fruit juice *(şerbet)*, then provide bathing, scrubbing, and foam massage for around an hour—but you can stay as long as you want (150 TL plus tip, women's hours daily 8:00-16:00, men's hours daily 16:30–23:30, reservation required, Kemankeş Mahallesi, Hamam Sokak 1, Tophane, tel. 0212/393-8010, http://kilicalipasahamami.com).

TAKING A COOKING CLASS

Spanning three continents, the Ottoman Empire united various peoples—and cuisines. Innovative palace chefs worked hard to please a discerning sultan, bringing together the culinary traditions of European, Asian, and Middle Eastern nations to create one of the world's most diverse cuisines. For an introduction to the tricks of the Turkish kitchen, consider spending a few hours (or a few days) learning how to cook—and then eat—a meal fit for a sultan.

Cooking Alaturka, a restaurant in the Sultanahmet area founded by Dutch ex-pat Eveline Zoutendijk, now has new owners—Rocco Strazzera and his Turkish wife Leyla. The couple teach students in English how to cook an entire Turkish meal—soup, cold appetizer cooked in olive oil, main course, and dessert—in about two hours (€65 or equivalent in other currencies, price includes five-course meal and beverages; several classes a week usually 10:30-14:30 or 16:30-20:30, but also on request, closed Sun; Akbıyık Caddesi 72A, a few blocks from the Blue Mosque, tel. 0212/458-5919, www.cookingalaturka.com).

Turkish Flavours is a small group of culinary specialists who teach cooking in their uptown condos on the Asian side of the Bosphorus. The half-day experience includes shopping in a food market followed by a hands-on cooking experience. You'll end up enjoying the food you prepared. Recipes are geared for home-cooking, and the menu changes seasonally. The team is headed by Selin, who can also share Jewish delicacies from her Sephardic heritage ($125/person, mobile 0532-218-0653, www.turkishflavours.com, turkishflavours@gmail.com).

Travelers also rave about **Istanbul Cooking School** in Tarlabaşı near Taksim, run by several young chefs (€65/class, cash only, sessions run daily 10:30-15:00 and 15:30-20:00; Kamer Hatun Mahallesi, Tarlabaşı Bulvarı 117/2, Beyoğlu, tel. 0545-554-6677, www.istanbulcookingschool.com, info@istanbulcookingschool.com).

HISTORIC CORE OF ISTANBUL WALK

Sultanahmet, the Blue Mosque, and the Hippodrome

Just like Rome, Istanbul's Old Town was built on seven hills. The district called Sultanahmet, on top of the first hill, is the historic core of the city. The Greek city of Byzantium was founded nearby, where Topkapı Palace stands today. Early Greek settlers—weary after their long journey—chose this highly strategic location, which could easily be fortified with walls on all sides. The site gave them control of all three surrounding bodies of water (the Bosphorus Strait, the Golden Horn, and the Sea of Marmara) and was convenient to the Greek colonies on the Black Sea.

Today, Sultanahmet is Istanbul's single best sightseeing zone for visitors—host to Istanbul's most important and impressive former church (Hagia Sophia) and mosque (the Blue Mosque), one of its best museums (Turkish and Islamic Arts), and its most significant Byzantine ruins (the Hippodrome and Underground Cistern).

Orientation

Length of This Walk: Allow about three hours, including sightseeing, for this short walk.

Getting There: If coming by tram, get off at the Sultanahmet stop, then walk to the park between the Blue Mosque and Hagia Sophia.

Hagia Sophia: 30 TL, daily 9:00-19:00, until 17:00 off-season, last entry one hour before closing, Sultanahmet Meydanı, tel. 0212/528-4500.

Underground Cistern: 20 TL, daily 9:00-18:30, until 17:30 off-season, Yerebatan Caddesi 1/3, tel. 0212/512-1570.

Blue Mosque: Free, generally open daily one hour after sunrise until one hour before sunset, closed to visitors five times a day for prayer, Sultanahmet Meydanı. To enter the mosque, knees and shoulders must be covered, shoes must be removed, and women should also cover their hair with a scarf (see page 63 for details).

Turkish and Islamic Arts Museum: 20 TL, Tue-Sun 9:00-19:00, until 17:00 off-season, closed Mon, Sultanahmet Meydanı, tel. 0212/518-1805.

The Walk Begins

• *Begin at the pond in Sultanahmet Park, sandwiched between Istanbul's two most famous sights: the Blue Mosque and Hagia Sophia.*

Sultanahmet Spin Tour

With your back to the gray-colored Blue Mosque, face the orange Hagia Sophia (eye-ah soh-fee-yah). We'll take a slow spin clockwise to get the lay of the land. Behind Hagia Sophia, not visible from here, are the Topkapı Palace grounds, which also house the Istanbul Archaeological Museum. To reach the main palace entry, you'd walk along the front of Hagia Sophia to the right, then turn left at the first corner and walk along the side of the church until you passed between the old walls through the Imperial Gate.

Now turn 90 degrees to the right. The long terra-cotta-colored building with different-sized domes is the 16th-century **Haseki Sultan Bath,** now a government-owned emporium (see photo). Keep turning right, and at the other end of this lively park is the famous **Blue Mosque.** Just to its right (out of sight) is the long, narrow Byzantine square called the **Hippodrome** (the green-domed German Fountain you can see through the trees marks the near end of the Hippodrome— where we'll finish this walk). Keep turning until you are again facing Hagia Sophia.

Sultanahmet Park is a fine example of a city determined to be people-friendly. In spring it's a festival of tulips. If the fountain is on, notice that the arcs of water are designed to mimic the domes of Hagia Sophia. This is perhaps the best photo op for both Hagia Sophia and the Blue Mosque. The large cobbled street at the end of the park (near the Blue Mosque) turns into a parking lot during festivals and on some weekends.

• *Across the very broad street, two red Turkish flags mark the entrance to Hagia Sophia. Now, let's cross the street and go to church.*

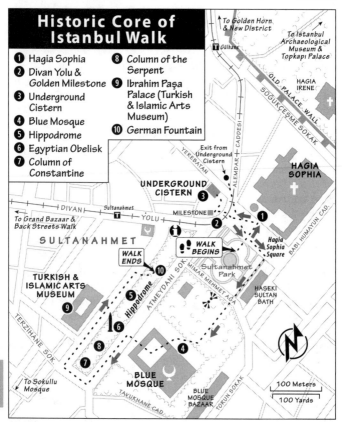

Historic Core of Istanbul Walk

❶ Hagia Sophia
❷ Divan Yolu & Golden Milestone
❸ Underground Cistern
❹ Blue Mosque
❺ Hippodrome
❻ Egyptian Obelisk
❼ Column of Constantine
❽ Column of the Serpent
❾ Ibrahim Paşa Palace (Turkish & Islamic Arts Museum)
❿ German Fountain

HISTORIC CORE

Hagia Sophia

Hagia Sophia—the name means "divine wisdom"—served as the patriarchal church of Constantinople for centuries (similar to the Vatican in Rome). When an earlier church on this site was destroyed during the sixth-century Nika Revolt, the Byzantine Emperor Justinian seized the opportunity—and this prime real estate—to build the most spectacular church the world had ever seen. He hired a mathematician named Anthemius to engineer a building for the ages,

with an enormous central dome unlike anything ever constructed. You could fit Paris' Notre-Dame Cathedral under Hagia Sophia's dome—or the Statue of Liberty, minus her torch. Nearly 1,500 years later, Hagia Sophia still dominates Istanbul's skyline.

When the Ottomans conquered Constantinople in 1453, Hagia Sophia (which they called Aya Sofya) was converted to a mosque, and minarets were added to this otherwise very Byzantine-looking church. Because of its grand scale, grace, and beauty, Hagia Sophia's design influenced Ottoman architects for generations. That's why many mosques built after the Ottoman invasion—and long after the Byzantines became a distant memory—continued to incorporate many Byzantine elements.

You could tour Hagia Sophia now (using the Hagia Sophia Tour chapter), or wait until the end of our orientation walk—we'll finish just up the street from here. (If you're visiting in peak season and the line is short, you'd be wise to pop in now—cruise groups can inundate the place at a moment's notice.)

• *Leaving Hagia Sophia, turn right and walk to the busy street corner. (Hop-on, hop-off tour buses leave near here, at the little red tour kiosk.) Head across the tram tracks to the 30-foot-tall stone-and-brick tower that looks like a large chimney, with a fountain built into it.*

Divan Yolu and the Golden Milestone

The busy street with the trams is Divan Yolu (dee-vahn yoh-loo), the main thoroughfare through Sultanahmet. To the left (uphill), it

leads to the Grand Bazaar. To the right (downhill), it heads to the Galata Bridge and New District. Notice the dramatic boomerang-shaped swoop made by the tram tracks as they pass Hagia Sophia. Since Istanbul's Old Town tram has only one line, it's remarkably user-friendly. If Istanbul is a jungle, consider this your vine. It swings to nearly all the places of tourist interest, and it can't get lost (trams run 6-8 times per hour).

Divan Yolu was also Constantinople's main transportation artery in Byzantine times, when it was named Mese ("Middle Way"). The road started right here, where the Golden Milestone (Miliarium Aureum) still stands (in a pit, to the left of the tower). Some 1,500 years ago, the Byzantines considered this point the center of the world. This ancient and once-gilded milestone showed the distances to key locations within the empire. Today it's a mere stub worn down by the centuries. Nothing remains of its decorative arches, or of the statues that once adorned it (of Constantine and his mother, Helen, holding a cross).

• *Go downhill to the first corner and turn left. Across the street from the old yellow police building is the low-profile, red-and-white striped entrance to the...*

Underground Cistern

This vast underground reservoir dates back to Byzantine Emperor Justinian's reign in the sixth century A.D. Because it was built on

the site of an earlier basilica, it's often called the "Basilica Cistern." Turks call it *yerebatan sarayı*, which means "sunken palace."

Buy your ticket and descend the stairs into the cistern. The visit is a level, 15-minute, 400-yard underground stroll. (You'll exit up stairs through a different gate, a block down the street.) While your eyes adjust to the dimness, ponder the history of this spectacular site. The Byzantine Empire enjoyed a Golden Age under Emperor Justinian; its currency was so strong that merchants in continental

Europe and Asia demanded to be paid in Byzantine imperial coins. The enormous wealth can still be seen in the monuments and even the functional structures (such as other cisterns) of that era. This massive reservoir—larger by far than any other in Constantinople—was built to meet the needs of a fast-growing capital city and to provide precious water in case of a shortage. It covers an area about the size of two football fields—big enough to hold 27 million gallons of fresh water.

A forest of 336 columns supports the brick ceiling. Most of them were recycled from earlier Roman ruins in and around the city. Note the variety of capitals (tops of columns). Clay pipes and aqueducts carried water 12 miles to this cistern. (A half-mile-long chunk of the Valens Aqueduct still stands, spanning Atatürk Bulvarı—Atatürk Boulevard—roughly a mile west of here.)

Gradually these pipes became clogged, and the cistern fell out of use. As time passed, neglect became ignorance, and people forgot it was even there. An Ottoman historian wrote that residents of this area were luckier than others, as they could easily drop a bucket into any garden well and collect what seemed to them like God-given water. (They didn't realize they were dipping their buckets into a Byzantine masterpiece.)

The platform you're walking on was constructed two decades ago to make the far reaches of the cistern more accessible to visitors. While water once filled this space halfway to the ceiling, today it's just a shallow pond, formed from rainwater that leaks in through cracks and compromised mortar in the ceiling. (Accumulated water is pumped out to prevent damage.) Before the walkway was built, the water was six feet deep, and the only way to see the cistern was to rent a boat and row in the dark—a perfectly evocative setting used for James Bond's adventures in *From Russia with Love*.

Walking toward the far end, notice that part of the cistern (which has suffered structural damage) is separated by a wall.

At the far end of the cistern, find the two recycled Medusa heads lying on the ground—one sideways and one upside-down—

squeezed under pillars. The Greeks often carved this fearsome mythological gorgon, with hair made of snakes and a gaze that could turn people to stone, into tombstones or cemetery walls to scare off grave robbers. In Roman times, she became a protector of temples. When Christianity took hold, Medusa was a reminder of the not-so-distant Roman persecution of Christians—so it may be no coincidence that these pagan fragments were left here in a dark corner of the cistern, never to see daylight again. Another theory proposes that the architect simply needed a proper base to raise the two small columns to ceiling height...and the Medusas were a perfect fit.

On the way out, you'll see huge, blocky concrete columns built more recently to support the structure, which are quite a contrast to the ancient, graceful Roman columns.

Near the exit, notice the stage in the water. The cistern serves as an exhibition hall for the Istanbul Biennial arts festival, and is a concert venue from time to time—mainly for traditional Turkish or Sufi music. Check the events schedule at the ticket office. You may be able to enjoy a great concert for no more than the regular cistern entrance fee.

• *Leaving the Underground Cistern, turn right and retrace your steps back up to the park where this walk began. Cross the park to find the towering Blue Mosque at the far end. You'll note that we've set out some nice wooden benches from which you can enjoy the view. Read the next page or so while seated here. Notice the schedule (posted by the souvenir kiosk) for the sound-and-light show performed some evenings near the mosque. Back in the 1970s, these shows were quite impressive.*

Blue Mosque

This famous and gorgeous mosque is one of the world's finest. It was built in just seven years (1609-

1616) by the architect Mehmet Aga, who also rebuilt Kaaba (the holiest shrine of Islam—the giant black cube at the center of the mosque in the holy city of Mecca). Locals call it the Sultan Ahmet Mosque for the ruler who financed it (see sidebar), but travelers know it as the Blue Mosque because of the rich blue color of the handmade ceramic tiles that dominate the interior.

• *As you face the Blue Mosque, to your right (with the multitude of mini-domes and chimneys) is the madrassa, a school of theology. Facing the mosque, you can see it has...*

Six Minarets

Aside from its impressive scale and opulent interior, the Blue Mosque is unique because of its six minarets. According to Muslim tradition, the imam (the prayer leader) or the muezzin (a man chosen for his talent in correctly voicing the call to prayer) would climb to the top of a minaret five times each day to announce the call to prayer. On hearing this warbling chant, Muslims are to come to the mosque to pray. Today, an imam or muezzin still performs the call to prayer, but now it's amplified by loudspeakers at the top of the minarets.

A single minaret was adequate for its straightforward function, but mosques financed by sultans often wanted to show off with more. A story popular with tour guides is that Sultan Ahmet I asked the architect for a gold *(altın)* minaret—but the man thought he said "six" *(altı)*. In all likelihood, Ahmet probably requested the six minarets to flaunt his wealth. But at the time, the central mosque in the holy city of Mecca also had six. The clergy at Mecca feared that Ahmet's new mosque would upstage theirs—so the sultan built a seventh minaret at Mecca.

• *The walkway by the benches leads to the Blue Mosque. Through the gate at the end of the walkway, you enter the mosque's...*

Outer Courtyard

Straight ahead, a staircase leads up to the inner courtyard (described next). To the right of the staircase, notice the line of water taps used for ablution—the ritual cleansing of the body before worshipping, as directed by Islamic law. These are comparatively new, installed to replace the older fountain in the inner courtyard (which we'll see soon). To the left, another set of stairs leads to an entrance into the mosque designated for worshippers (you may exit through this gate when you leave the mosque).

• *Now take the stairs up into the....*

Sultan Ahmet I and Kösem

Sultan Ahmet the First (1590-1617) ascended to the throne at the age of 14. Though young, he was well-educated and talented, spoke several languages, and proved to be an able statesman.

To prevent future conflicts for the throne, it was customary for a new sultan to kill his brothers. Regarded for his compassion, Ahmet went against two centuries of tradition to spare his brother's life. He allowed his brother, Mustafa, to live

(and Mustafa became sultan after Ahmet's death). But the tradition was soon revived: When Ahmet's son Murat IV took the throne, Murat had his young brother, Prince Beyazıt, strangled.

Ahmet's greatest achievement was the construction of the Blue Mosque, completed in 1616. He died of typhoid one year later at the age of 28. Ahmet's wife, Kösem (1590-1651), was one of the most influential women in Ottoman history. She became a *haseki* (favorite) of Ahmet when she was only 15. Notorious for her ambition, Kösem was kept away from the palace by Ahmet's successors. But when her young son Murat became sultan at age 11, Kösem returned to the palace and essentially ran the empire through him. Her control of the state continued through the reign of her second son, the mentally disturbed İbrahim I (a.k.a. İbrahim the Mad).

For nearly a decade, Kösem ruled the empire without intrusion. When İbrahim was murdered, Kösem introduced her grandson, Mehmet, as the next sultan. But Mehmet's mother, Turhan Sultan, would not tolerate Kösem's domination, and so she sent eunuchs to strangle Kösem in her sleep.

HISTORIC CORE

Inner Courtyard

The courtyard is surrounded by a portico, which provides shade and shelter. The shutters along the back wall open in summer for

ventilation. In the center of the courtyard is a fancy fountain, once used for ablutions but no longer functional. When the mosque fills up for special services, worshippers who can't fit inside pray in the large vaulted area in front of the mosque (on your left) and, if necessary, fill the rest of the courtyard. But today such jam-packed services are rare. Muslims are not required to go to the mosque five times each day; they can pray anywhere. The exception is the midday service on Friday, which the Quran dictates should be a time for all worshippers to come together in congregation—making mosques more crowded on Fridays.

• *Now go into the mosque. (For instructions and etiquette, see page 63.) The main door on this west end is where visitors generally enter. (If this door is closed, you should be able to go around the corner on the right.) As you enter, take a plastic bag from the container and use it to carry your shoes, which you should remove before you step on the carpet. Entering the mosque is free, but you can make a donation as you exit. If you have to wait in line, use the time to read the Understanding Islam chapter.*

Interior

Stepping through the heavy leather drape into the interior, you'll understand why this is called the Blue Mosque. Let your eyes ad-

just to the dim lighting as you breathe in the vast and intensely decorated interior.

Approach the wood railing to take a closer look at the apse (straight ahead from the main gate). The area beyond this barrier is reserved for worshippers, who fill the space at all times of day. The little shin-high wooden shelves are for storing worshippers' shoes.

On the far wall, look for the highly decorated marble niche with large candles on either side. This is the mihrab (meeh-rahb), which points southeast to Mecca, where all Muslims face when they worship. The surrounding wall is decorated with floral-designed stained-glass windows, many of them original.

On the right side of the apse is a staircase leading up to a platform with a cone on top. This is the *mimber* (meem-behr), similar to a pulpit in a Christian church. A *mimber* is symbolic of the growth of Islam—Muhammad had to stand higher and higher to talk to his growing following. It is used by the imam (prayer leader) to deliver a speech on Fridays, similar to a sermon in Christian services. As a sign of respect for Muhammad, the imam stands only halfway up the staircase.

Farther to the right, next to the main pillar, is a fancy marble platform elevated on columns. This is where the choir sings hymns a cappella (mainstream Islam uses no instruments) on important religious days.

Mosque services are segregated: The main hall is reserved for men, while women use the colonnaded area behind the barriers at the back, on both sides of the main entrance. Women can also use the upper galleries on crowded days. While many visitors think it is demeaning to women to make them stay in back, most Muslims feel it's respectful to women and more conducive to prayer. The men are better able to concentrate on God without the distraction of bent-over women in front of them, and the women feel more comfortable not having men behind them.

The huge dome—reaching a height of 141 feet and a diameter of 110 feet—is modeled after the one in Hagia Sophia, which was the first building to use pillars to support a giant central dome. As Turkish engineers improved on this concept over the years, they were able to create vast indoor spaces covered by cascading domes. The same fundamentals are still used today in many contemporary mosques.

Near the corners of the vast room, notice the giant pillars paved with fluted marble panels. These "elephant feet" support the arches, dome, semi-domes, and cupolas. Since the weight is transferred mainly to these four pillars, thick, bulky walls aren't necessary. As with flying buttresses in a Gothic cathedral, this technique allowed the architect to fill the walls with decorative windows. Compare the Blue Mosque (with its 260 windows) with the gloomy interior of the much older (and bulkier) Hagia Sophia.

The low-hanging chandeliers were made for oil lamps with floating wicks; they were designed to be raised and lowered to tend to the lamps (although now they hold lightbulbs). Years ago, a thick patchwork of handmade rugs covered the floor—these have been removed for preservation and replaced with the current machine-made carpeting. Notice that the carpets have lines to organize the worshippers—just like lined paper organizes words.

Islamic tradition forbids the portrayal of living beings in places of worship, which could distract people from worshipping Allah as the one God. As a result, the Muslim world excelled at nonfigurative art. In this and other mosques, instead of paintings of saints and prophets, you'll see geometric designs and calligraphy.

Along with the painted floral and geometric patterns, more than 20,000 ceramic tiles were used extensively to decorate the mosque. Lower parts of the wall—up to the height of the marble application on the giant pillars—are paved with mostly blue, early 17th-century İznik tiles. İznik (ancient Nicea) was the Ottoman Empire's tile-making center, and its tiles feature prominently in many museums around the world (including the Istanbul Archaeo-logical Museum, nearby).

Artful Arabic calligraphy (*hat* in Turkish; pronounced "hot") is another form of mosque decoration. To make the words appear more beautiful, the *hattat* (hot-taht; calligrapher) remains committed to grammar rules but takes liberties with forms of letters and comes up with decorative designs, though this makes reading difficult. Many of the examples of *hat* around the mosque are excerpts from the Quran or from the hadith (the collected teachings of the Prophet Muhammad). In a Chris-

tian church, you'd have God and Jesus front and center. Here, the two medallions high above the mihrab read *Muhammad* (left) and *Allah* (right).

The Blue Mosque represents the pinnacle of Ottoman architecture—and marks the beginning of the empire's decline. After its construction, the treasury was exhausted, and the Ottoman Empire entered a period of stagnation that eventually led to its collapse. Never again could the empire afford a building of such splendor.

Similarly, the mosque's patron, Sultan Ahmet I, was too young and inexperienced to effectively wield his authority and became mired in bureaucracy and tradition. While a few of his successors (including his son, Murat IV) managed to temporarily revive the dying empire, Ahmet marked the beginning of a long string of incompetent sultans who would eventually rule over an empire known in the early 20th century as the "Sick Man of Europe."

• *Leave the mosque and return to the inner courtyard. With your back to the mosque, walk to the back of the courtyard. Before you exit, consider taking a seat on the marble steps and soaking up the view of the mosque and the people mingling about. The crowd is a fun mix of Turkish tourists, travelers from across the world, wide-eyed cruise groups, and pilgrims. Try out a little Turkish: You can say, "Nasılsınız?" (nah-suhl-suh-nuhz; "How are you?") and "Merhaba" (mehr-hah-bah; "Hello"). Every school kid knows how to say in English, "What is your name?" and "How old are you?"*

As you leave, turn around when you step out of the courtyard for one more glance at the graceful cascading-domes design (go halfway down the stairs and look back for a good photo op, with the domes nicely framed by the portal).

As you step outside the exterior gate, you enter a long, skinny square that was the ancient Hippodrome of Constantinople. The Egyptian Obelisk is directly ahead of you.

Hippodrome

Built in the fourth century A.D., the Hippodrome was Constantinople's primary venue for chariot races. But it became the place where the people of the city gathered, and this racetrack has also been the scene of social and religious disputes, political clashes, and violent uprisings.

Chariot races were the most popular events in Constantinople, appealing to people from all walks of life. Winning teams became celebrities...at least until the next race. Between races, the masses were entertained by dancers, cheerleaders, musicians, acrobats, and performing animals.

The courtyard of the Blue Mosque marks the former site of the Hippodrome's *kathisma* (royal lodge). Supported by gorgeous marble columns, this grandstand was where the emperor and his family watched the races unfold. The lodge was connected to the Great Palace (on the site of today's Blue Mosque) for an easy escape in case the crowd got out of control.

Constantinople's social classes were identified by colors—Greens, Blues, Reds, and Whites—each with its favorite chariot team. Spectators at Hippodrome races, put on edge by social and economic gripes, often came to blows (not unlike today's soccer hooligans). Relations between the ruling and poor classes hit a low point in January of 532, when the Nika Revolt (named for the rebels' battle cry, *"Nika!"*—"Victory!") erupted at a chariot race. Emperor Justinian called in the Imperial Guard, who massacred some 30,000 protestors.

As big as today's gigantic football stadiums, the Hippodrome could seat 100,000 spectators. But when races went out of vogue, the once-proud structure became a makeshift quarry for builders scavenging precut stones.

The Hippodrome was in ruins long before the Turks arrived. The Ottomans named it Atmeydanı ("horsetrack") and used it for horseback riding and archery training. Through the years, dirt dug up to make way for foundations of surrounding buildings was dumped here, so today's ground level is significantly higher than during Byzantine times. If you look down around the base of the monuments that are still standing, you'll see the original ground level. The last remaining stones of the Hippodrome's "bleachers" were used to build the Blue Mosque. Today, none of the original seating survives, and the ancient racetrack has been replaced by a modern road.

Every year during Ramadan, the Hippodrome takes on a festive atmosphere in the evening, when Muslims break their fast at sunset (see page 64).

• *In its Byzantine glory days, the Hippodrome was decorated with monuments from all over the world. The most famous one is right in the middle of the long square.*

Egyptian Obelisk

This ancient, pointy pillar was carved about 1,500 years before the birth of Christ to honor the Egyptian Pharaoh Thutmose III; its inscribed hieroglyphs commemorate his military achievements. The obelisk was brought here from the Temple of Karnak on the Upper Nile sometime in the fourth century A.D. What you see today is only the upper third of the original massive stone block (take a moment to imagine its original height).

The most interesting part of the obelisk is its Byzantine base, which was cut out of local white marble and stands on four bronze feet. Reliefs on all four sides of the base depict Emperor Theo-

dosius the Great and his family at the royal lodge, watching the Hippodrome races. On the side facing the Blue Mosque, the emperor gives an olive wreath to the winner, while his servant hands out a sack of coins. On the opposite side, envoys bow down before Theodosius in homage. At the bottom of the base (facing Hagia Sophia), find the relief showing the column as it lay horizontal, and how pulleys were used to raise it.

Throughout Asia Minor (the Asian part of today's Turkey), the Latin and Greek languages coexisted during the early stages of the Byzantine Empire. At the obelisk's base, you'll see an inscription eulogizing the emperor, written in both Latin (on the side facing the Blue Mosque) and Greek (on the opposite side). Both inscriptions give basically the same information, but they differ when it comes to how long it took to raise the obelisk: The Latin version says 30 days, the Greek 32. This ancient typo perplexes archaeologists to this day.

• *The tall stone column (that looks like a stone-paved obelisk) at the left end of the Hippodrome (with the Blue Mosque to your back) is the...*

Column of Constantine

Like the Egyptian Obelisk, this column went up in the fourth century A.D. But unlike its Egyptian sister, it was constructed here. In the early 10th century A.D., Emperor Constantine VII Porphyrogenitus sheeted the column with bronze panels. But as the city was looted during the Fourth Crusade (in the early 13th century), the panels were pulled down to make weapons. You can still see the holes where the panels were attached to the column.

• *Between the Column of Constantine and the Egyptian Obelisk is the bronze...*

Column of the Serpent

This was a victory monument dedicated to the gods by 31 Greek city-states to commemorate their victory against the Persians at Plataea (479 B.C.). It stood at the Temple of Apollo in Delphi for 800 years, until—like the Egyptian Obelisk—it was brought to Constantinople from Greece in the fourth century A.D. The names of the sponsoring cities are inscribed at the base (currently underground, buried by earth accumulated over the centuries). Originally, this column showed three serpents twisted together, their heads supporting a golden trophy. The gold was gone even before the reign of Constantine the Great, but the heads survived until just 300 years ago—when they mysteriously vanished. Only the upper jaw of one snake still exists (on display in the Istanbul Archaeological Museum).

Other monuments that once decorated the Hippodrome are long gone, such as four famous cast-bronze horses from ancient Greece. During the Fourth Crusade, these were plundered and taken to Venice...where they're still on display at St. Mark's Basilica.

• *Across the Hippodrome from the Blue Mosque is the Turkish and Islamic Arts Museum, housed in the...*

İbrahim Paşa Palace

The palace—a gift from Sultan Süleyman the Magnificent to İbrahim Paşa in 1520—is one of the best examples of civil architecture in the city. The palace was once much bigger than what you see today, rivaling Topkapı Palace in both its size and opulence. The

HISTORIC CORE

only surviving bits are the reception hall and areas where guests were hosted, surrounding a small central courtyard. Looking at the facade, notice the Oriental-looking wooden balcony.

Through the years, the İbrahim Paşa Palace has been used as a palace school, a dormitory for single soldiers, and a prison. In 1983, it was restored and became the home of the **Turkish and Islamic Arts Museum** (see the Turkish and Islamic Arts Museum Tour chapter). The carefully chosen collection offers a representative glimpse of the richness of art and culture in this part of the world: metal and clay objects, ceramics, glassware, calligraphy, and an impressive collection of Turkish carpets, some dating from the 13th century.

• *Our walk is nearly finished. But if you're not mosqued out, first consider a 30-minute detour to the Sokullu Mosque, a few hundred yards south of the Hippodrome (described on page 33). Otherwise, continue down to the north end of the Hippodrome (with the Blue Mosque on your right). You'll run into an octagonal pavilion with a green dome on dark pillars, the...*

German Fountain

This pavilion—which seems a little out of place surrounded by minarets and obelisks—would be more at home in Berlin. The

fountain was a gift from the German government to commemorate Kaiser Wilhelm II's visit to Istanbul in 1898. It was constructed in pieces in Germany, then shipped to Istanbul in 1901 and reassembled on this location.

Kaiser Wilhelm II visited Istanbul three times to schmooze the sultan. By the early 20th century, it was obvious that a war between the great powers of Europe was imminent, and empires were choosing sides. Though the Ottoman Empire was in its waning days, it remained a formidable power in the east and a valuable ally for Germany. Sure enough, when World War I erupted in 1914, the Ottoman Empire joined the fray as Germany's unwilling ally. Less than four years later, the Ottomans had lost the war—and with it, what remained of their ailing empire. The last sultan was sent into exile with the establishment of the Turkish Republic in the 1920s.

• *We've come full circle—you're just up the street from Hagia Sophia. At the end of the Hippodrome, just before the street with the tram tracks (Divan Yolu), are a TI and some public WCs. Across the tracks are a*

pair of recommended local restaurants: Sultanahmet Köftecisi serves just meatballs, and the misnamed Pudding Shop (a.k.a. "Lale Restaurant")
offers meat and veggie dishes, döner kebab, *and sometimes fish in a cafeteria-style setting where you can see all of the choices (it may look crowded, but there's also seating upstairs). Just uphill from the restaurants on Divan Yolu is the Sultanahmet tram stop and the start of our "Old Town Back Streets Walk." Beyond that is a bustling commercial zone with more restaurants, a pharmacy, travel agencies, and banks (with ATMs). And farther up is the Grand Bazaar (from the Hippodrome, it's a 15-minute walk, or a quick ride on the tram from the Sultanahmet stop to the Çemberlitaş stop).*

HAGIA SOPHIA TOUR

Aya Sofya

For centuries, it was known as Megalo Ekklesia, the "Great Church" of Constantinople. The Greeks called it Hagia Sophia (eye-ah soh-fee-yah), meaning "Divine Wisdom," an attribute of God. The Turkish version is Aya Sofya. But no matter what you call it, this magnificent place—first a church, then a mosque, and now a museum—is one of the most impressive structures you'll ever see.

Emperor Justinian built Hagia Sophia between A.D. 532 and 537. For 900 years, it served as the seat of the Orthodox Patriarch of Constantinople—the "eastern Vatican." Replete with shimmering mosaics and fine marble, Hagia Sophia was the single greatest architectural achievement of the Byzantine Empire.

When the Ottomans took Constantinople in 1453, Sultan Mehmet the Conqueror—impressed with the Great Church's beauty—converted it into an imperial mosque. Hagia Sophia remained Istanbul's most important mosque for five centuries. In the early years of the Turkish Republic (1930s), Hagia Sophia was converted again, this time into a museum. It retains unique elements of both the Byzantine and Ottoman empires and their respective religions, Orthodox Christianity and Islam. In a sense, Hagia Sophia is Istanbul in architectural form: ancient, grand, gigantic, with some rough edges, but on the whole remarkably preserved—a fascinating, still-vigorous blend of East and West.

Orientation

Cost: 30 TL covers the entire museum, including the upper galleries. Unless the other windows are closed, avoid the right-hand ticket window, which is reserved for tour guides with groups.

Hours: Daily 9:00-19:00, until 17:00 off-season, temporary exhibits and upper galleries close 30 minutes earlier, last entry one hour before closing.

Crowd-Beating Tips: Buy your ticket in advance at www.muze. gov.tr/en or enter with a Museum Pass—either allows you to skip the ticket line and head directly to the security check. During peak season, avoid visiting on Tuesday, which is when Topkapı Palace is closed—and Hagia Sophia gets even more crowded.

Getting There: Hagia Sophia is in the Sultanahmet neighborhood in the heart of the Old Town, facing the Blue Mosque. The main entrance is at the southwest corner of the giant building, across the busy street with the tram tracks (Divan Yolu). If you arrive by tram, get off at the Sultanahmet stop, and walk a couple of hundred yards downhill along Divan Yolu. Cross the wide street at the traffic light. As you approach Hagia Sophia, loitering tour guides may offer to guide you around for a fee (generally 70 TL). But, with this self-guided tour, you won't need their help.

Getting In: A crowd generally gathers just before 9:00 outside the ticket office and rushes the doors when they open, so arrive at 9:15 to miss the mob. If you're early and also have the Underground Cistern in your plans, go there first (the cistern is across the street with the tram tracks—described in the Historic Core of Istanbul Walk chapter). Note that ongoing museum-entrance renovations may cause slow-moving lines. Guided tours often bunch up at Hagia Sophia's security checkpoint and ticket taker. Be patient—the logjam usually clears quickly.

Information: Tel. 0212/528-4500; most of the descriptions in the museum are in English.

Length of This Tour: Allow at least one hour for the main floor and 30 minutes or more for the upper galleries.

Security and Baggage: After buying your ticket, but before entering, you'll go through an airport-type security checkpoint. There is no bag check, so you'll need to carry your bags with you.

Services: The cafeteria is across from the main building entrance, to the left of the walkway that leads past ticket control. The WC is at the end of the walkway, past the cafeteria. The bookshop is in the interior narthex.

Photography: Photography is allowed, but no flash photos of icons, mosaic panels, or frescoes. English-language signs indicate where you should turn off your flash.

Nearby: Five *türbes* (sultans' tombs) along the south side of Hagia Sophia are open to the public and worth a look if you have extra time (daily 9:00-19:00). For details, see the end of this chapter.

Starring: The finest house of worship in the Christian and Muslim worlds.

BACKGROUND

Hagia Sophia was built over the remains of at least two earlier churches. After the second of these churches was destroyed in the Nika riots in A.D. 532, Emperor Justinian I (r. 527-565) wasted no time, immediately putting his plan for Hagia Sophia into action. He asked for the near-impossible: a church with un-believably grand proportions, a monument that would last for centuries and keep his name alive for future generations.

Justinian appointed two geometricians to do the job: Anthemius, from the Aegean town of Tralles, and his assistant, Isidore of Miletus (see sidebar on page 101). Both knew from the start that this would be a risky project. Making Justinian's vision a reality would involve enormous challenges. But they courageously went forward, creating a masterpiece unlike anything seen before.

More than 5,000 architects, stonemasons, bricklayers, plasterers, sculptors, painters, and mosaic artists worked around the clock for five years to complete Hagia Sophia—and drain the treasury—faster than even the emperor had anticipated. In December of 537, the Great Church of Constantinople held its first service in the presence of Emperor Justinian and the Patriarch of Constantinople.

The church was a huge success story for Justinian, who was understandably satisfied with his achievement. As the story goes, when he stepped inside the church, he exclaimed, "Solomon, I have surpassed you!" In the long history of the empire, the Byzantines would never again construct such a grand edifice, but its design would influence architects for centuries.

Hagia Sophia was a legend even before it was completed. People came from all over to watch the great dome slowly rise above the landscape of the city. It was the first thing that merchants saw from approaching ships and caravans. Hagia Sophia soon became a landmark, and it continues to hold a special place in the mystical skyline of Istanbul.

The structure served as a church for nearly a millennium. For a thousand years it stood as the greatest dome in the world, until the Renaissance, when Brunelleschi built his famous dome in Florence.

The day the Ottomans captured Constantinople in 1453, Hagia Sophia was converted into a mosque. Most of the functional elements that decorated the church were removed, and its figurative mosaics and frescoes were plastered over in accordance with Islamic custom. Today the interior holds elements mostly from the time when Hagia Sophia was used as a mosque (from 1453 until 1934, when it became a museum).

The Tour Begins

• *After you pass through security and ticket control, you'll see the official walkway leading straight ahead, toward the main entrance. Instead, we'll take a shortcut for a better entrance route: Turn right, cross the big paved path, and slip past the wooden kiosk toward the giant, ornate Rococo...*

Fountain

The Ottomans added this fountain in the mid-18th century. Across from the fountain, notice the water taps in the portico by the side of

the main building. When Hagia Sophia was a mosque, both of these were used for ablution (ritual cleansing before prayer) as part of Islamic tradition.

• *Enter the museum through its exit door at the far end of this courtyard (to the left). On the pillar before the door (to your right as you face the door, at the corner of the small museum bookstore), notice*

the Arabic translated into Turkish. According to Islamic tradition, in the seventh century, Muhammad himself predicted that Constantinople (which was Christian and ruled the Western world at that time) would be conquered, and he praised the commander and soldiers as "güzel" (elite or distinguished). Eight centuries later, his prediction came to pass.

Just past this pillar, before you enter the building, walk to the open chamber to your right, and take a few minutes to see the massive, presixth-century...

Baptismal Pool

This immense baptismal pool was hewn out of a massive piece of marble, and amazingly is still in one piece despite spending centuries buried amid construction debris in a corner of Hagia Sophia's courtyard. It was finally unearthed in 2010. More than 10 feet long and nearly four feet deep, the pool likely was used for communal baptisms common in early Christianity. Urns found nearby held olive oil, which—in the Byzantine Orthodox tradition—was added to water during baptism.

The pool sits in what was once the baptistery courtyard. The baptistery itself, next door, was converted into the tomb of Sultan Mustafa I in the 17th century (to the right as you enter the chamber, look through the glass to see the interior of the tomb). The pool and other items from the baptistery were moved here to make way for Mustafa's tomb.

• *Now backtrack and step into this historic place of worship through the...*

Vestibule of Guards

This entry is named for the imperial guards who waited here for the emperor while he was attending church services. Byzantine

emperors used this entryway because of its proximity to the royal palace, which stood where the Blue Mosque is today.

Scholars believe that the entrance's imposing **bronze doors** were brought here from an ancient temple in Antioch sometime after Justinian's reign. At the top of the flat panel (about eye-level on the first door), you can see traces of the silver imperial monograms that were once affixed to the bronze sheeting. Notice that these doors can't open or close—they became stuck in place when the marble floor was renovated and raised.

Stepping inside the vestibule, look up: The vaulted ceiling is covered with original mosaics, dating back nearly 1,500 years to Justinian's time. The mosaics in his church—such as these—depicted geometric patterns rather than people, as was the fashion at the time. Later, figurative mosaics were also added.

• *Above the doorway into the church, notice the gorgeous...*

Donation Mosaic

The mosaic dates from the 11th-century reign of Basil II. Scenes such as this became common in later Orthodox churches, and they usually depict the patron who funded the church's construction and to whom the church is dedicated. In the mosaic, you see Mary and the Christ child enthroned. Jesus holds the Gospels in his left hand and makes the three-fingered sign of the Trinity with his right hand. Two mighty Roman emperors flank the Holy Family: On the right, Constantine presents Mary and Christ with a model of his city, Constantinople (symbolized by city walls). On

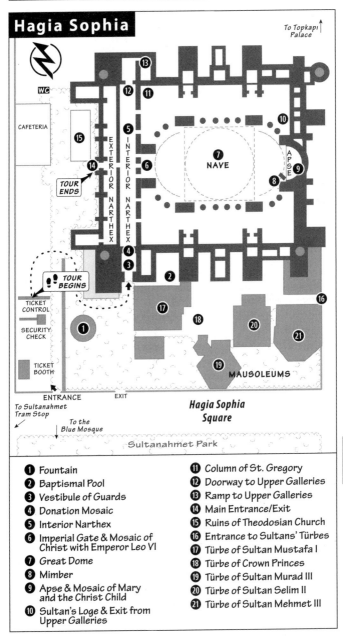

Hagia Sophia

To Topkapı Palace

WC

CAFETERIA

EXTERIOR NARTHEX

INTERIOR NARTHEX

NAVE

APSE

TOUR ENDS

TOUR BEGINS

TICKET CONTROL

SECURITY CHECK

TICKET BOOTH

ENTRANCE   EXIT

To Sultanahmet Tram Stop

To the Blue Mosque

MAUSOLEUMS

Hagia Sophia Square

Sultanahmet Park

❶ Fountain
❷ Baptismal Pool
❸ Vestibule of Guards
❹ Donation Mosaic
❺ Interior Narthex
❻ Imperial Gate & Mosaic of Christ with Emperor Leo VI
❼ Great Dome
❽ Mimber
❾ Apse & Mosaic of Mary and the Christ Child
❿ Sultan's Loge & Exit from Upper Galleries

⓫ Column of St. Gregory
⓬ Doorway to Upper Galleries
⓭ Ramp to Upper Galleries
⓮ Main Entrance/Exit
⓯ Ruins of Theodosian Church
⓰ Entrance to Sultans' Türbes
⓱ Türbe of Sultan Mustafa I
⓲ Türbe of Crown Princes
⓳ Türbe of Sultan Murad III
⓴ Türbe of Sultan Selim II
㉑ Türbe of Sultan Mehmet III

The Iconoclast Era (A.D. 730-840): The Banning of Icons

The religious use of icons—depictions of human figures in mosaics, frescoes, and other art forms—was a controversial subject throughout Byzantine history. Church and political leaders clashed over icons. Despite the disapproval of early Church fathers, the public liked the images. So did the emperors, who used icons to bolster their claim to divine power—often depicting themselves as holy figures on coins and church walls.

Opponents (called iconoclasts) argued that icons drove believers away from the very basis of Christianity. If Christ was divine, how could his nature be depicted in mere paint or stone? An icon would show only Jesus' human side, ignoring the divine part of his nature.

Fed up with the controversy, Emperor Leo III banned icons in A.D. 730, saying that people had begun worshipping them as idols. His ban did little to end the debate, instead leading to revolts.

Thanks to popular demand and political expediency, icons returned a century later. In the post-Iconoclast Era, craftsmen and mosaic artists were once again free to portray religious scenes. Emperors had artists add events and scenes that had nothing to do with religion—but instead furthered political objectives. They saw no harm in being portrayed with Mary, Christ, and the angels. Icons became like illustrations from a history book—projected from an imperial point of view—instead of tools to teach religion to the illiterate. Two great examples at Hagia Sophia are the mosaic of Emperor Leo above the Imperial Gate, and the Empress Zoe mosaic in the upper galleries.

the left is Justinian, presenting a model of his greatest achievement, Hagia Sophia. Note the differences between this model and today's Hagia Sophia: Justinian's version had no minarets and no retaining or garden walls, and its dome was topped with a cross. It's fortunate that this mosaic has survived so beautifully intact, because many such mosaics were destroyed during the Iconoclast Era (see sidebar). If your neck is sore, or just for fun, turn 180 degrees, block the light with this book, and see the same mosaic more comfortably.

• *Now walk under the donation mosaic and straight into the...*

Interior Narthex

Hagia Sophia's interior narthex is an attractive space, with nine vaulted bays richly decorated with mosaics. The walls on either

side are lined with inch-thick **marble panels,** which were glued to the wall with stucco and pinned with iron rods. In some parts of the building, such as the Vestibule of Guards, the iron rusted, and over time the marble pieces began to fall off (the Vestibule of Guards' walls are painted to replicate the original marble covering). But here in the interior narthex, which is more protected from the elements, after 15 centuries, the panels hang on.

On the narthex ceiling are original **Justinian mosaics** that survived the Iconoclast Era because they were nonfigurative. The church's designer, Anthemius, sought to give the impression of movement. These mosaic pieces—interspersed with randomly placed bits of semiprecious stones—change from muted shades to brilliant reflection, depending on the direction of the light. Since services generally took place after sunset, the mosaic artists designed their work to be vivid even in flickering candlelight: simple polychrome crosses and starry shapes on a golden background.

Five doors on the left wall lead into the narrow, unadorned **exterior narthex.** Less splendid than the interior narthex, it holds a few uninteresting relics and the occasional temporary exhibit, along with the main visitors' entrance. We'll skip this for now.

At the far end of the interior narthex, notice the huge doorway leading to the ramp to the upper galleries. We'll go up this ramp later, after visiting the nave.

• *Just ahead of you, the central (and biggest) door to the nave is called the...*

Imperial Gate

This majestic doorway was reserved for the emperor—it was opened only for him. Notice the **metal hooks** attached to the top of the doorway. The Ottomans added these to hold leather curtains—similar to those used in today's mosques—to protect worshippers from dust and to reduce the interruption of a giant door opening and closing.

Look at the panel glittering above the gate, the **Mosaic of Christ with Emperor Leo VI.** The emperor known as "Leo the Wise" is remembered more for his multiple marriages than for

his intellect. His first three wives died without giving him a child, so he married Zoe Carbonospina (meaning "Black Eyes")—his mistress and the mother of his son. This sparked a scandal: The emperor was excommunicated by the patriarch and barred from attending the Christmas service in A.D. 906. In this scene, Leo seems to be asking for forgiveness—prostrating himself before Jesus, who blesses the emperor. The Greek reads, "May peace be with you. I am the light of the earth." Mary and the Archangel Gabriel are portrayed in the roundels on either side of Jesus. Whitewashed over by the Ottomans, the mosaic was only rediscovered in 1933.

• *Now step through the Imperial Gate and into Hagia Sophia's...*

Nave

Overwhelming, unbelievable, fantastic: These are the words that fall from the open mouths of visitors to Hagia Sophia. Take a few steps into the grand space, close this book, shut your ears to the rumble of excited visitors, and just absorb the experience: You are in Hagia Sophia, the crowning achievement of the Byzantine Empire.

Paris' Notre-Dame would fit within Hagia Sophia's great dome, and New York City's Statue of Liberty could do jumping jacks here.

• *Take a few minutes to appreciate the feat of engineering that is Hagia Sophia. First, tune into the...*

Architecture

Hagia Sophia was designed as a classical basilica covered by a vast central dome. By definition, a "basilica" is characterized by a large, central open space, called a nave, flanked by rows of columns and narrow side aisles. It sounds simple, but even the two geometricians Justinian chose to build Hagia Sophia had doubts about whether the plan would work. Every so often, Anthemius would go to the emperor to tell him about potential risks. And every time, he got the same response: "Have faith in God." Anthemius was right to have worried. Despite his mastery of geometry, he made some miscalculations: A few decades after Hagia Sophia was completed, part of the gigantic dome collapsed. The dome was repaired using

Math in Practice

Emperor Justinian appointed two great scholars of geometry to design his Great Church: Anthemius of Tralles and his assistant, Isidore of Miletus. Anthemius' title was actually "*mechanikos*" (engineer), not "architect." (Architects of the time worked beneath the engineers and were considered contractors, ranking among the builders and masons.) The mission given to Anthemius was to "apply geometry to solid matter." Hagia Sophia's architectural unity is a testament to Anthemius' ability and genius. He knew how to create and integrate spaces within the confines of an architectural style.

In Byzantine architecture, a building's interior was more important than its exterior. The exterior was just a mask, but the interior aimed to impress and overwhelm the visitor with a specific message. Hagia Sophia's message was that the emperor—who created the sacred monument—was backed up by divine power. So in a way, the church was a very expensive propaganda tool.

Byzantines, like the Romans before them, mastered the use of the arch to bear weight. Anthemius wanted to create the feeling that the church's dome was hanging down from the heavens on gold chains. To achieve this, he designed a dome bigger and higher than anything built before, and placed a row of clear glass windows around its base. When you look up at the light streaming through these windows, you'll squint at the brightness—making the columns between the windows nearly disappear and creating the illusion that the dome is floating on air. (Later engineers in Europe's Gothic age opened up the space even more, through the use of flying buttresses.)

Anthemius is considered the greatest architect in Byzantine history. But after designing Hagia Sophia, he continued his career as a scholar, living a modest life in a small residence in Constantinople.

steeper angles than the original; even so, it would collapse and be rebuilt again in the sixth and 10th centuries.

The main dome—185 feet high and roughly 105 feet in diameter—appears to float on four great arches. The secret is the clear glass windows at the base of the dome. The triangular pendentives in the corners gracefully connect the round dome to the rectangular building below, and the arches pass the dome's weight on to the massive piers at the corners. Semi-domes at the ends extend the open space. Over 100 columns provide further support to the upper

parts of the building. Many of these columns were brought here from other, even more ancient monuments and temples.

Hagia Sophia was a worthy attempt to create a vast indoor space, independent of the walls. But in practice, quite a bit of the dome's great weight is held up by the walls, which is why there aren't very many windows. The Byzantines built additional arches inside the walls to further help distribute the weight. These "hidden arches" are visible here and there, where the stucco layers have worn away.

As you look around, note the basic principle of Byzantine architecture: symmetry. All the architectural elements, including decorative pieces, are placed in a symmetrical fashion. If symmetry demanded a window or door that would weaken a wall, then a false, painted-on one would be created in its place.

The artful use of light creates the interior's stunning effect. The windows at the base of the dome used clear glass, while other windows throughout the building used thin alabaster to further diffuse the light and create a more dramatic effect.

• *With the Imperial Gate directly behind you, face the apse and look up into the massive dome to see the...*

Dome Decorations

During the centuries that Hagia Sophia was used as a mosque, many of its original decorations—especially mosaics or frescoes depicting people—were covered over with whitewash and plaster. Ironically, in some cases, the plaster actually helped to preserve the

artwork. For others, damage was inevitable, as the stucco absorbed the whitewash. In the 19th century, the sultan invited the Swiss-born Fossati brothers to complete an extensive restoration of Hagia Sophia. They cleaned and catalogued many of the Byzantine figural mosaics before covering them up again.

At the base of the dome, between intersecting arches, are winged **seraphim.** Gold-leaf masks or medallions cover these angels' faces. The two nearest the apse are from the 14th century (the mask on the one to left of the apse was removed in 2010, and the face is now revealed); the other two are replicas by the Fossati brothers.

The Ottoman additions that immediately draw your attention are Arabic calligraphy, especially the eight 24-foot-wide **me-**

dallions suspended at the bases of the arches supporting the central and side domes. These huge, leather-wrapped wooden medallions were added in the 19th century and decorated by master Islamic calligraphers. In a church, you'd see paintings of Biblical figures and saints; however, in a mosque (which allows no depictions of people), you'll see ornately written names of leading Muslim figures. The two medallions on the arches flanking the apse are painted with the names of Allah (on the right) and Muhammad (on the left). The four at the center name the four caliphs, Muslim religious and social leaders who succeeded the Prophet Muhammad: Abu Bakr, Umar, Uthman, and Ali. The two medallions on the arches above the Imperial Gate bear the names of Muhammad's grandchildren and Ali's sons, who were assassinated.

• *Walk toward the front of the church. The heavy chandeliers hanging from the dome, additions from Ottoman times, held candlesticks or glass oil lamps with floating wicks. The highly decorated staircase before you, set diagonally away from the wall, is the...*

Mimber

The *mimber* (meem-behr) is the pulpit in a mosque, used by the imam (cleric, like a priest or rabbi) to deliver his sermon on Fridays, or to talk to the public on special occasions. The imam stands halfway up the stairs as a sign of respect, reserving the uppermost step for the Prophet Muhammad.

• *Go beyond the* mimber *and face the...*

Apse

When Hagia Sophia (the original church, facing Jerusalem) was converted into a mosque, a small off-center niche was added in the apse's circular wall. Called the mihrab, this niche shows the precise direction to face during prayers (toward the holy city of Mecca, which is south of Jerusalem). The stately columns flanking the mihrab are actually huge candles—standard fixtures in royal mosques.

High above the mihrab, on the underside of the semi-dome, is a colorful **Mosaic of Mary and the Christ Child** on a gold background (to see better, raise this book to block the light). Christ is also dressed in gold. Part of the background is missing, but most of the scene is intact. This mosaic, the oldest one in Hagia Sophia, dates from the ninth century. It may have been the first figurative mosaic added after the Iconoclast Era, replacing a cross-design mosaic from the earlier period. The gold "clubs" on Mary's forehead and both shoulders stand for the Trinity. Notice also the red "spades" among the "clubs" on the pillows.

On the right end of the arch, just before the semi-dome (behind the large medallion), find the **Mosaic of Archangel Gabriel** with his wings sweeping down to the ground. On the opposite end of the

arch, there was once a similar mosaic of the Archangel Michael.

To your left, by the side of the apse (the frilly gilded room under the big medallion), is the elevated prayer section for the sultans, or the **sultan's loge** (behind the gold-glazed metalwork). This area was added in the 19th century.

• *With your back to the apse, wander to the far right-hand corner of the nave. As you walk, notice the golden mosaics on the ceiling from Justinian's age. Past the large buttresses, separating the aisles from the nave, are rows of...*

Green Marble Columns

These columns carry the upper galleries and also provide support to the domes, easing the burden on the buttresses and the exterior walls. Notice the richly decorated white-marble capitals of these columns (with the joint monograms of Justinian and Theodora).

• *In the far corner (to your right, still facing the entry) is what looks like a five-foot-tall alabaster egg, but is actually an...*

Alabaster Urn

This is one of two Hellenistic-era **urns** (second century B.C., one on each side of the nave) that the sultan brought to Istanbul from Pergamon—the formidable ancient acropolis of north Aegean Turkey. Find the tap mounted in the side. Traditionally, Ottoman mosques had functional fountains inside, to provide drinking water for worshippers.

The two purple **porphyry columns** behind each urn are older than Hagia Sophia. Two columns stand at each corner—eight in all. Long ago, iron girdles were placed around the columns to prevent further damage (they already had cracks in them).

• *In the rear right-hand corner, about 10 yards beyond the alabaster urn, is the quirky and purportedly miraculous...*

Column of St. Gregory

This is the legendary "perspiring column"—the Column of St. Gregory, the miracle worker. For centuries, people believed this column "wept" holy water that could cure afflictions such as eye diseases and infertility.

How does it work? Put your thumb in the hole, and if it comes out feeling damp, your prayer will be answered. No? Try this. Put your thumb in the hole again, and this time, make a complete 360-degree circle with your hand, with your thumb still in the hole. The metal surrounding the hole has been polished by millions of hands over the years.

• *Walk through the door to the left of this column, leaving the nave and re-entering the interior narthex. The huge door to your right leads to the...*

UPPER GALLERIES

The upper level of the church holds Hagia Sophia's best-known mosaics. Go through this door and follow the long, stone-paved ramp up to the upper galleries (watch your step, as the stones are smooth and uneven). Why a ramp, and not stairs? Because those of exalted rank were either carried by their servants, or rode up on horseback. As you step off the ramp, keep to the right and enter the well-lit...

West Gallery

This gallery provides a direct view of the apse. Walk to the center of the gallery and look for a **green marble circle** in the floor right before the balustrade, with an ensemble of matching green columns on either side. This was the spot reserved for the empress' throne, directly across from the apse.

• *Turning left at the end of this gallery, you'll pass through the marble half wall—known as the Gate of Heaven and Hell—into the...*

South Gallery

This area originally was used for church council meetings. The frescoes on the ceiling are copies of ancient designs, redone by the Fossati brothers during their 19th-century restoration work.

Go to the first window on your right. To the right of the window is the **Deesis Mosaic,** one of the finest of Hagia Sophia's Byzantine mosaics—though certainly not its best preserved. It dates from the 13th or 14th century, and its theme—the Virgin Mary and John the Baptist asking Jesus for the salvation of souls—is common in Eastern Orthodox churches. Notice how Mary's and John's heads tilt slightly toward Christ. The workmanship is fascinating, especially the expression and detail in the faces. Get up close to examine how minuscule and finely cut the pieces are.

• *Walk to the far end of this gallery to see two more Byzantine mosaic panels, placed side by side.*

As you approach the end of the gallery, look for the 12th-century **Mosaic of the Virgin and Child with Emperor John**

Comnenus and Empress Irene. Mary stands in the center, holding the Christ Child in her arms. Christ's right hand extends in blessing, and he holds a scroll in his left hand. As in many such mosaics, the emperor offers Christ a bag of money (representing his patronage), and the empress presents a scroll. Their son, Prince Alexius, is portrayed to his mom's left on the adjoining pier—added to the scene only after he became co-emperor at age 17.

To the left is the 11th-century **Mosaic of Christ with Emperor Constantine IX Monomachus and Empress Zoe.** Constantine and Zoe are portrayed in ceremonial garments, flanking Christ on his throne. The inscription above the emperor's head reads, "Sovereign of Romans, Constantine Monomachus," while the empress is identified as "Zoe, the most pious Augusta."

Standard fare so far, but if we dig deeper, this mosaic gets quite interesting. If you look carefully, you can see that critical sections of text were erased and then restored (in what looks like a different font). Here's the story: Empress Zoe—the daughter of an emperor who had no male heirs—married Romanus Argyrus, but he was killed in his bath a few years later. Zoe then married her young lover, Michael IV, and, within a few years, he was dead, too. His nephew, Michael V, was named co-emperor and sent Zoe into exile. But the well-connected Zoe found a way back, had Michael V deposed, and at the age of 65 married a third time, to Constantine Monomachus.

That's three husbands in all—and a lot of extra work for the mosaic artists. So, instead of changing the image of Zoe's husband each time, they simply changed the title over his head. And Zoe's face, which was erased by Michael V, was restored to its youthful appearance after she resumed her reign and married Constantine Monomachus.

If you enjoy these mosaics, don't miss the Chora Church, out on the edge of the Old Town (see the Chora Church Tour chapter).
• *Retrace your steps back to the northwest corner (where you entered the galleries). This time walk along the North Gallery to the exit at the far end.*

North Gallery

As you walk, take a moment to look at the graffiti carved into the walls by bored, non-Byzantine church attendants during the long evening services. Graffiti is visible on the walls in the bays overlooking the nave, usually at upper-body height. Graffiti in the form of sailing ships makes you wonder whether these servants wished they could just sail away.
• *The exit ramp takes you down to the north aisle (you'll emerge by the Sultan's Loge). Head for the narthexes straight ahead, and exit the way others are entering. Just outside in a hole on your right are the remains of the earlier Theodosian Church.*

PREVIOUS CHURCHES

At least two earlier churches have stood on this spot. No trace remains of the first church, which was probably built in the fourth century A.D. as Constantine moved to strengthen his hold on the fledgling Byzantine Empire.

The next church, believed to have been built by Theodosius II, was grander in scale and more elaborate. But as fate would have it, this second church was also destroyed during a religious uprising—the Nika riots of 532 that caused the death of more than 30,000 people. Half of the city was reduced to ashes, including the church.

Some remains of the **Theodosian Church** are visible in the pit just outside the main entrance to Hagia Sophia. You can see part of the steps that led to the entrance portico, the bases of the columns that supported the entry porch, and fragments of marble blocks with carved designs of sheep. Other Theodosian Church artifacts, columns, and capitals are scattered nearby throughout Hagia Sophia's outdoor garden.

• *Your tour is finished. You're close to several other major sights, including the Blue Mosque, Hippodrome, and Underground Cistern (all described in the Historic Core of Istanbul Walk chapter). And directly behind Hagia Sophia is the wall of Topkapı Palace (see the Topkapı Palace Tour chapter).*

If you have a few minutes, it's worth a quick walk to see the Sultans' Türbes (mausoleums), which can only be accessed from outside the Hagia Sophia complex. To get there, exit the museum grounds through the turnstiles, head left along Hagia Sophia's garden wall, and find the entrance just around the southeast corner.

SULTANS' TÜRBES

A *türbe* (tewr-beh) is a monumental tomb—a mausoleum for high-ranking religious and political leaders. There are five *türbes* here in Hagia Sophia's garden, where sultans Selim II, Murad III, Mehmet III, and Mustafa I (all of whom ruled in the 16th and 17th centuries) are buried, side by side with their heirs and other relatives. To go inside a *türbe*, you'll need to remove your shoes on its entrance porch.

Walk past the first four elaborately decorated *türbes* to reach the simplest *türbe*, that of **Sultan Mustafa I.** This was built over the Hagia Sophia baptistery, after Mustafa's death. Through the glass (on the right as you enter the *türbe*), you can see the baptistery's former courtyard, which now holds the massive baptismal pool.

The twin-domed *türbe* of **Sultan Murad III** is particularly striking. Its interior is decorated in coral-red İznik tiles bordered with Arabic inscriptions—excerpts from the Quran—and inlaid wood. The octagonal *türbe* of **Sultan Selim II** (on the right as you return to the entrance) is one of the most elaborate in the city, with an exterior paved with marble. Notice the tile panels on either side of the entry: The one on the right is a 16th-century original, with traditional İznik designs. The one on the left is a replica: In 1895, a French art collector (who was also Sultan Abdulhamit's dentist) took the panel to France, ostensibly for restoration. It ended up in the Louvre.

HAGIA SOPHIA

TOPKAPI PALACE TOUR

Topkapı Sarayı

Topkapı Palace stands on the ruins of Byzantium, the ancient Greek settlement at the eastern tip of the Old Town peninsula. After capturing Constantinople, Ottoman Sultan Mehmet the Conqueror (a.k.a. Mehmet II) chose this prime location—overlooking the Sea of Marmara, the Bosphorus, and the Golden Horn—as the administrative center of his empire. In the 1470s, he built a large complex with offices, military barracks, a council chamber, and a reception hall. A century later, Topkapı (tohp-kah-puh) became the sultan's residence when Süleyman the Magnificent turned it into a home. Topkapı efficiently served as the sole administrative palace for Ottoman sultans for more than 400 years, until a new European-style palace was built on the Bosphorus in the mid-19th century (Dolmabahçe Palace, described on page 52).

The word "Topkapı" means "cannon door"—a reference to one of the gates on the old Byzantine wall along the Sea of Marmara. Originally known as the sultan's "New Palace," Topkapı was gradually enlarged over the centuries. Each reigning sultan contributed his own flourishes, according to the style of the era. So, unlike many European palaces, which were built all at once, Topkapı Palace was constructed gradually and organically over time. The result is a funhouse of architectural styles. Since no two buildings of the complex were built at the same time, they're all on different levels. As you pass through the doorways, you'll almost always step up or down. And yet this hodgepodge is totally functional—each addition had its purpose and was suited for its time. The visual mess of Topkapı Palace comes together to give visitors a vibrant, multilayered feel for the lifestyle of the sultans.

Orientation

Cost: 30 TL for palace, 15 TL for Harem, 20 TL for Hagia Irene church.

Hours: Palace open Wed-Mon 9:00-19:00, until 17:00 off-season, closed Tue, last entry one hour before closing, exhibits begin to close one hour earlier. Harem open Wed-Mon 9:00-17:00, closed Tue. Hagia Irene open Wed-Mon 9:00-19:00, until 17:00 off-season, closed Tue.

Renovations: Parts of the Harem and Imperial Treasury are under renovation into 2016 and other sections may close without notice. Popular items throughout may be missing, as they are sent to temporary exhibitions around the world.

Crowd-Beating Tips: Buy your ticket in advance at www.muze.gov.tr/en or enter with a Museum Pass—either allows you to skip the ticket line and head directly to the security check. If you arrive right at (or before) 9:00, when the palace opens, you'll have to wait outside the Imperial Gate. It's less chaotic to arrive later (10:00 or after). Because the museum is closed on Tuesday, it can be more crowded on Monday and Wednesday.

Planning Your Time: If you're here in the afternoon, visit the Harem first, as it closes earlier than the rest of the palace.

Dress Code: Women may need to cover their heads, knees, and shoulders to enter the palace's Hall of Holy Relics.

Getting There: It's located between the Golden Horn and Sea of Marmara, in the Sultanahmet district. The easiest approach, from the Sultanahmet tram stop, is described under "The Tour Begins," later. You can also take the tram to the Gülhane stop, go in the gate on the side wall of the Topkapı complex, and bear right up the hill. You'll pass the Istanbul Archaeological Museum on your left, then emerge into the First Courtyard (with the Gate of Salutation and inner Topkapı complex ahead and on your left).

Getting In: You can enter the outer Topkapı complex for free, but going into the inner part, with the palace museum, requires a ticket. As you face the Gate of Salutation (the entrance to the inner part of the palace), you'll see ticket windows on your right. (Some windows are reserved for tour guides—be sure you're in the correct line.)

To visit the Harem, you'll need to buy a separate ticket from the Harem's ticket booth (up the path to the left after you enter), unless you have a Museum Pass. You'll also need a separate ticket for the Hagia Irene church.

Information: Tel. 0212/512-0480, www.topkapisarayi.gov.tr. Most important items are well labeled in English.

Audioguide: You can rent an English audioguide. It's 15 TL for the palace and 10 TL for the Harem. While the information is scant, it's delightfully narrated and makes it easy to meaningfully navigate the sight.

Length of This Tour: Two hours, plus another hour if you visit the Harem.

Services: WCs and a top-notch souvenir shop are just outside the gate by the ticket office. Once inside the palace, you'll find more WCs in various places: outside the kitchen complex; as you exit the Harem (at the corner of the Third Courtyard); and at the restaurant in Mecidiye Pavilion (all are marked on the "Topkapı Palace" map). The museum bookstore is just inside past the security checkpoint, to your left before the exit. There is no cloakroom.

Photography: Indoor photography is not allowed in the Imperial Treasury's Armory (Second Courtyard) and in the sections surrounding the Third Courtyard (Imperial Treasury, Sultans' Clothing Collection, Sultans' Portraits, and Muslim Relics). Otherwise, photography is permitted.

Eating: At the far end of the palace (in the Mecidiye Pavilion in the Fourth Courtyard), the **Konyalı** restaurant serves Turkish fare in two sections: sit-down (slow service) or self-service (can be crowded). It's expensive (20-TL sandwiches at self-service section, 35-50-TL entrées in table-service section) but convenient and beautifully located, with sweeping views across the Bosphorus. You can also buy drinks and snacks at the little store next to the Harem entrance.

Starring: The jewel-encrusted Topkapı Dagger, an 86-carat diamond, some remarkable Muslim relics from Mecca, the famous Harem of the sultan (minus the dancing girls), and several centuries of Ottoman history.

OVERVIEW

The palace complex's main entry is near the back of Hagia Sophia, through the Imperial Gate in the outer wall. Nearby is the Ahmet III Fountain, the first stop on this tour. Past the Imperial Gate is the First Courtyard, home to the palace's ticket office and gift shop. After buying a ticket, you'll enter the inner complex of the palace itself and visit several increasingly intimate courtyards, which house the palace kitchens, council chamber, armory, treasury, and tulip garden. With a separate ticket, you can then tour the ornately decorated Harem. After exploring the palace and Harem, it's a short walk to the Istanbul Archaeological Museum (see next chapter).

The Tour Begins

• *From the Sultanahmet tram stop, walk across the street and face Hagia Sophia (with the Blue Mosque at your back). From here, walk around the right (eastern) side of Hagia Sophia, following the brown arrow for* Topkapı Sarayı. *(Notice Hagia Sophia's inclined retaining walls and two stone minarets, which the Ottomans added in the 16th century to reinforce the structure as they converted it into a mosque.) Straight ahead is the Topkapı Palace complex's main Imperial Gate. Just before it, on the right, is the...*

Ahmet III Fountain

In Istanbul, street fountains like this one are an important example of civic architecture (see sidebar). This early 18th-century structure

has a fountain on each facade, and each fountain is decorated with triangular niches on either side (similar to a prayer niche in a mosque, called a mihrab). The walls are decorated with tiles, gilded designs, and calligraphy—including the phrase, "Turn the tap with the name of Allah, the Protector, and the Merciful. Drink the water, and say a prayer for Sultan Ahmet."

• *If you have plenty of time, consider this detour: Before going through the Imperial Gate, side-trip about 100 yards to your left into a cobblestone lane called Soğukçeşme. This quaint street running between the church and the palace is lined with 19th-century townhouses, which are now part of a sterile-but-luxurious boutique hotel. Then return to the entry to the palace and pass through the...*

Imperial Gate (Bab-ı Hümayun)

This was the main entrance to the Topkapı Palace grounds. Mehmet the Conqueror built the gate when he chose this site as his ad-

ministrative center in the 15th century—just above the entryway, notice his imperial signature, or *tuğra* (too-rah). For centuries the Imperial Gate stayed open from the first prayer of the morning at sunrise, until the last in the evening at sunset. Originally, there was a wooden pavil-

Ottoman Fountains

Throughout old neighborhoods in Istanbul, you'll find elegant fountains, souvenirs of a genteel age. The most famous is the Ahmet III Fountain, just outside the Imperial Gate of Topkapı Palace.

In the 17th century, there were more than 10,000 fountains in Istanbul, easily accessible everywhere—near streets and street corners, mosques, parks, and gardens. Most private homes did not have plumbing, and people used public fountains as their water source. The fountains were generally simple structures, built to be functional. The tap was mounted on a marble panel and a basin was placed underneath.

Most of the fountains were connected to the water system, which had been constructed by the architect Sinan a hundred years earlier. Some fountains were built by the royal family and/or local administrators, but most were donated by the wealthy. It was considered prestigious to build a handsome fountain, and those commissioned by the rich were quite fancy and decorative.

The charming fountains (often drowned out by the noise of 21st-century traffic) come with decor typical of the Muslim Ottomans: no images, flamboyant Arabic script of a verse from the Quran, perhaps a local poem or proverb, the name of the benefactor, and a line thanking them for the donation.

Although no longer as common, the custom of building fountains continues today: People in the countryside sometimes build roadside fountains for travelers.

ion above the gate, from which the women of the Harem could watch the colorful processions into and out of the palace.

• *Going through the Imperial Gate, you find yourself in Topkapı's...*

First Courtyard

This wide-open space was reserved for public officials and civil servants. It was also called the Courtyard of Janissaries, for the royal soldiers who assembled here (see "The Janissaries" sidebar on page 122). Until a destructive mid-19th-century fire, the courtyard was cluttered with court buildings. Close to the Imperial Gate were the offices of state officials. The bakery supplied bread to the staff and palace residents. All of this, plus guard barracks, dormitories, and more, are gone without a trace, and now this grassy area resembles a large park.

• *As you walk from the Imperial Gate toward the palace through the First Courtyard, notice the terra-cotta church on your left.*

TOPKAPI PALACE

Hagia Irene

This important early-Christian church hides inside the outer Topkapı Palace wall. Often mistakenly interpreted as "St. Irene," the church's name actually means "Divine Peace," an attribute of God. The present structure dates back to the reign of Justinian in the sixth century. The original Hagia Irene church that stood on this site is thought to have been built by Constantine. Soon after Constantine split the Roman Empire between West and East—with the

Eastern capital here, in Byzantium (renamed Constantinople)—Hagia Irene hosted the Second Ecumenical Council to set the course for the new church (in A.D. 381). Decisions made in this building shaped Eastern Orthodox traditions for centuries to come. In the short term, the council—which discussed theological questions such as whether Jesus was human, divine, or both—sparked social struggles and riots in the early history of the capital.

Hagia Irene served as the patriarchal (main) church of Constantinople until Hagia Sophia was built. Under Ottoman rule, Hagia Irene was used as an arsenal by the imperial guards, and later to store artifacts from the Istanbul Archaeological Museum.

After being closed except for concerts and temporary exhibits, the stark and beautiful interior of Hagia Irene is now open to the public.

• *Past the church, the pronounced marble portal in the stone-and-brick wall is the entrance to the...*

Royal Mint (Darphane-i Amire)

This huge complex, with an indoor space of over 500,000 square feet, dates back to the early 1700s, but has undergone extensive renovations through the years.

For more than 200 years, and well into the Republic, this complex served as the central mint. The Ministry of the Treasury and the offices of treasury officials were housed here until the 1870s. (The ministry was relocated as the sultan and the administration moved to the new palace.) The first Turkish coins with Latin characters were minted here in 1934, and the mint remained operational until 1967.

• *Continue the rest of the way up through the First Courtyard. On the right, along the wall, you'll see a gift shop, WC, and ticket window. Buy your palace ticket here. Just beyond the ticket window, in the wall, notice the little fountain. This is called Cellat (jel-lot), or the Executioner's*

Fountain—where the executioner washed his hands...and blade. With that cheerful thought, turn your attention to the...

Gate of Salutation (Bab-üs Selam)

Also known as the Middle Gate, the Gate of Salutation dates from the mid-16th century, when the towers were used for defense as much as for decoration. It's reminiscent of European castles from the Middle Ages and was likely modeled after those fortresses. Guards who defended the towers (notice the slits for archers) lived on either side of the gate. Right above the doorway is the gilded *tuğra* (imperial signature) of Sultan Mahmut II. Above that,  in Arabic calligraphy, is the phrase, "There is no other God but Allah, and Muhammad is his Prophet." Beyond this point, everyone except the sultan had to leave their horse outside and walk in.

• *Unless you're a sultan, tie up your horse and go through the gate, noticing the original hand-beaten iron doors.*

As you pass through security and ticket control, look up to see the ornate decorations on the underside of the large eave. Once through the gate, you're now in the palace complex's...

Second Courtyard

This was not a private garden, but a ceremonial courtyard—host to centuries of coronations, successions, and other major benchmarks. Imagine the courtyard filled with hundreds of residents, royal family members, viziers, soldiers, and staff, all dressed in their finest attire, standing patiently in line for their turn to kiss the skirt of the sultan's caftan (gown) to show their respect and obedience.

To get your historical orientation, head around to the right side of the security checkpoint (with the gate at your back) to find two glass showcases with elaborate **models** of Topkapı Palace. Behind these, find the map showing the growing Ottoman Empire.

Now check your map and get your bearings. Stand with the Gate of Salutation behind you. Straight ahead, at the end of the long, central walkway, is the Gate of Felicity (which leads to the Third Courtyard of the palace). Along the right side of the Second Courtyard, marked by the domes and tall chimneys, are the palace workshops and imperial kitchens, which now house a porcelain and silver collection.

Now look to the left, to see the tall Divan Tower. In front of

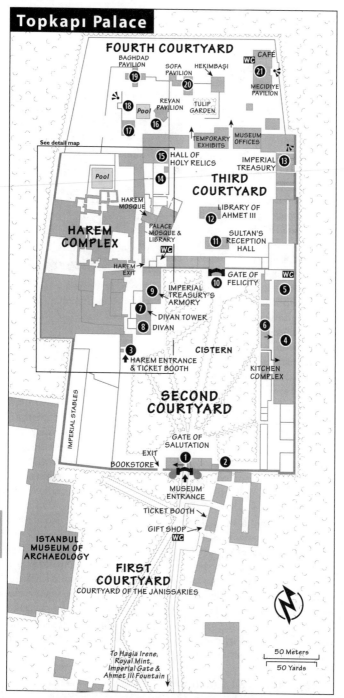

Topkapı Palace

FOURTH COURTYARD

BAGHDAD PAVILION
19

SOFA PAVILION
HEKİMBAŞI
20

WC CAFÉ
21

MECIDIYE PAVILION

18 Pool

REVAN PAVILION
16

17

TULIP GARDEN

TEMPORARY EXHIBITS

MUSEUM OFFICES

See detail map

15 HALL OF HOLY RELICS

IMPERIAL TREASURY
13

Pool

14

THIRD COURTYARD

HAREM MOSQUE

LIBRARY OF AHMET III
12

HAREM COMPLEX

PALACE MOSQUE & LIBRARY

SULTAN'S RECEPTION HALL
11

WC

HAREM EXIT

10 GATE OF FELICITY

WC

5

9 IMPERIAL TREASURY'S ARMORY

7 DIVAN TOWER

6

4

8 DIVAN

CISTERN

3 HAREM ENTRANCE & TICKET BOOTH

KITCHEN COMPLEX

SECOND COURTYARD

IMPERIAL STABLES

GATE OF SALUTATION

EXIT

BOOKSTORE

1

2

MUSEUM ENTRANCE

TICKET BOOTH

GIFT SHOP

WC

ISTANBUL MUSEUM OF ARCHAEOLOGY

FIRST COURTYARD
COURTYARD OF THE JANISSARIES

To Hagia Irene, Royal Mint, Imperial Gate & Ahmet III Fountain

N

50 Meters

50 Yards

TOPKAPI PALACE

Topkapı Palace Key

❶ Gate of Salutation
❷ Palace Models
❸ Harem Entrance
❹ Chinese Porcelain Collection
❺ Dessert Kitchen
❻ Kitchen Dormitory
❼ Divan Tower
❽ Divan
❾ Imperial Treasury's Armory
❿ Gate of Felicity
⓫ Reception Hall

⓬ Library of Ahmet III
⓭ Imperial Treasury
⓮ Sultan's Funeral Platform
⓯ Hall of Holy Relics
⓰ Revan Pavilion
⓱ Circumcision Room
⓲ Kiosk
⓳ Baghdad Pavilion
⓴ Sofa Pavilion
㉑ Mecidiye Pavilion

the tower, with a large eave, is the Divan—the council chamber where the viziers (ministers) of the imperial council met. To the right of the Divan Tower, at the far-left corner of the courtyard, is the Imperial Treasury's Armory. To the left of the Divan, just around the corner, is the Harem's ticket booth and entrance.

• *If there's no line at the Harem entrance, you'd be wise to visit it now (see page 129) and save the kitchen complex for later.*

If you're visiting the kitchen complex now (parts are under renovation into 2016), take the walkway leading diagonally to the portico running along the right side of the courtyard. Before going through the passage in the middle of this portico, notice the stone panels with Arabic calligraphy lined up along the wall behind the columns. A builder or architect would adorn his new building with an inscription like this, explaining the donor, construction date, architect, and so on— not unlike the bronze plaques on many public buildings in the West.

Through the passage is the...

Kitchen Complex

Much of Topkapı Palace burned down in the 16th century—thanks to a fire started in these kitchens (overheated oil in a pan, plus soot-clogged chimneys). Süleyman the Magnificent's royal architect, Sinan, rebuilt the grand-scale complex you see today, featuring 10 separate kitchen chambers, each with an elevated dome and a tall chimney for better ventilation (it worked—no more fires). Today this complex houses three different exhibits.

TOPKAPI PALACE

• *Through the long, narrow courtyard, a few steps to the right, and through the first door on the left are the actual kitchens. This section exhibits Topkapı's impressive...*

Chinese Porcelain Collection

This exhibit may be closed during your visit. If it's open, feast your eyes on a few hundred of the more than 10,000 pieces of Chinese porcelain that survive (about half of the sultan's original supply). Work your way counterclockwise around the collection, through 800 years of Chinese porcelain, covering four dynasties: Sung, Yuan, Ming, and Ch'ing.

First you'll come to plates, pitchers, vases, and cups fired with the green glaze called celadon, which supposedly changed color if touched by poisoned food. Most of these have traditional dragon and fish designs on them, but you'll also see a few with plant and geometric patterns.

Next, the blue-and-white porcelain items are in particularly exquisite condition, as most went into storage and never saw the light of day after being purchased. Some earlier examples carry abstract designs, Arabic script, and excerpts from the Quran; later ones have more traditional Chinese designs. The priceless blue-and-white pieces of china dating from the Yuan dynasty (1280-1368) are some of the most valuable pieces in the entire collection. A flask from the mid-1300s recently sold for over $5 million.

The rest of the collection features Chinese polychrome and Japanese Imari porcelain.

• *Leave the porcelain collection the same way you entered, then turn right and walk down the courtyard to the dead end. Go through the last door on the right, into the...*

Dessert Kitchen (Kitchen Exhibit)

This area was used to prepare traditional desserts, including *helva* (made with sesame oil and tahini)—so it's called the Helvahane (hehl-vah-hah-neh; Dessert Kitchen). This is also where the royal doctor concocted medicinal pastes, such as the "sultan's paste," an herbal mix famous for its strength-boosting (and aphrodisiac) qualities. Look for the round stone block across from the entrance, used to mix these ingredients.

Today, this section has been restored to its original form and shows off kitchen utensils, massive cauldrons, meat trays, coffee sets, and other copper objects (from the collection of about 2,000 pieces).

The narrow door on the left wall leads into the kitchen staff's

What's for Dinner?

The palace's imperial kitchens didn't feed just the sultan. They routinely dished up enough chow to feed thousands of people—up to 10,000 for religious festivals and when the hungry janissaries (soldiers) had their payday. In the 18th century, the imperial kitchens employed up to 20 chefs, 200 cooks and their assistants, 100 specialized cooks, another 100 dessert experts...and more than 300 busboys to clean up the mess. And this doesn't even count the bakers. As the head of such an immense staff, the master of the kitchens was as important as a vizier.

Sultans spent fortunes on buffet-style receptions for foreign envoys, weddings, circumcisions, and open-invitation public feasts on important religious days (such as the end of Ramadan). The circumcision gathering for one crown prince lasted several days. Each evening, the menu included rice pilaf for a thousand people and 20 whole roasted cows.

The catering complex had separate kitchens, each run by a specialized chef. For example, the Has (royal) Kitchen cooked only for viziers, Harem residents, and staff. There were two meals a day: midmorning and before sunset. Food was distributed by boys carrying large trays. The most commonly used ingredients in the kitchens were butter, saffron, and sugar.

The sultan's food was prepared in a special kitchen. Those cooking for the sultan were carefully chosen from among the best—the master chef and his crew of 12 cooks. The master chef was also the caretaker of the fine porcelain used by the sultan and viziers of the Divan, and for the banquets for visiting envoys and ambassadors. When the sultan went on a military campaign, his cooks went with him—and, occasionally, they'd have to grab a sword and join the battle.

Mealtime etiquette changed through time, but until the 19th century, there were still no dining tables at the palace.

The sultan sat cross-legged in front of a large tray and usually ate alone. Food and beverages were served in celadon porcelain ware and metal cups. The sultan's dinner menu would be something like this: mutton (steamed or kebab), a variety of grilled meats (mutton, quail, etc.), and baklava or rice pudding. The sultan didn't drink water during the meal, but instead sipped from a large bowl of chilled, stewed fruit juice (*şerbet*), as well as Turkish coffee. To set the proper mood, the room was filled with aloe-wood incense, and the sultan was entertained by mute dwarves.

mosque. Today it houses an exhibit of Turkish porcelain, which was in vogue here in the 19th century. You'll also see some traditional Ottoman glass filigree work: Colored glass rods (usually blue and white) are melted into crystal, creating a spiral design.

• *Exit back into the courtyard. Ahead on the right, just past the passage into the Second Courtyard, is the entrance to the...*

Kitchen Dormitory (Silverware and European Porcelain)

This collection is displayed in the former dormitory for the kitchen staff. First, you'll see several pieces of silverware that were gifts from European monarchs to the sultan. Then comes the Ottoman silverware, including a stunning silver model of the Ahmet III Fountain we saw just outside the Imperial Gate. Upstairs is an exhibit of European porcelain, which came into fashion after Chinese porcelain became passé in the 18th century. Most of the pieces are from Germany, France, or Russia.

• *Exit the kitchen complex the way you entered, back into the Second Courtyard. Directly across the courtyard is the Divan Tower. Go to the building just below it, to the intricately decorated door under the eave. This is the...*

Divan

The Divan (dee-vahn) was the council chamber where the viziers (ministers) got together to discuss state affairs. In other words, this was where the Ottoman Empire was governed for almost 400 years.

Like much of the rest of Topkapı Palace, the Divan was built by Mehmet the Conqueror in the 15th century; then it burned down and was rebuilt a century later by the royal architect Sinan. During the "Tulip Era" in the early 18th century (see sidebar, later), Sultan Ahmet III redecorated the rooms in Rococo style, which was the trend in Europe at the time.

Stepping inside, notice how the Divan's frilly Rococo flourishes clash with the rest of the Topkapı ensemble. The first room you enter is the office of the Record-Keeper, who kept track of every word spoken in the Divan. The larger second room was the actual Divan, or Council Chamber, decorated with original 16th-century tiles. The viziers would sit on the sofa according to their rank in the hierarchy.

(This is why some people call sofas "divans.") The Grand Vizier (prime minister) took the seat directly across from the door (see the red cloth with dark tulip designs). In the early years of the Divan, the sultan attended these meetings; later, the sultan would simply relax in the next room and eavesdrop as he liked through the window with the metal grill right above the Grand Vizier's seat. This window was known as "the Eye."

• *Exiting the Divan, turn left and walk to the brick-and-stone building next door, the...*

Imperial Treasury's Armory

This treasury held taxes collected from the provinces and was also where the janissaries and palace staff went to collect their paychecks. Today the building exhibits a small but interesting armory collection. Keep an eye out for several unique items: sultans' swords—including that of Mehmet the Conqueror, with Quran verses inscribed on the blade; the 18th-century ceremonial body armor of Sultan Mustafa III, embroidered with solid gold and brilliant gems; *yatağans*—lightweight, curved swords carried by janissaries; and artfully decorated helmets and body armor.

• *Leave the armory and continue to the top of the Second Courtyard—past some centuries-old sycamore trees—to the...*

Gate of Felicity (Bab-üs Saade)

This striking gate consists of a domed roof delicately carried by four slender columns. On either side of the gate, notice the antique designs, decorative columns, and landscape paintings (which were the trend during the last two centuries of the Ottoman Empire). Walking under the dome, notice the hole in the raised marble paving stone. This was used to hold the royal banner, which flew here when new sultans were coronated on this very spot.

The gate is also known as the "Gate of the White Eunuchs." White eunuchs were instructors, guards, and caretakers of the palace school, which occupied much of the Third Courtyard beyond this gate. Here the empire's top officials were educated, including ranking janissary leaders (see sidebar).

The Janissaries

When the Ottomans first rose to power, their military was made up of Turkish Muslim soldiers and cavalry from neighboring clans, who gathered only during times of war. The sultans would sometimes levy a "tax" of soldiers on large landowners, depending on the size of their holdings. Eventually, prisoners of war were also forced to serve in the Ottoman military.

But as the Ottoman Empire spread into Europe, the army—now made up of a hodgepodge of allies and POWs—became more diverse and difficult to control. So Mehmet the Conqueror re-envisioned his military as a reliable and controllable standing army. He updated and re-equipped the division of Christian converts to Islam, known as the janissaries. Young boys were taken from Christian families, converted to Islam, and raised to be soldiers for the sultan. Janissaries were professional soldiers—paid a salary even in peacetime—and eventually became the backbone of Ottoman military might.

Mehmet the Conqueror also founded the palace school at Topkapı Palace, where the brightest young janissaries were educated to prepare for serving the sultan and the state. Graduates of the palace school could work for the sultan's treasury, administration, and military—and the best of the best might even become viziers.

Many janissaries never saw their families again after they left their homes. But, while this system tore families apart, it was also beneficial for those who were left behind—a janissary's parents became exempt from taxes. And many janissaries went on to achieve a much greater degree of power and influence than they ever could have had as non-Muslim farm boys.

While this system began as a simple and efficient way to "draft" a powerful army, eventually the janissaries caused problems for the sultan. The janissaries—who generally preferred the status quo—often stood in the way of a sultan's reforms and, if angered, were known to dethrone or literally strangle a sultan to death. In fact, many historians fault the janissaries' influence for contributing to the empire's eventual decline.

• Walk through the Gate of Felicity, into the...

Third Courtyard

As you emerge from the gate, you're in front of the sultans' **Reception Hall,** a throne room designed to impress visitors. Recycled marble columns support the overhanging roof, creating an attractive portico around the hall. On the wall to the right of the entrance, notice the illustration showing a sultan receiving a foreign envoy. Flanking the door are imperial signatures.

Go right into the throne room—admiring the gorgeous 16th-century throne—and out the other side. The gray-white marble building straight ahead is the 18th-century **Library of Ahmet III.** The interior is decorated with cupboard doors inlaid with mother-of-pearl and tortoiseshell, and comfortable sofas next to the windows. If you're interested in going in, walk around to the far side of the building and up the marble staircase.

• *For now, go down the stairs on your right, and walk straight to the edge of the courtyard to reach the impressive...*

Imperial Treasury

The sultans used this building—with fireplaces and charming stained-glass windows—as a private chamber and occasional reception hall. Today it displays a sumptuous collection of the sultans' riches, though parts may be under renovation into 2016.

• *The Imperial Treasury is made up of four chambers linked together on a handy one-way route—just follow the signs. The first room is actually separate from the other three (you'll go in and out through the same door); the rest are all connected. Be warned that this area can be especially crowded—consider reading these descriptions before you enter.*

The **first room** shows off imperial thrones. As you enter, turn right to find the 17th-century ceremonial throne of Ahmet I. Along the opposite wall are three more, each one distinct in style: From right to left, you'll see an 18th-century Persian throne (a gift from an Iranian shah); the ebony throne of Süleyman the Magnificent (decorated with ivory and mother-of-pearl); and a gold-sheeted ceremonial throne from the 18th century. Notice the huge emeralds on the pendant hanging over this throne (more emeralds are in the showcase to the right of the thrones).

• *As you exit (the same way you entered), keep right to reach the second room.*

The **second room** is the least interesting, displaying jade objects and jewels—either designed by palace craftsmen or sent to the sultan as gifts.

• *Follow the crowds into the third room.*

In the **third room,** in a small showcase to the right of the fireplace, find the expertly crafted 16th-century gold helmet and mace, decorated with rubies and turquoise. On the left wall as you face the fireplace, notice the two massive candlesticks, designed in the 19th century to adorn the tomb of the Prophet Muhammad. These solid-gold candlesticks—weighing more than 100 pounds each—were brought here by Ottomans retreating from Mecca and Medina during World War I.

• *This room is connected to the next via a balcony*

The Tulip Era (1718-1730)

During the early 18th century, the Ottoman Empire enjoyed an unprecedented era of peace and prosperity: For a half-century, there were no wars, no border disputes, and no uprisings. The Ottomans signed treaties with long-standing rivals such as Russia, Austria, and Venice...and then found themselves out of enemies. Thus began the so-called Tulip Era.

Sultan Ahmet III (1673-1736), who took the throne in 1703, reigned over this era. But historians give more credit to his Grand Vizier (prime minister), İbrahim Paşa—called Damat (dah-maht; "Groom") because he married the sultan's daughter. (Don't confuse Damat İbrahim Paşa with plain old İbrahim Paşa, who was Süleyman the Magnificent's Grand Vizier and brother-in-law.) Aside from his fame as an able statesman, Damat İbrahim Paşa was an intellectual with a great interest in science and history, and a healthy appreciation for art and literature. He set the tone for the unusually cultured upper-class lifestyle of the Tulip Era.

Many scholars consider the Tulip Era an "Ottoman Renaissance"—a time of political, social, and cultural advancement. Free from the worries of a war-torn empire, people could explore and celebrate the finer things in life. The city's first print shop was established (more than two centuries after the printing press became commonplace in Europe). Literature, especially poetry, came into fashion—even the sultan was a poet. There was also a newfound appreciation for fine arts, particularly tile production. Turkish tiles from this period decorate monuments and

---

with a pretty marble fountain. Stop for a minute to enjoy the sweeping views from this grand perch: the Bosphorus, Bosphorus Bridge, Asian Istanbul, and Sea of Marmara.

The **fourth room** is more spectacular than the last three combined. As you enter, go to the far-right corner—past a bowl of emeralds and clear quartz crystals—to see the famous Topkapı Dagger, lying on a burgundy pillow. This was created here in the palace workshop in 1747 as a gift for the shah of Iran, but the shah was killed in an uprising, and so it never reached its intended recipient. The octagonal emerald on top of the handle hides a watch underneath. The plot of the 1964 Peter Ustinov film *Topkapi* centers on the theft of this dagger.

Now proceed counterclockwise around the room. A few steps to the left, on the right side of the fireplace, is the 86-carat pearl-shaped Spoonmaker's Diamond (surrounded by a double row of 49 diamonds)—one of the biggest diamonds in the world. They say a poor man found this diamond in the dirt in the 17th century and bartered it to a spoonmaker for wooden spoons; the spoonmaker then sold it to a jeweler for a few silver coins. How it ended up in

museums all over the world. Gardening caught on among the wealthy, as "Tulipmania" swept the country. A single sought-after bulb could sell for more than 30 ounces of gold. Hedonism took hold, as lavish waterfront parties sprawled along the Golden Horn at night—lit by candles placed on the backs of hundreds of roaming tortoises.

But as with any time of prosperity and decadence, the Tulip Era couldn't last. Because it was peacetime, the sultan's frivolity wasn't funded by the spoils of war, but instead by outrageous tax increases on the common people. Before long, revolution was in the air, led by a janissary named Patrona Halil, who was working as a bath attendant. Halil gathered a mob, recruited the royal guards, stormed Topkapı Palace, and beheaded Damat İbrahim Paşa. The rioters also executed several scholars, poets, and philosophers, and burned down tulip gardens all over the city. Ahmet III had to leave the throne to ease the anger of the rebels. When the dust cleared, Halil and several other rebels were executed as Sultan Mahmut I took the throne. Since Halil was Albanian, one of Mahmut I's first acts was to ban Albanian attendants in the city's baths.

the royal treasury is still a mystery...but it might have something to do with its enormous size.

Just to the right of the exit, look for the gold-sheeted wood cradle in which the sultan's newborn baby was presented to his daddy.

• *Exiting back into the Third Courtyard, proceed counterclockwise (to the right) around the courtyard to the next exhibit, the* **Hall of Holy Relics.** *As you walk along the portico, notice the stairs (to your immediate right) leading down into the Fourth Courtyard and its Mecidiye Pavilion, with a restaurant, cafeteria, and WC.*

After these stairs, you'll pass the so-called Pantry (now used for museum offices), where servants prepared and served the sultans' meals. Notice the river pebbles paving the floor of the domed portico in front. After the second passage leading into the Fourth Courtyard is the former Treasury Hall, which today houses free, good temporary exhibits (if the current offering seems interesting, drop in). Pass a third passage to the Fourth Courtyard to reach the Hall of Holy Relics. Before entering, look for the marble platform to the left of the door, next to the columns. This is the...

Sultan's Funeral Platform

According to Muslim tradition, after a dead body is washed and wrapped in a white shroud, it's laid on a slab like this one for a final religious service—to honor and pray for the deceased. You'll see platforms like this one in virtually every mosque. But this platform is special, since it was used to celebrate the last service of a deceased sultan. It was located here because it's near the important relics you'll see in the next section.

• *Now turn and face the highly ornamented door of the...*

Hall of Holy Relics

This collection shows off some of the most significant holy items of the Muslim faith. (Note that women may need to cover their heads, knees, and shoulders in this area due to the importance of these items to Muslim worshippers.) These relics were brought to Istanbul in the early 16th century from Egypt, Mecca, and Medina, when the Ottomans conquered those lands. In the past, the relics were only available to members of the Ottoman dynasty and handpicked guests, and presented to the public only on religious days. But today they're viewable at any time, offering an impressive glimpse into the world of Islam. (The location of the relics described here may vary—if you can't find a particular item, see if it's on display in another room.)

The **door** is a sight in itself, with gilded decorations and Arabic calligraphy reading, "There is no other God but Allah, and Muhammad is his Prophet." On either side of the entrance, you see the imperial signatures *(tuğra)*. As this is a very holy site for Muslims, you'll see many people praying with their hands open. Read the rules on the sign next to the entrance, and be respectful as you visit this exhibit.

Going through the door, you find yourself in the so-called **Fountain Room,** beautifully decorated with 16th- to 18th-century tiles and wall paintings. Listen for the chanting: An imam (cleric) reads verses from the Quran 24 hours a day—as imams have nonstop since the 16th century. (You'll see him soon.) The pool in the center is not just decorative: It was a tradition to wash your hands when you entered and left the chamber.

As you walk the room, look on the left (and in the case on the wall) for a collection of relics from the Kaaba—the big black cube in the center of the mosque at Mecca—the holiest of Muslim shrines. You'll see locks, keys, and even decorated rain gutters. At the far back end of the room (on the left corner) is the gold cover of the revered "Black Stone," which Muslims believe descended from heaven. According to Islamic tradition, the Prophet Abraham (the same Abraham as in the Old Testament) placed the stone at the eastern corner of the Kaaba—the temple he built in Mecca. At the right corner is the Repentance Door of Kaaba.

The room to the left, filled with strangely well-preserved everyday items from the lives of religious figures, may include the footprint of Muhammad, Muhammad's sandals, bone fragments of John the Baptist, Moses' staff, Abraham's granite cooking pot, David's sword, and Joseph's turban.

Backtrack into the Fountain Room and go through the door into the **Petition Room.** This room was a waiting lounge for those who wanted to address the sultan. The room holds relics from Muhammad: hair from his beard, a piece of his tooth, his sword and bow, and swords of the caliphs—the religious and social leaders of the Muslim community after Muhammad's death (similar to the early Christian apostles).

To your left as you enter the Petition Room is the door to the **Sultan's Chamber,** where the sultan received petitioners. The doorway is partitioned off, but the gold chest containing Mohammad's mantle is visible in front of the throne. In the connecting antechamber is the little kiosk where the imam reads from the Quran.
• *Go through the next room (which may house temporary exhibits). As you step outside, take the passageway to your immediate left into the...*

Fourth Courtyard
The most intimate and cozy of Topkapı's zones, the Fourth Courtyard enjoys fine views over the Golden Horn and Bosphorus and is dotted with several decorative pavilions, most of them built in the mid-17th century by Murat IV and his younger brother, İbrahim the Mad.
• *Go down the steps into the Tulip Garden of Ahmet III (we'll return here in a moment). Keep to the left along the wall and climb the stairs to the marble terrace. To your right is the...*

Revan Pavilion
Sultan Murat IV built this pavilion to commemorate a military victory against the Persians on the eastern front. Step inside to take a look at the interior, which is very typical of the style of the time: decorated with mostly blue-and-white 17th-century İznik tiles; window shutters and cupboard doors inlaid with mother-of-pearl and tortoiseshell; and roofed with a central dome, with three bays decorated with sofas and large pillows.
• *Exiting the pavilion, turn right and walk straight past the pool to the pavilion at the edge of the terrace, the...*

TOPKAPI PALACE

Circumcision Room

Murat's younger brother, İbrahim the Mad, built this pavilion, which was used over the next two centuries for the ritual circumcision of heirs to the throne. It's slathered inside and out with a contrasting patchwork of fine 17th-century İznik tiles.

• *Stroll along the pool and pop over to the left to the bronze-gilded...*

Kiosk

Stop for a minute to enjoy this perfect panorama of the Golden Horn and New District. The kiosk was also built by İbrahim the Mad, who enjoyed this view as he dined at the end of a long day of fasting for Ramadan.

• *With İbrahim's kiosk and that grand view on your left, continue straight ahead to the...*

Baghdad Pavilion

This pavilion was also built by Sultan Murat IV to celebrate the conquest of Baghdad. One of the more authoritarian sultans, Murat IV was feared by everyone. To intimidate dissenting janissaries, he'd lift a massive iron mace when he spoke to them at gatherings—as if to challenge them to defy him. (They rarely did.) Murat also banned alcohol use in the city,

not because he disapproved of drinking, but because it gave him an excuse to demonstrate his authority by executing violators. But after a long day of throwing his weight around, Murat IV retreated

to the Baghdad Pavilion to find peace. In strong contrast to his tough-guy image, he actually spent much of his time here reading poetry and listening to music.

As for the **pool** on the terrace, no one knows much about it. Tour guides love to spin tall tales of the wild fantasies enacted poolside by İbrahim the Mad and members of his harem, or how he would throw gold coins into the water to watch guards dive in after them.

• *When you're finished here, head back down the stairs into the...*

TOPKAPI PALACE

Tulip Garden

Ahmet III, also known as the "Tulip Sultan," had a short but sweet reign—an unusual time of peace, prosperity, and, of course, tulips (see sidebar, earlier). This is the private garden where Ahmet grew rare bulbs. Turks first brought tulips here from central Asia; in the late 16th century, they began shipping them to Holland. Tulip designs were a popular motif in Turkish art (such as on tiles or textiles) long before Ahmet III—but they became an obsession during his reign.

The first building on the left, just beyond the garden, is the late-17th-century **Sofa Pavilion.** Sultan Ahmet III spent a lot of time here, lounging on a sofa and gazing at his tulips after a long night spent enjoying worldly pleasures.

Behind the Sofa Pavilion is the tower-like **Hekimbaşı** (heh-keem-bah-shuh; "Chief doctor's chamber"). Dating all the way back to the 15th-century reign of Mehmet the Conqueror, this building was used by doctors as well as caretakers of the prince.
• *At the far end of the courtyard is the...*

Mecidiye Pavilion

Notice that this pavilion—built in the mid-19th century—looks more "European" than the other buildings at Topkapı. After centuries of living in the old-fashioned, Oriental-flavored opulence of Topkapı, Ottoman sultans began to realize that their European counterparts saw them as backward. To keep up with these Western-oriented neighbors, the sultans' architects began to adopt an eclectic mix of various European influences. The Mecidiye Pavilion marked a sea change in both the architecture and the culture of the time; just two decades later, Topkapı was abandoned in favor of the more modern, Western-style Dolmabahçe Palace on the Bosphorus (see page 52).

In addition to spectacular views over the Bosphorus Strait, Asian Istanbul, the Sea of Marmara, and (in clear weather) the Princes' Islands, the Mecidiye Pavilion hosts a restaurant (with self-service and sit-down sections) offering a convenient and scenic resting point after a busy palace visit.
• *This part of our tour is finished. When you're ready to leave Topkapı Palace, simply backtrack out to the Gate of Salutation (the exit is to the right of the security checkpoint, through the side door by the fountain). If you haven't yet, now's the time to tour...*

The Harem

The word "harem" refers to two things: the wives, favorites, and concubines of the sultan; and the part of the palace where they lived. Touring the Harem (hah-rehm) is an essential part of a Topkapı Palace visit, allowing curious Westerners to pull back the

TOPKAPI PALACE

veil on this mysterious and titillating phenomenon. As you'll learn, the Harem was not the site of a round-the-clock orgy, but a carefully administered social institution that ensured the longevity of the Ottoman Empire.

A separate ticket is required to enter the Harem (purchase at Harem entry ticket booth). The one-way route includes about 20 rooms, including stunning tile work, the mother sultan's private apartments, wives' and concubines' courts, and the grand reception hall. Although the following information should follow the route fairly closely, the route can change as various rooms close for renovation. Before visiting, read the "Harem 101" sidebar.

• *You'll begin by passing through the bronze-plated door (the Carriage Gate) into the antechamber known as the...*

Dome

In the 16th century, this was the entryway into the Harem grounds. Draped carriages would pull up to this gate to take the Harem women in and out, for shopping, a picnic, or a private visit. New women would enter the Harem and be introduced to the staff here. The only men who could enter the Dome—other than the sultan and young princes—were the sultan's close relatives and, when necessary, doctors. These guests were escorted by the black eunuchs (see next section), who were caretakers of the Harem.

• *Follow the attractive stone-paved corridor, through the Guards' Chamber, into a long, open courtyard surrounded by functional buildings. This was the...*

Courtyard of the Black Eunuchs

The black eunuchs were slaves from North Africa, Egypt, and Sudan who were trained and educated to serve in the Harem—to protect the women and take care of Harem administration. The sultan knew they wouldn't be tempted by their charges because they had been castrated by slave traders on the road from Africa. When this section was built in the 16th century, about 50 eunuchs were employed; in later years, that number doubled.

On the left, recessed from the court behind the portico, are the **Quarters of the Black Eunuchs.** Look through the windows to see the dormitories where the black eunuchs lived. The room with mannequins near the end of the portico was reserved for the chief black eunuch as a private apartment. You see the chief seated on his sofa, his assistant waiting for his orders.

Just past the eunuchs' quarters on the left, a porch with one column leads to the **School of the Princes.** This was where heirs to the throne received their primary education. Then, when they hit puberty, they were sent out of the Harem—often for field training in remote provinces of the empire.

• *At the end of the courtyard, you'll enter the women's quarters through*

The Harem

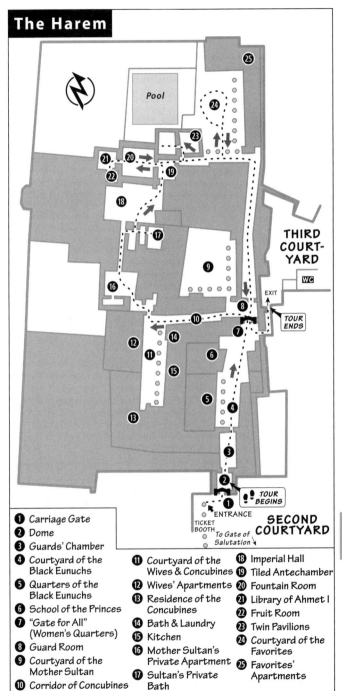

Pool

THIRD
COURT-
YARD

WC

EXIT

TOUR
ENDS

TOUR
BEGINS

ENTRANCE

TICKET
BOOTH

To Gate of
Salutation

SECOND
COURTYARD

TOPKAPI PALACE

1. Carriage Gate
2. Dome
3. Guards' Chamber
4. Courtyard of the
   Black Eunuchs
5. Quarters of the
   Black Eunuchs
6. School of the Princes
7. "Gate for All"
   (Women's Quarters)
8. Guard Room
9. Courtyard of the
   Mother Sultan
10. Corridor of Concubines

11. Courtyard of the
    Wives & Concubines
12. Wives' Apartments
13. Residence of the
    Concubines
14. Bath & Laundry
15. Kitchen
16. Mother Sultan's
    Private Apartment
17. Sultan's Private
    Bath

18. Imperial Hall
19. Tiled Antechamber
20. Fountain Room
21. Library of Ahmet I
22. Fruit Room
23. Twin Pavilions
24. Courtyard of the
    Favorites
25. Favorites'
    Apartments

Harem 101

"All the goodness and evil comes from the mother sultan."
—Paolo Contarini, Ambassador of Venice

To Westerners, the word "harem" conjures up images of a vast roomful of nubile young sex slaves, eager and willing to satisfy the sultan's every desire. But this dated notion is a romanticized and inaccurate picture painted by Europeans who'd never actually laid eyes on a real harem. The Arabic word "harem" actually means "forbidden." In common use, it usually refers to the part of a Turkish house that's reserved for family members, specifically women. To Turks, "harem" connotes respect and dignity—not sexual fantasy.

At Topkapı Palace, the Harem was more than just a living area. It was an institution—part of the state. Its primary role was to provide future heirs to the Ottoman throne, an essential responsibility that was too important to be left to coincidence. Thanks largely to the Harem, the Ottoman Empire was ruled by a single dynasty from start to finish, avoiding many of the squabbles and battles for succession that tainted other great empires.

The Harem at Topkapı Palace worked like this: The sultan was the head of the household, a role he shared with his mother (the "mother sultan"). The sultan could have up to four wives, with the first one being considered the senior, most influential wife. Also living in the Harem was a collection of several hundred concubines—female slaves who kept house but were not sexually active with the sultan. From among the concubines (his "harem"),

the Cümle Kapısı (jewm-leh kah-puh-suh), or "Gate for All." (You'll wind up back here at the end of the tour.) The gate opens into a guard room with large Venetian mirrors on the walls, surrounded by gold-leaf frames. As you enter, go to the mirror on the left wall; through the vault to the right of this mirror, you can peek into the fancy-looking, stone-paved...

Courtyard of the Mother Sultan

This courtyard—the centerpiece of the Harem complex—is where the various people living here could most easily mingle. The courtyard is fronted by apartments belonging to the sultan, his senior wife (wife #1), and in-between, the mother sultan. The tour takes us roughly clockwise around the interiors of these buildings.

• Now turn left and go down the **Corridor of Concubines.** Notice the long marble counter (on the left), used for service trays and cleaning up

the sultan—or, more often, his mother or wife—might select up to four "favorites," or *haseki* (hah-seh-kee), with whom he could become more, ahem, familiar. A favorite who bore a child of the sultan became known as a *haseki sultan* and was often treated as a wife. Again, the sultan could only have sex with chosen women, not with anyone he wanted. Every night he spent with a woman was written down.

Even though they were permitted up to four wives, sultans were often cautious about marriage. Many sultans chose to have just one wife—or no wife at all, but only favorites. One reason not to marry was to protect potential wives from getting caught in the crossfire of history. Legend holds that after Sultan Beyazıt was defeated by Tamerlane the Mongolian in the early 15th century, his wife swept the floors of Tamerlane's mansion as a slave. But sultans were also careful to guard the supreme power of the dynasty, and not to weaken this power through marriages. For example, Süleyman the Magnificent married Roxelana, who went on to wield tremendous influence over the empire, kick-starting a "reign of the ladies" that would last for a century and a half.

When the sultan died or was replaced, the new sultan's mother (who was almost always a member of the previous sultan's harem) was the only one who could stay. Wives and favorites alike had to leave the Harem and were given a house and a healthy pension.

after meals. At the end of the corridor, you'll walk along the edge of a courtyard surrounded on three sides by a portico, the...

Courtyard of the Wives and Concubines

This courtyard was reserved for the use of the **non-senior wives** of the sultan. The building complex on the right is divided into three apartments—one each for wives #2, #3, and #4, plus their children and servants. Although they were neighbors, the sultan's wives were hardly friends. Rather, each one vied with the others to promote the interests of her own son. The wives received lavish gifts from the sultan, which they often invested in real estate, bazaars, baths, shops, and so on. The more wealth they had squirreled away, the better they could protect themselves from internal enemies. And their most hated enemy was often the wife next door—or, worse, the elderly woman up the hall: the mother sultan.

The quarters at the far end of the court were the residence of **concubines,** or female servants. (Notice the water taps on the left along the way—used for ablution, or ritual cleansing—marking a bath and a laundry room, followed by a small kitchen.) Concubines began as young slave girls who were brought into the Harem and trained to serve the senior women. Being a concubine could be a major opportunity: Many were granted their freedom after just a few years in the Harem, and others attracted the attention of the sultan (or, more often, his mother) and were granted favorite *(hase-ki)* status. Again, the concubines were not sex slaves at the beck and call of the sultan; rather, the mother sultan and the sultan's wives carefully orchestrated which concubines the sultan could unveil. (In other words, the man's mother and wives chose his girlfriends.)
• *Leave the courtyard and continue into the...*

Mother Sultan's Private Apartment

Notice how the mother sultan's apartment is strategically situated between the sultan's quarters and his wives'—yet another reminder of her strict control over her son's liaisons.

Beyond the antechamber with the fireplace, you enter the mother sultan's main hall and dining room. The 17th-century

decor includes Kütahya tiles and landscape paintings (notice there are no people because Islam discourages the depiction of humans in art). You can also see later, 19th-century touches that show the influence of European trends: Western-style paintings and cupboard doors inlaid with tortoiseshell and mother-of-pearl. To the right of the fireplace is the entrance to the mother sultan's bedroom and prayer chamber.

As you explore, ponder the tremendous influence wielded by the mother sultan. Traditionally, she always had a word in state affairs. But the mid-16th to the 17th centuries are known as the "reign of the ladies," when the sultans' mothers and wives (aided by the chief of the black eunuchs) essentially ran the Ottoman Empire. This began with the incompetent, do-nothing heirs of Süleyman the Magnificent in the mid-16th century; by the time İbrahim the Mad took the throne a century later, the only thing his mother, Kösem, didn't do was lead armies into war.
• *Next are the...*

TOPKAPI PALACE

Take My Wives...Please!
A Few Words on Polygamy

Contrary to popular belief, the majority of Turks have always been monogamous. Even though the Quran permits a man to marry up to four times, this is reserved for extraordinary situations. When the rule was instituted, wars had decimated the male population, leaving more women than men. With no modern social-welfare network to care for war widows, men began to take additional wives. The Quran sets strict criteria for polygamy: The man must have the financial means to support all his wives, and he must treat each one equally. Under Ottoman rule, polygamy was practiced only among minorities, traditional Arab communities...and, of course, the ruling class who could afford it. Polygamy is illegal in Turkey—it exists today only on the fringes of Turkish society (such as in some mostly Arab communities of eastern Turkey). In most of the country, today's progressive Turkish women would never accept their husbands' taking second wives. Legally, Turkish women have had equal rights with men since the days of Atatürk, including the right to vote and run for office.

Sultan's Private Apartments

At the end of the corridor, turn right and enter the **sultan's private bath**. This is basically a smaller-scale version of any Turkish bath, with a dressing room and a hot section for bathing, all paved with marble. The large marble tub at the end was added in the 18th century, when this room was renovated in the Western style. Traditional Turkish bathing doesn't use a tub; rather, the water should always be running. Also notice the locked gold-leaf cage separating the sultan's private area from the rest of the bath.

• *Backtrack and turn right. (On the way, watch for an "Oriental toilet" to the left—porcelain footprints on either side of a hole in the ground—*

with gilded taps on the wall for hot and cold water.)

The **Imperial Hall,** used as a reception hall for special occasions, is the largest room in the sultan's private apartments. The gallery with windows was reserved for the senior women. On the right, under a canopy carried by four slender columns, is the sultan's throne—actually a long sofa. Dutch Delft tiles with geometric designs decorate the walls; higher up is a line of Turkish İznik tiles. Excerpts from the Quran are written in calligraphy.

• *Next is an antechamber with beautiful 17th-century tile work. Take the door on the left.*

Named for the marble fountains set into the wall, the **Fountain Room** is covered with colorful 16th-century İznik tiles, many inscribed with Quran verses. Through the doorway at the far end of the room (notice the elaborate little carved fountain on the left), you enter the **library of Ahmet I**—better-lit, more tranquil, and more private-feeling than the Fountain Room. Notice the shutters and drawers with more inlaid mother-of-pearl, tortoiseshell, and ivory. To the left is a tiny chamber known as the **Fruit Room.** Built in the early 18th century, it's decorated with wood panels with fruit and flower designs.

• *Pass back through the Fountain Room, go through the doorway, and continue. On the left, just before the big courtyard, is the entrance to the...*

Twin Pavilions

These two connected pavilions, richly decorated with stained-glass windows and floral tiles, were the living quarters for young heirs to the throne.

The rooms used to be mistakenly identified as "the Cage," where brothers (and potential rivals) of the sultans were kept under house arrest. As draconian as that sounds, it was an improvement on the original tradition, when sultans would kill their brothers to avoid conflicts over the throne. Sultan Ahmet I, the patron of the Blue Mosque, chose imprisonment for his brothers rather than death. This caused a new problem: If a sultan died or became unable to rule, his brother would take the throne after having spent his entire life under lock and key—and without any knowledge of how to run an empire. Many historians blame these incompetent brother-sultans for hastening the decline of the Ottoman Empire.

• *Now continue into the...*

Courtyard of the Favorites

As the name implies, this is where the sultan's favorites—the *haseki*—resided (in the white two-story building that surrounds the courtyard). These favorites had a great view; belly up to the marble banister and enjoy it yourself.

The mother sultan selected

the favorites from among the concubines. Despite birth-control methods—and the disapproval of the wives—a favorite would often bear the child of a sultan. In this case, she became a *haseki sultan*, joined the ranks of the senior women...and her life would change forever. Now she was powerful, envied...and in danger of attack.

• *From here, continue down a long corridor to eventually reach the Harem exit. Once you exit, you'll find yourself in the Third Courtyard of the palace complex. To go back where you started, turn right and follow the wall until you pass through the Gate of Felicity, which puts you back in the Second Courtyard (if you have yet to visit the kitchen complex and the rest of the palace, see page 117).*

ISTANBUL ARCHAEOLOGICAL MUSEUM TOUR

İstanbul Arkeoloji Müzesi

The Istanbul Archaeological Museum's collection rivals any on earth, with intricately carved sarcophagi, an army of Greek and Roman sculptures, gorgeous İznik tiles, ancient Babylonian friezes, the world's oldest peace treaty, and an actual chunk of the chain that the Byzantines stretched across the Golden Horn. The complex is divided into three parts: the Museum of Archaeology, the Tiled Kiosk Museum, and the Museum of the Ancient Orient. These underrated but impressive museums are worth consideration, even for visitors who normally couldn't care less about ancient artifacts.

Orientation

Cost: 15 TL includes entry to all three sections.

Hours: Tue-Sun 9:00-19:00, off-season until 17:00, closed Mon, last entry one hour before closing.

Renovations: The Museum of Archaeology will be under renovation in 2016, but highlights of the collection will be displayed in temporary galleries. The Tiled Kiosk Museum and Museum of the Ancient Orient remain open.

Getting There: It's inside the outer wall of the Topkapı Palace complex, at Osman Hamdi Bey Yokuşu. It's easiest to reach by tram; get off at the Gülhane stop. From the stop, walk two blocks away from the Golden Horn along the old palace wall, go through the entryway with three arches into Gülhane Park, and bear right up the cobbled lane. The museum is near the top of this lane, on the left.

You can also approach the museum from the First Courtyard of the Topkapı Palace (see the Topkapı Palace Tour chapter). After entering the First Courtyard through the Imperial Gate, go diagonally to the left (with the Hagia Irene church on your left), pass through the arched entryway, and follow the alley down the hill to the museum (on your right).

Getting In: Pass through the museum complex's big entrance gate and find the ticket seller to the left. Tickets in hand, go through the turnstile: The Museum of the Ancient Orient is directly to your left; the Tiled Kiosk Museum is ahead on the left; and the main Museum of Archaeology is ahead on the right, across the courtyard.

Buying an **advance ticket** online (www.muze.gov.tr/en) or entering with a Museum Pass allows you to skip the ticket line and head directly to the security check.

Information: Exhibits throughout are labeled in English. Tel. 0212/520-7740, www.istanbularkeoloji.gov.tr.

Expect Changes: With the Museum of Archaeology under renovation in 2016, a number of popular items will shift to temporary exhibits. Look for signs at the entry gate that list temporary displays and closures.

Length of This Tour: Allow at least two hours to tour all three parts (if the Museum of Archaeology is closed when you visit, an hour will suffice). If you're in a hurry, spend an hour at the Museum of Archaeology, sprint through the Tiled Kiosk Museum, and skip the Ancient Orient.

Services: The cloakroom and WCs are in the main building (Museum of Archaeology).

Photography: Photography without a flash is generally allowed.

Eating: An outdoor café hides among trees and columns on a pleasant terrace overlooking Gülhane Park (between the Museum of the Ancient Orient and the Tiled Kiosk Museum, limited menu, may be closed in winter). Having a bite or drink here is like living out your own archaeological fantasy. The Museum of Archaeology has a small coffee shop serving sandwiches and cookies.

Starring: A slew of sarcophagi (including the remarkable Alexander Sarcophagus), sumptuous İznik tiles, the ancient Kadesh Treaty, and several millennia of Turkey's past.

OVERVIEW

The main collection—the Museum of Archaeology—features the world-renowned Alexander Sarcophagus, a selective and engaging collection of ancient sculpture, and archaeological finds from the Trojans and the Byzantines (predominantly from the sixth century B.C. on). The 15th-century Tiled Kiosk Museum, one of the oldest examples of

ARCHAEOLOGICAL MUSEUM

Ottoman civic architecture, contains an outstanding collection of
centuries-old Turkish tiles. And the Museum of the Ancient Orient displays artifacts from early Mesopotamian and Anatolian cultures, mostly dating from before the sixth century B.C. (with some
going all the way back to 2700 B.C.).

There's a lot of ground to cover here. If your time is limited,
spend most of it at the Museum of Archaeology. The Tiled Kiosk
Museum and the Museum of Ancient Orient are small enough to
merit at least a quick walk-through.

The Tour Begins

• *We'll begin at the museum's highlight: the Museum of Archaeology.
Recent renovations may have shifted the location of some collections described below, so use this tour to get an overview, and then just enjoy
what's currently on display. Enter the long courtyard and walk toward
the end (passing the Museum of the Ancient Orient, a little park with
a café, and the Tiled Kiosk Museum on your left). Near the end of the
courtyard, on your right, is the entrance to the...*

Museum of Archaeology

This ornamental building has two entrances,
framed by pediments supported by four tall
columns—resembling the designs on some of
the museum's sarcophagi. Inside you'll find
those sarcophagi, as well as piles of artifacts
from the Greeks, Romans, Byzantines, Trojans, and more.

After entering, you'll find yourself in a
lobby with a bust near the staircase. The **bust**
depicts the museum's founder, Osman Hamdi,
and is surrounded by backlit panels about his
life and paintings. Famous in his own time as
a painter, Hamdi (1842-1910) is now regarded
as the father of Turkish museums.

• *The halls on either side of the lobby display the museum's...*

SARCOPHAGI COLLECTION

Hamdi brought these sarcophagi here in the 1880s from the royal
necropolis of Sidon (in present-day Lebanon, but part of the Ottoman Empire back then). Discovered accidentally by a villager
digging a well, these sarcophagi are among the most important
classical works ever unearthed. Hamdi, who personally directed
the excavations, found the marble sarcophagi miraculously intact in

two separate burial chambers, where they had been insulated from humidity and water damage.

• *Go through the door to your left to see the...*

Alexander Sarcophagus

The museum's star exhibit is inside a large, red-framed glass case. Other than a few dents in the marble caused by careless movers,

this fourth-century B.C. sarcophagus is in excellent condition. Although it's known as the Alexander Sarcophagus—that's Alexander the Great portrayed in the scenes of battle and hunting on the sides—it was actually carved to hold King Abdalonymos of Sidon.

While faded after two thousand years, some of the sarcophagus' colors remain, and the bas-reliefs that decorate the casket and its lid are impressive. Some figures are almost freestanding, giving the impression that their next step will take them right out of the scene and into the room with you. Nearby, look for a color model of the "Alexander on his horse" scene, offering a better idea of how the relief may have looked in full sarcophi-color.

One side of the casket shows Alexander's army battling the Persians in the Battle of Issus in 333 B.C. Alexander's victory here

paved the way for him to conquer the Middle East. The battle also changed the life of Abdalonymos, the sarcophagus' likely "owner": Distantly related to Sidon's royal family, he was appointed as the new king when the Macedonians marched into Sidon. It's easy to tell who's who: Persian troops wear long pants, several layers of loose shirts, and turbans. The Macedonians are either naked or half-naked, in short tunics. On the far left, Alexander wears a lion pelt as he attacks a Persian soldier from horseback. His arm is raised as he prepares to hurl a (missing) spear.

Move counterclockwise around the sarcophagus. The battle scene continues on the short end of the casket to the right. The relief on the lid, in the triangular pediment, is another battle scene—likely the battle of Gazze (312 B.C.), in which King Abdalonymos

was killed. The dominant red color is best preserved on this side.

The next, long side of the sarcophagus depicts two separate hunting scenes. This relief, less crowded than the battle scene, is dominated by the lion hunt at its center. The lion's body is pierced at several points, and blood flows from his wounds. Still, he manages to bite and claw at the horse's shoulder. The rider of the horse is King Abdalonymos, dressed in a traditional Persian outfit. Pay attention to the different garb of the soldiers—here, they're all hunting together. This was a scene Alexander fought for: to create a united empire. The Macedonian on the horse behind the lion is Alexander's general, Hephaestion, who appointed Abdalonymos as king. Alexander is on horseback to the left of Abdalonymos.

On the final short end is a panther hunt, but this time all the hunters are dressed in the same Persian style. There's more fighting in the pediment, but the figures here are not as refined as the rest. Apparently the first sculptor ran out of time to complete his work, so another took up the hammer.

• *Near the Alexander Sarcophagus is another perfectly preserved sarcophagus, the...*

Sarcophagus of the Mourning Women

The museum building you are in was modeled after this mid-fourth-century B.C. sarcophagus, arguably the best example of its kind. Although Greek in style, it has Eastern influences that are apparent in the mourning figures' wailing gestures and long robes (called chitons).

The sarcophagus belonged to King Straton of Sidon. Professional mourners—women hired to cry and wail at funerals—were common when he died around 360 B.C., but the women portrayed on this sarcophagus were members of Straton's harem, and seem genuinely affected by his death. Notice that their gestures are very natural, almost lifelike. Scholars believe the sculptor may have used models to create such realistic emotion. The designs along the lid's long sides represent the funerary procession. From right to left, find the young man leading the cortege, two horses to be sacrificed at the service, a Persian quadriga (chariot with four horses), and a funeral cart pulled by four horses, followed by the attendants.

• *Step through the doorway at this end of the hall to take a quick look at the...*

Grave Steles and Egyptian-Style Sarcophagi

Besides several fairly well-preserved pre-Hellenistic and Hellenistic grave steles, this room contains several Egyptian-style sarcophagi from Sidon and other sites in the Middle East. These sarcophagi are called "anthropoid" because they were crafted in the shape of the human body. Some of these were imported from Egypt, while others were knockoffs made by local craftsmen.

• *If you have the time and interest, continue on to the next series of rooms to see more sarcophagi. Two standouts are the second-century **Sarcophagus of Meleagros**, decorated with mythological figures and motifs (in the next room), and the third-century **Sidamara Sarcophagus**, known for its sheer size and detailed sculptures (in the following room).*

To stick with this tour, return to the lobby and walk straight through to the other side, to enter the second hall of Sidon sarcophagi. The first one is the...

Satrap Sarcophagus

A "satrap" was a Persian governor, akin to a viceroy ruling in a king's name. This sarcophagus dates back to the fifth century B.C.

Its specific occupant is unknown, but the scenes on the sides of the casket trace the life of a powerful satrap. The once-bright colors of the palm- and lotus-flower borders faded long ago. On one long side, the satrap and his men prepare his chariot for a ride. As you walk around the sarcophagus to the right, the short end shows the satrap reclining on a bench in his private chamber, accompanied by his wife (who's resting her back on the border). A servant pours wine, while a second servant stands by with a cloth in one hand and an unseen fan in the other. In the next scene, on the opposite long side, the satrap uses a spear to hunt a panther. The final short end shows the satrap's grooms with their spears, helping him out of a potentially embarrassing situation.

• *Near the Satrap Sarcophagus, you'll see the...*

Istanbul Archaeological Museum

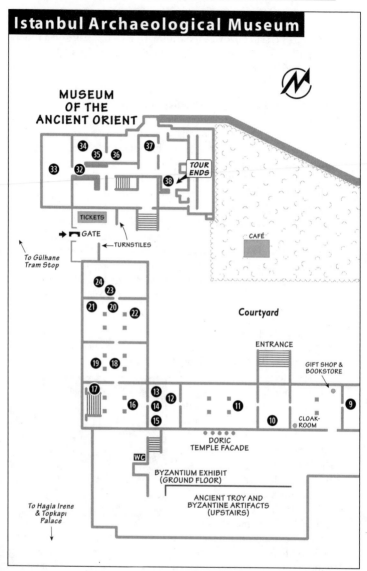

Lycian Sarcophagus

Dating from the late fifth century B.C., this sarcophagus is named for Lycia—a small area in Mediterranean Turkey—because its shape resembles the distinctive, monumental Lycian tombs there. But that's where the connection ends: The three-quarter poses of this sarcophagus' figures and their Thracian attire—popular in Athens at the time—instead link it to the Greek mainland, as does the layered portrayal of horses and hunters on the casket's long

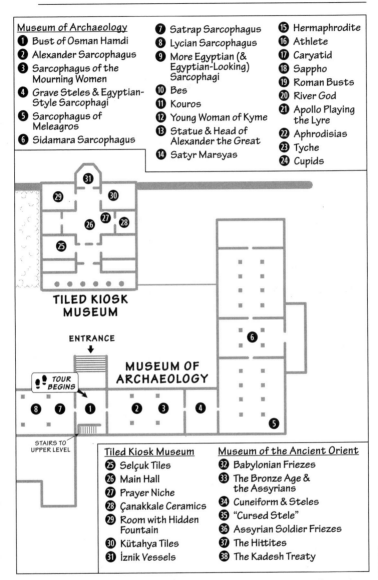

Museum of Archaeology
1. Bust of Osman Hamdi
2. Alexander Sarcophagus
3. Sarcophagus of the Mourning Women
4. Grave Steles & Egyptian-Style Sarcophagi
5. Sarcophagus of Meleagros
6. Sidamara Sarcophagus
7. Satrap Sarcophagus
8. Lycian Sarcophagus
9. More Egyptian (& Egyptian-Looking) Sarcophagi
10. Bes
11. Kouros
12. Young Woman of Kyme
13. Statue & Head of Alexander the Great
14. Satyr Marsyas
15. Hermaphrodite
16. Athlete
17. Caryatid
18. Sappho
19. Roman Busts
20. River God
21. Apollo Playing the Lyre
22. Aphrodisias
23. Tyche
24. Cupids

TILED KIOSK MUSEUM

ENTRANCE

MUSEUM OF ARCHAEOLOGY

TOUR BEGINS

STAIRS TO UPPER LEVEL

Tiled Kiosk Museum
25. Selçuk Tiles
26. Main Hall
27. Prayer Niche
28. Çanakkale Ceramics
29. Room with Hidden Fountain
30. Kütahya Tiles
31. İznik Vessels

Museum of the Ancient Orient
32. Babylonian Friezes
33. The Bronze Age & the Assyrians
34. Cuneiform & Steles
35. "Cursed Stele"
36. Assyrian Soldier Friezes
37. The Hittites
38. The Kadesh Treaty

sides. This experimentation with 3-D perspective winds up as a clutter of horse heads and hooves—like equine Rockettes.

The two long sides feature detailed, lifelike hunting scenes: a lion on one side, a wild boar on the other. The horses show their Arabic and European ancestry, with large foreheads, deep chests, and lean bellies—similar to the horses in friezes at the Parthenon in Athens.

On one narrow end, two centaurs fight over a deer. One is

ARCHAEOLOGICAL MUSEUM

naked, while the other—wearing a panther skin—is about to spear his opponent in the eye. On the other short end, the centaurs beat a man to death. This half-buried man is Kaineus, the mythological centaur-slayer. The centaur on his left is about to hit him with an amphora jug. The simple lid is decorated with seated (and remarkably sexy) sphinxes on one side and griffons on the other.

• *Beyond the Lycian Sarcophagus and the mummified corpse of a king who would have inhabited one of these sarcophagi are...*

More Egyptian (and Egyptian-Looking) Sarcophagi

Just before the exit is an Egyptian sarcophagus carved from dark diorite (a rock similar in texture to granite). Dating from the sixth

century B.C., this is the oldest sarcophagus found in the Sidon excavations. Hieroglyphs on the lid describe the owner, an Egyptian commander named Penephtah. He was later moved from his tomb to make room for the local king, Tabnit of Sidon. The inscription at the foot is Tabnit's epitaph.

Nearby, two light-colored, Egyptian-style sarcophagi lie side by side. Beginning in the fifth century B.C., Greek sculptors carved Egyptian-looking sarcophagi for their wealthy clients. Although the basic style was Egyptian, the Greeks felt free to play around with the design. The result: archaic Greek statues trapped in an Egyptian sarcophagus. The extensions at the shoulders were used to lift or carry the sarcophagus, then usually chopped off once they reached their final destination.

• *Continue ahead, past the museum store and the cloakroom. WCs are nearby. Straight ahead, through the lobby, is a statue of...*

Bes

This colossal statue of Bes is from the first century A.D. Often confused with Hercules, Bes was a demigod of ancient Egypt and a popular figure in the Cypriot pantheon of gods at the time. Here we see Bes holding a lion by its legs. Scholars' best guess is that the statue served as a fountain.

• *Walk through the doorway ahead of you, into the exhibit of...*

GREEK AND ROMAN SCULPTURE

• *Just past the doorway, you're greeted by the head of a...*

Kouros

This kouros (a Greek statue of a boy), dating from 600 B.C., was brought from the Greek island of Sámos. His face is round, with a blunt profile, almond eyes, and raised eyebrows. His lips are closed and straight, but grooves at the corners give the impression that he's smiling. In south Aegean art, kouros statues represented the idealized Greek youth. Similar heads and statues have been found in excavations on Sámos, Rhodes, Cos, and other Greek islands. Two other kouros statues stand stiffly at either side of the bay.

The rest of the hall is dedicated to a time period when Anatolia was under Persian rule (from the mid-sixth century B.C. to the Hellenistic age).

• *Continue about 30 yards into the next hall, dedicated to...*

Hellenistic Sculpture (330 B.C.-First Century B.C.)

This hall contains a beautiful example of the Hellenistic period: a fine statue of a **young woman** from ancient Kyme. Rather than noble, idealized gods, the Hellenistic artists gave us real people with real emotions.

But the highlight of this exhibit is a pair of Alexander the Great artifacts. Both were discovered at Pergamon, the world-famous acropolis in Aegean Turkey.

Swooping down from ancient Macedonia (located in present-day Macedonia and the far north of Greece) in the fourth century B.C., Alexander the Great's father conquered the Greeks and embraced their culture—one of Alexander's tutors was Aristotle. When Alexander took the throne after his father's assassination, he spread Greek customs and philosophy as he marched across the Middle East. By the time he died, in 323 B.C., his empire—and Greek culture—stretched all the way to India. Every city's main square had a Greek temple, and Greek was the language of his vast domain.

From an artistic perspective, Alexander's conquests marked the end of the Greek Golden Age (when balance was celebrated). The Hellenistic period that followed was characterized not by idealized and composed beauty but by rippling energy and jump-off-the-stage exuberance.

Carved from fine white marble, the powerful **statue of Alexander the Great** dates from the second century B.C. It's likely

he once held a bronze spear in his right hand, although his right arm and hand are missing. The hilt of the sword he held in his left hand remains. The statue bears a rare inscription naming its sculptor: "Menas of Pergamon, son of Aias."

The very natural-looking **head of Alexander the Great** also dates from the second century B.C. Some believe it was carved to decorate the renowned "Altar of Zeus" in Pergamon (the altar is now in Berlin). This head is a copy of the fourth-century B.C. original, by the renowned sculptor Lysippus. Alexander has a slightly tilted head, round eyes with heavy eyelids, and an open mouth that doesn't show his teeth. Gentle lines, deep furrows on the forehead, and the overall natural rendering of the face are characteristic of Hellenistic Pergamon sculpture.

Look for the third-century B.C. statue of the **satyr Marsyas.** Marsyas isn't stretching—he's tied to a tree by his arms, his face contorted in terrible pain. According to myth, Marsyas, provoked by peasants, invented a flute and challenged Apollo to a musical contest. Marsyas lost the contest, and Apollo hanged him from a branch and skinned him alive. Usually portrayed alone, this Marsyas statue was found in a group, next to Apollo... with a slave by his side, ominously sharpening his knife.

Also found in Pergamon was a fine, if surprising, statue of a **hermaphrodite**.

• *The next hall is dedicated to statues from two other ancient Aegean cities.*

Magnesia and Tralles

These statues were found in the late 19th century in Magnesia and Tralles. As you enter this larger hall, you'll see a statue of a cloaked **athlete** (some say he was a wrestler), which probably decorated the gymnasium at ancient Tralles in the first century A.D. The muscular young man with the playful smile relaxes against a column, having just finished his exercise.

A beautifully shaped **caryatid**—a support column—is carved as a woman. Dressed in a traditional gown, she looks well-suited for her architectural role.

• *Enter the doorway on the right to a hall with bays on either side, separated by columns.*

At the center of this hall is the head of the poet **Sappho,** born 2,700 years ago on the island of Lesbos. Her romantic poems to other women, including Aphrodite, gave us the words "lesbian" and "Sapphic." The left bay is dedicated to **Roman portrait busts.** The statue and bust (second century A.D.) of Emperor Marcus Aurelius, and the bust of Empress Faustina, are particularly interesting and realistic.

• *The next hall displays findings from renowned...*

Ancient Cities in Turkey

This hall is marked by a reclining **river god** (second century A.D.). Brought to the museum from Ephesus, this is Oceanus, a personification of the river thought by ancients to encircle the world. He's shown here as an old man, but his arms still ripple with muscle.

In the left bay are more statues from Miletus and Ephesus. Find the statue of **Apollo playing a lyre.** In this second-century

Roman copy of the Hellenistic original, Apollo is portrayed as more graceful than divine. His missing fingers were on the strings, and his right hand holds the plectrum (used to pluck the strings)—ready to play. Here and there are traces of the reddish brown and blue paint that once decorated the statue.

The right bay is dedicated to the ancient city of **Aphrodisias,** which had its own school of fine arts and a distinct artistic style. The room is named for Kenan Erim, the professor who spent a lifetime excavating at Aphrodisias. (Asked why he never married, Erim said he already was married—to Aphrodite.) Erim was buried at the site, next to the monumental entry to the Temple of Aphrodite.

• *Past the river god, enter the last exhibition hall, with statues from the...*

Roman Imperial Period

Although of lesser importance, a few of these statues stand out for their intricate work—like **Tyche,** the city goddess. Also check out the two **cupids**—betting on a rooster fight (in a glass case).

• You've now seen the best of the Museum of Archaeology. If you're getting museumed out, head for the exit and skip down to the Tiled Kiosk Museum.

Or, if you can't get enough of ancient Turkey, consider an optional detour upstairs to see artifacts from...

ANCIENT TROY AND BYZANTIUM

• To go upstairs, backtrack to the lobby where you first entered (near the sarcophagi). Head up the stairs and pass through the hall with a bronze statue of Emperor Hadrian to find the annex.

Start by touring the humble exhibit of artifacts from the ancient city of **Troy.** At the end of this long hall, dip into the section

to the left, which displays findings from a **tumulus** (ancient burial mound). Then backtrack to the end of the Troy exhibit, and take the stairs (across from the tumulus exhibit) down to the mezzanine level. Halfway down the stairs is an exhibit of **Byzantine artifacts.** Follow the zigzag tour route past a few interesting items, including part of the impressive chain the Byzantines pulled across the mouth of the Golden Horn to block enemy fleets (to your immediate left as you enter); fine Byzantine church frescoes; and massive Byzantine water pipes carved out of marble and caked with lime deposits. You'll also have views down into the atrium, where you can see a replica of the facade from the Doric Temple of Athena at Assos (580 B.C.).

At the bottom of the far staircase is the entrance (and exit) for the **Byzantium** exhibit (on the ground level, by the WC), which may be worth a few minutes if you have the interest in even more late Roman and Byzantine artifacts. You'll wind up in the gift-shop area.

• As you leave the Museum of Archaeology, the small, older building directly ahead of you—fronted by a gorgeous two-story colonnade, and to the right of the little park and café—is the...

Tiled Kiosk Museum

The word "kiosk" comes from the Turkish word *köşk*, meaning "mansion" or "pavilion." This kiosk contains some of the finest ex-

amples ever assembled of Selçuk, Ottoman, and regional tiles. As you tour the sumptuous collection, keep in mind that in Turkey, "tile" (*çini;* chee-nee) refers to a high quartz-content material that can be used to decorate architectural surfaces (with flat tiles) or to create functional vessels (such as bowls, vases, and cups). While much of what you'll see inside might be called "ceramics" or "pottery" in English, Turks consider them all "tiles."

The collection is displayed on one easy floor, so you can treat it like eye candy, lingering only at your favorite pieces to read the fine English descriptions.

The steps leading up to the entrance are in the center of the lower gallery, hiding behind the stone wall with the barred window. The Arabic **inscription** above the doorway explains that the building was constructed in A.D. 1472, during the reign of Mehmet the Conqueror—roughly 20 years after the Ottomans had taken Constantinople from the Byzantines. The building represents the earliest stages of Ottoman civic architecture and is the only one of its kind in Istanbul dating from this period.

As you step into the lobby (its floor is covered in glass to protect the original pavement), head for the large **map** on the opposite wall, which shows the historically important tile-manufacturing regions in Turkey and throughout the Middle East and Asia.

• *This entrance lobby is flanked by two small rooms. Enter the room on the left, which contains some of the oldest objects in the exhibition.*

Selçuk Tiles

This room is dedicated to the early tiles of Selçuk (the Turkish empire before the Ottomans) and Middle Eastern origin. As you enter the room, the case in front of you displays Syrian and Iranian pieces; the one behind it has some fine designs of Selçuk pottery.

At the end of the room, on the right wall, are decorative tile pieces with colored glaze from a 13th-century mosque. This turquoise-colored glaze is still in use, although only a few master potters who can apply it correctly remain. On the opposite wall are **star-shaped wall tiles** with animal and floral designs. Dating from the 13th century, these are from the summer palace of the Selçuk sultans in Konya (central Turkey).

• *Return to the lobby, and take the door to your left into the main hall, where you'll see...*

More Tiles and Ceramics

These objects are showpieces of Selçuk, Anatolian, and Ottoman tiles and ceramics. The pieces that look like vases are actually **ceramic lamps** (in the larger case in the center). These 16th-century oil-burning lamps were hung from the ceilings of mosques by those little handles. From the tile-making center of İznik, these were probably the best available lamps in the market at the time.

The colorful circa-1430 **prayer niche** was brought from a mosque in Konya in central Turkey. Its pieces are fired with colored glaze.

An annex off the main hall displays curiously designed 18th- and 19th-century **ceramics** from Çanakkale (a city on the Dardanelles).

• *Now walk to the end of the room, across from the entrance.*

Find the two world-renowned **glazed plates,** displayed in the side walls, across from each other. Dating from A.D. 1500, these are two of the finest surviving pieces of İznik tile—frequently showing up in reference books as textbook examples of Turkish tiles.

• *Walk past the plates, and go through the doorway on your left, which opens into a highly decorated room.*

The walls contain color-glazed tiles and intricate gold designs. Part of this so-called gold embroidery was redone over the centuries. It may look a little chintzy, but it was the height of style in its day. At the end of the room, on the left corner, is a beautiful **hidden fountain.**

The room to your right displays **Kütahya tiles.** The town of Kütahya (south of the Sea of Marmara) began making tiles during the 18th century, using techniques similar to those of the master potters at İznik, but never quite matching the quality of their work.

For the real deal, head into the next room, with outstanding blue-and-white **İznik vessels** from the early 15th century.

• When you're done in the Tiled Kiosk Museum, exit back into the court-yard and turn right. Head back toward the entrance gate to the complex. Just inside the gate, on the right-hand side, are stairs leading up to the third and final part of the museum.

Museum of the Ancient Orient

Well worth a look, this small collection offers an exquisite peek at the ancient cultures of the Near and Middle East. Most of what you'll see here comes from Mesopotamia, between the Tigris and Euphrates Rivers (parts of present-day Iraq and Syria). On this one-way loop tour you'll meet Sumerians, Akkadians, Babylonians, and Assyrians (all of whom were sovereign in the Middle East), as well as the Hittites (who ruled today's Turkey)—peoples who paved the road to modern civilization.

• The entry area offers some maps and other posted information worth skimming for a background understanding of the "Ancient Orient." As you head for the collection, notice the cuneiform script in the floor, which says that flash photography is prohibited.

Walk through the first room of the museum—stopping to see the Babylonian sundial (on the left)—and head for the doorway on the right (next to the adorable little sphinx). Turn left into a corridor, and take a moment to enjoy the tile friezes lining the walls.

Babylonian Friezes

These tile friezes once decorated the gate of the ancient city of Babylon (located in today's Iraq). The colorful designs of lions,

bulls (which, thanks to stylized perspective, look more like unicorns), and dragons (up top, looking like snakes with lions' paws in front and eagles' feet in back) represented Babylon's mighty gods.

• Beyond the friezes, at the end of the corridor, you'll emerge into a room with artifacts from...

The Bronze Age and the Assyrians

The marble head of Lamassu—a half-human, half-bull Assyrian creature—guards the doorway. Turn left and tour the collection clockwise. First you'll see early Bronze Age objects from the Sumerian and Akkadian civilizations. If you know your prehistory, you'll notice that Anatolia and Mesopotamia were technologically advanced, progressing through the metal ages (such as the Bronze Age) thousands of years ahead of continental Europe. So while a Mesopotamian sword was made around 3000 B.C., its European counterpart wouldn't have been created until 1000 B.C.

Continuing around the room, you reach a small showcase with **weight and measurement units** used in Mesopotamia, including the talent, mina, and shekel. Using these units, along with accurate scales, the ancients developed the first formal monetary system, based on the weights of gold and silver.

Keep going, into the collection of **Assyrian objects.** The two tall, free-standing statues of kings (ninth century B.C.) were carved from basalt; although the shorter statue is unfinished, the big one shows fine detail, with cuneiform script pressed into his uniform.

• *For more cuneiform, head back toward the corridor, then take the first left into the collection of...*

Cuneiform and Steles

On the back wall is a group of five steles—small pillars used to commemorate major events. The cases on either side of the steles display **cuneiform tablets.** The wedge-shaped script is the world's first writing system, invented 5,000 years ago by the Sumerians (of southern Iraq) and developed into a syllabic alphabet by their descendants, the Assyrians.

The case on the left traces the progress of cuneiform script. At the bottom left is one of the oldest tablets in the museum (2700 B.C.). The nail-shaped object nearby is actually an inscribed piece. To its right, the item shaped like a roll of paper towels chronicles the acts of the Babylonian king Nebuchadnezzar, describing the temples he built and the reconstruction of Babylon's city walls.

The case to the right of the steles holds interesting tablets, such as the Ur-Nammu law, a legal code of ancient Mesopotamia dating from 2050 B.C. Another tablet records the Assyrian kings' genealogy, while others list sacred marriage rites, poison remedies, and the court verdict for a man who put off an engagement. There's also a resume and job application, a book of proverbs, and a steamy love poem that conveys the timelessness of passion ("My groom, lover of my heart/Your beauty is unques-

Who's Who in the Ancient Orient

Who were the peoples of the Ancient Orient, and how did they relate to one another—and to today's Middle East? While ethnic lines are rarely clear-cut, here's an admittedly oversimplified family tree to help you get your bearings.

One of the clearest ways to track an ethnic group's lineage is to examine its language. Today's Arabs and Jews share a common Semitic language, meaning that they probably also share common ancestors. Today's Turks, Persians (most Iranians), and Kurds speak non-Semitic languages, which indicates that they aren't related to the Arabs.

The earliest of the peoples you'll meet in this museum are the **Sumerians** (c. 3000-2000 B.C.). While their origins are unclear, they weren't Semitic. The Sumerians invented a writing system called cuneiform, which marks the beginning of humankind's recorded history.

The **Akkadians** (c. 2300-2100 B.C.) and the **Babylonians** (c. 1900-1600 B.C.) were of Semitic origin—meaning they're the ancestors of today's Arabs. Because the city of Babylon is located in today's Iraq, you could say the Babylonians were "ancient Iraqis."

The **Assyrians** (c. 1900-600 B.C.) were descendants of the Akkadians, and also Semitic (Arab). They created a very efficient trade system throughout the lands they conquered. To secure their borders and prevent uprisings, the Assyrians forced the people they conquered to migrate to other areas of the empire, contributing to the Middle East's ethnic complexity. Today's Assyrian descendants speak Syriac, a form of Aramaic.

The **Hittites** (c. 1700-1200 B.C.) spoke an Indo-European language—meaning their language, and probably their ethnicity, were closer to Europe than to Asia. The Hittites came from the north and ruled today's Turkey and the Middle East for centuries.

tionable, sweeter than honey. Lion, my heart's treasure.../Let us take joy in your beauty").

Notice the **"cursed stele"** on the wall (to the left of the doorway to the next room). This eighth-century B.C. stele records the will of an Assyrian palace administrator, Bel-Harran. He tells about a city that he founded and a temple he constructed and dedicated to the gods. He declares that his citizens will be protected and exempt from tax. And at the end, he tacks on a curse to scare away vandals: "I pray that the great gods of Assyria destroy the future of whomever might destroy my words and my name, and the gods shall have no mercy on them." Maybe that explains how this stele has survived intact for 2,700 years.

• *Continue into the next room. On the right, notice the long army of knee-high Munchkins marching along the wall.*

Assyrian Soldier Friezes

The first few of these Assyrian troops carry taxpayers' money on the trays balanced on their heads. At the front of the line (at the opening in the wall) is a highly decorated basalt altar from Cappadocia, in central Turkey. The altar dates from the fifth century B.C. Both the reliefs and the altar have Aramaic text—a "newer" style of writing that replaced cuneiform. Aramaic is also the language spoken by Jesus Christ, most other New Testament figures, and Mel Gibson.

• *After a quick look around in this room, backtrack through the previous room (with the cuneiform tablets and steles). From there, turn left into the main corridor and follow it to its end, into a room with artifacts from...*

The Hittites

The Hittites once controlled a big chunk of Anatolia, reaching their peak in the 13th century B.C. The huge relief on the wall depicts

a king praying to Tarhunza, the Hittite storm god. Although the king stands on a tall mountain, he still can't reach the height of the gigantic god. Tarhunza was also the god of plants—he carries grapes in one hand and wheat in the other. His curly beard and hair, as well as the flares on his skirt, reflect Assyrian influence, while the helmet is Hittite-style. The horns on the helmet are a barometer of his divine importance: The more horns, the more important the god.

• *Go through the doorway on the right, and look to your right. A small case displays the exhibit's highlight.*

The Kadesh Treaty

These few clay fragments are a record in cuneiform script of the world's oldest surviving peace accord: the Kadesh Treaty. This document, created in 1283 B.C., ended the decades-long war between the Hittites and the Egyp-

tians. Even the United Nations recognizes the importance of this early peace agreement: A large copy of the treaty is displayed at the UN headquarters in New York City.

The text was initially engraved on silver tablets that have been lost to time. Three ancient copies exist. The version you see here was found in the archives of the Hittites' capital, Hattusha (100 miles north of present-day Ankara). It's written in Akkadian cuneiform, the language of diplomacy at the time.

Egyptian King Ramses II and Hittite King Hattusili III each had his own copy of the treaty—and each version claims victory for that copy's owner. But otherwise, the copies are similar, and they include many elements still common in modern-day peace agreements, such as provisions for the return of prisoners and refugees, and a mutual-aid clause. The treaty ends with a curse: "To whomever acts against these words, may the thousand gods of the Land of Hatti and the thousand gods of Egypt destroy his home, his land, and his servants." These final words dictate that the treaty's conditions would be honored by the kings' successors forever. After the Kadesh Treaty, the Middle East enjoyed uninterrupted peace for seven years—which, back then, was a pretty impressive run.

• *Your tour is finished. You're just a short walk from Topkapı Palace: Leave through the main gate to the museum complex, turn left, and head up the hill into the palace's First Courtyard; once there, the entrance to the palace is on your left, and the gate to the Sultanahmet district (and the back of Hagia Sophia) is on your right.*

TURKISH AND ISLAMIC ARTS MUSEUM TOUR

Türk-İslam Eserleri Müzesi

With a thoughtful and manageable collection of artifacts spanning the course of Turkish and Islamic civilizations, this museum is a convenient place to glimpse the rich cultural fabric of Turkey and the Middle East. You'll see carpets, calligraphy, ceramics, metalwork, woodwork, and lots more. Almost as interesting as the collection is its setting: the İbrahim Paşa Palace, one of Istanbul's great surviving Ottoman palaces.

Orientation

Cost: 20 TL.

Hours: Tue-Sun 9:00-19:00, until 17:00 off-season, closed Mon.

Getting There: It's centrally located in the Old Town's Sultanahmet area, across the Hippodrome (with its Egyptian Obelisk) from the Blue Mosque. From the Sultanahmet tram stop, simply cross through the park toward the Blue Mosque, then jog a few steps to the right when you hit the Hippodrome.

Information: Tel. 0212/518-1805, www.muze.gov.tr/tr/muzeler/turk-ve-islam-eserleri-muzesi.

Length of This Tour: Allow one hour.

Services: WCs are located under the staircase that leads up to the central courtyard.

Photography: No flash and no tripods.

Cuisine Art: The cafeteria is to the right as you enter the central courtyard. On the left side of the courtyard, the terrace has a great view of the Hippodrome and the Blue Mosque.

Starring: Carpets, ceramic tiles and containers, rare calligraphy, and other artifacts of the Islamic world's religious and cultural heritage.

OVERVIEW

Originally, the İbrahim Paşa Palace was much bigger, rivaling that of the Sultan. But today, its smaller size makes the museum's  U-shaped layout easy to figure out. The palace's original reception hall is today's south wing, with a small wooden balcony facing the Hippodrome. Its north and west wings were once palatial guest rooms. Today the museum's upstairs north, west, and south wings focus on historical artifacts, while the downstairs (garden level) south wing focuses on lifestyles (may be closed for renovation). Temporary exhibits are located on the entrance level. In the chamber behind the ticket/information desk, you'll find the remains of the Hippodrome's Byzantine infrastructure. On this tour, we'll start in the north wing, dip into several rooms along the west wing, then enter the large south wing.

Dates on the artifacts I mention are according to the Western calendar, though a few items in the museum are dated only by the Islamic calendar.

The Tour Begins

• *After you enter the large central courtyard, turn 180 degrees, and then go through the first door (to the right of the cafeteria) to enter the north wing.*

North Wing

• *At the top of the entry staircase, turn around. On the back wall of the corridor (on the elevated section behind the staircase) are the...*

❶ SAMARRA PALACE ARTIFACTS

The Abbasid dynasty ruled the Muslim world for more than five centuries, from A.D. 700 to 1250. Abbasid caliphs (political and religious leaders) employed non-Muslim slave-soldiers, mainly Turkic people from the north who had been abducted by slave traders or sold into slavery by impoverished parents. In time, these soldiers became a powerful military caste, establishing their sovereignty in North Africa and the Middle East.

The presence of these troops caused friction with the public in

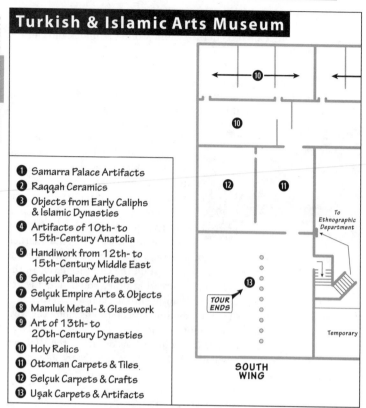

Turkish & Islamic Arts Museum

❶ Samarra Palace Artifacts

❷ Raqqah Ceramics

❸ Objects from Early Caliphs & Islamic Dynasties

❹ Artifacts of 10th- to 15th-Century Anatolia

❺ Handiwork from 12th- to 15th-Century Middle East

❻ Selçuk Palace Artifacts

❼ Selçuk Empire Arts & Objects

❽ Mamluk Metal- & Glasswork

❾ Art of 13th- to 20th-Century Dynasties

❿ Holy Relics

⓫ Ottoman Carpets & Tiles

⓬ Selçuk Carpets & Crafts

⓭ Uşak Carpets & Artifacts

Baghdad, capital city of the Abbasid dynasty. In 836, largely pressured by local leaders in Baghdad, the caliph decided to move the center of the caliphate from Baghdad to the new city of Samarra, which was then a simple military garrison. Thousands of masons were brought in from all over the Middle East to build immense structures. Even the homes of officials and administrators were huge palaces. The masons created some of the finest examples of early Islamic civil architecture, with summer and winter sections that incorporated baths, canals, and pools.

The display case holds composite column capitals, wall frescoes, tiles, and other decorative pieces unearthed during early 20th-century excavations.

• *Before you continue, notice the attractive ceramic vase with a dark blue glaze (13th century,*

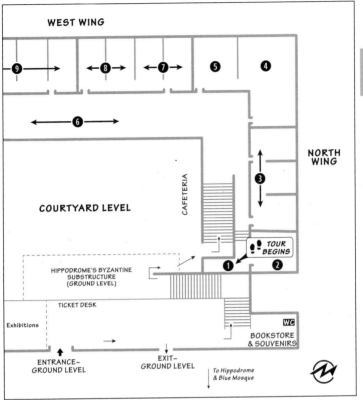

Raqqah, Syria) in the wall display to your left. This gives you an idea of what is through the doorway to the left, in the chamber dedicated to...

❷ RAQQAH CERAMICS

Through the middle ages, Raqqah (in north Syria) produced both polychrome and monochrome ceramics. The monochrome Raqqah-ware, in a dominant turquoise color and transparent glaze, were the most popular. The collection displayed here comes from archaeological digs done in 1905.

• *Leave the room, start down the main corridor, and go through the first door on the right (behind the staircase) to three connecting rooms showcasing art from the...*

❸ OBJECTS FROM EARLY CALIPHS AND ISLAMIC DYNASTIES

These three rooms are dedicated to Islamic art dating back to the early caliphates. Following the first four caliphs of the newborn religion, the two caliphate dynasties—the Umayyad (660 to 750) and the Abbasid (700 to 1250)—carried the influence of Islam be-

İbrahim Paşa

The museum building is the former palace of İbrahim Paşa, the Grand Vizier (prime minister) of Süleyman the Magnificent. İbrahim was appointed to serve young prince Süleyman, and when Süleyman succeeded to the throne, İbrahim advanced quickly. He became the sultan's right arm and also married the sultan's sister, Hatice.

İbrahim appreciated art, and after the Ottomans conquered Budapest, he brought back bronze statues of Apollo, Artemis, and Hercules, and placed them in front of his palace. However, these pagan symbols offended the public. One poet even said, "Two İbrahims came to this world. One destroyed idols (Prophet Abraham), and the other re-erected them." İbrahim could not stand this criticism—he forced the poet to crawl the streets of Istanbul and then hanged him.

The Grand Vizier's arrogant and self-centered attitude produced some strong enemies, among them Süleyman's wife, Roxelana. İbrahim was very powerful, so Roxelana had to get rid of him to guarantee her sons' succession. One day, the Grand Vizier was invited to Topkapı Palace for dinner, and the next morning, his dead body was found outside the palace walls (apparently Roxelana was...a bad cook). Süleyman had İbrahim buried in an unmarked grave, and his enormous wealth was confiscated.

yond the Arabian peninsula. During their reign, territories of the Islamic Empire extended from central Asia to Spain (see sidebar).

The first room displays objects from the Umayyad period. In the display case, the eighth-century Quran chapter *(Juz)* deserves particular attention.

The stones you see here on the wall, dating from the seventh and eighth centuries, are some of the oldest pieces in the museum's collection. The slab on the left is a milestone, with an inscription in Arabic that states that you are only at the beginning of your journey.

The next room boasts fine decorative pieces of ninth-century Abbasid palace art. Cases in the room display wall frescoes from the palace harem (the larger fresco of the two dancers is particularly attractive), wooden fragments used for wall decoration, an intricate marble bowl, and ceramics.

The last room is dedicated to the so-called Damascus documents (they were kept in the Damascus Umayyad Mosque for centuries), a vast collection of Islamic calligraphy. Among these are

The Great Caliphates

After the death of the Prophet Muhammad in A.D. 632, Islamic leaders created the position of caliph to serve as the religious and social leader of the Muslim community (similar to the apostles or popes in Christian history). But as the first four caliphs (who served consecutively) began to die off, people wondered how to choose their replacements: Some Muslims thought caliphs should be elected, while others felt the position should be hereditary and pass only to direct descendants of Muhammad.

First the title of "caliph" was handed down through family dynasties, taking on more of a political significance. The **Umayyads** (661-750) became the first significant caliphate dynasty, who ruled from Damascus, in present-day Syria.

Then the **Abbasids**—the descendants of Muttalib, the uncle of Muhammad—used the lineage argument to seize the caliphate, moving its base from Damascus to Baghdad, and eventually to Samarra. Beginning in the early eighth century, the Abbasids ruled the Middle East and the Islamic world. Although their power waned over time, they kept the caliphate title until the early 1500s, when the Ottomans took over.

Because the **Ottomans** were Turks rather than Arabs, their claim to the caliphate was less convincing to the Arab communities within their empire. But once the Ottoman sultan's name was officially recorded as the caliph, his authority was accepted.

In the early 20th century, as Turkey was poised to become a modern republic, the caliphate came into question again. Because Atatürk's vision for the new republic included a separation of mosque and state, Turkey's parliament abolished the caliphate in 1924, once and for all.

the earliest Quran copies, including parchment sheets on which the Quran was initially written.

• *Head back to the corridor and enter the next room on the right.*

❹ ARTIFACTS OF 10th- TO 15th-CENTURY ANATOLIA

In the last quarter of the 11th century, the Selçuk (the first of the powerful Muslim Turkish states) invaded Anatolia, aiding an extensive migration of Turkic tribes into Anatolia (Asia Minor, the Asian part of present-day Turkey). The Artuqid State (1100 to 1400) is one of the many states that

were founded during this transition period, in what is the south-eastern part of Turkey today.

As insignificant as the Artuqid State was, it produced some remarkable metalwork—some of the most attractive pieces in the museum are in this section, such as the two intricate bronze drums. However, the main attraction here is the monumental gate of the mid-12th-century Grand Mosque of Cizre (jeez-reh, today a small town in eastern Turkey west of the Tigris River) in the large corner room.

This magnificent door is made of wood, sheeted with copper, held together with iron nails, and reinforced with brass rods. Patches were made from recycled metal items and used to replace

missing sheets on the doors' panels. Look at the dragon-shaped handles. The one on the left was stolen in 1969 and somehow showed up in a Copenhagen museum. The lion-shaped middle piece is still on the door wing. Lions and dragons, considered talismans, were common designs in Anatolia in the Middle Ages.

• *As you face this monumental gate, the doorway on the left leads into a display of artifacts from the...*

❺ HANDIWORK FROM 12th- TO 15th-CENTURY MIDDLE EAST

Founded by Selahaddin Eyyubi, the Eyyubid State (1170 to mid-15th-century) ruled Egypt and the entire Middle East at its height. Eyyubi, known in the West as Saladin, led the Muslim opposition against the Crusaders in the Levant. On display here are two 13th-century intricate wood columns, turquoise Raqqah ceramic ware, and vessels for daily use.

• *Step through the doorway, back to the corridor.*

West Wing

• *Beyond this point, the corridor through the West Wing is dedicated to Selçuk palace art and artifacts, with additional audio-visual displays. On the left and just behind the visual depicting Kubadabad Palace (in central Turkey), the display case shows some of the rare and attractive pieces of...*

❻ SELÇUK PALACE ARTIFACTS

Attached to the back wall of the case (and marked as a 13th-century archivolt, or ornamental molding inside an arch) is a fine example of figurative stone carving. Artuqid in origin, the archivolt features

traditional geometric and floral patterns, and a pair of eagles flanked by a griffin. The inscription in Kufic-style calligraphy (an early form of Arabic script with straighter lines) is an excerpt from a love poem.

The decorative star-shaped tiles in blue, turquoise, and purple represent the favored patterns of the time. With high quartz content, these tiles were made to last for centuries.

Further down the corridor, to the right and hidden behind the screen, the second display case has more pieces related to palace entertainment. The case features everyday objects that were both decorative and functional, including a 12th-century Persian ewer, metal and ceramic bowls, and candlesticks.

The 12th-century Minai tiles, painted both under and over the glaze, have their roots in central Asia. Even at the time they were made, these were unique and precious items. Their designs are intriguing—a halo indicates aristocratic status, while armbands on kaftans and jackets indicate social rank. Most figures depict classic Turkic features: round faces, almond eyes, and small noses and mouths.

Admire the outstanding miniatures and decorations in the *Kitab al-Aghani*, or the *Book of Songs*. This is the masterpiece of Al-Isbahani (897-967), a Persian literary scholar and poet who lived much of his life in Baghdad and Aleppo.

Moving a few more steps along the corridor, you will find some intimate objects, including a star-shaped 12th-century tile piece depicting a courting couple. It is a reminder of the many behind-closed-doors affairs that took place in the Selçuk palace.

• *Now walk back to the beginning of the West Wing corridor, and go through the door across from the display case to enter the...*

❼ SELÇUK EMPIRE ARTS AND OBJECTS

The Selçuk Turks governed from 1000 to the early 1300s, maintaining power over the Near East (mainly present-day Iran), the Middle East, and Anatolia. While the Selçuks ruled where Islam

TURKISH & ISLAMIC ARTS

was the dominant culture, you will find extensive traces of their Turkish roots and the influence of local cultures in their art. The decline of the Selçuks in the early 14th century cleared the way for the autonomy of future Turkish dynasties—just over a century later, the Ottomans would unify the Turks once again.

The first room boasts some very fine examples of 11th- to 13th-century Selçuk calligraphy and illumination. The adjacent room is reserved for everyday items, from earthenware objects to metalwork. Check out the decorative bowl in the wall display (on the left as you enter) and the bronze mirrors in the large display case.

❽ MAMLUK METAL AND GLASSWORK

The next two rooms display artifacts of Mamluk origin. The Mamluks (1250-1500) were slave-soldiers of non-Muslim origin under the Abbasid caliphs. This powerful military caste ruled over Egypt and the Middle East until the Ottoman occupation in the early 1500s.

The giant 15th-century brass lantern (third room, wall display) shows off skilled craftsmanship. Beaten metal parts were painstakingly decorated by carving and punching.

Marked as *badiye* (bah-dee-ych), the 15th-century brass bowl in the wall display (fourth room, next to the door) is a true work of art. Further decorated with silver and gold, the inscriptions praise the Mamluk sultan for his victory.

Also note the intricate glass lanterns in the large case across the room. The colorful designs on the exterior were applied using enamel techniques.

• *Step through the doorway, back to the corridor. If you have time for a detour, turn right and enter the next door, into a section dedicated to...*

❾ ART OF 13th- TO 20th-CENTURY DYNASTIES

The work in these rooms is from the two Turco-Mongolian dynasties—the Ilkhanids (1255 to 1350) and Timurids (1370-1500)—along with the Safavids (1500-1720, founded by the Safavviya Sufi order) and the Turkmen Qajars (1795-1925, who ruled Persia—today's Iran).

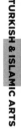

TURKISH & ISLAMIC ARTS

You'll see some fine examples of religious calligraphy and decoration, as well as other diverse items of interest, such as the 642-page, 14th-century album of Persian poetry that also includes attractive landscape paintings (*Mecmua*, Timurid, second room). Notice the highly decorated, boat-shaped brass bowl from the 17th century, used by dervishes to collect alms and offerings (marked as *Keşkül*, Safavid, third room in the wall display).

• *Continue to the end of the corridor. The last section in this wing contains...*

❿ HOLY RELICS

The long, single case on the corridor wall displays a 19th-century Kaaba Belt. It was a tradition for the house of the ruling caliph to annually present embroidered fabric covers and belts to decorate the stone walls of the Kaaba, the holiest Muslim shrine, located in

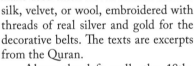

Mecca, Saudi Arabia. Ottomans used thick woven textiles such as silk, velvet, or wool, embroidered with threads of real silver and gold for the decorative belts. The texts are excerpts from the Quran.

Along the left wall, the 18th-century Kıblenüma (compass pointing in the direction of the Kaaba, toward which Muslims pray), and the 13th-century scroll *(Hac Vekaletnamesi)* deserve particular attention. Devout Muslims are expected to make the *hac* (pronounced hahdge), or pilgrimage, to the Kaaba at least once in their lifetimes. In the Middle Ages, this was a long, arduous journey. Believers who were unable to do this journey for some reason would sponsor someone else's pilgrimage, which would be undertaken on the donor's behalf, as inscribed in this scroll.

Items in the connecting rooms include hair from the Prophet Muhammad's beard, his footprint, and two highly decorated verbal descriptions of his qualities—all the more important in Islam in the absence of physical portraits. Called a *hilye* (heel-yeh), or *Hilye-i Şerif*, the poetic text describes the Prophet's attributes, such as generosity, honesty, and gentleness. It combines two traditional arts—*hat* (calligraphy) and *tezhip* (decoration)—into one piece of artwork.

Traditionally, a *hilye* was given to a young man about to get married with the hope that he would read it and be inspired to model himself after the Prophet. Similarly, a bride's dowry chest contained a Quran, so that she could pattern herself after the woman to whom an entire chapter in the holy book is dedicated—Mary, the mother of Jesus.

• *Now continue into the...*

South Wing

• *As you enter the south wing, the left wall of the entrance hall is covered with fine examples of...*

⓫ OTTOMAN CARPETS AND TILES

The European love affair with Turkish, or "Oriental," carpets began in the 13th century. For centuries, upper-class Europeans considered a Turkish rug the ultimate status symbol. If you couldn't afford to buy an actual rug, you'd pay an artist to paint one to hang on the wall—or to paint a rug hanging in the background of a portrait.

A few of the carpets here are named for the German painter Hans Holbein the Younger (1497-1543). Holbein served as a court painter to Henry VIII, was considered a master portrait artist, and illustrated the first German translation of the Bible. He liked to paint Oriental carpets (and other handicrafts) in the backgrounds of his paintings and court frescoes. Europeans who had seen these designs in the paintings wanted to own a similar carpet in real life...and Turkish weavers happily obliged.

Even though the designs carry his name, Holbein didn't originate them. For example, Holbein carpets often have large eight-pointed stars, which were unusual in Ottoman carpets of the time; rather, this motif is more common in earlier Selçuk carpets (shown in the next section). The carpets you see here are mainly based on designs from the Turkish towns of Uşak (oo-shahk) and Bergama (behr-gah-mah; known in ancient times as Pergamon). Today, limited numbers of Bergama carpets are still being woven  there, but none are made in modern Uşak. (For more examples of Uşak carpets, see the next section.) Crafted in a predominantly red color, these carpets have a traditional design and are extremely fine, especially considering the density of their wool.

The prayer rugs on display here—or what's left of them after centuries of constant use—have worn bare spots from the foreheads, knees, and toes of worshippers. They have repeating prayer-niche designs that reflect their purpose.

In the large central case, you will find a few examples of early Ottoman tiles and ceramics, including decorative fragments of a 15th-century inscription. Pieces called Milet İşi (mee-leht ee-shee), or Miletus Ware, are named so because scholars initially thought they resembled the ceramics of Miletus (ancient city along the Aegean Sea, near Ephesus). But they're actually late 14th- and 15th-  century ceramics manufactured in İznik (ancient Nicaea), a town to the east of the Sea of Marmara. Milet İşi, which were produced for just a short time and represent a transition from traditional Selçuk to fine Ottoman tiles, usually feature purple and cobalt-blue colors on a white undercoat, with basic geometric shapes and plant and animal motifs.

• *Walk through the doorway by the fireplace into the next section, which is reserved for...*

⓯ SELÇUK CARPETS AND CRAFTS

Only a handful of 13th-century **Selçuk carpets** have survived, and more than half of those still in existence are displayed in this room. They were gathered from mosques and shrines in central Turkey, especially in Konya, the capital city of the Selçuk Empire. The rare carpets on display here show different colors and designs, making each one unique. They are quite stylized, almost to the point of abstraction, as the creators adapted floral and animal motifs into geometric  forms. The patterns are often repeated. Their designs include stylized eagles, arrowheads, crescents, and eight-pointed stars, as well as Kufic letters (which are also commonly used to decorate borders). These carpets, made of pure wool, are knotted with a double-knot technique known as the "Turkish knot."

On the opposite wall, you will find rare and highly intricate examples of traditional wood carving. The larger, 13th-century walnut window shutters, brought from a monumental tomb in the early 1900s, represent painstaking craftsmanship. Arabic script on the upper panels reads, "There is no greater virtue than to avoid ambition and earthly desires." The nicely detailed, ceremonial wood sarcophagus dates back to 1250. The smaller walnut doors are more recent, and not Selçuk.

On the north wall hangs a 13th-century tiled-brick panel made in a traditional fashion. The Selçuk Turks used tiles to decorate both the interiors and the exteriors of their monuments. The secret to their artistry was the fine clay they used, which contained a large amount of quartz. The quartz made the tiles durable enough to survive even the harsh weather of the steppes of central Asia. To create the tiles, Selçuk artisans spread a layer of clay several inches thick on a tray, and cut it into smaller shapes such as triangles, rectangles, and stars. Then they painted the pieces with colored glazes and fired the tiles. Unlike thin-surface tiles used elsewhere, the Selçuks' thick, glazed tiles were integrated into the walls, ceilings, and minarets.

To the right of the panel, note the rare pieces of Selçuk stone carving, including a relief with two Selçuk warriors and two others with griffin motifs. In the Selçuk tradition, stylized reliefs display birds, beasts of prey, and griffin and dragon motifs embedded in intricate, floral designs. The Selçuk Turks used these motifs extensively in wood and stone to decorate facades and entrances on civil as well as religious architecture.

• *Pass through the doorway next to the stones, and into the last and largest hall of the museum to see...*

⓫ UŞAK CARPETS AND ARTIFACTS

The museum has a large inventory of Uşak "palace carpets," many of which are on display here and at the new Carpet Museum (at the northeast corner of the Hagia Sophia, by the Imperial Gate of Topkapı Palace). Dating to the 16th and 17th centuries, Uşak marks the pinnacle of traditional all-wool carpet weaving in Turkey. An average Uşak carpet has about 103,000 knots in ten square feet. (Wool carpets don't come any denser.) There are two types: those designed with medallions (the more common type), and those with repetitive star patterns.

After admiring the rugs, take a look at the other objects. The first case (to the right as you enter, behind the carpet display) has some attractive items from the Ottoman era. The two 17th-century gilded copper candlesticks (decorated with floral motifs and semi-precious stones) and the highly decorated 15th-century copper lantern stand out. The 17th-century incense burner-candlestick, featuring curved arms that end in tulips, also has an unusual design.

Continuing around the room counterclockwise, the next case displays an incomplete scroll that carries the *tuğra* (pronounced too-rah), or the imperial signature of Sultan Süleyman the Magnificent. This particular type of scroll is called a *ferman* (pronounced fehr-mahn), meaning "the word of the monarch." The visible part of the scroll has words of praise for the sultan.

The scroll (and thus the signature) is a great example of traditional *hat* (pronounced hot) art, which combines Arabic writing with artistic calligraphy. The calligrapher *(hattat)* plays with the shape of letters, creating beautiful forms that remain grammatically correct but can be hard to read. (For more on this art, including information about how to see it being made, see page 346.)

The next display case boasts ornate woodwork and outstanding decorations. This late 16th-century Quran holder (the taller of the two displayed) was brought here from the library of Hagia Sophia. The wood is studded with ebony, ivory, turtle shell, and mother of pearl, and the interior of the domed cover has exquisite paintwork.

Also on display are two 17th-century *rahles*, or Quran stands. A *rahle* (pronounced rah-leh) supported the fragile binding of the Quran (or other books) while it was read.

The last case displays a masterpiece of Ottoman calligraphy and traditional book decoration. Renowned calligrapher Seyyid

Lokman created the book, *Religions, Islam, and Ottoman History*, at the end of the 16th century on the order of the sultan. The book's miniatures and decorations were painted by skilled artisans of the time in watercolor and glaze. The 55 miniatures in the book depict personalities of religious significance, as well as Ottoman sultans.

• *Exit down the staircase to return to the central courtyard. Next to the base of the stairs is the entrance to the...*

Ethnographic Department

This section of the museum is closed for renovation, with no set date for reopening. If it is open when you visit, it's worth a look, but keep in mind that the exhibits may have moved. It describes Turk-

Where Were the Men?

Except for one man, the fabric merchant, you'll see only female models in this exhibit. There are two main reasons. In Turkish culture, women traditionally passed down folk-art traditions to the next generation. Particularly in the countryside, men were not usually involved in domestic activities within the home. Women were in charge of what took place beneath the roof of the house—the cooking, cleaning, sewing, and child-rearing. Men built the house, tended the  flock, sold the produce, chopped the wood, cleaned the stable, cultivated the field, did the jobs that brought in hard cash...and sometimes hung out in the town coffee shop.

ish lifestyles, from nomadic life in central Asia to 19th-century city living.

• *On the left wall as you enter is a panel about...*

NOMADIC LIFESTYLES

A map traces the lands where the *kara çadir* (kah-rah chah-duhr), the traditional, black goat-hair tent of nomads, has been used—from the shores of the eastern Atlantic Ocean to the Caspian Sea. Nomads in eastern Turkey still follow this traditional lifestyle, occasionally crossing borders while herding their animals.

Considering the nomads' mobile lifestyle, a portable tent that they can fold and pack on an animal is the ideal home. The black tent is made of woven goat hair and connecting wood pins, with a central wood pole for support. Although the tent material looks simple, it is quite difficult to make. The fabric is made of coarse goat hair, which makes the weaver's hands bleed and become calloused.

• *Now, go straight ahead to the display of kilims across from the entrance. On the right wall is a panel about the...*

WOMEN OF ANATOLIA

Stop here for a look at these photos of Turkish women from different walks of life, to whom this exhibit is dedicated. In Turkish, the term used to describe the ideal woman—generous, hardworking, nurturing, caring, loving, and protective—is "Anadolu Kadını" (ah-nah-doh-loo kah-duh-nuh), meaning "Woman of Anatolia." The word "Anatolia" (Anadolu in Turkish) has a double meaning. Literally, it means "east" in Greek and refers to the Asian part of Turkey. Culturally, it is translated as "full of mothers" by breaking the word into its syllables ("ana" meaning mother and "dolu" meaning full). Given the importance Turkish society places on women, translating Anatolia as "full of mothers" makes sense.

• *Look behind the glass wall to see a big weaving hanging on the wall, called a...*

KILIM

Textiles, especially those that can be used as furniture in a Turkish home, are the flagship of Turkish arts and crafts. Once produced for basic needs, textiles eventually turned into a pleasing art form, especially as the Turks prospered under Ottoman rule.

Kilims (kee-leem) are flat woven rugs, consisting of warp (horizontal) and weft (vertical) layers (without the knots added for carpets). These weavings are quite similar to Navajo Indian rugs, and tribal designs are passed down from one generation to the next. The large kilim you see here has two long and narrow parts, like two runners, which were successively woven on the same narrow loom and later connected to form a large rectangle. This was a common way to create large kilims, instead of making a bigger loom. On the left, you'll see a typical wooden kilim loom used by nomads.

• *Continue to your left, under the arch near a huge **wooden wheel**. This wheel is the circular roof of a wood-frame tent (shown behind the glass wall on your right) known as a...*

YURT

This is a style of tent that has been commonly used throughout Central Asia and by the Turks. The yurt (which also means "motherland" in Turkish) consists of a cylindrical wooden frame that is covered on the outside with thick felt made of sheep's wool, with kilims lining the inside. Behind the same glass wall, outside the yurt, on the right, is a thick felt cloak worn by shepherds, still commonly seen in the countryside.

• *Continue to your left to find the...*

LOOM AND CARPET

Turkish carpets are usually known by the name of the regions where they are made, and the traditional wool-on-wool carpets from the same region almost always have similar designs and colors. This is not only because traditional designs are passed down through the generations, but also because the plants used to dye the wool are grown only in certain areas.

The carpet on this big wooden loom has traditional geometric designs and is colored with natural dyes. Around the loom are different tools used in weaving: heavy wood combs—called *kirkit* (keer-keet)—used to beat down the pile to tighten the threads, a spinning wheel, and simple drop-spindles. To the right of the carpet loom, on either side of the hall, are two panels showing **dye-making techniques** and the plants—and even insects—used in the process. An interesting example is the cochineal, a small insect used to make red dye. The Italian liqueur Campari also gets its color from the cochineal.

• *Turn left and walk under the wide arch to find the replica...*

BLACK TENT

This actual-size black goat-hair tent is filled with models of women going about their daily routines. The tent's interior is multifunctional: During the day, it serves as the living room, kitchen, and dining area, while at night, mattresses, quilts, and pillows are rolled out to transform it into a bedroom. A nomad's multipurpose tent was the prototype of today's rural Turkish home.

The goat hair, with its high oil content, hardly absorbs any rain—the water slides right off. For extra protection in winter, today's nomads stretch nylon covers over their tents.

• *Continue along the hallway to find (on the right) the stone walls of a...*

MOUNTAIN HOME

Behind the glass wall is a model interior of a typical country home

from the Yunt Mountain region in western Turkey. Like the tent, this village house is multifunctional. The family cooks, cleans, eats, and sleeps in one room. Mattresses piled during the day behind a white embroidered curtain are unfolded at night on the carpeted floor. The house is illuminated by a gas lamp (find it on the central shelf of the wooden cupboard). In Turkish, a gas lamp is a *lüks* (lux), which means "light" in Latin.

The model on the far left wears a red bridal headdress and carries a baby on her back. Red, the color of chastity in Turkish tradition, is used in traditional wedding clothes.

• *Continue down the hallway to find the...*

BURSA HOME

This reconstruction shows the interior of the upper-middle-class home of a family in the 19th-century Turkish city of Bursa. The walls of the wood-and-brick house are covered

with fine plaster and painted a saffron color. This house's several rooms were typically used for multiple purposes. Notice the fine embroidered curtains on the left-hand windows. Between the windows, on the wall, is a gold-embroidered velvet case that holds the Quran. Below the windows is a wood divan, draped with more finely embroidered cloths. In most homes, the divan doubled as a storage unit with drawers (the material hid the drawers).

The two women sitting on the couch are the ladies of the house; one is embroidering, while the other threads vegetables to be dried on a line. Their garments are made of fine velvet, embroidered with gold threads. The way they cover their hair and necklines with embroidered scarves signifies their social status.

Sitting on the floor are two more women—the servants, their status made clear by their simple outfits. They cover their hair in the traditional style; while their scarves pull back their hair, it's not completely covered—nor are their necklines. One does embroidery while the other makes Turkish coffee on a grill (also a good source of heat during the winter).

• *Turn left to find the...*

FABRIC SHOP

Here's a scene from a 19th-century city street. A merchant shows his wares to a wealthy woman (her clothing signals her status: a velvet dress embroidered with gold threads). To the right, a commoner passes by a typical Ottoman street fountain.

• *The last few exhibits leading back toward the entrance door show examples of 19th-century Istanbul homes. In these displays, you see early glimpses of Westernization: rooms built for a specific function, furnished with armchairs and chairs instead of divans, and models wearing non-traditional clothes. The first room next to the fabric shop shows a...*

DINING ROOM

Note the marble table and many chairs, and the dresser heavily inlaid with mother-of-pearl, evidence of the family's wealth. This kind of furniture came from what is today southeastern Turkey and northern Syria. On the floor, the fancy carpet with intricate designs represents the 19th-century style favored by the ruling class. There are no figurative paintings; the framed decoration instead shows the art of *hat* (calligraphy).

The two women sitting on the armchairs wear jewelry rather than traditional headdresses. When city women of the time went outside, they covered themselves from head to toe. The common village women in the countryside never followed this trend. The traditional headdress—a square scarf folded into a triangle, with the ends tied at the back of the head—is still in use today.

• *Directly behind you is the...*

LIVING ROOM

The ladies of the house are seated in armchairs, admiring the samples brought by the tailor (she's the woman in blue, with the handmade silver belt). On the table in front of the tailor are drawings of the latest fashions.

• *Down the hall and on the opposite side is the...*

BRIDAL CHAMBER

The big brass bed is covered in heavily embroidered bedspreads and pillows, and the furniture is inlaid with mother-of-pearl. The bride's white dress is embellished with gold threads. The traditional Turkish bridal dress was either completely red or dominated by red, but as Western influence grew, more brides began wearing white.

• *Turn around to see the last exhibit, which shows a...*

TURKISH BATH

The woman on the very left is dressed for the bath, covered in a wrap called a *peştemal* (pehsh-teh-mahl). Commoners wore simple,

wooden non-slip slippers called *takunya* (tah-koon-yah), while the rich would wear the fancier silver or bronze *nalın* (nah-luhn) you see here, inlaid with mother-of-pearl. The bowls in the display are similar to those still used today in Turkish baths. Notice the bowls on the right side with the Arabic words. These are prayers from the Quran, talismanic bowls that people believed gave them strength—allowing them to wash away some of their troubles. Bath towels and a *peştemal* hang on the wall, over the metal taps.

• *Our tour is over. As you walk back across the garden, notice the terrace overlooking the Hippodrome, with sweeping views of the Hippodrome monuments and the Blue Mosque.*

OLD TOWN BACK STREETS WALK

From Sultanahmet to the Spice Market

This walk leads you through the back streets of Istanbul's Old Town, giving you a taste of the authentic city (rather than its tourist-filled historic core). You'll share sidewalks with natives going about their daily routines, and walk streets that haven't changed in centuries, lined with shops that cater to locals.

The major themes of this walk are markets and mosques. First, the Old Town has been a bustling commercial center for centuries, and you'll enjoy two of its most famous and bustling marketplaces: The Grand Bazaar's aggressive salesmen and tempting souvenirs will threaten to empty your wallet, while the Spice Market's intoxicating aromas and offers of "Turkish Viagra" will titillate your senses. Second, we'll drop into two of the city's most interesting and important mosques: one grand (the Mosque of Süleyman the Magnificent, the finest of all Ottoman mosques in Istanbul), and one cozy (the gorgeously tiled Rüstem Paşa Mosque). In between these main attractions, we'll see a side of Istanbul few tourists experience.

Orientation

Length of This Walk: Allow at least four hours, not counting the Grand Bazaar; if you linger in the shops at the Grand Bazaar and Spice Market, it could fill an entire day.

Getting There: We'll start at the Sultanahmet tram stop in the heart of the Old Town.

Grand Bazaar: Mon-Sat 9:00-19:00, shops begin to close at 18:30, closed Sun and during religious holidays, across the parking lot from the Çemberlitaş tram stop, behind the Nuruosmaniye Mosque.

Mosque of Süleyman the Magnificent: Mosque—Free, generally open daily from one hour after sunrise until one hour before sunset, closed to visitors five times a day for prayer. Mausoleums—Free, daily 9:00-17:00, until 18:00 in summer. Located on Sıddık Sami Onar Caddesi, in the Süleymaniye district.

Rüstem Paşa Mosque: Free, generally open daily from one hour after sunrise until one hour before sunset, closed to visitors five times a day for prayer, on Hasırcılar Caddesi, Eminönü.

Spice Market: Free to enter, Mon-Sat 8:00-19:30 (until 19:00 off-season), Sun 9:30-18:00, closed during religious holidays, at the Old Town end of the Galata Bridge, near the Eminönü tram stop.

Dress Code: To enter a mosque, knees and shoulders must be covered, shoes must be removed, and women should also cover their hair with a scarf (see page 63 for details).

Starring: Some of Istanbul's best markets and mosques...and its people.

The Walk Begins

• *Begin at the Sultanahmet tram stop (200 yards uphill from Hagia Sophia and the Underground Cistern). From here, we'll walk five gradually uphill blocks along the tram tracks to an ancient column from Byzantine Constantinople (at the Çemberlitaş tram stop).*

Divan Yolu

The bustling street called Divan Yolu—now reserved mostly for trams and buses, and lined with shops and restaurants—has been the city's transportation thoroughfare since Byzantine times. The small mosque near the Sultanahmet tram stop is the 15th-century **Firuz Ağa Camii.** Just beyond the mosque, enter the **park** to your left and climb the stairs to the red-brick platform, which offers grand views of the Blue Mosque (including all six minarets). The Byzantine ruins scattered in and around the circle in front of the platform probably once belonged to the ancient Hippodrome (chariot racecourse) or a related building.

After enjoying the view, continue up Divan Yolu (with Hagia Sophia behind you). The bust you pass as you leave the park depicts the poet **Mehmet Akif,** who wrote Turkey's national anthem.

Walk another block up the street, and cross the tracks at the traffic lights (just past Starbucks). Ahead, an old **cemetery** filled with Ottoman bigwigs is behind the wall on your right. Enter near the corner, walk in 15 paces, and look to your right. Amid the traditional pillar- and turban-shaped tombstones, find the unique stone resembling a ship's sail (it belongs to Cudi Paşa, apparently a high-ranking official). The big mausoleum at the far end of the cemetery honors Sultan Mahmut II, who ruled in the first half of

OLD TOWN BACK STREETS

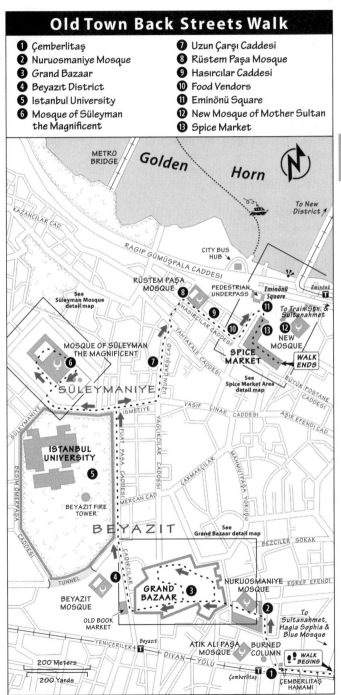

Old Town Back Streets Walk

1. Çemberlitaş
2. Nuruosmaniye Mosque
3. Grand Bazaar
4. Beyazit District
5. Istanbul University
6. Mosque of Süleyman the Magnificent
7. Uzun Çarşı Caddesi
8. Rüstem Paşa Mosque
9. Hasırcılar Caddesi
10. Food Vendors
11. Eminönü Square
12. New Mosque of Mother Sultan
13. Spice Market

METRO BRIDGE

Golden Horn

To New District

KAZANCILAR CAD.

RAGIP GÜMÜŞPALA CADDESI

CITY BUS HUB

See Süleyman Mosque detail map

RÜSTEM PAŞA MOSQUE

PEDESTRIAN UNDERPASS

Eminönü Square

Eminönü

To Train Stn. & Sultanahmet

HASIRCILAR CADDESI

TAHTAKALE CADDESI

MOSQUE OF SÜLEYMAN THE MAGNIFICENT

NEW MOSQUE

SPICE MARKET

WALK ENDS

SÜLEYMANIYE

UZUN ÇARŞI CAD.

BÜYÜK POSTANE CADDESI

See Spice Market Area detail map

SÜLEYMANIYE

İSMETİYE

VASIF ÇINAR CADDESI

AŞIR EFENDI CAD.

FUAT PAŞA CADDESI

YAĞLIKCILAR CADDESI

ISTANBUL UNIVERSITY

BEYAZIT FIRE TOWER

ÇAKMAKCILAR

MAHMUTPAŞA YOKUŞU

BESIM ÖMERPAŞA CADDESI

MERCAN CAD.

See Grand Bazaar detail map

BEYAZIT

BEZCILER SOKAK

CADIRCILAR

TUNNEL

NURUOSMANIYE MOSQUE

EŞREF EFENDI

BEYAZIT MOSQUE

GRAND BAZAAR

OLD BOOK MARKET

To Sultanahmet, Hagia Sophia & Blue Mosque

YENIÇERILER CAD.

Beyazit

ATIK ALI PAŞA MOSQUE

BURNED COLUMN

WALK BEGINS

200 Meters

200 Yards

DIVAN YOLU

Çemberlitaş

ÇEMBERLITAŞ HAMAMI

the 19th century. His mausoleum represents the eclectic taste of the time (it includes a beautiful crystal chandelier hanging down from the center of the dome). To go inside, find the entrance at the far corner of the cemetery (free, donation requested, remove shoes before entering). Two other sultans, plus some relatives, share this grand space with Mahmut. As was traditional, the "caskets" you see are actually empty—the bodies are buried underground. Caskets with hats were for men; flowers were for women. You may see a visitor saying a prayer for the soul of the deceased (see sidebar on page 382).

• *Back on Divan Yolu, continue along the tram tracks. After one block, you'll see a towering Byzantine column called...*

❶ Çemberlitaş

Also known as the Burned Column, Çemberlitaş (chehm-behr-lee-tahsh) consists of six drums held together by hoops. ("Çemberlitaş"

means "stone with hoops.") Dating from the fourth century A.D., Çemberlitaş once held aloft a larger-than-life statue of Constantine, who was depicted as the god Apollo. When the statue was lost (well before the Ottomans took over the city), it was replaced with a golden cross—which is also now missing. In Constantine's day, this column marked the center of the Forum, the city's main square, ringed with public buildings and churches. Now the column stands empty, forlorn behind the tram stop. Adding insult to injury, frequent fires in this district left the column permanently scorched. After all those years of abuse, it's finally being restored—so it may be covered with scaffolding when you visit.

• *At the column, turn right (passing a recommended Turkish bath, Çemberlitaş Hamamı, on your right—see listing on page 72) and head down the hill toward the big, ornate, late-Ottoman ❷ Nuruosmaniye Mosque (noo-roo-os-mah-nee-yeh; "Sacred Light of Osman"). Continue straight past the line of tour buses, and walk along the outer wall of the mosque. The tourist shops on the left were built as part of the complex, to provide funds to maintain the mosque.*

Walk one block along the mosque wall to find the entrance into the mosque courtyard on your left (across from a pedestrian street). Go into the courtyard and continue straight past the mosque (drop in if you like—but be careful not to get mosqued out, as we'll be visiting two more mosques on this walk).

After passing the mosque through the courtyard (WCs at the far

end, on the left), you'll enter the Grand Bazaar. Above the gate, between the Arabic inscription and the emblem on top, find the name of this entrance (the same as the mosque)—Nuruosmaniye Kapısı (kah-puh-suh), or Nuruosmaniye Gate. As you enter "How much you pay?" land, button away your valuables and watch your money.

❸ The Grand Bazaar

This remarkable roofed warren of shops—with Byzantine foundations and an Ottoman floor plan, bustling with merchants and

shoppers—is one of Istanbul's top attractions. Of course, this is a colorful and convenient, if predictable, place to do your souvenir shopping. But it also hides nooks and crannies rarely seen by tourists that offer rich, vivid insights into the Turkish culture of yesterday and today.

For a self-guided tour of the bazaar, 📖 see the Grand Bazaar Tour chapter.

• If you follow the self-guided tour, you'll wind up at the far end of the Grand Bazaar to continue this walk (see "Beyazıt District," next). To skip the bazaar and get on with this walk, simply walk straight up the main street on which you entered the bazaar (Kalpakçılar Caddesi) and continue out through the exit at the far end (Beyazıt Kapısı).

This next stretch—through the Beyazıt district, connecting the Grand Bazaar and the Mosque of Süleyman the Magnificent—involves about a half-mile walk, with relatively little to see in between...but it's worth the trek.

❹ Beyazıt District

Exiting the bazaar (through the Beyazıt Gate), go right and walk a couple hundred yards through the outdoor textile market. At the end of the textile alley, you'll be facing the wall of Istanbul University's main campus (across the street). This area, called Beyazıt, is where the market crowds and the student population mix, giving it a special spice.

• Continue straight down the busy street (Fuat Paşa Caddesi) with the university wall across the street on your left. Go a block or so along the *right side of the road, then cross the street to the left side (along the wall). We'll continue about a quarter-mile straight downhill along this road.*

Notice that many stores along here sell **kitchen utensils.** This district was once Istanbul's coppersmith center. Even up until the early 1980s, many people still used copper utensils. But modern materials and methods have taken over, coppersmiths are mainly a thing of the past, and most of the utensils along here are now made of steel, aluminum, or pressed copper or brass.

• *At the fenced gate in the wall, the landmark Beyazıt fire tower marks the grounds of...*

❺ Istanbul University

This partly state-subsidized school (closed to tourists) is the city's biggest university, with thousands of students from all over Turkey. This is the larger of Istanbul University's two main campuses.

• *After the shops end, the wall continues. Keep going until the end of the wall. Now's the time to decide if you'll visit the massive Mosque of Süleyman the Magnificent (worth an hour visit, following the wall 300 yards uphill to your left) or turn right steeply downhill toward the Rüstem Paşa Mosque.*

❻ Mosque of Süleyman the Magnificent

Perched high on a hill overlooking Istanbul, this stately mosque befits the most "Magnificent" sultan of the Ottoman Empire. De-

signed by the empire's greatest architect (Sinan) and dedicated to one of its greatest sultans, the Mosque of Süleyman the Magnificent gives the Blue Mosque a run for its money. Its pastel interior is a serene counterpoint to the Blue Mosque's vivid colors. The mosque complex holds the mausoleums of Süleyman and

his wife, Roxelana, and its "backyard" offers sweeping views of the city below. The surrounding Süleymaniye neighborhood includes a former *madrassa* (seminary) that now hosts restaurants and tea gardens.

• *For a self-guided* **tour** *of the mosque,* 📖 *see the Mosque of Süleyman the Magnificent Tour chapter. If you follow the tour, come back to this intersection afterward.*

To skip the mosque (or if you're rejoining this walk after touring the mosque), head downhill about 150 yards to the second street on your left (Uzun Çarşı Caddesi—look for a sycamore tree on the corner and a fast-food kiosk across the street). Turning downhill and left onto this street, you'll see the brick minaret of a 15th-century mosque straight ahead and, behind it, the minaret of our next stop—Rüstem Paşa Mosque.

❼ Uzun Çarşı Caddesi

As you walk straight ahead along this street—which soon becomes a narrow alley, near the brick minaret—you'll be jostled by shoppers and nudged by delivery trucks trying to sneak their way into the commercial sprawl. Shops on either side cater to locals: hardware stores, stationery shops, toy stores, quilt-makers, sportswear vendors, shoe stores, and so on. If you're looking for a traditional backgammon board—without all that shiny, fake mother-of-pearl and wood inlay that strain your eyes as you play—you'll find it here, and dirt cheap.

• *The alley runs directly into a two-story stone building with an arched entryway. Go through the humble doorway and take the stairs up into the courtyard of the...*

❽ Rüstem Paşa Mosque

Built by Sinan in the 16th century, this mosque stands on an elevated platform, supported by vaults that house shops which once provided income for the mosque's upkeep. The mosque's namesake, Rüstem Paşa (ruhs-tehm pah-shah), was a Grand Vizier of Süleyman the Magnificent (after the mysterious death of İbrahim Paşa—see page 162). He found great success in this role, not just because he was Süleyman's son-in-law (he married Süleyman and Roxelana's daughter Mihrimah, whose tomb is next to Süleyman's), but also because he was clever and efficient. Like King Midas, Rüstem

Paşa could turn anything into revenue, and he filled the sultan's treasury. But the public hated him because he taxed everything in sight, and he was frequently accused of embezzling funds.

Admire the giant portico that covers most of the courtyard, and notice that the Rüstem Paşa mosque seems to be missing one feature found at almost every mosque: a fountain for ablution. Because of the limited space in this courtyard, Sinan placed the fountain at street level (down the stairs across the courtyard from where you entered).

The mosque's facade is slathered in gorgeous 16th-century İznik tiles, but the interior is even more impressive. To enter, go around the left side to find the visitors' entrance. Inside, virtually every surface is covered with floral-designed tile panels. (Locals say that if the Blue Mosque is Istanbul's Notre-Dame, this tiny gem is its Sainte-Chapelle.)

• *Because the next alley we'll be using is always packed with people—especially on Saturdays—consider reading the following section before you start walking. Leave the mosque complex through the door you entered, passing some enticing tile souvenirs. Turn left and walk down...*

❾ Hasırcılar Caddesi

Hasırcılar (hah-sur-juh-lahr) Caddesi ("Mat-Weavers' Alley") is a real-life market street—part of the commercial sprawl surrounding our next sight, the Spice Market.

As you walk, notice the porters and the carts squeezing their heavy, wide loads through the alley. You'll pass old *bedestens* (traditional commercial buildings) and stores, many of them family-owned for generations. If you had strolled this street a century ago, only the shoppers' clothes would have been different.

At the first corner on your left, notice the store selling hunting knives and rifles. Turkey has strong gun-control laws, but they don't extend to hunting rifles—you just need a hunting license to own one of these weapons.

One block before the Spice Market entrance, you'll smell the aroma of fresh-roasted coffee and spices. If you're in the market for spices, dried fruits, sweets, and nuts, start checking the prices along here—they're cheaper than in the high-rent Spice Market. Ask for a sample, and don't feel obligated to buy. While bargaining has become common in the Grand Bazaar, around here you'll generally pay what's on the price tag for food and spices—though you can haggle for souvenirs and exotic items (such as saffron and imported caviar).

• *Half a block before the arched entry to the Spice Market (the big brick-and-stone building at the end of the alley), you'll be immersed in a lively bazaar of...*

❿ Food Vendors

On your left, look for the thriving deli, **Namlı Şarküteri** (a.k.a. NamPort), with the large containers of olives, pickled peppers, and hanging pastramis out front (get a sample inside). It's been here for over a century, selling a wide range of traditional cold *mezes* (appetizers): dry salted fish, spicy tomato and pepper pastes, pickles, *sucuk* (soo-jook; spicy veal sausage), Turkish pastrami, and a variety of white cheeses made from sheep's and cow's milk. They also make a high-cholesterol sandwich called *kumru* (koom-roo; meaning "dove"), stuffed with spicy sausages, salami, and smoked cow's tongue. Wander through to get a feeling for what locals buy at the grocery store, and say hello to Zeki, the guy who runs the place. Upstairs is an oasis of a cafeteria (air-con, bright, cheery, and fast).

A little farther ahead on the right, just before the Spice Market entrance, is one of the best coffee vendors in town: the venerable **Kurukahveci Mehmet Efendi Mahdumları** (say it three times fast). This is the locals' favorite place to get ground coffee. Remember that only sealed packets can be taken through US Customs, and pick up the leaflet with preparation instructions when you check out. There's often a long line of loyal customers waiting at the cashier. If you can't find it on the map, just follow your nose.

• *Just after the coffee shop is the Spice Market's Hasırcılar Gate. Rather than entering the market here, let's walk around the side of the L-shaped building to the main entrance, facing the Golden Horn. Turn left and continue along the street (following the Spice Market wall).*

Along this alley you'll spot several more shops displaying spices, dried fruits, and sweets, alongside butcher, fishmonger, and dairy shops. The Turks have a word for this vibrant scene: *pazar* (pah-zahr), which gave us the English word "bazaar."

The alley opens into the large ❶ **Eminönü Square,** with the Golden Horn (not quite visible from here) on the other side of the busy street.

Before or after you tour the Spice Market, consider these options. You could take a break, sitting with locals on the platforms by the side of the square, watching the people pass by. (If you've bought some munchies, here's a good place to picnic. You can get a beverage from a nearby store, or from the newsstand straight ahead.)

If you'd like a cup of coffee or tea, walk down the alley (bordering the square) to your immediate left as you face the Golden Horn. You'll soon come to **Ender Çikolata,** a chocolate and candy store (on the left). It has tables and chairs across the alley, where you can sit down and relax. Or if you're hungry for a meal, go next door to the recommended **Hamdi** (hahm-dee) **Restaurant,** which specializes in meaty kebabs.

• *Continue around the corner of the Spice Market to the right to reach the main entrance.*

In Front of the Spice Market

The square in front of the Spice Market is dominated by the ❷ **New Mosque of Mother Sultan** (or simply "New Mosque")—one of the latest examples of classical, traditional-style Ottoman mosques.

This square was once a huge outdoor bazaar. You may still see a few makeshift stands with vendors hawking anything from clothes to fake jewelry to giant posters of pop stars. The vendors, who "forget" to pay taxes, are routinely rounded up by local police—so don't be surprised if you see a string of people running up the street with merchandise in their hands, chased by municipal inspectors.

Also notice the **pigeons:** Consider that most Turks believe it's good luck if a pigeon leaves its mark on you. Unless you're interested in putting this to the test, don't get too close to the buildings (where the birds are likely to be perched overhead, just waiting to bestow luck).

With the mosque on your left, you're facing the front of the Spice Market. Notice the outdoor plant and pet market to the left.

A WC is just around this corner, in the inner corner of the "L" formed by the Spice Market.

• *Now go through the main entrance into the...*

⑬ Spice Market

Built in the mid-17th century, this market hall was gradually taken over by merchants dealing in spices, herbs, medicinal plants, and pharmaceuticals. While it's quite a touristy scene today, most stalls still sell many of the same products, and the air is heavy with the aroma of exotic spices. Locals call it the Mısır Carşışı (Egyptian Bazaar) because it was once funded by taxes collected from Egypt.

While smaller and less imposing than the Grand Bazaar, the Spice Market is more colorful, with the ambience of a true Oriental market. On either side of the long, vaulted central hall are a wide range of merchant stalls, most of them with sacks and barrels out front showing off their wares. While merchants once sat quietly, cross-legged, next to their shops, today they engage in a never-ending game of one-upmanship, competing for the attention of passersby. If you're offered a sample of something (such as Turkish delight), feel free to accept—but be warned that it can be difficult to pry yourself away from the sales pitch that's sure to ensue. (To the left as you enter, the staircase to the second floor leads to the recommended and historic **Pandeli Restaurant**.)

Aside from the spice shops, you'll also see stores slinging natural sponges, lentils and beans, dried vegetables, dried fruits (especially figs and apricots), pistachios and hazelnuts, and several kinds of sweets—including, of course, Turkish delight. While most Westerners think of Turkish delight as being colored and fruit-flavored, locals prefer more adventurous varieties: with double-roasted pistachios, or the kind with walnuts in grape or mul-

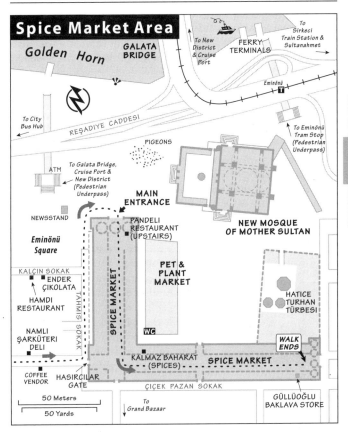

Spice Market Area

Golden Horn

GALATA BRIDGE

To New District & Cruise Port

FERRY TERMINALS

To Sirkeci Train Station & Sultanahmet

Eminönü **T**

To City Bus Hub

REŞADIYE CADDESI

To Eminönü Tram Stop (Pedestrian Underpass)

PIGEONS

ATM

To Galata Bridge, Cruise Port & New District (Pedestrian Underpass)

MAIN ENTRANCE

NEWSSTAND

PANDELI RESTAURANT (UPSTAIRS)

NEW MOSQUE OF MOTHER SULTAN

Eminönü Square

KALÇIN SOKAK

ENDER ÇIKOLATA

HAMDI RESTAURANT

PET & PLANT MARKET

TAHMIS SOKAK

SPICE MARKET

HATICE TURHAN TÜRBESI

NAMLI ŞARKÜTERI DELI

WC

WALK ENDS

COFFEE VENDOR

HASIRCILAR GATE

KALMAZ BAHARAT (SPICES)

SPICE MARKET

ÇIÇEK PAZAN SOKAK

GÜLLÜOĞLU BAKLAVA STORE

50 Meters

50 Yards

To Grand Bazaar

OLD TOWN BACK STREETS

berry molasses called *sucuk* (soo-jook; also the name of the spicy veal sausage).

Look for the granddaddy of spices, **saffron.** Locals still use saffron (mostly in rice pilaf and dessert), though not as much as they used to. The best saffron is Spanish; the local kind—cheaper and not as dark-red—usually comes mixed with other herbs. The **caviar** you see isn't local; it's mostly from Iran or Russia. More authentic are the Turkish dried **apricots** and **figs.** Dried vegetables, eggplant, and green peppers hang from the walls. Cooks use these to make dolma (dohl-mah; "to stuff"), stuffing them with rice and raisins, or rice and meat. You'll also see lots of sacks full of green powder. This is **henna,** traditionally used by women as a hair dye and for skin care. In the countryside, young women stain the palms of their hands with henna the night before they get married. For tips on what to buy in the Spice Market, see the Shopping chapter. Lately these old-fashioned shops are being joined by souvenir shops and jewelry stores, making this a mini Grand Bazaar of sorts.

• *Walk to the far end of the hall, at the intersection with the side wing of the Spice Market (to the left). Straight ahead is a gate leading to an always-busy street that heads five blocks up to the Grand Bazaar; to the right is the Hasırcılar Gate, leading to the alley we just came down.*

Go left and start walking down the side wing—less crowded and less colorful than the main concourse. After a few steps, look for a tiny shop on the left (second from the corner) called **Kalmaz Baharat.** *Baharat* (bah-hah-raht) means "spice," and this is one of the few shops that still sells the exotic spices of the past. Adnan, the owner, has herbal teas, thick aromatic oils, natural-fiber bath gloves, and olive-oil soap (white is better than green). He also sells the aphrodisiac called "sultan's paste" (more recently dubbed "Turkish Viagra"). This mix of several kinds of herbs and exotic spices supposedly gave the sultan the oomph to enjoy his huge harem, and is still used as an all-purpose energy booster today.

Browse your way to the end of this side wing (notice the great **Güllüoğlu Baklava** store on the right, the third shop before the exit), then head back the way you came. For more suggestions in the Spice Market, see page 349 of the Shopping chapter.

• *When you're ready to finish this walk, retrace your steps and leave the Spice Market through the main entrance. You'll be facing the Galata Bridge over the Golden Horn, with the **New District** beyond it. If you want to visit these sights, walk to the pedestrian underpass ahead of you (a little to the left, with an ATM kiosk nearby) that will take you under the busy street to the Galata Bridge. (Notice the many restaurants on the lower level of the bridge; this area is described in the Golden Horn Walk chapter.)*

*To reach the Eminönü tram stop—where you can catch the tram to go to the **Old Town** (Sultanahmet stop)—walk to the right between the New Mosque and the busy street. Where the mosque ends, you'll see the entrance to another pedestrian underpass. Halfway through the underpass, steps lead up to separate platforms: The first one is for the Old Town. The second platform—a little farther on—is for the New District (for those who want to cross the Galata Bridge to reach the Karaköy tram stop in the New District).*

Alternatively, you can generally wave down a cab along the main street right in front of the Spice Market. Or, to walk all the way up to Sultanahmet, turn right, walk with the New Mosque on your left, go straight ahead five blocks to the Sirkeci train station, and follow the tram tracks uphill.

GRAND BAZAAR TOUR

Kapalı Çarşı

The world's oldest shopping mall is a labyrinthine warren of shops and pushy merchants—a unique Istanbul experience that shouldn't be missed, even if you're not a shopper. While parts of the bazaar are overrun with international visitors, it also has many virtually tourist-free nooks and crannies that offer an insightful glimpse into the "real" Istanbul.

Orientation

Cost and Hours: Free to enter and browse, Mon-Sat 9:00-19:00, closed Sun and during religious holidays.

Information: www.grandbazaaristanbul.org.

Getting There: It's behind the Nuruosmaniye Mosque, across the parking lot from the Çemberlitaş tram stop. For detailed instructions on getting here from Sultanahmet (in the center of the Old Town), see the beginning of the Old Town Back Streets Walk chapter.

Length of This Tour: Allow one to three hours, depending on how much shopping you want to do.

Shopping Tips: This tour goes hand-in-hand with the Shopping chapter. Consider reading that chapter beforehand, perhaps while nursing a cup of Turkish coffee in the bazaar (focus on the bargaining tips if you plan to buy anything). For advice on dealing with overly zealous shopkeepers here (and elsewhere), see the "Dealing with Aggressive Merchants" sidebar, later in this chapter.

Navigating the Bazaar: The Grand Bazaar is a giant commercial complex with named "streets" *(caddesi)* and "alleys" *(sokak)*. But few of these streets and alleys are well marked, or the signs are covered by merchandise, so relying on these names isn't always successful. Complicating matters is the bazaar's maze-like floor plan. To make things easier, navigate using the map in this chapter and by asking people for help. (But be warned that asking a merchant for help may suck you into a lengthy conversation about the wonders of his wares.) Most of the specific shops we describe in this tour are well-established landmarks that are unlikely to go out of business before your visit.

Pickpocket Alert: The Grand Bazaar probably contains the highest concentration of pickpockets in Istanbul. Watch your valuables.

Rainy Day: This tour is a good bad-weather activity, since almost the entire bazaar is covered.

BACKGROUND

Sprawling over a huge area in the city center, Kapalı Çarşı (kah-pah-luh chahr-shuh; "Covered Market") was the first shopping

mall ever built. During Byzantine times, this was the site of a bustling market; when the Ottomans arrived, it grew bigger and more diverse. The prime location attracted guilds, manufacturers, and traders, and it grew quickly —its separate chunks were eventually connected and roofed to form a single market hall. Before long, the Grand Bazaar became the center for trade in the entire Ottoman Empire. At its prime, the market was locked down and guarded by more than a hundred soldiers every night, like a fortified castle.

The Grand Bazaar remained Turkey's commercial hub—for both locals and international traders—through the 1950s. Its 4,000 shops were bursting with everything you can imagine, from jewelry to silk clothing, and from traditional copperware to exotic Oriental imports. But then the Grand Bazaar was discovered by travelers seeking the ultimate "Oriental market" experience. Prodded by shopaholic tourists with fat wallets, prices and rents skyrocketed, and soon modest shopkeepers and manufacturers found themselves unable to compete with the big money circulating through the bazaar's lanes. These humble merchants moved outside the bazaar, displaced by souvenir and carpet shops.

Today's Grand Bazaar sells 10 times more jewelry than it used to. And, while tourists find it plenty atmospheric, locals now consider its flavor more Western than Oriental. And yet, even though the bazaar has lost some of its traditional ambience, enough artifacts remain to make it an irreplaceable Istanbul experience. This tour takes you through the schlocky tourist zones...but it also takes you by the hand to the market's outer fringe, still frequented by more Turks than tourists.

The Tour Begins

• *Enter the Grand Bazaar through the* ❶ *Nuruosmaniye Gate behind the Nuruosmaniye Mosque. As you walk through the gate, you're at the start of the bazaar's main street, called...*

❷ Kalpakçılar Caddesi

Step through the entryway, past security police and under the Ottoman coat of arms, with its red and green flags (green for the Islamic caliph, and red for the Ottoman dynasty). You'll notice the temperature rise by several degrees—the air inside is heated by thousands of watts of electric bulbs, and by bustling shoppers and merchants. This scene is a little overwhelming at first sight. Welcome to the Grand Bizarre...er, Bazaar.

You're standing on the bazaar's main street, Kalpakçılar Caddesi, which leads straight from the Nuruosmaniye Mosque to the Beyazıt district, where we'll exit, though we'll take a very roundabout route to get there. On this walk, everything of importance is to the right and downhill of this main drag. Kalpakçılar Caddesi (kahl-pahk-chuh-lahr jahd-deh-see) means "Hatmakers' Street." Historically, each street, alley, or corner of the bazaar was dedicated to a particular craft or item, and they still bear those names.
• *All those lightbulbs are illuminating...*

❸ Jewelry Showcases

Today's high-traffic, high-rent Kalpakçılar Caddesi is dominated by these glittering displays, which contain bigger-ticket items than the traditional Turkish hats. Turks love gold, not because they're vain or greedy, but because they're practical: Since local currency has a tendency to be devalued, people prefer to invest in something more tangible. Traditionally, Turks celebrating special occasions—such as a wedding or a boy's circumcision—receive gold as a gift. In fact, in the most traditional corners of Turkey, the groom's family still must present the bride's family with gold bracelets before the couple can marry.

Because all this gold is used primarily as an investment, and only secondarily as an accessory, it's most commonly sold in the form of simple 22-carat bracelets (24-carat is too soft to wear). If you see a woman whose arm is lined with five or six of these bracelets, she's not making a fashion statement—she's wearing her family's savings on her sleeve, literally. Recently, jewelers have started selling more elaborately decorated designer pieces. These are more expensive and less appealing to thrifty locals (since you're paying for the workmanship, not just the gold itself). Instead, locals who want jewelry for fashion buy cheaper 14- or 18-carat bracelets.

• *A few steps into the bazaar from the Nuruosmaniye Gate (after the fifth shop on the right), look for the entrance marked* Old Bazaar—Sandal Bedesteni *over the doorway, a little off the main street. Duck into the courtyard called...*

❹ Sandal Bedesteni

The Grand Bazaar is made up of a series of *bedestens* (beh-dehs-tehns)—commercial complexes of related shops. The Sandal Bedesteni is one of the oldest, dating from the late 15th century. After the Ottomans arrived and took over a Byzantine marketplace here, the bazaar grew organically—new buildings sporadically sprouted up, each one devoted to a particular trade or item. For the convenience of both the shopkeeper and the customer, shops dealing with similar items clustered together. These distinct units, many of which survive today, are called *bedesten* or *han* (hahn; see the "What Is a *Han?*" sidebar, later). The most traditional *bedestens* like this one have a central courtyard surrounded by shops and workshops on two floors. Later, developers roofed these commercial units and connected them with alleys, creating a unified central market hall. But if you pay attention, you'll notice that each part of the bazaar still has its own unique characteristics (and characters).

The Sandal Bedesteni once housed merchants of valuable fabrics (such as silk and velvet), turban makers, and jewelers specializing in precious stones. Today it carries ordinary textile products and assorted tourist knockoffs.

• *Backtrack out to the main drag (Kalpakçılar Caddesi), turn right, and continue to the first intersection, where you'll turn right on Sandal Bedesteni Sokak. Look high above, where signs point to various landmarks. Walk straight downhill on this alley—with a high concentration of souvenir shops, carpets, tiles, leather and kilim bags, and chandeliers—toward the intersecting arches. On the right, you'll pass another entrance to the Sandal Bedesteni we just visited. After that, take the next alley on the right. Walk 50 yards to the...*

❺ Free Exchange Market

You'll hear it before you see it. From about 10:00 until 17:00, the little alleys branching off this strip are squeezed full of hundreds of boisterous men shouting into their mobile phones and waving their arms. These are currency brokers, and this zone of the bazaar

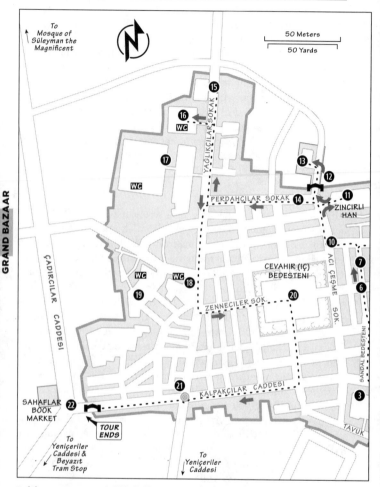

is like a poor man's Wall Street. In this humble setting, people are cutting deals involving hundreds of thousands of dollars and euros every minute.

The Turkish lira is (by European standards) an unstable currency. So, in addition to gold, many Turks still invest in euros or dollars to shore up their savings. Turkey tried to grow with controlled inflation in the 1980s, in order to be more compatible in the international markets. But inflation got out of control—reaching almost 100 percent annually in the 1990s. During this time, people began buying US dollars or German marks. Exchange offices popped up on every corner. On payday, you'd immediately take your paycheck to be converted into dollars, then convert it back to lira when you were ready to buy something with it. Gradually, $100 billion worth of non-Turkish currency was circulating

Grand Bazaar Tour

1. Nuruosmaniye Gate
2. Kalpakçılar Caddesi
3. Jewelry Showcases
4. Sandal Bedesteni
5. Free Exchange Market
6. Ağa Sokak
7. Pawn Shops
8. Mahmutpaşa Gate & To Spice Market
9. Kalcılar Han
10. Oriental Kiosk
11. Zincirli Han
12. Mercan Gate
13. Kızlarağası Han
14. Perdahçılar Sokak
15. Eğin Tekstil
16. Astarcı Han & Brothers Restaurant
17. Pedaliza Restaurant
18. Şark Kahvesi Coffee Shop
19. Havuzlu Lokanta Rest.
20. Cevahir Bedesten
21. Fountain
22. Beyazıt Gate & Sahaflar Book Market

GRAND BAZAAR

in Turkey, and one-third of this huge amount never showed up in bank accounts. On January 1, 2005, the New Turkish Lira (Yeni Türk Lirası, or YTL) went into circulation, trimming off six zeroes and sporting a fresh new look. In 2009, the central bank changed the currency's name back to Türk Lirası (TL), omitting the word *yeni* (new). Now $1 is worth about 3 TL...and travelers can leave their calculators at home.

• *Backtrack to the alley called Sandal Bedesteni Sokak, turn right, and continue one block to where it intersects with the wider...*

⑥ Ağa Sokak

Since the "ğ" is a vowel lengthener, without any sound of its own, the word "ağa" is pronounced "aaa-aah." Looking to the left up Ağa Sokak, you'll see the entrance to Cevahir Bedesteni, where

Dealing with Aggressive Merchants

Throughout the Grand Bazaar—and just about everywhere in the Old Town—you'll constantly be barraged by people selling everything you can imagine. This can be intimidating, but it's fun if you loosen up and approach it with a sense of humor. The main rule of thumb: Don't feel compelled to look at or buy anything you don't want. These salesmen prey on Americans' gregariousness and tendency to respond politely to anyone who offers a friendly greeting. They often use surprising or attention-grabbing openers:

"Hello, Americans! Where are you from? Chicago?! I have a cousin there!"

"Are you lost? Can I help you find something?"

"Nice shoes! Are those Turkish shoes?"

"Would you like a cup of tea?"

The list is endless—collect your favorites.

If you're not interested, simply say a firm, "No, thanks!" and brush past them, ignoring any additional comments. This may seem cold, but it's the only way to get through the market without constantly getting tied up in unwanted conversations.

If, on the other hand, you're looking to chat, merchants are often very talkative—but be warned that a lengthy conversation may give them false hopes that you're looking to buy, and could make it even more difficult to extract yourself gracefully from the interaction.

people sell antiques, semiprecious stones, and silver items. We'll pass through that *bedesten* later on the walk.

• *Continue up the narrow alley called Sandal Bedesteni Sokak. Notice that the shops become less colorful and the clientele becomes more local. This section of the bazaar is mostly devoted to...*

❼ Pawn Shops

Many of these shops look empty, with signs on the windows and a few gold items and coins on display. This is where locals can exchange those "investment bracelets" and valuables for some hard cash. When these shops buy jewelry, they deduct whatever the seller paid for workmanship, charge a small commission, and pay for the actual value of the gold.

• *Continue to the end of the alley, where it ends at Aynacılar Sokak (eye-nah-juh-lahr; "Mirror-Makers' Alley"). Looking to your right, you'll see another gate of the bazaar, named after the neighboring district.*

❽ Mahmutpaşa Gate

If you went through this exit and walked about 15 minutes down the hill, you'd reach the Spice Market. The area between here and there is a huge outdoor textile bazaar, with retail shops, wholesalers, and workshops. Vendors sell a range of textile products, from underwear and socks to wool sweaters and jackets, to more conservative clothing, turbans, and raincoats. The week before schools open (usually the second week of September), the area is packed with bargain-hunters seeking back-to-school deals.

• *Step outside the Mahmutpaşa Gate and continue straight. Walk about 50 yards down to a second gate, which opens onto Mahmutpaşa Yokuşu Sokak. Immediately beyond this second gate, on the left (after a window filled with dandy circumcision outfits), is the entrance to...*

❾ Kalcılar Han

This is also known as the Gümüşçüler ("silversmith") Hanı, because it's a center for the production and sale of all sorts of handcrafted silver objects.

The Kalcılar Han, like others of its kind, resembles a factory. In each workshop, an artisan completes a different step of the production process. A single silver object goes from one workshop to another, as in a factory production line, with artisans working together to create a finished piece.

As you walk the long entryway to the open courtyard, you're looking at a typical *han*—built on two floors around a central courtyard. The first (ground) floor contained stables and storage, while travelers stayed in upper-floor rooms. Today, all the rooms on the upper floor are workshops.

Take time to visit a silversmith. Turn to your immediate right as you step into the courtyard, walk in, and take the stairs on the left (mind the low iron bar) to the upper floor. Turn right at the top and find the workshop of **Kapik Usta** at #10. Kapik Usta (kah-peek oos-tah; "Kapik the Master") is a master *sıvamacı* (suh-vah-mah-juh), a silversmith who uses molds. As a potter shapes clay, Kapik shapes silver into plates, bowls, and other everyday items using a power lathe and steel molds (in the past, the molds were made of walnut). If he's not too busy, he may show you how he does it. Stay away from the lathe, and watch as Kapik transforms a flat piece of metal into a three-dimensional object.

Kapik is kind and modest, and doesn't speak much English. Like many others working in this complex and throughout the Grand Bazaar, Kapik is of Armenian origin. But he's a native of

What Is a *Han*?

An important element of commerce in Ottoman times, a *han* (hahn) was an inn located in an urban business district to accommodate tradesmen, diplomats, students, and travelers. The concept brings to mind the caravanserais (lodging for caravans) along eastern trade routes. The *hans* eventually developed into commercial centers, with production facilities and markets for various handicrafts. Later, *hans* specialized in the trade and production of a particular item. Most were (and still are) owned by state trusts, although some were privately owned.

Traditional *hans* usually have a rectangular floor plan, with rooms and passages around a central courtyard. The main gate into the complex was designed to be large enough to accommodate animals loaded with goods. While some of Istanbul's *hans* have three floors, most have two: The first (ground) floor contained a storage area, stables for animals, and repair shops. Dormitory-style guest rooms were located on the second floor. Guests spread sleeping mats on the floor at night, and tucked them away in wall niches during the day.

A typical *han* had a *mescit* (mehs-jeet; small mosque) in the courtyard. In *hans* frequented mainly by non-Muslims, synagogues and Christian chapels were common.

the city, and this is his family business; his son, Alex, works with him as an apprentice, and is enthusiastic when it comes to demonstrating his skill.

Head to the opposite side of the *han* (past the stairs). On your way, you can step into other workshops, but ask for permission first—especially if there is work going on—and try to keep your visits brief. At the workshop at #20, Master Zavel uses sand molds to shape melted silver.

Find **Barocco Silver** at #31. It's owned by Kapik Usta's Armenian business partner, Aruş Usta (ah-roosh oos-tah; "Aruş the Master"). He is a master *dövücü* (dew-vew-jew), a silversmith who uses a hammer to shape flat metal. Walk into his shop, where he works with his son, Dikran, who is also a master craftsman. He's a *kakmacı* (kahk-mah-juh), a silversmith who uses a hammer and other tools to create designs. Dikran worked as an unpaid apprentice for a decade, studying under a master until he himself became one. He reveres his retired master. Now the other masters in this complex say that Dikran is one of the best at what he does—anywhere.

The master-apprentice relationship is still an important aspect of commerce here on the outskirts of the bazaar, despite the fact that nowadays the masters are having a hard time recruiting apprentices. In the past, a volunteer apprentice often had to work hard to persuade a master to accept him as an apprentice. Today's young men are more reluctant to enter a field in which business is down and incomes are limited, although it is still considered an honor to be an apprentice to a reputable master.

• *Head down the stairs, turn right, and backtrack to the Mahmutpaşa Gate. Step back inside the Grand Bazaar, and walk straight on Aynacılar Sokak until you hit the intersection marked by a charming little...*

❿ Oriental Kiosk

This adorable structure, originally built as a teahouse in the 17th century, sells jewelry today. Notice the fountain next to the kiosk. The alley it's on is Acı Çeşme (ah-juh chesh-meh), which means "Bitter Fountain." Avoid the water here...just in case. (In the thrilling chase scene at the opening of the James Bond movie *Skyfall*, a motorcycle crashes through the roof here and into this delicate—and now rebuilt—kiosk.)

• *Turn right at the kiosk onto Acı Çeşme, and walk to the end of the alley. On your right, just before the bazaar exit, marked by an arrow hanging from the vaulted ceiling, is the entrance to...*

⓫ Zincirli Han

Rough steps take you into Zincirli Han (zeen-jeer-lee hahn; "Chain Han"), which is surrounded mostly by jewelry shops, with some workshops on the upper floor. The shops here are less polished and fancy, and less aggressive, than those in the more touristy zones back in the heart of the bazaar.

At the far end of the courtyard, on the right (unmarked, at #13), is **Merim Kuyumculuk** (koo-yoom-joo-look; "jewelry"). Rather than selling lots of jewelry, this place focuses on production and wholesale—one of the few jewelers in the bazaar with its own workshop nearby. If the owner, Ferdi, is around, ask him nicely if you can take a look into his tiny workshop upstairs (he may say no if they're very busy).

To the left of Merim, fronting the courtyard, is **Osman's Carpet Shop.** Run by a hard-to-miss

"professor of carpets" nicknamed Şişko (sheesh-koh; "Fatty"), this shop is regarded as *the* place to go to get a high-quality, expensive carpet and expert advice. Şişko—often assisted by son Nurullah or nephew Bilgin—won't hustle you or try to talk you into something, like the cheap carpet hawkers elsewhere in the bazaar. He prefers to equip customers with information to be sure they get the carpet that's right for them. This fifth-generation shop is hardly a secret—notice the celebrity photos, magazine clippings, and guidebook blurbs hanging on the wall.

• *Leave Zincirli Han, return to Acı Çeşme, turn right, and step outside the Grand Bazaar. The jewelry shop to your left immediately outside the* **⑫ Mercan Gate**—*with hundreds of 22-karat gold bracelets—will give you an idea of what most jewelry around here looked like a decade or two ago, before fancier bracelets came into fashion.*

Continue a few steps beyond the Mercan Gate, and go through the first building entrance to your left (#94). You're now in...

⑬ Kızlarağası Han

The *kızlarağası* was the master of all eunuchs (castrated slaves who looked after the sultan's palace and harem). This humble court-yard is where you'll find middlemen who recycle secondhand gold and silver—or shavings and unwanted fragments from other work-shops—and turn them into something usable.

Notice the low-profile teahouse in the center, serving simple glasses of tea to an almost exclusively local crowd. If you've got some time, buy a glass of tea and join the gang playing backgam-mon at the little table. If any children or teenagers are around—as they usually are in the summer—they might know a few words of English, and can translate for you.

Ayhan Usta (eye-hahn oos-tah; "Ayhan the Master") is one of the goldsmiths who works here. His shop is the third one on the left as you enter, across from the teahouse. Ayhan speaks only Turkish, but if you peek into his shop and if he's up for visitors and not too busy, he'll motion you inside to watch him at work. Cautious at first, but sweet and  easygoing, Ayhan enjoys showing travelers what he does. You need not pay or tip him in return—he simply likes to share his craft with curious travelers. Stay safely away from the fire (burning at 2,200°F)—especially when he tosses in some white powder to in-crease the temperature as he melts the gold.

Ayhan belongs to a dying breed. Not much gold production

still takes place near the Grand Bazaar, and the few goldsmiths who remain may soon be moved to a plant outside the city. Craftspeople such as Ayhan like where they are and loudly oppose this new plan. In the opinion of locals, the Grand Bazaar needs both shops and workshops to be successful. Traditionally, if a customer wants to buy something, but it's not ideal—such as a garment that doesn't quite fit—the shopkeeper can send it to his workshop (or a neighbor's) for an adjustment to make it just right. But if all of the workshops are forced out by high rents, and replaced with nothing but "Made in Taiwan" gift shops, locals fear the soul of the Grand Bazaar will be lost.

On the way out (a few steps from Ayhan's shop), note the tiny shoeshine hut with Cafer (jah-fehr) happily polishing shoes (2-4 TL). Let him give you a shine, and he'll get you tea. You'll step out with slick shoes and a shiny memory.

• *Now go back in the Grand Bazaar, and take the first right as you step in. You'll walk down the big lane called...*

GRAND BAZAAR

⓮ Perdahçılar Sokak

Perdahçılar Sokak (pehr-dah-chuh-lahr soh-kahk) was once the main clothing section of the bazaar; now it's a combination of carpet stores, souvenir shops, "genuine fake items" stands, and shops selling tourist knockoffs of traditional clothes—like fake pashminas or a tongue-in-cheek "one size fits all" belly-dancing outfit.

• *Continue to the T-junction, and turn right onto Yağlıkçılar Sokak (yaah-luhk-chuh-lahr soh-kahk), with items similar to what you've just seen. Walk all the way to the bazaar exit. To the right, just inside the exit door, notice the textile store called...*

⓯ Eğin Tekstil

This unassuming little shop provided many of the costumes for the 2004 movie *Troy* (an adaptation of Homer's *Iliad*). Go inside and say hello to owner Süleyman or his assistants, who'd be happy to tell you all about their shop's history...and, of course, what they're selling. Eğin Tekstil (eh-een tehks-teel) has been in the same family for five generations, nearly 150 years. In fact, Süleyman—who continues the family tradition even though he's actually a doctor by trade—still has the Ottoman deed to the store. Their specialty is the *peştemal* (pehsh-teh-mahl), the traditional wrap-around sheet for visits to a Turkish bath. I think the quality is reliable, and the prices are marked, fixed, and fair. This is one of the Grand Bazaar's few stores that actually has an annex behind the main shop that was built during Byzantine times, which is now used for storage (the entrance is on the back wall).

• *Stepping outside the store, turn left and head back the way you came on Yağlıkçılar Sokak. After about 50 yards, on the right—marked with a colorful electronic WC sign—you'll see the entrance to...*

⑯ Astarcı Han

Go through the doorway, between shops and stands, into Astarcı Han (ahs-tahr-juh hahn; "Courtyard of the Cloth Lining"). Historically, this courtyard was home to textile workshops. A few still remain here: As you enter, notice the workshop in the right-hand corner (where workers braid golden trim with a century-old technology). Peek inside with a smile to see the textile makers in action.

On the left as you enter the courtyard is the recommended **Brothers (Kardeşler) Restaurant.** This place specializes in southeastern Turkish cuisine and has peaceful outdoor seating upstairs. Squat WCs are across from the restaurant.

• *Exit Astarcı Han and turn right onto Yağlıkçılar Sokak, continuing in the same direction as before. Within 50 yards look for a sign (on the right) for Cebeci Han. The popular ⑰ Pedaliza Restaurant is to your right as you enter this courtyard. (If you'd like a cup of Turkish coffee after your meal, the perfect spot is coming right up.)*

From Cebeci Han, head back out to Yağlıkçılar and go right. After a few blocks, keep an eye out on the right-hand side for the tiny, green, box-like wooden balcony (attached to the wall above the jewelry store). Used for the call to prayer, like a low-tech minaret, it marks one of the bazaar's mosques (next to it are steps leading up to the mosque).

Go 50 yards past the mosque on the right-hand corner to find a venerable tea and coffee house called...

⑱ Şark Kahvesi

The recommended Şark Kahvesi (shark kah-veh-see; "Oriental Coffee Shop") is an Istanbul institution and a good place to sample Turkish coffee if you haven't yet. For more on Turkish coffee, see the Experiences chapter.

• *Just past Şark Kahvesi on Yağlıkçılar Sokak, a lane on the right leads to the recommended ⑲ Havuzlu Lokanta restaurant. But instead, we'll head left, going downhill on Zenneciler Sokak (zehn-neh-jce-lehr soh-kahk). After about 100 yards, you'll emerge into a courtyard we saw earlier, from the other side...*

⑳ Cevahir Bedesten

Cevahir Bedesten (jeh-vah-heer beh-dehs-tehn) was built as a freestanding warehouse for merchants in the 15th century. It has been used for many purposes since, but the basic structure—with domed bays supported by eight massive pillars—is still intact. Entering the courtyard, you may notice it's taller than the rest of the bazaar, and, since it's devoted to big-ticket items, it's a bit quieter. Most merchants here are antique dealers, selling icons, metal objects, miniatures, coins, cameras, daggers, and so on; others here sell semiprecious stones, either by the piece or on chains. There are also a few silver shops and places where you can buy worry beads with semiprecious stones.

• *From here, you can explore the bazaar on your own. But first, we'll head back to the main drag (uphill 50 yards) and get oriented; we'll also suggest a possible detour to an enjoyable book market nearby.*

From the center of Cevahir Bedesten, turn 90 degrees to the right and leave through the door into the bustling alleys of the bazaar—this zone is packed with shops selling souvenirs, as well as carpets and traditional metal items. Soon you'll run into the main street, Kalpakçılar Caddesi.

To leave the market now and go back the way we came, turn left (downhill) on this main stretch and walk back to the Nuruos-

maniye Gate (at the Nuruosmaniye Mosque, near the Çemberlitaş tram stop—you can take the tram from here back to Sultanahmet).

If you want to see more, instead turn right on Kalpakçılar Caddesi and walk about 200 yards to the gate leading to the Beyazıt (beh-yah-zuht) district, where you can follow the self-guided 📖 Old Town Back Streets Walk. Halfway to the Beyazıt exit, keep an eye on your right, behind the ㉑ **fountain,** for a stretch of shops selling leather, denim, and other textiles. At the end of Kalpakçılar Caddesi, you'll exit through the...

㉒ Beyazıt Gate and Sahaflar Book Market

You may feel that you've only seen a small part of the very Grand Bazaar. You're right—there are another 4,000 shops we haven't passed on this tour. Entire trips, books, and lifetimes are devoted to the wonders of the Grand Bazaar.

But for now, let's look at one more interesting corner of the Grand Bazaar scene. As you exit through the Beyazıt Gate (with a tram stop 100 yards to your left), turn right and walk toward the crowded market area for textiles, clothes, and shoes—popular with local bargain-hunters. After about 20 yards, look on your left for steps leading to Sahaflar (sah-hahf-lahr), the old book market. For two centuries, this was a magnet for bibliophiles—even 20 years ago, you could find rare old collector's items with fancy illustrations. But today only a few shops sell those items (or handmade replicas of them), while most others carry textbooks, titles that are hard to sell at a mainstream bookstore, and religious texts.

• *Our bazaar tour is finished. To head home, you can go to Beyazıt Square and catch a tram back to Sultanahmet and beyond. To continue the Old Town Back Streets Walk from the Beyazıt Gate, turn to page 181.*

...turn to page 181.

MOSQUE OF SÜLEYMAN THE MAGNIFICENT TOUR

Süleymaniye Camii

Built for the sultan by his prolific architect, Sinan, and completed in 1557, the Mosque of Süleyman the Magnificent almost outdoes the Blue Mosque in its sheer size, architecture, and design. Its subtly understated interior is decorated in pastel tones.

The term "Süleymaniye" applies not just to the mosque, but to the huge network of related buildings that nestle around it on a hilltop overlooking the city. Within this complex are the ornate mausoleums of Süleyman and his wife, Roxelana, as well as a former madrassa (theological school).

Imagine the pomp and circumstance on the summer day in 1550 when construction began: Sultan Süleyman the Magnificent arrives on his horse, along with the clergy. He orders his guards to give alms to the poor and to sacrifice rams for a fortunate start. As the crowd recites verses from the Quran, the head of the clergy sets the first stone of the foundation. Within six years, the dome would be complete; the following year, the mosque would open for worship. The whole shebang took only a decade to finish.

Today the mosque is almost as clean and shiny as it was the day it opened, thanks to a renovation completed in 2010.

Orientation

Cost and Hours: Mosque—Free, generally open daily from one hour after sunrise until one hour before sunset, closed to visitors five times a day for prayer. Mausoleums—Free, daily 9:00-17:00, until 18:00 in summer.

Dress Code: You'll need to remove your shoes. Modest dress (covered knees and shoulders) is expected for men and women, and women should cover their hair with a scarf. For more tips, read "Visiting a Mosque" in the Experiences chapter (see page 62).

Getting There: This is an easy stop on the Old Town Back Streets Walk. It's on a hill near Istanbul University, on Sıddık Sami Onar Caddesi in the Süleymaniye neighborhood. It is a short walk from most places in the Old Town, but if you are coming from Taksim or further north, take the Metro to Vezneciler Station.

Length of This Tour: Allow one hour.

Services: WCs are located just outside either end of the mosque wall. Two recommended restaurants and a coffee shop are located within the former madrassa alongside the mosque.

Starring: One of Sinan's great mosques; the mausoleums of Süleyman and his wife, Roxelana; and the Süleymaniye neighborhood.

The Tour Begins

• *Enter the mosque complex at its southern corner, by the large street fountain.*

Standing in the square with the mosque behind you, you're facing the corner of the **madrassa.** Originally, this school of theology was divided into three sections: The first two were devoted to interpreting the Quran, while the third (at the far end, with the flagpole at its entrance) was a medical school—now it's a hospital.

This peaceful space, stretching along the mosque's outer courtyard wall, is lined with decent restaurants, including the recommended Darüzziyafe and Kanaat Lokantası. There's a WC just outside the wall at this end of the mosque, and another at the opposite corner of the mosque's outer courtyard.

• *Now use the gate near the big fountain to enter the...*

Outer Courtyard

As you enter this courtyard, walk straight ahead to the gate leading into the cemetery. Just before you enter the cemetery, look to your left to see two elevated stone slabs—these are used to support the coffin during a funeral service. According to Muslim tradition, the body of the deceased is washed and wrapped in a white shroud, then placed in a wood coffin and brought to stone slabs such as these. Relatives and friends gather nearby, and the imam (cleric) leads them in one last prayer for the soul of the deceased. The body is then taken into the cemetery and buried, still in the shroud but without the coffin. Just as a Muslim faces Mecca to pray, the body of a Muslim is buried so that it points eternally toward Mecca.

• *Go through the gate into the cemetery with the...*

Mosque of Süleyman the Magnificent

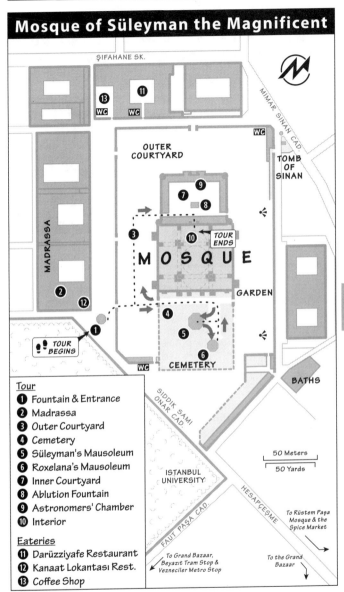

Tour
1. Fountain & Entrance
2. Madrassa
3. Outer Courtyard
4. Cemetery
5. Süleyman's Mausoleum
6. Roxelana's Mausoleum
7. Inner Courtyard
8. Ablution Fountain
9. Astronomers' Chamber
10. Interior

Eateries
11. Darüzziyafe Restaurant
12. Kanaat Lokantası Rest.
13. Coffee Shop

Mausoleums of Süleyman the Magnificent and Roxelana

As you walk through the headstones (some dating back to the early 17th century), notice that each tomb has two stones. The larger stone was inscribed with the epitaph, while the smaller one was for decoration.

Süleyman the Magnificent (1494-1566) and Roxelana (c. 1498-1558)

Süleyman the Magnificent, the 10th sultan of the Ottoman Empire, ruled for nearly a half-century (1520-1566). His reign was the Golden Age of Ottoman history, when the Ottoman Empire was the world's greatest power. The treasury was bursting, and the empire's borders stretched from North Africa to Central Europe to the Near East. The Mediterranean Sea, which the Romans had once called Mare Nostrum ("Our Sea"), became a Turkish lake. One-third of the Western world's population lived under the Ottoman flag.

Süleyman ruled during the age of powerful leaders. His contemporaries were Charles V of the Holy Roman Empire, François I of France, and Henry VIII of England. A peace treaty ending a dispute with Austria refers to Süleyman as the "Emperor of the East and the West"—the first time someone laid claim to this title since the Byzantine Emperor Justinian. In signing the treaty, Charles V accepted Süleyman's superiority despite his own title of "Holy Roman Emperor."

While Westerners know him as Süleyman the Magnificent, the Turkish people call him "Süleyman the Legislator" or "Süleyman the Law Giver." His greatest contribution was to codify Ottoman law. As the ruler of a multinational empire, Süleyman realized that different regions and different peoples needed different laws.

Süleyman's biggest weakness was a woman. His first son, Crown Prince Mustafa, was born to Süleyman's chief consort, Gülbahar. But Süleyman later fell deeply in love with one of his concubines, Roxelana.

Said to be the daughter of an Orthodox priest from Ukraine, Roxelana was bought at a slave market and sent to the palace harem. She wasn't the most beautiful, but Roxelana was ambitious and managed to get herself presented to the sultan, draw-

• *Follow the stone path to the first and bigger mausoleum (on your right).*

In 1566, the aging Süleyman the Magnificent went on one last military campaign to Zigetvar, where he died silently in his tent. His clever Grand Vizier knew that the army would disband if they found out the sultan was dead, so he covertly had Süleyman's body mummified. (Meanwhile, the Grand Vizier sent a note to Süleyman's son, Selim, telling him to grab the throne before another one of his relatives did.) The magnificent sultan's death was kept secret until after the army returned in victory to Istanbul, when his body was interred next to the mosque that bears his name.

ing his attention by daring to laugh in his presence. Süleyman named her "Hürrem"—his "Cheerful One."

Underestimating this simple Ukrainian girl, the jealous Gül-bahar snubbed Roxelana, addressed her as "slave," and even physically attacked her. Süleyman had Gülbahar banished, and Roxelana became his chief consort. She persuaded Süleyman to legally marry her—a first for a slave concubine—and bore the sultan five children (four sons and a daughter).

Gülbahar's son, Crown Prince Mustafa, remained an obstacle for Roxelana, who hoped one of her sons would become sultan after Süleyman. She convinced Süleyman that Mustafa was plotting against him, and Süleyman had him strangled.

Of Roxelana's four sons, two died of natural causes, and a third was strangled at his father's orders. The remaining son survived to eventually take the throne...but, never able to quite fill daddy's shoes, became known as Selim the Blonde.

During her lifetime, Roxelana grew in influence as Süleyman turned to her for advice in all his decisions. She was the first of several powerful women who ruled the Ottoman Empire from "behind the curtain" for the next 150 years. Relentless in her ambition, Roxelana is said to have orchestrated dozens of murders to secure her surviving son's crown. In what may have been a sort of public apology, Roxelana later spent her personal fortune creating charitable institutions.

When Roxelana died in 1558, Süleyman had a separate mausoleum built for her. After Süleyman's death eight years later, he was buried in a mausoleum of his own—forever separated from the strong-willed woman who'd compelled him to do things he may later have regretted.

• *At the entrance porch, remove your shoes and stow them on the wooden shelves, then step inside.*

A year after Süleyman's death, the best stonemasons and marble-workers in the empire came here to build a *türbe* (tuhr-beh), or mausoleum, that would mirror Süleyman's fame. They were led by Sinan, the master architect who'd also built the mosque. The mausoleum was considered complete when it was decorated with precious tiles from İznik (bordered with Arabic inscriptions—excerpts from the Quran). Candles and oil lamps were lit, Süleyman's robe was laid over the green cover of the ceremonial coffin, and imams began reading from the Quran...and didn't stop for years.

On either side of the entrance are some of the most beautiful tile frames anywhere. Above the door are inscribed the words,

"There is no other God but Allah, and Muhammad is his Prophet." The larger tomb (cenotaph) at the center of the mausoleum is Süleyman's. On either side are Süleyman's two heirs, their relatives, and Süleyman and Roxelana's daughter (to his right). Notice the room's gorgeous details: floral-designed İznik tiles, marble paintwork, beautiful woodwork on the window and door shutters, and decorative ostrich eggs and colored replicas in the frame hanging from the ceiling.

As you exit, the entrance to Roxelana's mausoleum is to your right. While not as impressive as her husband's, it's worth a look. Enjoy the attractive tiles, and notice the "stalactites" decorating the niches between the windows. Roxelana's cenotaph is the first one, surrounded by an attractive inlaid wood panel. Take a close look at the workmanship—thousands of tiny wood pieces were studded in to create its elegance.

• *Exit the cemetery back into the outer courtyard, turn right, and walk along the mosque. You'll see stairs leading up to a gate reserved for worshippers (usually no visitors are allowed). Continue beyond this gate to the far end of the mosque, and climb a few stairs into the...*

Inner Courtyard

Like the rest of the Süleymaniye complex, this courtyard was designed by the architect Sinan. He was a master of creating spaces that were at once plain and tranquil. Looking around the courtyard, appreciate Sinan's command of architectural grace: It's not ostentatious, but the surrounding porticos and soaring minarets make it feel appropriately majestic. Take a moment to consider the architectural beauty of what is not only the finest mosque in Istanbul, but also one of the finest in all of Islam.

If you've already been to the Blue Mosque, you'll notice some similar features here: The domed porticos around the perimeter look decorative, but they're also functional, providing shade in summer and shelter in winter. The shutters are opened for ventilation in the

Turkey's Greatest Architect: Mimar Sinan (1489-1588)

Mimar Sinan was one of the greatest architects the world has ever seen. Named Joseph by his parents, he was born to a Christian family in a small village in Kayseri (ancient Caesarea, in central Turkey). His father was a mason and carpenter, and young Joseph spent his childhood as his father's apprentice. At the age of 23, Joseph was conscripted into the elite janissaries, converted to Islam, and changed his name to Sinan. (For more on the system of janissaries, see the sidebar on page 122.)

Sinan received the customary janissary education, living with a Turkish family to learn the Turkish language and culture. He built tile kilns in İznik, developing an appreciation for tiles (and later using them to adorn his most important works). He also worked in the construction of government and military buildings, polishing his skills and learning techniques that would serve him well as an architect.

Sinan traveled extensively with the army, from Vienna to Baghdad. He was a student of architecture everywhere he

went, examining what made structures strong or weak, beautiful or ugly. During military campaigns, Sinan built bridges, forts, siege towers, and canals. His abilities, which literally paved the way for the army, impressed the sultan. Sinan became the royal architect in 1539, serving Süleyman the Magnificent and two of his successors. Sinan worked until the day he died, at age 99. During his prolific career, he built over 450 monuments, including 20 royal mosques in Istanbul alone. Most of his buildings are still standing—including his masterpiece, the Mosque of Süleyman the Magnificent.

Less visually striking, but arguably more important, were Sinan's improvements to Istanbul's water-distribution infrastructure. Süleyman was so happy with the results that he allowed Sinan to pipe running water into the architect's own home, a privilege previously enjoyed only by the sultan.

Sinan was an intellectual, a researcher, and an avid reader who spent extravagant sums on books. One of his greatest joys upon becoming the royal architect was gaining access to the royal library. Though he achieved personal glory and success, Sinan always remained a loyal servant to the Ottoman dynasty, praising those who encouraged him to follow his passion. While largely unfamiliar to Westerners, this contemporary of Leonardo da Vinci and Michelangelo certainly ranks among those greats.

SÜLEYMAN MOSQUE

summer. The portico that runs along the front of the mosque is elevated, giving it a grand appearance; this area is reserved for overflow when services fill up. The old marble **fountain** in the middle of the courtyard was used for ablution—ritual cleansing before worship.

The main gate of the courtyard is across from the entrance to the mosque. (This door is usually kept closed, but we'll see it from the other side later on this tour.) Notice the first shutters on either side of this door and the windows above them. These appear identical to the other shutters around the courtyard, but they actually hide the entrance to a special **chamber** used by astronomers—who had the important responsibility of calculating the exact time for worship, five times each day, based on the position of the sun.

This mosque has four minarets. Mosques financed by sultans often had more than one minaret, to show off the sultan's wealth. Here, the extra minarets symbolize the initial four caliphs (religious and social leaders who succeeded the Prophet Muhammad). Notice that there are a total of 10 balconies on the minarets. This is also symbolic: Süleyman was the 10th sultan of the Ottoman dynasty.

• *Enter the mosque, removing your shoes and placing them on the wooden shelves. Notice the beautiful stalactite designs on the niche over the door, and the woodwork on the door wings. There's no fee to enter the mosque, but you can leave a donation as you exit. Now go through the leather curtain and into the mosque's...*

Interior

Tranquility. Especially compared to the riot of color and design in the Blue Mosque, the sedate interior of Süleyman's mosque puts the worshipper at ease. Appreciate the genius of the architect Sinan: Somehow the seemingly plain pastel decoration and tasteful stained-glass windows merge in a harmonious whole.

The architect behind this building—whom Turks call "Sinan the Great"—struggled his whole life to engineer a single dome that could span an entire building, without bulky support arches and pillars. He considered this mosque an important milestone in his quest. (He later succeeded with the Selimiye Mosque in Edirne, near the Turkish-Bulgarian border.)

For this mosque, Sinan used four irregularly shaped "elephant's feet" pillars to support the arches and the dome. His simple and elegant design masks the pillars with an arcaded gallery. The bulky buttresses blend in with their surroundings, giving the impression of an uncluttered space. You have to look hard to see the pillars (unlike the Blue Mosque, where the pillars immediately pop into view).

The impressive dome (flanked by two semi-domes, as at Hagia Sophia) has a diameter of 90 feet. While Renaissance architects in Europe were struggling to sort out the basic technical difficulties of building domes, Sinan succeeded in creating an elegant, masterful dome that included such niceties as open earthenware jars embedded between the brick layers to enhance acoustics.

Look around to find the typical features of a mosque: The wooden barrier marks an area reserved for worshippers. At the end of the apse, a marble niche, the mihrab, shows the direction of the holy city Mecca (toward which Muslims face to pray). To the right is the decorated staircase called a *mimber,* where the imam stands to deliver his sermon. In front of that is an elevated marble platform for the choir. And in the left corner, behind the giant support leg, is the sultan's lodge (on pillars). The decor is nonfigurative: floral designs, stained-glass windows, tiles, and calligraphy *(hat).*

• *Your tour is over. For a sultan's view of the Bosphorus, Europe, and Asia, visit the garden on the far side of the mosque (see map earlier in this chapter). Also, consider the recommended* **Süleymaniye Hamamı** *Turkish bath just outside the complex walls (listed in the Experiences chapter). To rejoin the Old Town Back Streets Walk, retrace your steps to the entrance of the mosque complex.*

GOLDEN HORN WALK

From the Galata Bridge to Sirkeci Train Station

The famous Golden Horn—a strategic inlet branching off the Bosphorus Strait—defines Istanbul's Old Town peninsula. The city's fate has always been tied to this stretch of sea: The Golden Horn is Istanbul's highway, food source, and historic harbor all rolled into one. While much of the Old Town area feels dedicated to tourists these days, a visit to the Golden Horn has you rubbing elbows with fishermen and commuters.

This walk offers a handy orientation to the city, since it affords a sweeping panorama of the Old Town peninsula. Because it's near the terminals for the various Bosphorus ferries, this walk also works well either before or after a cruise of the strait (see the Bosphorus Cruise chapter). The walk is short (about a third of a mile), but allow around 45 minutes if you like to linger.

GETTING TO THE GALATA BRIDGE

The walk begins on the New District (north) end of the Galata Bridge, across the bridge from the Old Town.

From the Old Town: Take the tram (direction: Kabataş) to the Karaköy neighborhood. Get off at Karaköy, the first stop after you cross the Galata Bridge over the Golden Horn. You want to be on the side of the bridge that faces the Bosphorus (to the left, as you face the Old Town). To get to that point from the tram stop, take the pedestrian underpass—if you get turned around in the poorly marked underground zone, simply do the prairie-dog routine: surface, figure out where you are and where you're going, then burrow your way back down and repeat as necessary until you get to your destination.

From Taksim Square, in the New District: You have two options: Take the funicular down to Kabataş, then take the tram to Karaköy. Or, to follow our self guided New District Walk (next chapter), walk down İstiklal Street to Tünel (with less time, you can head down İstiklal Street on the Nostalgic Tram). From Tünel you can either take the old funicular down to the bottom of the hill, or walk down on Bankalar Caddesi ("Bankers Street").

The Walk Begins

• *Start at the Galata Bridge (at the east side of the north end—see map). If you wind up on the wrong side of the bridge, take the pedestrian underpass (with a WC) connecting the two sides. Position yourself on the riverbank, noticing the tulip shapes decorating the railing. With the water at your back, you're facing the neighborhood called...*

Karaköy

The New District covers the area from Karaköy to Taksim Square, a few blocks up the hill. In Byzantine times, this area was inhabited by the commercial colonies of Genoese and Venetian settlers. In the late Ottoman era, it was also a residential area

for non-Muslims, including Jews, Catholics, and Eastern Orthodox Christians. Today, this part of the city is dominated by the famous Galata Tower (you can just see its cone-shaped top up the hill).

Karaköy is also Istanbul's main passenger port. As you turn and face the Old Town across the Golden Horn, you'll see public ferry and seabus docks along the embankment to your left. The port is the scene of an extensive rebuilding project, as run-down buildings make way for art galleries and convention centers. A deluxe hotel is also planned. Locals grumble about political connections that made the project possible, but it's too late to go back now.

• *Notice that the bridge has two levels. We'll start by walking across the top level, then duck down to the lower level. Climb the stairs and wander across the bridge—dodging fishing poles as you walk.*

Fishermen

Enjoy the chorus line of fishing rods, dancing their little jig. While some of these intrepid folks are fishing for fun, others are trying to land a little extra income. They catch mostly mackerel or anchovies—better than nothing, especially during the commercial fishing ban (no nets or sonar) that's in effect from June to September.

GOLDEN HORN

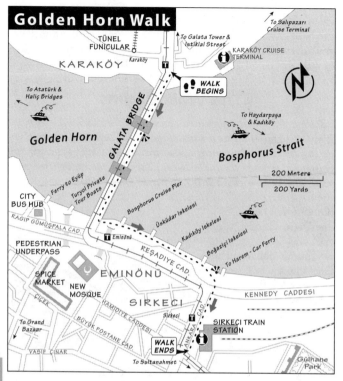

Golden Horn Walk

TÜNEL FUNICULAR

To Galata Tower & İstiklal Street

KARAKÖY

Karaköy

KARAKÖY CRUISE TERMINAL

To Salıpazarı Cruise Terminal

To Atatürk & Haliç Bridges

WALK BEGINS

Golden Horn

GALATA BRIDGE

To Haydarpaşa & Kadıköy

Bosphorus Strait

Ferry to Eyüp

Turyol Private Tour Boats

200 Meters
200 Yards

CITY BUS HUB

RAGIP GÜMÜŞPALA CAD.

Bosphorus Cruise Pier

Üsküdar İskelesi

Kadıköy İskelesi

Boğaziçi İskelesi

PEDESTRIAN UNDERPASS

Eminönü

REŞADIYE CAD.

To Harem - Car Ferry

SPICE MARKET

NEW MOSQUE

EMİNÖNÜ

ÇİÇEK

HAMIDIYE CADDESİ

SIRKECI

KENNEDY CADDESİ

To Grand Bazaar

BÜYÜK POSTANE CAD.

Sirkeci

ANKARA CAD.

SIRKECI TRAIN STATION

VASIF ÇINAR

WALK ENDS

To Sultanahmet

Gülhane Park

GOLDEN HORN

During the ban, most of what you find in the market is the expensive daily catch, imported frozen fish, or farm-raised fish.

Approach a fisherman and wish him well, saying *"Rastgele"* (pull your lips to your ears and say "rust-geh-leh"; "May you catch some"). Ask to see his catch of the day: *Bakabilir miyim?* (bah-kah-bee-leer mee-yeem; "May I see?"). Each one has a jar, jug, bucket, or Styrofoam cooler full of wriggling

fish he'd love to show off. If you're having fun with the language, try this: Point to someone's bucket of tiny fish and ask playfully, *"Yem mi, yemek mi?"* (yehm mee yeh-mehk mee; "Is that bait or dinner?").

Be careful as you walk among the fishermen—occasionally they get careless as they swing back for a cast.

• *The part of the bridge between its two low-profile towers can be raised to let big ships pass. This is a good place to find a spot out of harm's way and ponder the famous...*

Golden Horn (Haliç)

This four-mile-long horn-shaped inlet glitters like precious metal at sunset. But its strategic value is also worth its weight in gold. Protected from the prevailing north winds, the Golden Horn has served as a natural harbor for centuries—the history of Istanbul is steeped in it.

This was once the main commercial port of Constantinople and a base for the Byzantine fleet. To block enemy fleets sailing into the heart of the city, and to more effectively levy taxes on ships, the Byzantines hung a massive chain across the entrance of the Horn (you can see some of the historic links in the Istanbul Archaeological Museum). The chain was breached only a couple of times, by the Vikings (10th century) and by the Crusaders during the Fourth Crusade (1204).

In 1453, when the young Ottoman sultan Mehmet set out to capture Constantinople, he knew it was crucial to gain control of the Horn. Rather than breaking the chain, he decided to bypass it altogether. His troops pulled their fleet of ships out of the waters of the Bosphorus, slid them on greased logs over the hills through what later became the New District, and launched them back into the Horn—all in just one night.

During Europe's Industrial Revolution, the Ottoman Empire was slow to adapt to the fast-changing new world. It began the industrial race well after the West, then rushed to catch up, often without careful planning. The Horn became more and more polluted as industrial plants and shipyards were built along its banks.

In the 1980s, a clever Istanbul mayor with light blue eyes used a great gimmick to clean things up: He got people on board by saying his project would make the Horn as blue as his eyes. Factories were closed down and moved outside the city. Rotting buildings along the water with no historic significance were torn down, and empty space was converted into public parks. The area's entire infrastructure was renewed—a process that's ongoing.

• *Now look inland over the tram tracks and up the Golden Horn (with your back to the Bosphorus), to see the...*

Bridges over the Horn

Five bridges over the Golden Horn connect the Old Town to the New District. The first one you see is the brand-new Metro Bridge, completed in 2013 as part of the project to extend the underground Metro line to the Old Town.

Right behind the Metro Bridge is the low-lying Atatürk

Bridge, on floating platforms, and beyond that is the taller main highway bridge, called Haliç (hah-leech)—also the local name for the Golden Horn.

The old Galata Bridge was the first and, for decades, the only bridge spanning the Horn. It's the one you see in historic postcards from Istanbul. But the huge platforms it was built on blocked water circulation, worsening the Horn's pollution woes. So, in 1994, this historic bridge was replaced with the new Galata Bridge—the one you're standing on. A public outcry of nostalgia eventually compelled city leaders to reassemble the original bridge farther down the Horn (between the Atatürk and Haliç bridges—not visible from here).

• Now take in the...

Old Town Panorama

Use this sweeping vista of the Old Town to get your bearings. Straight ahead from the end of the bridge, you can see the main entrance to the famous **Spice Market** (stone-and-brick building with three small domes), which sells souvenirs, caviar, dried fruits, Turkish delight, "Turkish Viagra"...and, oh yeah, spices.

The handsome mosque just to the left of the Spice Market (partly obscured by the bridge tower) is the New Mosque of Mother Sultan, or simply **New Mosque.** Dating from the 17th century, it's one of the last examples of classical-style Ottoman mosques. After that time, mosques were built in an eclectic style, heavily influenced by Western architecture.

Behind the Spice Market, twisty streets lined with market stalls wind their way up the hill toward the famous **Grand Bazaar.** While the Spice Market and Grand Bazaar are deluged with tourists, this in-between zone sells more housewares and everyday textiles than souvenirs—meaning that it's packed tight with locals looking for a bargain, particularly on Saturdays. Thanks to these crowds—and a steady stream of delivery trucks and carts blocking the streets—it can take a half-hour to walk just the four blocks between the markets. This is the "real" Istanbul—gritty and authentic.

Farther to the right, past the open space and near the Golden Horn, you see the **Rüstem Paşa Mosque.** This tiny mosque, with its single dome and lone minaret, is dwarfed by the larger mosques around it. But a visit there offers a peek into a more intimate and cozy mosque, with some of the finest 16th-century Ottoman tiles around.

On the hillside just above the Rüstem Paşa Mosque is the 16th-century **Mosque of Süleyman the Magnificent,** with its handsome dome and four tall minarets. Elaborate and impressive, yet tastefully restrained, this mosque offers an insightful contrast to the over-the-top and more famous Blue Mosque.

To the left of Süleyman's mosque is the single, tall **Beyazıt Tower.** Sometimes referred to as the "fire tower," it marks the location of bustling Beyazıt Square and Istanbul University's main campus (next door to the Grand Bazaar).

Now look to your left. At the end of the Historical Peninsula, you can see the lush gardens marking the grounds of **Topkapı Palace.** Most of what you see from here are the palace's lower gardens, called Gülhane, now a public park. You can also see the tower marking the entrance to the Harem complex.

To the right of the palace (up the hill, above the modern buildings), notice the gorgeous dome and minarets of **Hagia Sophia**— once the greatest church in Byzantium, then a mosque, and today one of Istanbul's best museums. The famous Blue Mosque, which faces Hagia Sophia from across Sultanahmet Park, is not quite visible from here.

If you look far to the left, beyond the Topkapı Palace gardens, you can see the Bosphorus Strait and **Asian Istanbul** (the hilltop that bristles with TV towers, like a sea of giant minarets). The Bosphorus Bridge, an impressive suspension bridge, is visible from here (unless it's really hazy).

• *Continue along the bridge to the second tower. Go inside the tower and take the stairs down...*

Under the Bridge

As you descend the stairs, look up for a fun view of dozens of fishing rods twitching along the railing of the bridge. As you walk down here, watch your head—sometimes an amateur fisherman carelessly lets his weight swing under. And keep an eye out for the flicker of a little silvery fish, thrashing through the air as he's reeled in by a happy predator.

Walk along the bridge (toward the Old Town), enjoying this "restaurant row." Passages lead to the other side of the bridge,

which is lined with still more restaurants. As you walk, aggressive waiters will try to lure you into their restaurants. Don't be shy—look around, get into a conversation, and compare prices. You may end up here tonight for a fish dinner or, better yet, on the other side of the bridge, where you can watch the sun set over the Golden Horn. Even if you don't want a full meal, consider picking up a sandwich or having a drink at a café. The last restau-

GOLDEN HORN

rant, with dozens of simple brown tables, sells barbecued fish sandwiches to go—handy to eat as you walk (you'll smell the outdoor barbecue before you see it). If you cross under, you'll find a line of trendy teahouses and bars facing up the Golden Horn—great for backgammon, drinks, and sunsets. At the end of the bridge on the Old Town side, venerable "fish and bread" boats sell cheap fish sandwiches literally off the boat.

• *If you have the time and interest, you can take a short cruise from here to see more of the Golden Horn. The Haliç ferry pier is a short walk away, to the west (to your right facing the Old Town), past the "fish and bread" boats and the bus stops (Eminönü-Haliç Pier/İskelesi, Mon-Fri at :45 past the hour from 7:45-16:45 and on the hour from 18:00-20:00, Sat-Sun 10:45-16:45 and 18:00-20:00, also Sun at 21:00; 35 minutes; one-way trip covered by single-ride public transit tickets/passes—see page 26). Passengers are mostly devout Muslims on a trip to Eyüp (the last stop; for its religious significance—see page 59, or those few intrepid travelers looking for "Back Door" scenes).*

At the end of the bridge, turn left and continue along the...

Commuter Ferry Terminals

This embankment bustles with thousands of commuters heading to and from work (during morning and evening rush hours) and shopping chores (especially Saturdays). Peek into the pedestrian underpass beneath the bridge for a taste of the shoulder-to-shoulder commute that many locals endure.

This area is also a hub for intercontinental traffic. Public ferries carry millions of commuters every year between the European and Asian districts of Istanbul. Until the first bridge over the Bosphorus was built in the early 1970s, boats were the only way to cross from Europe to Asia. Locals still prefer the ferries, which are a convenient and cheap (a little over $1 one-way) way to avoid the gridlock on the bridges.

From this vantage point, you can assess how crowded with tourists Istanbul is at the moment. The cruise-ship port is just opposite (at the New District harbor). Big boats routinely unload several thousand tourists apiece. If three ships are in port, more than 6,000 tourists are inundating the city's top three sights: the Blue Mosque, Hagia Sophia, and Topkapı Palace.

The first terminal, the **Bosphorus Cruise Pier,** is where you can catch a public ferry for a cruise up the Bosphorus (25 TL round-trip, allow 5.5-7 hours with stop at fishing village; seasonal schedule and route described in the Bosphorus Cruise chapter). Just beyond are **private tour boats** (look for the *Bosphorus Tours* sign). For only 12 TL (hawkers ask more), these boats take you as far as the second bridge on the Bosphorus and back again in 1.5 hours. Ignore the posted schedule: Boats leave when they fill up, so just hop on board whenever you're ready. While we prefer taking a public ferry for our Bosphorus cruise, these tour boats—which don't go as far up the strait, and don't make any stops—are faster and worth considering if you're pressed for time and just want a taste of the strait.

The next terminal is **Üsküdar İskelesi,** with boats heading to Üsküdar, a lively commercial district on the Asian side (2-4/hour in peak times, 20 minutes).

It's followed by **Kadıköy İskelesi,** with boats heading to Asian Istanbul's commercial hub, the busy Kadıköy district (every 30 minutes, 25-minute trip; rush-hour service is more frequent but goes via Haydarpaşa—near the train station but takes a little longer). Next is the new **Boğaziçi İskelesi,** a commuter port.

The last terminal is for the car ferry to **Harem**—not a place with sultans' wives, but the major commercial harbor in Asian Istanbul (near Üsküdar). Harem is a handy shortcut to the Asian side, and it's definitely the cheapest intercontinental crossing for cars (every 30 minutes, 25 minutes). One-way passenger trips on the Üsküdar, Kadıköy, and Harem ferries are covered by single-ride public transit tickets/passes—see page 26.

• *When you spot the Harem ferry, it's time to head inland. For a nice panorama over the Galata Bridge and the New District, you could climb the pedestrian overpass. But for where we're going next, it's better to cross the street at the stoplight in order to stay on the proper side of the tram tracks.*

After you cross the street, you're in the Sirkeci neighborhood, and a few steps from the historic train station of the same name.

Sirkeci Train Station

This is a surprisingly low-profile train station for having once been the terminal of the much-vaunted Orient Express. An old locomotive decorates the corner of the station, honoring this footnote in history. Pass the locomotive and turn left, finding your way to the station's main entrance (along the modern wall with the white doors, under the sign for *İstanbul Gar*). Once inside the door, a TI and well-signed ticket windows are to your left—and a statue of Atatürk is staring down at you from the head of the tracks.

Wander deeper into the station, past the ticket windows, and go left to find evidence of a more genteel, earlier age. Consider popping into the humble little **Railway Museum,** with its old photos and equipment (free, Tue-Sat 9:00-12:30 & 13:00-17:00, closed Sun-Mon). To the right of the museum is the old passenger waiting room, with wooden benches and stained-glass windows that recall the station's former glory.

The **Orient Express** train line began in the 1880s. You could board a train in Paris and step off into this very station three days later (after passing through Munich, Vienna, Budapest, and Bucharest). Traversing the mysterious East, and headed for the even more mysterious "Orient," passengers were advised to carry a gun. The train service was rerouted to avoid Germany during the Nazi years, and was temporarily disrupted during both world wars, but otherwise ran until May of 1977. While this is the most famous route, almost any eastbound train from Western Europe could be called an "Orient Express." The train line was immortalized in literature and film—most famously by Agatha Christie, whose *Murder on the Orient Express* takes place on the Simplon Orient Express (Paris' Gare de Lyon station to Milan, Belgrade, Sofia, and Istanbul).

Due to renovation work on the tracks, regular train operations at the station are suspended until late 2016, when Intercity services are planned to restart. Currently, travelers to Bulgaria are bused to the border where they switch to a train, and the lines to Greece are closed. But, the station is still busy as it is a major stop on the Marmaray commuter rail line that runs under the Bosphorus Strait to the Üsküdar district in Asia.

• *Your walk is finished. To head back to Sultanahmet, you can take the tram (which departs from directly in front of the station) two stops uphill to the Sultanahmet stop, or follow the tram tracks on foot (10-15 minutes).*

NEW DISTRICT WALK

Taksim Square and İstiklal Street

To fully appreciate the urban Istanbul of today, you must leave the Old Town and plunge into the lively, sophisticated, and oh-so-European New District. Start at the vast Taksim Square and stroll the length of teeming İstiklal Street (İstiklal Caddesi)—the city's jam-packed main pedestrian drag. Lined with Art Nouveau facades, cafés, restaurants, pubs, bookstores, music shops, art galleries, cinemas, theaters, and a rainbow of shops, İstiklal Street is the most cosmopolitan—and most European—part of Istanbul. Pastry shops and restaurants that once served only the upper crust now open their doors to commoners like you and me.

Orientation

Length of This Walk: Allow one hour for the walk itself...but you'll need much longer if you succumb to the many temptations along the way.

Getting There: From the Old Town, ride the tram to Kabataş (the end of the line) and follow the crowds directly into the funicular station. Take the handy little one-stop funicular up to Taksim Square, and exit following signs for *İstiklal Caddesi*.

Nostalgic Tram: This tram runs quietly up and down İstiklal Street between Taksim Square and Tünel. It's a handy way to quickly skip ahead or backtrack during this walk (4 TL for single ride—see page 24).

The Walk Begins

• *Start at Taksim Square, next to the Republic Monument.*

Taksim Square

Taksim Square (Taksim Meydanı; tahk-seem may-dah-nuh) is the New District's transportation hub, connected to other parts of Istanbul by bus, Metro, funicular, and the Nostalgic Tram. Taksim Square also marks the beginning of modern Istanbul's trendiest business and residential neighborhoods, which stretch in the direction of the big park behind the line of buses.

At the top of Taksim Square is the big, black, blocky **Atatürk Cultural Center,** the setting for classical music concerts, opera, and ballet performances. Currently undergoing renovation, it is closed indefinitely.

• *In the center of the traffic circle opposite, check out the...*

Republic Monument (Cumhuriyet Anıtı)

This patriotic monument, unveiled in 1928, commemorates the fifth anniversary of the founding of the Turkish Republic. When

the government ran out of money to fund the monument, the people of Turkey reached into their own pockets to finish it.

The sculpture shows the two sides of Atatürk, the father of modern Turkey. On one side, he's wearing his military uniform, as the hero of the War of Independence. On the flip side, civilian Atatürk is modern Turkey's first president, surrounded by figures representing the proclamation of the Republic.

The other two sides—with soldiers and waving flags—symbolize victory. And the two images/medallions near the top represent women before (veiled) and after the founding of the Republic. Scholars say the woman depicted is actually Sabiha Bengütaş—the Republic's first female sculptor, the first female student admitted to the sculpture department at the Turkish Academy of Fine Arts (today's Mimar Sinan University of Fine Arts), and the first Turkish woman to win the Prix de Rome scholarship (to attend the Academy of Fine Arts in Rome). Later, Bengütaş worked with Italian sculptor Pietro Canonica and assisted him with this monument.

• *From Taksim Square, the Nostalgic Tram loops around the monument and runs the length of İstiklal Street. That's precisely the course we'll walk: from the Republic Monument to the end of İstiklal Street (and the top of the Tünel funicular, which leads down to the Galata Bridge).*

Let's start at the top of...

İstiklal Street

İstiklal Caddesi (ees-teek-lahl jahd-deh-see; "Independence Street") was born after a devastating 1870 fire. The Ottoman government took the opportunity to rebuild the area as a showpiece of Art Nouveau style.

While immersed in the crowds that enliven this boulevard, stand still for a moment just to watch the river of people. İstiklal Street is today's Turkey. Where is everyone going? Just "out." Are they Turkish? Yes. Nine out of every 10 people you see on this promenade are Turks—modern Turkey is a melting pot of some 20 different ethnic groups. Observe the haircuts and fashions as everyone from teenagers to businesspeople makes the scene. Stop and talk with someone in this living celebration of diversity.

From here, this walk slopes gradually downhill. Along the way, cafés and eateries offer second-floor refuges from the crowds, and fine vantage points from which to view the scene below. To make the route super-simple to follow, we've posted handy red-metal numbered plates on the buildings, and keyed them to this book's walk (ignore the old blue plaques). Simply follow the tram tracks and match the numbers with this text (odd numbers on left, even on right).

Thronged with people, İstiklal Street is no fun for claustrophobes. (The crowds can be so thick that occasionally the tram simply cannot run.) When the street is jammed, it's easier to go with the flow by sticking to the right, as local strollers do.

• *Start out at the...*

Top of İstiklal Street: Food Corner

This first corner has long been a fast-food stop. Fresh-squeezed orange juice and newly sliced *döner kebab* are traditional favorites, but American fast-food joints are also popular.

• *A few steps down, take a closer look at a truly local fast-food place...*

Simit Sarayı (at #3)

A *simit* (see-meet) is sort of like a bagel: bread dough dipped in *pekmez* (grape molasses), rolled in sesame seeds, then baked. You'll see street vendors with old-fashioned carts selling these sesame-seed bread rings all over town (a filling snack starting from 2 TL). The popular Simit Sarayı (see-meet sah-rah-yuh) chain has all of

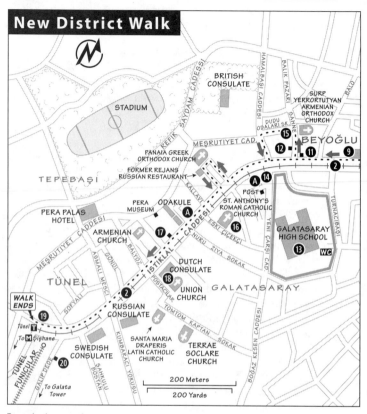

New District Walk

Istanbul munching on its sesame-seed-bread-ring sandwiches of cheese, sausages, and olives.

• *Across the street from #3 is a...*

Water Fountain

This water fountain is a physical reminder that "Taksim" means "distribution," and that this square was once part of the town's water system. Also on the square (just behind the fountain) is the free **Republic Art Gallery** (Cumhuriyet Sanat Galerisi), which showcases temporary exhibits of contemporary art.

Coffee Wars: Gloria Jean's (at #17), Starbucks, and Kahve Dünyası

The green mermaid is here. Since Turks already love coffee (heck, they claim to have invented it), Turkey is an appealing market. Australia's Gloria Jean's was the first modern coffee shop to hit Istanbul, with Starbucks close behind. The local Kahve Dünyası ("Coffee World") boldly challenges the big chains by selling coffee at a fraction of the others' prices.

Across the street (opposite #13-39) is the **French Consulate**. As

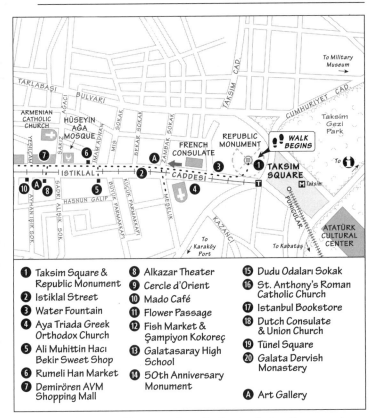

1. Taksim Square & Republic Monument
2. Istiklal Street
3. Water Fountain
4. Aya Triada Greek Orthodox Church
5. Ali Muhittin Hacı Bekir Sweet Shop
6. Rumeli Han Market
7. Demirören AVM Shopping Mall
8. Alkazar Theater
9. Cercle d'Orient
10. Mado Café
11. Flower Passage
12. Fish Market & Şampiyon Kokoreç
13. Galatasaray High School
14. 50th Anniversary Monument
15. Dudu Odaları Sokak
16. St. Anthony's Roman Catholic Church
17. Istanbul Bookstore
18. Dutch Consulate & Union Church
19. Tünel Square
20. Galata Dervish Monastery

A. Art Gallery

this was the most European-friendly district during Ottoman times, many European consulates and churches were located in this district.

• *Continue down İstiklal Street, and after half a block, turn left at the alley (Meşelik Sokak). On your left is the...*

Aya Triada Greek Orthodox Church

Aya Triada—or, as the locals call it, the Grand Church—is the largest active Orthodox church in town. While it's often closed, the guard will usually let you in (for a donation to the church offering box). Built in the Neo-Gothic style in 1880, the church has some interesting flourishes, such as the delicate paintings that line the sanctuary walls. Also enjoy the colorful frescoes and Baroque-style decorations on the ceiling and dome. This is the first of many Christian churches we'll see along the walk today—constant reminders that

"I Was in Taksim"

Taksim Square has always been a gathering point for crowds—the place to come if you want to draw attention to your cause. Any event organized here makes the news.

For decades, labor-union members celebrated Labor Day (May 1) in Taksim Square. For years the rally was a scene of low-level tension between unions and the government, with the occasional clash between workers and police, but the rallies always ended peacefully. May 1, 1977, was different. Half a million workers crowded the square that day, and tempers flared. Suddenly, gunshots were heard, though it wasn't clear who'd fired (some blamed the secret service, but the shooter or shooters were never identified). In the ensuing panic and chaos, 37 people died. The event is still fresh in the minds of many locals, who consider it a particularly dark day in the city's history.

The following year, union members again assembled at the square, this time to protest against the government they held responsible for the previous year's melee. In response, the government banned May 1 gatherings on the square for three decades. In 2009, the unions finally got permission for a Labor Day rally, and in 2010, more than 100,000 workers demonstrated peaceably.

But Taksim Square had never seen anything quite like the massive anti-government demonstrations that took place here in May of 2013, sparked by police action against a group of young environmentalists.

It all started as a small gathering to protest the government's plan to turn a public park (Gezi Parkı) in Taksim into a commercial project. But after a brutal police intervention, the peaceful environmental demonstration turned into a prolonged anti-government rally, with protesters decrying increasing intrusions into their private lives by a government attempting to regulate its citi-

historically, this was one of the most diverse, cosmopolitan areas of Istanbul.

• *Head back out to İstiklal Street and continue our walk.*

AkSanat Art Gallery (at #8) and the Art Gallery Scene

Several art galleries are located on İstiklal Street and nearby. These galleries, primarily sponsored by banks, display permanent and temporary exhibitions of both well-established artists and rising stars in the art world. This is a good opportunity to check out Turkey's often-overlooked contemporary art scene (most galleries have free admission).

Megavizyon Music Store (at #57)

Pop music is ever more popular among young Turks, with new stars seeming to crop up every day. You'll see their posters decorating

zens' social behaviors.

In the last few years, the country has seen a major shift from the liberal policies and ideals that originally brought the ruling party, AKP, to power in 2003. Civil unrest and a faltering economy have led the AKP to adopt more authoritative, conservative policies in order to retain power—and conservative votes. These were unexpected changes for some; for others they came as no surprise. Among the controversies: restrictions on freedom of speech, a ban on alcohol sales, crackdowns on public displays of affection, and plans to build a gigantic new mosque.

The driving force behind the huge May 2013 demonstrations came from an unexpected (to the government) source: Turkey's apolitical young generation, not the older, pro-secular members of society. These persistent, computer-savvy kids used methods that were hard for the government to deal with—social media and humor—and attracted large numbers of supporters.

Successive waves of protests rippled across the nation, even reaching remote, traditionally pro-government towns in the east. Officials say three million citizens took to the streets, but the number was undoubtedly higher. Local authorities called it the largest anti-government uprising in the history of the Republic. Authorities also said that it was the first time the three-term prime minister and his party had suffered a defeat at the hands of the opposition.

The protests and the government's violent reactions left deep scars in the Turkish psyche. To many, Taksim Square is considered Turkey's version of Tiananmen Square. Depending on what happens next, to say, "I was in Taksim," may take on an even greater meaning in the future.

NEW DISTRICT

music-store showcases and billboards. As in many countries, music and book piracy are problems in Turkey. The rumor is that pirated CDs sell better than the real thing—so music companies are now selling their own versions "under the counter."

As you explore İstiklal Street, note the many flagship stores like this one. If something sells here, it is likely to sell in the rest of the country.

Turkey's retail electronics giant Teknosa has taken over Megavizyon, so you are likely to see the *Teknosa* sign along with *Megavizyon*. As in other parts of the world, corporate takeovers are increasing in Turkey. No matter how popular or successful a business is, it is becoming increasingly difficult to withstand serious competition.

Mustafa Kemal Atatürk (1881-1938)

Atatürk, the George Washington of the Turks, almost single-handedly created modern-day Turkey. As the map of Europe was being redrawn at the end of World War I, this confident war hero put forth a clear and complete vision that persuaded the Turks, on the brink of crisis, to forge a modern nation.

By the early 20th century, the Turkish people were in dire straits. After centuries of decline, the Ottoman Empire—known as the "Sick Man of Europe"—allied itself with Germany and was pulled into World War I. But even as the Ottoman Empire floundered, a wily officer named Mustafa Kemal proved his military mettle, successfully defending Gallipoli against a huge armada with a handful of poorly equipped soldiers.

As the war came to an end, victorious European armies occupied Istanbul and made plans to dole out pieces of the former Ottoman Empire to their allies. In 1919, the Greeks took the city of İzmir (on the south coast of Turkey) and began pushing toward Istanbul. With lightning speed, the war hero Kemal gathered an army to defend Turkish territory. Over a three-year period (the Turkish War of Independence), he chased out French and Italian troops and repelled the Greek invasion. With the Treaty of Lausanne in 1923, the Ottoman Empire was history, the Turkish Republic was born, and Mustafa Kemal became the most beloved Turkish leader in centuries. The National Assembly elected Mustafa Kemal as the first President of the Republic, and dubbed him Atatürk. Translated literally, Atatürk means "father of the Turks";

NBA Store (part of the Adidas Store, at #59)

American professional basketball is hugely popular in Istanbul. This is the first NBA store to open anywhere outside the US. In 2000, Hidayet "Hido (hee-doh)" Türkoğlu became the first Turkish-born player in NBA history. Following Türkoğlu's footsteps, Mehmet Okur played for the 2004 NBA champion Detroit Pistons and became the first Turk to play in an All-Star game (other Turkish NBA stars include Ersan İlyasova and Cenk Akyol). In 2006, the NBA began actively promoting the sport in Europe, including Italy, Spain, Britain...and Turkey. Turks have a hunch that the NBA could expand its league to Europe in the future.

Ali Muhittin Hacı Bekir (at #83)

Turkish delight (*lokum* in Turkish; loh-koom) is a sweet, flavorful cube of gooey gelatin dusted with powdered sugar, sometimes embedded with nuts. Turkish kids cheer when their parents bring

in this context, it also means "great leader" or "grand Turk."

Rescuing his nation from the chopping block would have been enough to get his name in the history books, but Atatürk was not finished. He envisioned a modern, progressive Turkey that would eschew the outmoded values of the Ottoman Empire in favor of a European-style democracy. Rarely in history has anyone exerted such power with such effect in so short a time. In less than 10 years, Atatürk

- aligned Turkey with the West,
- separated religion and state (by removing Islam as the state religion and upholding civil law over Islamic law),
- adopted the Western calendar,
- decreed that Turks should have surnames, similar to Western custom,
- changed the alphabet from Arabic script to Roman letters,
- distanced Turkey from the corrupt Ottoman Empire by abolishing the sultanate and caliphate, and outlawing the fez and veil,
- abolished polygamy, and
- emancipated women (consider that Swiss women didn't receive the federal right to vote until 1971).

Atatürk died at 9:05 on November 10, 1938—and every year, all of Turkey still observes a minute of silence at 9:05 on that day to honor the man they regard as the greatest Turk. For a generation, many young Turkish women worried that they'd never be able to really love a man because of their love for the father of their country. Because of Atatürk, millions of Turks today have a flag—and reason to wave it.

home a box of *lokum*—and Hacı Bekir's is considered the best. Browse their selection; the *lokum* comes in boxes of all shapes and sizes, packed with many different flavors and add-ins (pistachios are favorites). Their almond paste, hard candies, and *helva* (a sesame oil and tahini treat) are also good. Prices are by the kilogram—

buy a small amount to taste. About 2 TL will buy you 50 grams, about five pieces of Turkish delight. For an assortment, ask for *karışık* (kahruh-shuhk) *lokum*. Or pay 3 TL to get the same amount of double-roasted pistachio *lokum* (the real stuff).

Rumeli Han Market (at #48)

Notice the eclectic decorations on the entrance to this old shopping market—Greek Ionic columns, lions' heads, Arabic script, and more.

In Istanbul, North Is "West"

The New District, part of Beyoğlu County, was once called Pera (peh-rah; "The Side Across"). Many locals still use this term, which dates from the Middle Ages. When Constantinople's Orthodox Christians clashed with its minority Roman Catholics, the Catholics moved outside the city walls—to "The Side Across," north of the Golden Horn. Ever since, the northern part of Istanbul (the New District) has looked west to Europe, while the southern part (the Old Town) identifies more with the East.

During the Fourth Crusade, in 1204, the gap between Constantinople's Orthodox and Catholic populations widened. The Crusaders stayed here for half a century, establishing relations with Venetian and Genoese merchants, who dominated world trade. For political and economic reasons, the emperors reluctantly gave up their claim to "The Side Across," offering it to the Genoese as a self-governing commercial base.

When the Ottomans conquered Constantinople in the 15th century, the Genoese immediately recognized the rule of the young Ottoman sultan. In return, they were granted privileges and commercial rights that would last for centuries.

As the Ottoman Empire became a more powerful player on Europe's political stage, "The Side Across" became a home base for visiting envoys and ambassadors. Genoa, France, Spain, England, Holland, and many of Europe's other great powers built

The *han* (a combo marketplace and inn for merchants) was built in the 1870s for the sultan by the same architects who designed the seaside Dolmabahçe Palace. Later it became a commercial complex with shops, cafés, art studios, and office space on the upper floors. It's hard to tell from here, but this huge complex takes up about a third of the block.

• *Continue down İstiklal Street. To your right, just past the 16th-century Hüseyin Ağa Mosque (the only mosque on the street) and covering an entire city block is the...*

embassies here. Beginning in the 16th century, these embassies became deeply involved in business interests. Foreign merchants wanted to live near their embassies, turning "The Side Across" into a particularly desirable and genteel corner of the city. Schools, churches, and communal buildings were built to meet the needs of the ever-growing expatriate population. Soon İstiklal Street became known as the Grand Rue de Pera, and the district became a "little Europe" within the boundaries of greater Istanbul. This cosmopolitan area also began to draw the city's other non-Muslim minorities, such as Greeks, Armenians, and Jews.

The mid-19th century was a time of great change. A new bridge over the Golden Horn connected the still very Eastern-feeling Old Town to newer, European-style neighborhoods in the north. Tired of being viewed as backward by his European contemporaries, the sultan moved out of the historic, Oriental-style Topkapı Palace and into the new, Western-style Dolmabahçe Palace in the New District.

The ties between "The Side Across" and Europe are still palpable today. Strolling down the very European-feeling İstiklal Street, tourists sometimes forget they're just a short boat or train trip from Asia. Like the Genoese merchants, ambassadors, and clever sultans before them, today's visitors are figuring out that here in Istanbul, you go north to find the West.

NEW DISTRICT

Demirören AVM Shopping Mall

Construction of this modern shopping mall caused a great deal of controversy. The years-long project to build the mall—which covers the entire block to Yeşilçam Sokağı and has four subterranean floors in addition to five stories aboveground—was opposed by many neighborhood shop owners and residents. But none were as powerful as the company building the mall—the Demirören group, one of Turkey's leading development companies. The mall's grand-opening ceremony was hosted by the head of the Demirören

The Brave Grocer Against the Supermarket (Kahraman Bakkal Süpermarkete Karşı)

This was the title, and the plot, of a satirical play that drew full houses in Istanbul for several seasons in the 1980s.

Istanbul's first modern shopping mall opened in 1988 to newspaper headlines and public acclaim. It was large, there was plenty of parking, fine brands filled the many shops, you could eat on-site, there was even an ice-skating rink...and it was expensive. Luxury wasn't cheap, and Turkish shoppers were willing to pay for the convenience.

Contractors noticed the trend, and soon malls were going up throughout the city, and across Turkey. Supermarket chains followed the trend, supersizing themselves and securing locations in or next to the malls.

As a result, Turkish shopping trends changed radically. Locals who had been accustomed to shopping in neighborhood markets abandoned their familiar haunts and rushed to these giant shopping utopias. Small businesses, groceries, neighborhood eateries, and bakeries tried very hard to survive, but some were forced out of business.

Today, many shoppers have realized that while the big malls offer one-stop convenience, they lack the personal touch. Many consumers are again seeking out their neighborhood shops, and starting the day with a chat with the corner baker. While malls are still everywhere, now they are the ones trying to survive.

group (he's also president of one of Turkey's top soccer teams, Beşiktaş) with a special guest appearance by the popular Brazilian soccer player Ronaldo. Nearby shop owners had to close up early or risk being overrun by the chaotic crowd of soccer fans. Turkey's first Virgin Megastore was located in this mall.

• *Across from the mall, at #111, is the...*

Alkazar Theater (Alkazar Sineması, at #111)

This narrow storefront—with a fancy pseudo-arch supported by little statues on pedestals—hides one of the first movie theaters built in Istanbul, dating from just after World War I. Ultimately doomed by its prime location, the theater recently closed—a victim of developers hungry for commercial real estate.

In those first years of the early Republic, it was a gathering place for the aristocracy. Later,

when cinema fell out of fashion and other theaters closed down, this one kept its doors open. In the 1970s and 1980s, the only way it could pay the bills was to show erotic films. With the Turkish film industry on the upswing—thanks to bigger-budget attractions, foreign films, and the buzz created by Istanbul's International Film Festival—this theater survived another two decades. Today the building serves as the flagship store of Teknosa, the Turkish version of Best Buy.

Yeşilçam, the Turkish Hollywood (across from #115)

Look down the first street to the right. This alley, called Yeşilçam (yeh-sheel-chahm; "Green Pine"), was once the heart of the film industry—the "Turkish Hollywood." While the actors, directors, and producers have moved on to other parts of town, "Yeşilçam" is still the nickname for the local film industry. In Turkey, filmmaking is all about making a good movie on a small budget.

Turkish soap operas are giving Bollywood and Brazilian productions a run for their money—both in Turkey and abroad. In some countries, the ratings for Turkish soaps surpass even those of Hollywood productions. They pull the best ratings in the Middle East and the Balkans, including in Greece, where the Bishop of Thessaloniki warned citizens against watching *Magnificent Century* (about Süleyman the Magnificent, who conquered Rhodes), saying that Greeks surrender to Turks simply by watching the show. In Iran, authorities blame Turkish soaps for pushing a liberal lifestyle.

Cercle d'Orient and Emek Theater

This building (in the block that stretches from Yeşilçam to the Greek Consulate) combines various architectural elements and was designed in the 1880s by architect Alexander Vallaury for Abraham Paşa, a wealthy Armenian Catholic. For a long time it was used by Cercle d'Orient, a gentlemen's club (more like a political and financial-interest group) that still exists today under the name Büyük Kulüp. Early club members included top-ranking Ottoman officials and officers and foreign diplomats. The balls once organized here were the talk of the elite.

The renowned **Emek Theater,** built in 1924 in the Cercle d'Orient complex, is now gone—demolished to make way for commercial development. The entire complex is being turned into another shopping mall, despite huge protests led by intellectuals fighting to save one of Istanbul's cultural landmarks.

• *Across the street at #121 is...*

NEW DISTRICT

The Turkish Flag

While the modern Turkish Republic was founded only in 1923, its heritage is much older. Today's flag is very similar to the design used by the Ottomans for centuries, often with a red or green background. All were decorated with a crescent moon (and sometimes a verse from the Quran) as a symbol of Islam. Under Ottoman Sultan Selim III (1789-1807), an eight-point star was added to the flag. That star was replaced with today's five-point version some 150 years later. The design and exact proportions of the Turkish flag were standardized by law in 1937.

The red color of the flag is said to represent the blood that was shed to create the Turkish nation. The crescent and star are the subject of a curious legend. Following the Ottoman victory at the Battle of Kosovo, the Sultan Murat I was killed by a Serbian captive. The legend says that the crescent moon and a star were seen reflected in a pool of Turkish blood at the scene—inspiring the design for the flag. Interestingly, the date of the battle (July 28, 1389) actually was a night when Jupiter and the moon were side by side in the night sky over this part of the world. So it is possible that someone could have seen a reflection that matches the moon and the star on the Turkish flag.

NEW DISTRICT

Mado Café (at #121)

This chain is a local favorite for its Turkish-style ice cream. Made with goat's milk and wild orchid pollen, it has a thick, stretchy texture. The café also serves good *börek* (savory pastries) and traditional Turkish desserts such as baklava. Two scoops of their ice cream over a serving of baklava is a real treat.

Traditional Food at Otantik Anadolu Yemekleri (at #80A)

In the window of this recommended restaurant, a woman prepares and bakes *gözleme* (gohz-leh-meh) in the traditional way. *Gözleme* is thin, flat bread rolled with a rolling pin, folded over the ingredients (such as cheese, potatoes, and spinach), and baked. It's simple, delicious...and a good quick snack midway along this walk. Pick the ingredients (10 TL, depending on fillings). To get it wrapped to go, say, "*Paket, lütfen*" (pah-keht lewt-fehn).

Flower Passage (Çiçek Pasajı, at #80)

The original Flower Passage was built in the Neo-Baroque style in the 1870s. Until the 1940s, it was filled only with flower shops.

Then, over time, lively pubs and taverns began to sprout inside. It became a gathering place for writers, newspaper correspondents, students, and intellectuals sitting around beer-barrel tables.

But in 1978, a century after it was built, the Flower Passage collapsed due to lack of maintenance. It remained in ruins for a decade until the city decided to rebuild it. What you're looking at is a nostalgic reproduction of a place that's long gone. While some people enjoy the new version (and travel writers who pen guidebooks seem to love it), most locals are skeptical. Part of the original Flower Passage's charm was its casual, spontaneous atmosphere—nothing like the white-tablecloth uniformity of today's incarnation.

Fish Market (next to the Flower Passage)

A wrought-iron arch with a plaque in the center decorates the alley ·entrance to the Fish Market (Balık Pazarı; bah-luhk pah-zah-ruh). True to its name, this is *the* place in the New District to shop for fresh fish. But you'll find other uniquely Turkish taste treats here, too.

A few steps into the alley, notice **Şampiyon Kokoreç** on the left. *Kokoreç* (koh-koh-retch; sounds like—but doesn't taste like—"cockroach") is chopped-up sheep intestines, grilled and served with toma-

toes, green peppers, and fresh seasonings and herbs. You can get *kokoreç* by itself on a plate, or in a sandwich. Ask for a stand-alone *porsiyon* (pohr-see-yohn), a half-sandwich (*yarım;* yah-ruhm), or a quarter-sandwich (*çeyrek;* chey-rehk). Try the *çeyrek* first, to be sure you like it, before digging into a *porsiyon.* To enhance the flavor, doll up your sandwich with the hot peppers in the jars.

As you munch, ponder how seriously Turks take their *kokoreç.* A few years ago, a rumor flew through the streets that stringent new EU regulations would outlaw the beloved *kokoreç.* Before the story was proved untrue, many Turks did some soul-searching and decided that if they had to choose, they'd gladly pass up EU membership for *kokoreç*.

As you wander along the fish stalls and tiny shops selling herbs, dried fruits, and nuts, you're seeing the reality of workaday Istanbul. About halfway down the alley on the right, a narrow door leads into the courtyard of the Holy Trinity Armenian Orthodox Church (also known as the Armenian Church of the Three Altars, or Surp Yerrortutyan). Just beyond (also on the right) is the intersection with the street called Nevizade Sokak, lined with lively, down-to-earth restaurants and *meyhanes* (mehy-hah-nehz; taverns). The ambience here is local, and the service is usually attentive. It's busiest near sunset, when district residents stop by after work to chat with friends and have a drink or an extended dinner.

• *Down İstiklal Street, behind the tall, fancy gate is...*

Galatasaray High School

Set in the middle of a huge garden surrounded by a wall marked with a gigantic ornamental gate, this "Royal School" (Mekteb-i

Sultani), founded in 1870, was designed to properly raise and educate a new generation of public servants and officials. Its founders hoped to boost the Westernization of the struggling Ottoman Empire. Classes were taught in Turkish and French (the lingua franca of Europe at the time). The school's first principal was a visionary Frenchman who pursued a secular curriculum years before this was common in Europe. The secular teaching outraged the Catholic Pope, the Greek Orthodox Patriarch, and the leading Muslim clerics.

As the Ottoman Empire declined, so did the quality of education. Many of the school's teachers were sent to fight in World War I and never returned. In 1917, the year before the war ended, only five students graduated. But after the Turkish Republic was founded, Galatasaray High School's fortunes improved. Today it's one of the best schools in the country, with a primary school, a high school, and a university.

Across from the high school, at #90, is a fine example of Art Nouveau architecture. Built in 1875 for the Sivajian family, this building was later converted into a post office. The post office is

NEW DISTRICT

now gone, and the building has been turned into a center for culture and the arts.

Just past the high school wall is a small square decorated with an abstract **monument** celebrating the 50th anniversary of the Turkish Republic (1923-1973). This is the halfway point of İstiklal Street. This little square is the usual scene for colorful demonstrations, and talented and sometimes not-so-talented street musicians and jugglers.

• *Take the intersecting street to the right and walk a block. Straight ahead is the wall of the British Consulate. The first alley on the right is...*

Dudu Odaları Sokak

Packed with shops that sell a variety of foods, this narrow alley is the best place in town for one-stop picnic shopping. (It's a bit like the Fish Market, but with specialties of its own.)

Businesses open quite early here, and many stay open late into the night. Bakeries start it off around 7:00, gradually joined by more shops and eateries. Some don't open until noon, since they're open late—until at least 21:00 (one soup shop, described below, is open virtually all night).

The prices you see are per kilogram, but you can buy items in any amount you want (half a kilo is roughly a pound). With simple gestures, you can signal that you'd just like a small sample, or a handful.

Petek Turşuları (#1D) is a gourmet sour-pickle shop. Turks love sour pickles (*turşu*, toor-shoo) and pickle juice (*turşu suyu*, toorshoo soo-yoo). Even if pickles aren't your thing, they're displayed so well that this shop makes a great photo op. The shop's specialties are plum-and-okra pickles (15-18 TL/kg), beet juice (6 TL/liter), and marinated grape leaves for dolma (10 TL/kg). The store carries some of the finest olives and virgin olive oil from Ayvalık, a town on Turkey's Aegean coast.

Sakarya Tatlıcısı (#3) makes more traditional Turkish desserts, including varieties of baklava (about 35-45 TL/kg). A serving of their specialty, quince dessert, with *kaymak* (kai-mahk; clotted cream made from water-buffalo milk) is 8 TL.

Üç Yıldız Şekerleme (#7) is one of the oldest confectionery shops in the city, famous for its Turkish delight (2.50-4 TL/100 grams—about 8-10 pieces), including varieties flavored with resinous *mastic* and jelly candies. The shop carries a variety of hard candies as well. It's owned and managed by a father-son duo who speak excellent French; the son also speaks English. If you understand some French, it's a delight to hear Feridun, the father, recount stories of good old Istanbul.

Cumhuriyet İşkembecisi (#15B) is a historical shop known for its tripe soup (yes, as in intestines—but remember, sausages are made using animal guts, too). In Turkey, if you're hungry—or drunk—late at night, you go out for tripe soup (this shop stays open until 5:30 in the morning). Try a bowl; it's a great Turkish experience. Locals dress it with vinegar, garlic, and red-hot chili peppers. The shop also serves head of sheep—the brain, tongue, and eyes (you can opt out on the eyeballs). The specialty salad is brain salad. Soups are around 11 TL a bowl, a portion of sheep head is 13 TL, and brain salad is 12 TL.

Beyoğlu Şarküteri (#20) is the best deli on the street. They have a great variety of picnic-ready foods, from dried and smoked fish to cheese and *mezes* (appetizers). You can buy ingredients separately, or ask them to prepare a sandwich with the fixings of your choice. For a local taste, try the "Albanian liver" (*Arnavut ciğeri*, ahr-nah-voot jee-eh-ree)—chopped liver pieces fried in bread crumbs.

Zek Erkek Kuaförü (#1A) is a barber shop. Men, if you haven't yet tried a Turkish shave, this is the place to go. You can have a haircut for 20 TL and a shave for an additional 10 TL. Barber Zekai can get rid of your facial hair with a silk thread, or with fire (may sting a bit). Both methods are pretty standard in Turkish barber shops.

• *Back on İstiklal Street, duck into the...*

Hazzopulo Passage (at #116)

Need a short break or a Turkish coffee? A narrow and not-so-special entryway leads to the spacious atrium of this century-old historic passage. Here you'll find a traditional-style coffee shop (Café Grand Boulevard; see page 65) that's frequented by locals. Sip your coffee or tea while seated at short legged-tables, and watch the commotion of people going about their daily routines.

• *Back on İstiklal Street, look for the...*

State Lottery Administration (at #120A)

Private casinos and gambling were made illegal in Turkey several years ago after authorities discovered they were being used for money laundering. (When the tax office would ask someone shady about a sudden, huge influx of cash, the predictable answer was, "I won it gambling.") So the nationwide lottery is hugely popular, with prizes in the millions of dollars. The government runs the lottery and all other legal betting opportunities in Turkey (except horse races; your bet on a winning horse is handled by a private broker). Also popular are the *kazi kazan* (scratch-to-win) cards and İddia (eed-dee-ah; literally "to bet"), a lottery game in which players bet on Turkish and European soccer scores. Conservative Muslims debate the morality of state-organized betting games, and yet lottery agents are everywhere, even in the remote ghettos of the city.

İpek Silk Shop (at #120)

In this fine shop, just inside the passage entrance, prices are fixed, the quality is reliable, and the help is friendly and knowledgeable. Isaac and his staff speak English and are happy to demonstrate the latest in scarf fashion. Ask to see the various ways to wear a scarf, depending on your religious leanings. (For more, see the Shopping chapter.)

Koska Helva Shop (at #122)

It's time to taste another delicacy: *helva* (hell-vah). The word *helva* is Arabic and means "sweet." Today, several countries claim the original recipe. Turkish *helva* is made of crushed sesame seeds, wheat flour, and sugar. Pistachios, vanilla, or cacao is added to create different flavors. *Helva* is also associated with social rituals. For example, when someone dies, loved ones will prepare a certain type of wheat *helva* (without the sesame seeds) and serve it to visitors offering condolences. *Helva* is prepared in large blocks (10-20 TL/kg). If you go inside and ask for 2 TL of *karışık* (kah-ruh-shuhk; assorted) *helva*, you'll end up with a mixed bag of about 100 grams (roughly a quarter-pound).

• *A one-block detour off the main drag takes you back in history: Take a right on Emir Nevruz Sokak, and then jog left to the site of the closed historic Rejans Russian Restaurant (there may still be a sign), which was a New District landmark for decades.*

Former Rejans Russian Restaurant

After the 1917 Russian Revolution, many of the deposed czar's officers fled to Turkey. For the next 30 years, the New District was an enclave of Russian culture, with Russian restaurants, pubs, music, shows, and dances. Though they had lost the war for their homeland, these Russian transplants spent the rest of their lives pretending they were still living high on the hog in Mother Russia. The locals continued to call them by their former titles: Baron Colonel, Count General, Grand Duke, and so on.

Founded by Russian aristocrats, Rejans (reh-zhahn)—named for Le Régence Restaurant in Paris—retained the caviar-and-vodka trappings of that era for decades to come. The owners were proud of the restaurant's heritage and were eager to share stories of famous patrons, including Atatürk, founder of the Republic. During World War II, German ambassador Franz von Papen dined here frequently. Since Turkey was neutral, Istanbul became a hotbed for under-the-table negotiations and espionage—a Turkish Casablanca. And Rejans was a part of the action.

While some Turks think President İsmet İnönü should have entered World War II to regain territory lost in World War I, today most historians agree that his decision to stay neutral helped spare Istanbul (and the rest of the country) from the devastation that swept across Europe.

• *The alley named Olivya Geçidi Sokak leads back to İstiklal Street. It's lined with people sucking big water pipes* (nargile) *at the Sefa Nargile Café (at #1B, daily 10:00-24:00). (For more on trying out a water pipe, see the Experiences chapter.)*

St. Anthony's Roman Catholic Church (between #167 and #173)

Remember that even back in Roman times, today's New District was the place where Western-oriented minorities settled. Franciscan priests built a church here in the 13th century. That church became known as the Hagia Sophia of the Roman Catholic minority in Constantinople (which was then mostly Eastern Orthodox). After that church burned down in the late 17th century, the Franciscans chose to rebuild on this site. The current Neo-Gothic building, with a particularly impressive facade, dates from 1912. St. Anthony's still serves an active Roman Catholic congregation with weekly Mass, and the Christmas service here has become a major social event in

Istanbul, attended by Turkey's jet set (even many Muslims). If the church is open, feel free to take a quick trip west by popping inside.

• *Now's a good time to side-trip to the worthwhile* **Pera Museum** *to see its displays of Kütahya tiles, Oriental paintings, and ancient weights and measures (described on page 48). To reach the museum, take the pedestrian lane under the tall, brown Odakule office building. The museum is on the left corner at the end of the passage.*

Fans of Agatha Christie or opulent hotels may want to visit the historic Pera Palas Hotel (see page 49), down the street from the Pera Museum (see map in this chapter). When you're done with the museum and hotel, backtrack to İstiklal Street to continue our walk.

Istanbul Bookstore (at #146)

This bookstore, specializing in books on Istanbul (many in English), is owned and operated by the Greater Istanbul Municipality. You're welcome to grab a chair and flip through some of its delightful titles (open daily 9:00-20:00).

Dutch Consulate (#197) and
Union Church of Istanbul

Behind this consulate is the Union Church of Istanbul, which holds English services each Sunday (walk a half-block down Postacılar Sokak, entry on left). The Union Church of Istanbul was founded by American missionaries from the Congregational Church in the 1830s. Soon after, the Dutch ambassador invited the congregation to build a permanent home on the embassy grounds. In the years since, the church has attracted many English-speaking, Protestant worshippers. Unfortunately, the chapel's interior is generally closed except for Sunday services: at 9:30 (contemporary worship in English), at 11:00 (traditional worship in English), and at 13:30 (in both English and Turkish; tel. 0212/244-5212, www.ucistanbul. org).

Paşabahçe Glass Store (at #150,
across from Dutch Consulate)

Browse here for fine handmade Ottoman-style glassware in the Beykoz and Çeşm-i Bülbül styles. Beykoz glassware is made of transparent or opalescent glass with painted and cut designs, often with gold accents. Çeşm-i Bülbül (also known as "eye of the nightingale") bowls and vases have swirling blue-and-white strips twisted within clear crystal. Paşabahçe is famous for producing fine, traditional Turkish-Ottoman glassware, along with more casual daily ware. For locals, a piece from this store is considered a prestigious treasure. Paşabahçe is owned by Turkey's largest bank, Türkiye İş Bankası (whose largest shareholder is the People's Republic Party, founded by Atatürk).

• *Continue walking down İstiklal Street. Just past the Swedish Consulate, the tracks for the Nostalgic Tram bend to the right and arrive at its final stop, marking the end of this walk. It also marks the top of the funicular called...*

Tünel

To Istanbul natives, "Tünel" (tew-nehl) refers both to this neighborhood (at the bottom point of İstiklal Street) and to the underground funicular that goes from here to the bank of the Golden Horn, below. Look for the entrance to the Tünel funicular at the terminus of the Nostalgic Tram.

In the 19th century, as the Golden Horn became Istanbul's bustling commercial hub, it became clear that the narrow alley connecting İstiklal Street to the waterway below was too narrow to transport the increasing volume of goods and people. When French engineer Henri Gavand visited and saw 50,000 people walking or riding their horses up and down this hill each day, he decided there must be a better way. Funded by the British government, and

NEW DISTRICT

approved by the sultan, Gavand spent four years building a tunnel for an underground funicular.

When finished in 1875, Tünel became the second subterranean people-mover in the world (after London's Tube). The roofless cars were lit by gas lamps and had no seats, so passengers had to stand. At first the public was uncomfortable traveling underground, so most of the cars carried goods and livestock. But ultimately the efficiency and ease of the Tünel trip won out. (Locals still use this old-fashioned underground funicular to get between İstiklal Street and Karaköy, a few blocks down the hill, near the Galata Bridge on the Golden Horn.)

Opposite the Tünel terminus, Tünel Pasajı (passage) is a fun place to celebrate the end of your walk with a drink. Enjoy the festive, cozy atmosphere.

• From here, you have several options. You can ride the Tünel funicular down to the Galata Bridge and Karaköy (4 TL for single ride, covered by transit passes, explained in sidebar on page 26). From Karaköy, you can catch the main tram line, which connects to the Old Town (Sultanahmet stop) and beyond.

Or skip the funicular, and stroll the colorful streets leading downhill to the Galata Bridge—the left fork (Galip Dede Sokak) goes down to the Galata Dervish Monastery (see page 352) and the Galata Tower (described in the Sights chapter), then steeply downhill to the Galata Bridge.

Or catch a taxi to your next destination (a taxi stand is just beyond the Nostalgic Tram terminus).

Or you can ride the romantic Nostalgic Tram back to Taksim Square, along the same street you just explored. The tram runs every 5-10 minutes daily 7:30-22:45.

CHORA
CHURCH TOUR

Kariye Müzesi

Certain art forms are indelibly associated with a specific place, time, or civilization. The trademark art form of the Byzantines is the wall mosaic, and this tiny, underrated museum—hiding out on the edge of town—is home to some of the best examples of late-period Byzantine mosaics anywhere. Mosaic art existed in this region a thousand years before Christ, but originally was found only in floors. It was the Byzantines who refined the technique, used lighter material with better plaster, and mastered the application of mosaics to walls and ceilings. The mosaics in the Chora Church are among the most beautiful surviving examples of this classic Byzantine art form. The formal name of the church is St. Savior in Chora, but most locals know it by its Turkish names, Kariye Müzesi or Kariye Camii.

Note that parts of the church are being renovated. While it remains open to visitors, various areas will be unavailable for viewing as the work progresses.

Orientation

Cost: 15 TL.

Hours: Late March-late Oct Thu-Tue 9:00-19:00, off-season until 16:30, closed Wed, last entry one hour before closing.

Getting There: The church is just inside Istanbul's old city walls, about four miles northwest of the historic core, in a district called Edirnekapı (eh-deer-neh-kah-puh). The church is on a little square, facing a big café with outdoor tables and lots of souvenir stands. It's easiest to get there by **taxi** (about 20-25 TL each way from the Sultanahmet area).

You can also reach the church efficiently by **bus.** From Taksim Square in the New District, bus #87 takes you right there (4-5/hour, bus stops under Taksim Square—take escalator down at the corner of Gezi Park; it's at north end of square, across from Marmara Hotel, behind Metro entrance). From the Old Town, take the tram to the Eminönü stop, near the Galata Bridge, then go beyond the bridge to catch bus #32 (Eminönü-Cevatpaşa) or #910 (Eminönü-Otogar) beneath the yellow signs directly across from the Spice Market. Buses #37E and #38 also link Eminönü to the church's neighborhood.

Get off at the Edirnekapı stop (it's just after the huge, sunken stadium and right before the big fragment of the city wall). At Edirnekapı, face the city wall: The church is down the hill to your right (follow signs for *Kariye Oteli,* a hotel right next to the church, and look for the old dome with the simple minaret).

A third option is **tram and light rail** (which makes sense from Sultanahmet, but less so from the New District, unless you're near the tram line): Ride the tram to the Topkapı stop (nowhere near Topkapı Palace; direction: Zeytinburnu), then transfer to light rail and ride three stops to Edirnekapı (direction: Habibler). This leaves you outside the old city walls, but within walking distance of the church: Facing the walls, head left and cross the highway at the traffic light. Continue to a second traffic light behind the wall and cross Fevzipaşa Street. Take the first left (Vaiz Sokak, just past the bus stop) and then the third right (Kariye Camii Sokak) to reach the church.

Information: A small bookstore is inside the church building. Museum tel. 0212/631-9241, http://kariye.muze.gov.tr/en.

Length of This Tour: Allow one hour.

Services: Free WCs are on the left down the stairs just after you buy your ticket, but before you pass through the turnstile.

Photography: Photography is permitted, but no flash or tripods.

Eating: Basic tourist restaurants, cafés, and souvenir stands line the leafy square in front of the church. For better (and more expensive) cuisine, consider the **Asitane** restaurant, in the Kariye Hotel next to the church.

Nearby: Consider combining your visit to the Chora Church with a walk along the nearby city walls (described in the next chapter). If you're short on time, it's worth at least climbing the walls for the view (described at the beginning of the next chapter's tour).

Starring: Thousands upon thousands of glittering little tiles, plus several walls and ceilings slathered with vivid frescoes, all from about 1300.

CHORA CHURCH

Chora vs. Ravenna

Visitors tend to compare the mosaics at the Chora Church with the mosaics in the Basilica of San Vitale in Ravenna, Italy (near Venice). But they were completed in very different historical periods.

Ravenna's sixth-century mosaics were commissioned by Emperor Justinian. The basilica was an imperial project intended to show off the emperor's power and wealth. It was a gigantic self-made shrine, and Justinian spent a great deal of money from the royal treasury to bring it to completion.

The Chora's mosaics are from a much later date (14th century) and were commissioned by the wealthy Byzantine

bureaucrat Theodore Metochites. Instead of showing emperors and empresses standing proudly next to holy figures, as at Ravenna's basilica, the Chora's donors are generally portrayed as being more humble and vulnerable. The mosaics' style, use of light, and perspective are also different. Compared with the classical Byzantine mosaics at Ravenna, the newer Chora mosaics show a better sense of 3-D perspective, with more realism, action, and emotion.

While Justinian's reign marked the heyday of the Byzantine Empire, by the time Metochites was decorating the Chora Church, the empire was approaching its final days. The Black Death had killed hundreds of thousands. To the west, the Serbs were a serious threat, while to the east the Turks were at Constantinople's gates. Amid this chaos, the Chora's artists managed to produce works that are glorious in every respect, with mosaics that shine brighter than the troubled era of their creation.

BACKGROUND

The Chora Church can be crowded inside, and you'll be craning your neck to see all of its little details. Read the information in this chapter before you arrive, or at the small café across the square from the church.

Locals call this church Kariye (kah-ree-yeh)—the Arabic interpretation of the Greek word *chora*, which means "territory" or "land." When a church was first built here in the fourth century, it was outside Constantine the Great's city wall. A century later, the walls were enlarged, and the church was folded within the city limits. But the name "Chora" stuck, likely because the word had other meanings and interpretations. In Byzantine religious literature, Mary herself is often referred to as "Chora," in the same sense as an uncultivated field—in other words, a virgin. When she became pregnant with Jesus, Mary (or the "Chora") became "a container for the uncontainable." Greek inscriptions in the church refer to this, as in *"He chora ton zon ton"* ("the house of the living") and *"He chora tou achoretou"* ("the house of the uncontainable"—the One that cannot be kept within boundaries, a.k.a. Jesus Christ).

The current church—built after an earthquake damaged the original—dates back to about 1100. Then the church was damaged by Crusaders in the 1200s.

In the early 1300s, the Byzantine prime minister Theodore Metochites was selected as Chora's patron, and he oversaw the church's reconstruction. It was the first time someone other than a royal was honored with the title of patron for an imperial monastery. Metochites was powerful and rich, and he invested generously in the project, commissioning the sumptuous mosaics that attract tourists today (see sidebar on Metochites).

In the early 16th century, 60 years after the Ottomans took Constantinople, the church was converted into a mosque. A mihrab (prayer niche) was built off-center in the main apse (to face Mecca), and the bell tower was replaced with the minaret you see today. The frescoes and mosaics were whitewashed over and remained hidden from daylight until the late 1940s, when they were rediscovered and restored.

Artistically, the Chora Church's decorations represent a set of early and very influential models for depicting Christian figures and events. After the Church split between east and west (Eastern Orthodox and Roman Catholic) in the 11th century, western Christians wriggled free of Roman rule. Western churches became provincial, focused on their own local customs and saints—causing church art to splinter into many different, idiosyncratic visions. Meanwhile, the Eastern Orthodox Church remained consolidated under the stable and wealthy Byzantine Empire. Church power was centralized, so artistic decisions made in Constantinople filtered down to churches throughout the Eastern Orthodox world, bringing a great consistency to medieval Eastern Orthodox church art. For example, an artist's depiction of Mary, Joseph, and Baby Jesus at the Nativity here became the norm for church art throughout the realm. Lacking a similarly coherent Western Christian artistic tradition, artists across the generations have embraced these

Theodore Metochites

You're here today because of Theodore Metochites, the man who commissioned these mosaics. Metochites was born in Constantinople in 1270, a few years after the city was taken back from the Crusaders. His father supported the unification of the Eastern Orthodox and Roman Catholic churches—a view that earned the family exile in Nicaea (the present-day Turkish city of İznik, south of Constantinople). Metochites' parents tried to steer him away from politics, encouraging their son to devote his life to science. But politics was in his blood. By the time he reached his 20s, Metochites was writing essays and critiques.

His work came to the attention of Emperor Andronicus II, who invited Metochites to serve in the palace in Constantinople. He got his start arranging political marriages for royal family members—including a wedding between the emperor's five-year-old daughter and a middle-aged Serbian king. In the early 1300s, Metochites became treasurer, and then prime minister. Anyone who wanted access to the emperor had to see Metochites first. He acquired land and wealth, but wasn't the most effective bureaucrat. Decorating the Chora Church distracted him from the Italian merchants who were becoming superior in naval trade.

As the Ottoman Turks became a clear threat to the empire, panic and chaos led to civil war between Andronicus II and his grandson Andronicus III. The grandson won, and in 1328 Metochites lost his protector. A mob burned his palace, his wealth was confiscated, and Metochites was exiled. Metochites was eventually allowed to return to Constantinople, where he entered Chora's monastery, took the name Theoleptos, and died in 1332.

Eastern Orthodox archetypes. The artistic vision realized here in Chora eventually trickled down to decorations in today's Christian churches in Italy, Indonesia, and Iowa.

OVERVIEW

Theodore Metochites said of Chora Church, "The mosaics and frescoes in the church show how God became a mortal on behalf of human beings." On this tour, we'll concentrate on important events in the lives of Jesus and Mary, to whom the church and its monastery, respectively, were dedicated.

The decoration in the church is meant to transform Eastern Orthodox liturgy into reality. Standing before these images of

Christ, the Virgin, and the saints, the believer feels present with them at that very moment and place. A pilgrimage to the Holy Land has never been a priority for Orthodox Christians, because the neighborhood church brings the Holy Land to them.

The church contains some images of holy figures and biblical stories that seem unconventional to Western eyes. They are drawn from apocryphal writings—versions of scripture that are not part of the Hebrew Bible.

The layout of the church is fairly straightforward. The main part is a single nave, facing east (like all European Christian churches of the time). Behind the nave are two narthexes: inner and outer. These narthexes hold most of the mosaics. Running next to the nave is a long corridor called a *parekklesion*, or side chapel. This section is decorated with frescoes, not mosaics.

While the church can be confusing, if you use the map intelligently, everything is easy to find.

Give your neck a good stretch before you begin—most of what there is to see is a few feet above eye level. You'll be whirling like a dervish trying to see all the details. To make things easier, we'll focus on the most interesting or important scenes—explaining some Bible stories out of order and skipping lesser figures and events, such as Church fathers, no-name angels, and so on.

The Tour Begins

• *The "front" door of the church you see from the square is used as the tourist exit today. The ticket booth is around the left side of the church: Go through the gate, buy your ticket, pass through the turnstile, and circle the church until you reach the entry. As you walk, notice the giant buttress at the back of the church. This originally held up the church...but now, due to settling over time, the church supports the buttress.*

Orientation Walk

The interior visit has four parts—outer narthex, inner narthex, central nave, and *parekklesion*. The art tells a story that unfolds as the worshipper enters the building, so we'll view it as a Christian would have during Byzantine times (and with the same mind-set). Begin your survey by the current exit door in the outer narthex (refer to map).

Take a quick walk around to understand the general structure of the church before studying its many mosaics: The **outer narthex** tells the story of Jesus—from his conception and childhood through his baptism as an adult. Behind you (above the exit door) is a mosaic with Jesus in Mary's womb. A mosaic above the door leading toward the nave and altar shows Jesus, finished with childhood—and now an adult creator—ready to work.

Walking into the next chamber, the **inner narthex,** you encounter art that teaches the delicate balance between Jesus (on the right, curing the sick and working miracles) and Mary (on the left, with scenes from her life).

Stepping into the **nave,** you enter a place of worship that functioned as a mosque for 500 years. The centuries-old Christian altar was replaced by the Islamic prayer niche, or mihrab. Notice that the mihrab is made with marble cut from the same quarry to match the exquisite original walls of the much older interior. Rather than destroy the Christian frescoes and mosaics, the Muslim Ottomans covered them over with whitewash.

The last part of your visit is the *parekklesion* (to the right of the nave), a chapel for important tombs and decorated with frescoes.

Now, return to the outer narthex and study some of the Bible scenes depicted in the fine mosaic art. (Use the map with keyed numbers to locate each scene.)

Outer Narthex

❶ **Incarnation of Jesus Christ:** Here the Virgin Mary holds the divine Baby Jesus in her womb. She is the Chora, the dwelling place of the uncontainable. The placement of this scene—just above the door to the outside—is interesting. It's likely that when the panel was made, you could see the walls of Constantinople through this door. When the city was in danger, the people would bring icons of Mary to the walls to protect the city. Perhaps this panel was part of that tradition.

❷ **Joseph Dreaming:** In Joseph's dream, the angel explains Mary's pregnancy to him. Behind him are the Virgin and a companion.

❸ **Journey to Bethlehem:** Mary is seated on a donkey; in front of her is Joseph's son (not Jesus—explained later). Joseph walks at the back, trying to catch up. The city behind the hill is Nazareth.

❹ **Enrollment for Taxation:** The governor of Syria is seated upon a throne, wearing the outfit and hat of Byzantine's high government officials. He likely represents Theodore Metochites, who served as a tax collector on his way to becoming prime minister. At the center, another official holds an unrolled scroll. On the right is pregnant Mary, her tunic stretching to contain her belly. Joseph is behind her.

❺ **Nativity:** This representation of the birth of Jesus Christ is typically Byzantine, with all the events related to Jesus' birth shown next to one another. Notice the stable, animals, Joseph in deep thought, Mary resting, and maids bathing the newborn Christ.

❻ **John the Baptist Bearing Witness of Christ:** John talks with a group of priests and Levites and gestures toward Christ.

CHORA CHURCH

Chora Church Museum

↑ To Edirnekapı
Bus Stop

ENTRANCE ➡ - - - - - - -

EXIT
←

TOUR
BEGINS

INNER NARTHEX

OUTER NARTHEX

PAREKKLESION

BOOKSTORE

CHORA CHURCH

1. Incarnation of Jesus Christ
2. Joseph Dreaming
3. Journey to Bethlehem
4. Enrollment for Taxation
5. Nativity
6. John the Baptist Bearing Witness of Christ
7. Temptation of Christ
8. Miracle of Cana
9. Multiplication of the Loaves
10. Journey of the Magi
11. Magi Before Herod
12. Massacre of the Innocents
13. Mothers Mourning for Their Children
14. Ancestors of Mary
15. Annunciation to St. Anne
16. Annunciation to Mary at the Well
17. Joseph Taking Mary to His House
18. Birth of Mary
19. Mary Entrusted to Joseph
20. St. Peter
21. St. Paul
22. Dedication Panel
23. Presentation of Mary to the Temple
24. Deesis Mosaic
25. Biblical Genealogy of Christ

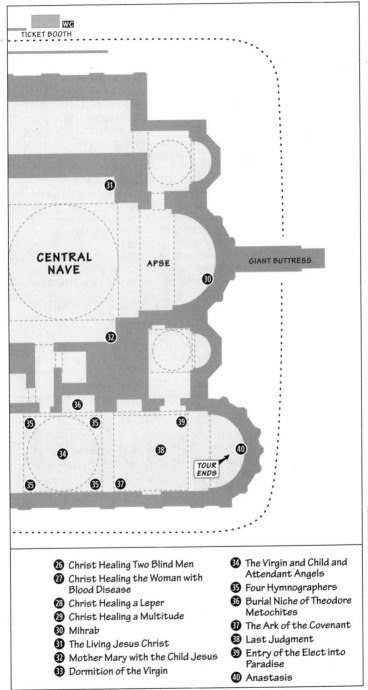

26 Christ Healing Two Blind Men
27 Christ Healing the Woman with Blood Disease
28 Christ Healing a Leper
29 Christ Healing a Multitude
30 Mihrab
31 The Living Jesus Christ
32 Mother Mary with the Child Jesus
33 Dormition of the Virgin
34 The Virgin and Child and Attendant Angels
35 Four Hymnographers
36 Burial Niche of Theodore Metochites
37 The Ark of the Covenant
38 Last Judgment
39 Entry of the Elect into Paradise
40 Anastasis

Mosaics 101

Mosaic art was expensive and time-consuming, which is why it's generally seen only in royal residences or churches decorated by

wealthy patrons. Mosaicists usually worked in groups, like a small union or guild. The most experienced—the master—was usually the leader. A metropolis like Constantinople supported several competing mosaicist groups.

Mosaics are made of tiny pieces of glass or other materials (tesserae) stuck to moist plaster to create a larger image. It took about three years to complete the mosaics in the Chora Church. The Chora's art was ahead of its time, and in a way anticipated the Renaissance: art for the sake of religion, but without neglecting aesthetics. You'll notice an attempt to create emotive faces, moving bodies, and realistic perspective. The Chora Church was often used after sunset, lit by candles and oil lamps. Imagine the flickering light sweeping across the walls, each tile glittering in turn.

Feeling inspired? Here's a recipe for your own Byzantine mosaic:

1. Prepare a blueprint. Mosaics require detailed planning.
2. Gather the mosaic pieces. Common materials include glass, stone, marble, and brick. Gold and silver tesserae are not solid metal, but a thin layer of metal sandwiched between two

The fiery-eyed Baptist is dressed in his usual animal-skin outfit and sports the long beard of a hermit.

❼ Temptation of Christ: The story of the temptation of Christ is told in four scenes arranged in a semicircle in the vault, with the Devil represented as a dark, ugly winged creature appearing four times. In the first section, the Devil appears above a box full of stones, asking Jesus to turn them into bread. Next, the Devil offers Jesus the world's many kingdoms (the tiny kings with crowns make the place look like Legoland). In the third scene, we see Jesus on a hill, overlooking the kingdoms. In the last scene, Jesus stands on a tower, as the Devil asks him to prove his divinity by jumping down without hurting himself.

❽ Miracle of Cana: Here we see Jesus turning water into wine at a wedding party. Jesus is holding a small scroll with the Virgin Mary behind him. A servant is pouring water into one of five huge jars. Notice that the jar mosaics are made of terra-cotta—the same material the actual jars would have been made of.

❾ Multiplication of the Loaves: By blessing five loaves of

glass pieces. A very thin, pink marble can represent the color of human flesh.

3. Stud the walls at random with nails, leaving about one inch of the nail exposed. This helps the plaster adhere to the wall. (Make sure you don't use iron nails—in the past, rusting iron nails ruined many mosaics when they expanded and forced chunks of plaster to crack and fall from the wall.)

4. Apply three layers of plaster, up to two inches thick. The first layer—made of crushed lime and straw—should cover the entire work surface, and then be scored so the next layer will adhere better. When the first layer is completely dry, apply a second layer of more finely crushed lime and straw pieces. While the second layer is still damp, apply the third and finest layer of plaster, of crushed lime and marble dust.

5. Transfer your blueprint to the plaster in the form of a rough painting. This will serve as your guide. (Often, the underlying blueprint can be seen in older mosaics where pieces have fallen out.)

6. Begin by applying smaller pieces to define the contours of your mosaic design, then fill in the rest with the bigger pieces. The frame, hands, feet, face, and hair require the most skill and are traditionally completed first by the master mosaicist. Then the other mosaicists fill in what's left. Place your pieces at different angles to capture the light.

7. Stand back and enjoy.

bread, Christ feeds a multitude. Jesus is seen behind three big baskets of bread, giving pieces of bread to his disciples, who pass them to the crowd. If you follow the vault to the right, you'll see the happy conclusion: After everyone was fed, the remaining bread filled 12 large baskets.

❿ Journey of the Magi: Three wise men on horseback—Melchior, Balthasar, and Caspar—follow the star to find the newborn Christ Child.

⓫ Magi Before Herod: The wise men offer their gifts to Herod, who sits on a throne.

⓬ Massacre of the Innocents: Herod orders the murder of all young male children, in an effort to find and kill the baby Jesus. The flying cloaks imply motion and action.

⓭ Mothers Mourning for Their Children: Grief-stricken mothers cradle the bodies of their brutally slain children. Above the next window to the right you see Elizabeth and her baby, John the Baptist, hiding safely in a cave.

Inner Narthex

⓮ Ancestors of Mary: At the center of the dome, in the medallion, is Mary with the baby Jesus. Notice the two figures in each section between the ribs. The upper figures are the genealogical ancestors of Mary and Jesus, starting with King David; the lower figures are ancestors outside the official lineage.

⓯ Annunciation to St. Anne: St. Anne, the mother of Mary, wears a long, red scarf over a blue garment and a red shawl that falls down to her knees. Above the fancy fountain before her is a flying angel giving the good news that she will bear a daughter.

⓰ Annunciation to Mary at the Well: Now it's Mary's turn. Mary is dressed in a blue tunic and holds a golden pitcher. She's surprised by the angel approaching her, who tells her she will give birth to the Christ Child.

⓱ Joseph Taking Mary to His House: A young and helpless-looking Mary follows her new husband. In front of them is Joseph's son. While this figure may be surprising to Roman Catholics, Eastern Orthodox tradition—based on the apocryphal Gospel of St. James—holds that Joseph was a widower with several children when he wed Mary. Joseph seems a little confused, too—which way is he walking?

⓲ Birth of Mary: The newborn, naked baby Mary is held by a midwife as a maid prepares a bath. Another maid fans St. Anne while attending women present gifts.

⓳ Mary Entrusted to Joseph: On the left side, the local priest Zechariah is behind young Mary, his hand protectively on her head as he presents her to Joseph. Other suitors stand to the side.

⓴ St. Peter and **㉑ St. Paul:** St. Peter is on the left side of the door, holding the keys to heaven. On the right side is bald and wrinkled St. Paul, holding the codex of Epistles in his left hand (the wrinkles on Paul's broad brow are said to represent his intellect). The Byzantines often decorated either side of a church's nave door with the twin figures of St. Peter and St. Paul—fathers of the early Christian Church.

㉒ Dedication Panel: The enthroned Jesus Christ is at the center, holding the Bible and making the sign of the Trinity. On his right side, squeezed in the corner, is church patron Theodore Metochites, offering Jesus a model of the church (a common Byzantine way to represent a donation). Metochites wears a fancy garment and a big hat reminiscent of a Turkish turban—both are symbolic of his status.

㉓ Presentation of Mary to the Temple: Mary's parents enthusiastically urge their daughter to go to the priest—Zechariah,

Mary Rules the Orthodox World

Christianity has always proved remarkably adaptable to local traditions. From the Christmas tree to the Easter egg, many

"Christian" traditions actually have pagan roots. It was no different in Anatolia (Turkey), where the long tradition of a female "mother-goddess" figure provided a convenient foundation for Mary.

Turkey has a long history of reverence for female deities. The idea of a mother-goddess originated in Anatolia (likely in the early sixth millennium B.C.), and her popularity spread to encompass virtually all of Mediterranean Europe, western Asia, and North Africa. No matter what she was called or how she looked, the mother-goddess always displayed the maternal qualities of fertility and nurture. She also possessed miraculous gifts. For example, the Phrygian goddess Cybele was a figure of power and protection. Often, a mother-goddess figure would give birth to a deity. Leto was impregnated by the Greek god Zeus and gave birth to the twins Apollo and Artemis—both highly revered as gods. The mother-goddess Aphrodite (Venus) was born pregnant with her child, Eros, the god of love.

By the time Christianity arrived, the stage was set for a powerful mother-goddess figure, and Mary easily took her place in the pantheon. Like so many mother-goddesses before her, Mary is looked to for comfort and healing in times of trial. As the "container of the uncontainable," she gave birth to the son of God, Jesus Christ. And according to Christian tradition, when she completed her earthly life, she was transported ("assumed") body and soul directly to heaven, as no other mere mortal has been.

father of John the Baptist—who welcomes the Virgin. Behind them, in a separate scene, we see Mary receiving holy bread from an angel.

❷❹ Deesis Mosaic: In Greek Orthodox churches, a *deesis* mosaic such as this one would traditionally show Christ flanked by both Mary and John the Baptist, interceding on behalf of sinners. But John must have been late for his Chora Church sitting, because he's not depicted here. Instead, behind Jesus and Mary are two small figures representing church donors. Mary is asking Jesus to forgive their sins. The woman kneeling before Christ is Melanie, the illegitimate daughter of a Byzantine emperor (the head below Mary) who married a Mongolian king. After the king died, she came back to Constantinople and lived as a nun.

❷❺ Biblical Genealogy of Christ: In the center, Jesus Christ—

in the usual pose—holds the Bible in one hand and makes the sign of the Trinity with the other. In the flutes of the dome are Christ's Old Testament ancestors. Though most of us can't read the Greek names, many of the figures come with attributes that help to identify them. The cycle starts in the upper level with Adam, standing on a snake (he's the one with a long white beard under Jesus' left hand).

If your neck isn't killing you, spend some time here and try to identify other familiar figures—such as Noah carrying an ark. Hmm...a vessel for holding precious life...yet another metaphor for the Virgin. Nearby, many of Christ's miracles are depicted: ㉖ **Christ Healing Two Blind Men;** ㉗ **Christ Healing the Woman with Blood Disease;** ㉘ **Christ Healing a Leper;** and ㉙ **Christ Healing a Multitude.**

Nave

This square, domed room is the oldest section of the building, probably dating from around 1100. Straight ahead is the main apse—the holiest section of the church, where the altar once stood.

• *The marble niche a little to the right of center is the...*

㉚ **Mihrab:** This was added by the Muslim Ottomans when this church became a mosque. Representing a symbolic doorway leading to the holy city of Mecca, the mihrab shows Muslims the correct direction in which to pray.

• *Two mosaics in the central nave use the word "Chora" to describe Jesus and Mary. On the left side of the wall, before the apse, is a framed mosaic depiction of...*

㉛ **The Living Jesus Christ:** The inscription originally read "Dwelling-place (Chora) of the Living."

• *On the right wall before the apse is...*

㉜ **Mother Mary with the Child Jesus:** The inscription originally read "Dwelling-place (Chora) of the Uncontainable." (The mosaic lettering HXOPA spells "Chora.")

• *Turn around and look above the door where you entered. This is one of the church's most impressive panels, the...*

㉝ **Dormition of the Virgin:** Byzantine Christians struggled with the theological issue of who Mary was. In the early fifth century, the Church declared her the "Mother of God." This was actually good marketing, as Anatolians were already comfortable with goddesses (see sidebar, earlier).

Whether Mary died at the end of her life, or fell asleep (which "dormition" seems to imply), is debated among theologians. But

either way, she passed from this life (or was "assumed") into heaven. August 15 is celebrated as the feast of the Assumption of Mary by both the Eastern Orthodox and Roman Catholic worlds.

Mary is shown here on her last earthly bed. The scene is made of very small mosaic pieces, allowing the artists to show palpable emotion in the faces of the apostles and other mourners around her deathbed. Behind her, in a large heavenly halo, is Jesus Christ. He holds the innocent soul of Mary, in the form of a baby. Angels appear in the outer ring of the halo. To the left of the bed, St. Peter swings an incense burner, while on the right, St. Paul bends toward the bed in sorrow.

A gray bubble is taking her soul to heaven. Follow this: In heaven Mary has morphed into a baby (as a child of God). Since God and Jesus are one, baby Mary is the mother of Jesus...or God. It's beyond us. But the point is that she made it to heaven, where she's a busy part of God's administration in both the Eastern Orthodox and Roman Catholic churches to this day.

Take a few moments in the nave to study the marble, and notice the slender recycled pieces in the panels placed higher on the walls—these were columns before being cut into panels.

Parekklesion

This side chapel, which functioned as a mortuary chamber for Theodore Metochites and his family, is decorated entirely with frescoes. A fresco is painting applied to wet plaster, which provides a smooth surface for the artist. The plaster absorbs and preserves the pigment, making frescoes more durable than regular wall paintings.

Most of the frescoes on the *parekklesion* walls deal with the afterlife and

The Marble of Marmara

Most of the marble used in the Chora Church came from Marmara Island, which is in Turkey's Sea of Marmara. (In fact, *marmara* means "marble" in Greek.) But some of the marble was recycled from buildings in Italy, Greece, and North Africa. These pieces were cut again before being reused.

Most of the marble panels in the building are slices of stone, cut in half and placed next to one another. The workmanship involved in cutting marble was as painstaking as the workmanship of the mosaics. Only a couple of inches of marble could be cut each day, using a smooth piece of metal that—combined with sand—was used as a saw.

Notice the marble slabs of the nave's upper level. These tall, slender, recycled pieces were formed from columns cut into slices.

The marble lintels above the church's doors and door frames, and most of the column capitals, were recycled as well. The marble arches decorating the *parekklesion* are the best examples of stone carving from the late Byzantine period.

Whether recycled or newly quarried, Chora's marble decorations fit harmoniously with the rest of the structure. Originally, many of the marble works were painted or glazed with gold. The small holes and niches in the marble (which you'll see throughout the church) once held icons, crosses, lamps, and holy relics.

salvation—appropriate themes for a burial chamber. Unlike most other Byzantine churches, here the dead were not interred in the ground, but instead were laid to rest in the now-empty niches in the chapel walls.

• *Again, referring to the map, you'll see the following scenes:*

❸❹ The Virgin and Child and Attendant Angels: Mary is depicted here as the Queen of Heaven, dressed in her usual blue tunic, now decorated with gold. This is another ribbed dome, made more impressive by the light from windows at its base. Within the dome's sections are winged angels worshipping Mary and Christ. The angels wear clothing typical of Byzantine officials.

❸❺ Four Hymnographers: These four serious-looking Byzantines are poets who were renowned for their verses in Mary's honor: John of Damascus, in the northeast corner wearing a turban; Kosmas the Poet, in the southeast corner with a blank book in his lap; Joseph the Poet, in the southwest corner holding a scroll;

and Theophanes Graptos, in the northwest corner, where he's writing verses.

③⑥ Burial Niche of Theodore Metochites: The largest of all the chapel's burial niches, this probably belonged to Theodore Metochites. Most of its decorations were lost over the ages, although the inscriptions and decorations in some of Chora's other burial niches are among the best sources of information about the lives of 14th-century Byzantine aristocrats.

③⑦ The Ark of the Covenant: Men are carrying something that looks like a coffin. This is the Ark of the Covenant being taken to Solomon's Temple. This ark, like Noah's ark, is a metaphor for the Virgin Mary: All three contain the treasures of God.

• *Look above the vault to see the most impressive fresco in the church, the...*

③⑧ Last Judgment: This colorful fresco depicts scenes from the Book of Revelations: Christ's victory over death and the sal-

vation of the righteous. Jesus sits on a glorious throne in the center, flanked by the Virgin Mary and John the Baptist. The 12 apostles, holding books, are seated at either side. Behind them are groups of angels. The white shell-like object held aloft by an angel represents the sky at the end of time. All around the vault are choirs of the chosen, floating in clouds.

Below this triumphant scene is the dramatic Weighing of the Souls. Christ's right palm is turned up, showing the lucky bunch who will go to heaven. His left hand is turned down and points toward the condemned (the ultimate "thumbs up" or "thumbs down"), as does the river of fire flowing from his left foot.

Notice the stigmata (marks of Crucifixion) on Jesus' hands. Try to imagine his gold-colored robe and the halo behind his head as they once appeared, covered in sheets of gold (some of the gold still remains in his halo).

Beneath Jesus are the figures of Adam and Eve on their knees. Farther down, you can see a scale. Naked bodies on the right are the souls awaiting judgment. At the center, another naked soul trembles while he is judged. Barely visible is a little demon, craftily trying to pull down the scale. Look closely at the river of fire to see ugly little demons giving the condemned a helpful push.

③⑨ Entry of the Elect into Paradise: A cherub with closed wings protects the entrance into heaven. On the left, St. Peter unlocks the door. The Good Thief—carrying a cross—greets the chosen and points toward the Virgin Mary on her throne.

⓵ Anastasis: This fresco depicts the standard Byzantine representation of the Resurrection, when Christ descends into hell to save the righteous people of the Old Testament. You can see Jesus (like a biblical Rambo) pulling Adam and Eve by their arms out of their coffins. Under Jesus' feet are the broken gates of hell, scattered keys, and Satan, bound and powerless.

• *With that promising image, this tour is over. Congratulations. Give yourself a well-deserved rest and neck rub. From here you might explore the city walls and the colorful Lonca, Balat, and Fener neighborhoods (see next chapter), or catch a taxi to the most conservative religious scene in town at the Eyüp Sultan Mosque (see page 59).*

CITY WALLS AND NEIGHBORHOODS WALK

City Walls • Lonca, Balat & Fener
Neighborhoods

The Walls of Constantinople rank among the most impressive city walls in the world. Istanbul was born on this peninsula, flanked by the waters of the Golden Horn and the Bosphorus, in part because it was so easy to fortify: Simply build a wall across the narrow thumb of land. The first wall was built by Greek settlers. Constantine the Great's version was replaced by Theodosius II (ruled A.D. 408-450), who expanded the wall to encompass a greater area, creating the mightiest city wall anywhere in medieval Europe. In total, the land and sea walls stretched 13 miles around the city and remained a virtually impenetrable fortification for more than 1,000 years. These massive walls were breached only twice—by the Fourth Crusade in 1204 and by the Ottoman invasion in 1453.

The walls that stretch across the Old Town peninsula lie about four miles northwest of the historic core. The first half of this walk focuses on the walls and nearby sights (between the Chora Church and the Golden Horn). Then we'll cut through colorful neighborhoods as we head back toward downtown, learning more about the ethnic diversity that shaped Istanbul's past and present. As this is a conservative neighborhood, you'll see more scarves and traditional dress here.

Orientation

Length of This Walk: Allow 2.5 hours for the entire 1.5-mile walk. Figure on one hour for the first part—from the Chora Church to the Eğrikapı Gate (with an optional detour to the view outside the walls). For most people, the first part of the walk is enough. The second part, which takes 1.5 hours, goes from the Eğrikapı Gate to the Greek Orthodox Patriarchate, passing through untouristed, gritty, residential neighborhoods that might make some tourists feel a bit on edge.

You'll need to take public transit or a taxi to the starting point of the walk. Whether you do just the first part of the walk or the whole thing, you'll also need to rely on public transit or a taxi to get back to downtown Istanbul.

When to Go: The walls are best viewed by day. If you plan to visit the Chora Church (see previous chapter) before the walk, go any day except Wednesday, when the church is closed. Many travelers find the area scary and unsafe after dark.

Getting There: Start at the Chora Church (for info on how to get to the museum, see "Getting There" at the beginning of the previous chapter).

Note that the hop-on, hop-off bus runs the entire length of the city walls (see page 28); its closest stop to the start of this walk is Edirnekapı.

If you've taken a taxi to visit the Eyüp Sultan Mosque (a recommended sight outside the city walls—see page 59), it's easy to have your cabbie drop you off at the Chora Church on your way back from the mosque.

Starring: The Walls of Theodosius, Tekfur Palace (the only surviving Byzantine palace), the Dungeons of Anemas, and various religious sights (churches and synagogues and mosques, oh my).

The Walk Begins

PART 1: CHORA CHURCH TO EĞRIKAPI GATE

• *Begin at the Chora Church. With the church behind you (and the street fountain to your right), walk uphill for about 50 yards and take the first right on Kuyulu Bahçe Sokak (labeled* Şeyh Eyüp *on the left). Follow Kuyulu Bahçe as it bends left and then right. Take the narrow alley to the left to Hoca Çakır Caddesi. You are now facing the...*

Walls of Theodosius

Constantinople surrounded itself with land walls and sea walls. Because the sea itself provided natural fortification (like a giant moat), the land walls were stouter and more impressive. Built by Emperor Theodosius II, these early fifth-century walls stretch for 3.5 miles north to south, from the shores of the Golden Horn up the hill to the Edirnekapı district, and then downhill to the shoreline of the Sea of Marmara. (If you arrived at Istanbul's Atatürk Airport and drove into the city along the coastal road, you passed a portion of the land walls and bits of the sea walls.)

Fortified with 185 towers, each about 65 feet high, the Walls of Theodosius were actually two separate walls—an outer wall and a stronger inner ring, separated by a defensible no-man's land about 55 feet wide. And just outside the outer wall, a huge moat further protected the fortification.

After the Ottoman conquest, the walls fell into disrepair, as they were no longer needed for protection. While most of the inner walls are long gone, the outer walls still stand.

• *To climb the wall, face it, turn left, and walk 150 yards up Hoca Çakır Caddesi (with the wall on your right). You'll see a staircase set into the wall leading up to a platform at the top. Another staircase, slightly farther along the street, will take you up to a longer platform. Take this second staircase for a wider view (the metal gate halfway up these stairs is usually open during the day). Warning: The steep, narrow staircases have no railings, and neither do the 10-foot-wide platforms on top. Be very careful—or you'll give new meaning to "the fall of Constantinople."*

If you don't want to climb the wall, turn around and continue back down Hoca Çakır Caddesi to Tekfur Palace (see directions at the end of the following section).

View from the Wall

The view from the top is rewarding. Look out beyond the wall, with the Old Town at your back. You'll see some of Istanbul's centuries-old cemeteries—they're the patches of green on either side of the busy road (one is Muslim, and the other is Greek Orthodox). This location outside the city boundaries was a hygienic, logical place to bury the dead. Off in the distance are the Golden Horn and the Haliç Bridge with its eight busy lanes of traffic.

From the top of the wall, you have a chance to look inside what little survives of the fortified towers. Historically, there was no access between a tower's upper and lower levels: If enemy troops captured the lower section, defenders above could continue to fight.

The massive tower farther to your left (as you face away from the Old Town) was built to guard Edirnekapı (eh-deer-neh-kah-puh), the grand gate of ancient Constantinople (as well as the modern-day name for this district of Istanbul). The physical gate is long gone, with Fevzi Paşa street passing unchallenged through a large opening in the wall. But the two huge towers that once protected and flanked the gate still stand like sentinels.

Sultan Mehmet the Conqueror (Mehmet II) rode triumphantly through the gate into Constantinople in 1453, ending the Byzantine era and ushering in the Ottoman age. In Ottoman times, Edirnekapı continued as the "official

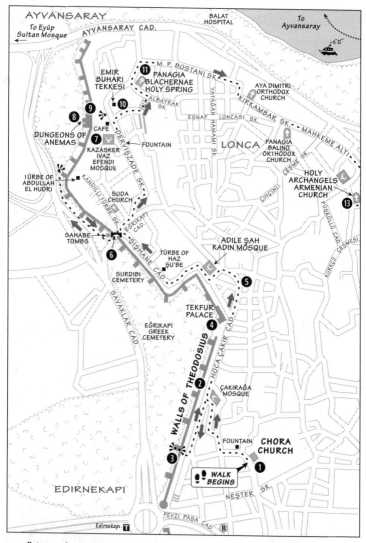

gate" into the city—and it was a busy one. Sultans left the city through this gate when visiting the Eyüp Sultan Mosque for Friday prayers. Common folk, caravans of merchants, and soldiers on the way to their posts also passed through Edirnekapı. Guarded by a squad of janissaries, the gate was locked at the end of the day.

• *Descend, retrace your steps, and continue on Hoca Çakır Caddesi roughly 100 yards. Beyond the Çakırağa Mosque on the right, watch for a wide opening in the wall. On weekends this area is a market where pigeon fanciers buy and sell "Turkish tumblers," a domesticated pigeon prized for its acrobatic, back-flipping skills. The hobby, of Mesopotamian*

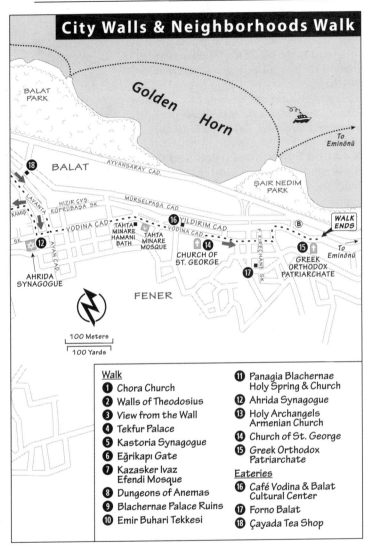

City Walls & Neighborhoods Walk

Walk
1. Chora Church
2. Walls of Theodosius
3. View from the Wall
4. Tekfur Palace
5. Kastoria Synagogue
6. Eğrikapı Gate
7. Kazasker Ivaz Efendi Mosque
8. Dungeons of Anemas
9. Blachernae Palace Ruins
10. Emir Buhari Tekkesi
11. Panagia Blachernae Holy Spring & Church
12. Ahrida Synagogue
13. Holy Archangels Armenian Church
14. Church of St. George
15. Greek Orthodox Patriarchate

Eateries
16. Café Vodina & Balat Cultural Center
17. Forno Balat
18. Çayada Tea Shop

origin, has many avid fans; prices for some birds can reach into the thousands.

Where the wall sharply bends to the left, you'll see a more recent structure—with fancy, arched windows and a balcony out front—built into the top of the wall. This is part of the...

Tekfur Palace (Tekfur Sarayı)

Tekfur Sarayı (tehk-foor sah-rah-yuh), at the southern end of the larger Blachernae Palace complex, is Istanbul's only surviving Byzantine palace. Other than this facade, all that remains of the palace is its three-story outer wall. Built during the 13th and 14th centuries, the palace grounds are closed to the public while undergoing renovation and are unlikely to reopen before late 2016.

• *Keep to the right and continue on Hoca Çakır Caddesi down the hill. In less than 100 yards, the street curves to the left. To your right are the...*

Kastoria Synagogue Wall and Gate

These are the scant remains of a synagogue built in 1453 by Jewish immigrants from

Kastoria, Macedonia. The building was renovated in the 1800s, but over the ensuing decades, many well-to-do Jewish families moved away from this neighborhood. Without its congregation, the synagogue fell into disrepair and was transferred to a state trust. Eventually it was rented to a businessman, who tore down the building and turned the space into a parking lot, earning the ruins the nickname "the drive-in synagogue."

On the still-standing main gate, among other Hebrew writings, you'll see the year "5653"—which, in the Hebrew calendar, equals 1893, most likely the year the synagogue was last renovated.

• *Continue down the hill. Take the first left (Sulu Sokak), then turn right at the Adile Şah Kadın Mosque onto Şişhane Caddesi; follow it as it twists through a residential neighborhood. Just ahead, the street makes a left turn (by the wall of the Alparslan vocational high school). A block later, stick with the street as it bends sharply to the right. Continue down the hill to the intersection with Eğrikapı street. Turn left onto Eğrikapı and walk a few steps to the...*

Eğrikapı Gate and Surdibi Cemetery

Eğrikapı (eh-ree-kah-puh; "bent gate") is one of the minor city gates. Step through the gate and outside the city walls to see a small Muslim cemetery, often frequented by tour groups. The cemetery is known as the legendary burial site of several of the *sahabe* (companions of the Prophet Muhammad—the Muslim equivalent of the Christian apostles). The *sahabe* are said to have been buried here in unmarked graves, having fought and died as members of the Arab army that attacked Constantinople in the seventh century.

When Sultan Mahmut II started a major westernization project in the early 19th century, his opponents tried to discredit him by portraying him as an infidel who had turned away from Islam. To prove his faith, the sultan initiated a search to pinpoint and mark the burial sites of the *sahabe* who had fallen during the Arab siege of Constantinople. The historical legitimacy of these *sahabe* gravesites is—for Muslims—authenticated by faith. Look for the gravestones marked *Sahabe'den*.

• *From here, those willing to brave the traffic can detour for an impressive view of the walls from the outside. Otherwise, skip to "Part 2: Lonca, Balat & Fener Neighborhoods," to continue this walk through these three residential areas inside the walls. The people you're meeting along the way don't see many tourists. Greet them with a friendly "Merhaba" as you pass.*

If you choose to end the walk at Eğrikapı Gate or after the short detour outside the walls, here are your options for moving on: You can catch a cab back to the Eminönü neighborhood (east), walk to the Ayvansaray dock to catch a boat back to Eminönü (cheaper than a cab), or continue to the Eyüp Sultan Mosque by taxi (west—see page 59). Or retrace your steps to the Chora Church, then take a taxi, bus, or the tram-and-lightrail option back to central Istanbul.

Detour Outside the Walls

To get the great view of the walls, you'll need to walk on a sidewalk alongside a busy highway. Don't go beyond the viaduct, or you'll end up in the middle of the highway.

Take the walkway on the right (through the cemetery), and keep walking along the wall. Farther down the road, the wall bends again and gradually splits off from the road. Here you'll see the final section of the wall leading all the way to the Golden Horn. Look down about midway along the last stretch of wall, where two towers stand next to each other, sharing a common base. The first tower (on the right) is the Bastion of Isaac II Angelus. The tower on the left marks the Dungeons of Anemas, built as a prison in the early seventh century as part of Blachernae Palace (described later). Just behind the towers is the 16th-century Kazasker İvaz Efendi Mosque (we'll see the bastion, dungeons, and mosque again later, from inside the wall).

Beyond the Dungeons of Anemas, the rest of the wall forms a fortress with huge hexagonal towers. This is where the land walls connected to the sea walls on the Golden Horn. The sea walls, which ran a little less than four miles, were shorter and largely unfortified, making them the weak link in Constantinople's defenses. As additional security, the Byzantines sealed off the Golden Horn to enemy vessels by stretching a thick chain across its entrance. But a clever attack rendered the entire network of walls irrelevant. In 1453, in a remarkable feat of military ingenuity and engineering prowess, Mehmet the Conqueror dragged his warships on rollers through today's New District under cover of darkness, deposited them into the Golden Horn, and launched a successful surprise attack on Constantinople—ending Byzantine rule and opening a new chapter in the city's history.

• *To continue on the second part of the walk, backtrack to the Eğrikapı Gate. Head toward the Old Town, and take the third alley to the left (Dervişzade Sokak). It's next to a little grocery store and a manly tea house. (1 TL for tea, free backgammon—drop in and make some friends. At this price, the drinks are on you.)*

PART 2: LONCA, BALAT & FENER NEIGHBORHOODS

As you walk along, imagine how the city walls lost their protective function as the centuries went by. No longer needed for fortification, they became a handy quarry for locals needing stone for home additions or to build walls of their own. Many homes were actually constructed right up against the wall (to save on building materials), ensuring that the Walls of Constantinople would always remain integral to the foundation of this grand city.

An ongoing urban rehabilitation project (supported by UNESCO and the European Union) seeks to preserve the authenticity of these neighborhoods while being mindful of the inhabitants and their needs. A few years ago, tourists walking these alleys would have faced a tough, local attitude. Residents feared that the renewal project would force them from their homes. To bring them around, tour guides were hired to take locals on cultural tours of their own neighborhoods to learn what the project is all about.

Follow Dervişzade Sokak as it curves to the right and then left (and gets wider). Straight ahead, you'll see an old fountain in the middle of the alley.

• *To the left of the fountain is the entrance to the...*

Kazasker İvaz Efendi Mosque

This mosque, built in 1585 by the architect Mimar Sinan or one of his students, honors Kazasker İvaz Efendi, one of the highest-ranking military judges in the Ottoman Empire, who conferred directly with the Grand Vizier. Located on what was one of the terraces of the sprawling Blachernae Palace (described

CITY WALLS

later), this mosque is unusual for its entry, which has double doors (women right, men left) at either side instead of the traditional central entrance. You're welcome to enter the courtyard and mosque. Peer over the balustrade into the cemetery with its Arabic calligraphy and turbans carved in stone. If the imam is around, ask him to open the mosque so you can see its delightful original interior. Wander upstairs behind the jalousies.

• *Return to the alley and follow the mosque's courtyard wall to the viewing platform next door (next to Anemas Café). Approach the fence. Here you have a fine view of the...*

Dungeons of Anemas

The dungeons are named for their first prisoner—a Byzantine soldier of Arab origin named Michael Anemas. He was imprisoned here after a failed attempt to murder the Byzantine emperor in 1107. Legend says the emperor's daughter later helped Anemas escape, while historians believe he served jail time but was spared being blinded, thanks to the daughter's fervent pleading.

This prison was also where overthrown emperors were locked up and tortured. Emperor Isaac II Angelus was blinded and held in the dungeons (next to his bastion) for years when his elder brother usurped the throne.

All three floors inside the tower have collapsed, so what you'll see is an empty shell. The basement (not visible from the platform and currently closed for restoration) contains remnants of the walls that once separated the cells. Imagine the sunlight beaming through narrow openings.

• *A section of the Blachernae Palace, now in ruins, lies before you along the wall.*

Blachernae Palace Ruins

The palace dates back to the sixth century. Over time, it grew larger and more extensive, incorporating part of the city wall. In the 12th century, the run-down royal palace (located where the Blue Mosque stands today) was abandoned, and the royal family moved here. Blachernae (vah-lah-hehr-nah) became the official administrative center of the Byzantine Empire. The emperor brought royal traditions with him to the new palace, where a priest locked the doors of the palace each afternoon and opened them again at sunrise the next day.

Everything at Blachernae was designed to impress. Visitors and envoys were admitted with much pomp and circumstance to the highly decorated throne room, where the emperor and his officials awaited in fine robes and jewel-encrusted crowns.

The showiness backfired. Latin envoys, who were as impressed as they were envious, brought home stories of the wealth on show

The Roma of Lonca and Balat

Long ago, Istanbul's Roma (Gypsy) families wearied of traveling and settled in the neighborhoods of Lonca and Balat. Lonca's residents are known for being talented musicians, fortune-tellers, and street florists. The musicians you come across in *meyhanes* (mehy-hah-nehz; taverns) all across Istanbul are usually from this neighborhood. And if you wander Lonca's alleys, you may hear music coming from "musicians' coffee shops," which function as a sort of informal musicians' guild.

Laundry hanging from lines stretched across the street; young children running around, hollering for attention; and elderly women sitting out on doorsteps, chatting and sipping tea—these are common scenes in the alleyways of Lonca and Balat. You won't see many older kids around during the day—if they're not at school, they're usually on a mission to help the family economically. As the Roma say, "The wealth of a Roma family is determined by the number of their children."

The Roma of Lonca are famous for their "street fights." Don't worry; these aren't violent conflicts. When a family has a problem to resolve with another family, they invite that family to a "fight." A date and time are set, and a location selected (it could be outside on a common street, or inside a coffee shop). Neighbors are invited to attend as witnesses, and both families prepare food to serve the audience. At the appointed date and time, musicians and dancers from both families take turns trying to outdo one another's performances. The family that receives the most applause from the audience wins the "fight"—and prevails in whatever issue it was that needed to be settled.

here, and in 1204, Crusader armies plundered Constantinople and the riches of Blachernae Palace. The palace was still standing when the Crusaders left, but likely never regained its former glory, even after the Byzantine emperor retook the throne. By the 14th century, the treasury was empty, the palace was in disrepair, and the emperor was drinking his wine from an earthenware cup.

Today, the remains of the foundations, vaulted galleries, and underground tunnels of the Blachernae Palace are still visible here and there, all along the wall. Excavation and restoration work has been going on for some time now, closing this site to visitors. If by chance you are permitted to enter, watch out for unstable, loose ground.

• *Next, take the narrow alley (Ahmet Rufai Sokağı) across from Anemas Café. To your left as you walk is the...*

Emir Buhari Tekkesi (Emir Buhari Lodge)

The popular dervish spiritual leader Emir Buhari lived in the late

15th and early 16th centuries. As his name suggests, he came from the city of Bukhara (Buhara in Turkish), in today's Uzbekistan. Buhari introduced a dervish sect with roots in the spiritual side of Islam. This lodge (not open to the public) was built by the sultan to serve as a gathering place for Buhari's followers. To the left of the lodge are the burial places of sect leaders who followed Emir Buhari.

Religious orders, dervish lodges, and sheiks like Buhari played an important role in Istanbul's social, religious, and political life in the past—and to some extent, they remain influential even now. When the Turkish Republic was established in 1923, religious organizations like this were banned, and *tekkes* (lodges) were closed down. But the sects lived on, practicing dervish traditions unofficially, in secret, under different names. These sects still exist—unofficially. While the Greek Orthodox patriarch resides near here, there are only a couple of thousand Greek Orthodox people in Istanbul today.

• *Continue until the alley ends (keep left) at a staircase. Looking straight down from the top, you'll see the Panagia Blachernae Church, our next stop. At the bottom of the staircase, turn left and keep the wall to your right as you go around the block to the church entrance.*

Panagia Blachernae Holy Spring and Church

The word *panagia* refers to the Mother Mary and means the "all holy." Many churches in Istanbul dedicated to Mother Mary are named *panagia*—this one is Panagia Blachernae, or the All Holy of Blachernae.

A holy spring (one of the Orthodox faith's three most sacred springs in Istanbul) was once part of the Blachernae Palace complex, with a small church at the site. The church housed a sacred relic—a scarf purported to have been Mary's—that was believed to protect the city from disasters. When the church and scarf were destroyed in a fire, churchgoers believed that the city would fall to invaders. Two decades later, the Ottomans conquered Constantinople.

Step inside the church to take a quick look at the holy spring (inside the church building by the end of the courtyard—look for the basket of small plastic bottles). The water is believed to have healing properties. A large number of visitors come here from Greece, filling their bottles at the spring to take home.

Superstitious Turks believe in charms and spells, and that a certain type of spell (involving prayers in Aramaic) can only be undone by a faithful Orthodox priest. You may see Muslims—mostly women—visiting this church to ask the priest for help.

As you step outside the church, look across the street to the shop with many colorful and extravagant cabaret costumes hang-

CITY WALLS

ing outside. This is the atelier of **Kobra Murat,** a Roma fashion designer known as the Versace of Istanbul. Nearly all Roma performers and those attending special events come here when they need fancy garb.

• *With the church entrance behind you, turn right and walk along Mustafa Paşa Bostanı Sokak (called Bostan Sokak by locals).*

Roughly 100 yards into the alley, on the right, a recently restored building is home to the Plato College of Higher Education. Its location here mirrors a new trend in the city. Instead of moving to more spacious suburban campuses, educators are picking locations within the heart of the historical city to connect students to real life.

• *Continue on to the end of Bostan Sokak, where it sharply bends to the right and connects to Kırkambar Sokak. You are now in the **Lonca neighborhood,** home to a significant Roma population (see sidebar). Turn left onto Kırkambar Sokak. The Aya Dimitri Orthodox Church is to your immediate left.*

On Tuesdays, this is the start of a lively street market—with its crush of people and pickpockets—making this a good time to secure your wallet. Walk straight ahead another 100 yards onto Mahkeme Altı Caddesi. To your right, within a few steps, you'll see the entrance to the Panagia Balino Greek Orthodox Church.

In 250 yards at the fork, keep to the left, following Lavanta Sokak as it turns into Ayan Caddesi (the elaborate portal of the historic Kastoria Synagogue is to your right).

Balat

Ahead of you is the Balat neighborhood and its commercial zone (Balat Çarşısı, bah-laht chahr-shuh-suh). Until the 1950s, Balat

was a bustling Jewish neighborhood with a lively market. But in the decades since Turkey became a republic, many well-to-do Jews have moved to more desirable neighborhoods elsewhere in Istanbul. Today's Balat is missing the taverns, jewelers, fabric merchants, and bankers of the past—they've been replaced by hardware stores, metal repair shops, butchers, wholesalers, and green grocers. And yet this little downtown somehow retains a hint of its traditional charm.

• *At the intersection, turn right onto Kürkçü Çeşmesi Sokak. To your left is the...*

Ahrida Synagogue

This synagogue is the only one in the city that can be dated with

The Jews in Turkey

The Byzantines were not very tolerant of Jews. Jewish people couldn't ride on horseback within Istanbul's city limits; they weren't allowed to build houses taller than those of their Christian neighbors; and their synagogues couldn't have domed roofs. Emperor Justinian was particularly harsh. He outlawed the reading of the Torah in Hebrew and ordered that it must be recited in Greek. The emperors who followed imposed heavy taxes on the Jewish minority. In the sixth century, the Jews were expelled from the city and required to live outside the walls in Haskoy and Galata (today's New District). These Greek-speaking "Romaniots" made up the small Jewish minority in Constantinople when the Ottomans took over the city.

The Jews fared better under the Ottomans, who encouraged more Jewish immigration as a way to populate the city and boost the economy. The first to come were Jews from the Balkans (Ashkenazi Jews). Then, in the late 15th century, 200,000 Sephardic Jews were expelled from Spain. Ottoman Sultan Beyazıt II welcomed a number of them to Turkey, saying, "Ferdinand of Spain is a wise king, however, he is making his land poor and ours rich."

Later, under the Turkish Republic, the Jews were unfairly targeted by a WWII "wealth tax." Despite being neutral during the war, Turkey increased its military spending and levied taxes on wealthy citizens to pay for arms and soldiers. The tax was applied more heavily to non-Muslims, and although it was later lifted, it caused many Jews to leave the country.

At the same time, Turkey offered refuge to many prominent German Jews escaping from Hitler during the war. Later, Jewish professors played an important role in the development of the Turkish education system.

Today, Turkey's Jewish community is estimated at 25,000 people, about 95 percent of whom are Sephardic Jews—descendants of those Spanish exiles. The vast majority of Turkey's Jews live in Istanbul, with about 2,500 in İzmir, on the Aegean. Turkish Jews are legally represented by a chief rabbi, a post currently held by Istanbul native Izak Haleva.

certainty to the Byzantine period. It was built in the early 15th century by Jewish settlers from the Macedonian city of Ohrid, and has been welcoming worshippers ever since. The last renovation was in 1992, during the Jewish community's quincentennial celebration (marking the 500th anniversary of the arrival of Sephardic Jews in Istanbul).

The synagogue is open to the public only during the first week of September (Jewish Week in Europe). The rest of the year you'll need advance permission from the Chief Rabbinate (www.turkyahudileri.com, click on "Admissions").

Catching Your Breath in Balat

Thanks to a European Union project, Balat has had a facelift in recent years. With many of its once-dilapidated buildings restored, the neighborhood is evolving into a trendy design district, with a smattering of artists' studios and craftsmen's workshops. Nowadays, it's cool to hang out here. A handful of newly opened, rustic, and cozy cafés and restaurants are ideal for a short rest stop or simple lunch.

Look for homey **Café Vodina** on the main street, on the route of this walk. It is housed in the Balat Cultural Center (Balat Kültür Evi), the meeting place of the Turkish Soroptimist Federation, an organization of professional women. The café and the cultural center are focused on increasing the education level of the women of Balat—who staff and run the entire facility (daily 10:00-18:00, Vodina Caddesi 39, tel. 0212/531-0057, www.balatkulturevi.org).

Forno Balat is a small and friendly *pide* shop that feels more like a large kitchen than a restaurant. The chef works at a long marble counter running along one wall, while regulars socialize at the large central table (most *pides* 12-16 TL, Tue-Sun 10:00-20:00, closed Mon, off Vodina Caddesi at Fener Kireçhane Sokak 13, tel. 0212/521-2900).

With coffee shops trimming every corner of the city, **Çay-ada** ("Tea Island") is a haven for tea enthusiasts. The simple interior is colorful and cheerful with wall paintings, flowers in pots, and a kaleidoscope of glass chandeliers; a pleasant outdoor terrace has views of the Golden Horn. They serve cold sandwiches as well as cookies and tea (most sandwiches 7.5-10 TL, daily 9:30-24:00, Mürselpaşa Caddesi 201, tel. 0212/531-3148).

If you get a chance to peek inside, look for the bema, the elevated platform from which the Torah is read to the congregation. Built in the shape of Noah's Ark, it's the most interesting part of this synagogue. Because Byzantine restrictions didn't allow for a domed synagogue, this dome was hidden under the roof and is visible only from the interior. Although this synagogue is almost 600 years old, the oldest Torah kept here is from the 1920s, as Jews have a tradition of burying worn Torahs.

• *From here, if you're interested, take a short detour to Holy Archangels Armenian Church. With your back to the synagogue entrance, take the alley (Düriye Sokak) directly across from you, and turn left onto Kamış Sokak by the church wall.*

Holy Archangels Armenian Church (Surp Hıreşdagabet)

Dating from the 19th century, this church replaced an earlier Greek Orthodox structure. In the 1600s, the sultan gave it to the

The First Patriarch After the Ottoman Conquest

When Mehmet the Conqueror took Constantinople in 1453, the patriarchal throne had been empty for a few years. Even before the conquest, ongoing discussions about the reconciliation of the Catholic and Orthodox churches were creating friction. Realizing that a unified Church would be a threat to his throne, Mehmet sought to derail the negotiations. He picked the theologian Gennadius Scholarius—a strong opponent of unification—as patriarch of the Orthodox Church. Unfortunately Gennadius wasn't around: He'd been taken captive during the conquest of Constantinople and was being held in a slave market in a neighboring city. Mehmet's soldiers found Gennadius and brought him back to Constantinople, where he became not only the patriarch of Constantinople, but also the ethnarch—the political representative of the entire Orthodox population living under Ottoman rule.

Gennadius was an important scholar and theologian even before his ascension to the patriarchal throne. He's best known for writing the *Confession*, a book about Christianity that was presented to Mehmet. Today a mosaic panel, depicting Sultan Mehmet the Conqueror and Gennadius, decorates the entrance hall of the Patriarchate administrative building.

Armenian congregation to return a favor. The holy spring in the basement—a typical feature of a Greek Orthodox church—is dedicated to St. Andonios (church open to the public Thu 8:30-10:30 & 12:00-14:00, Sun 9:30-14:00, closed Mon-Wed and Fri-Sat).

• *Whether you stayed at the synagogue or detoured to the Armenian Church, backtrack to the junction of Kürkçü Çeşmesi and Ayan Caddesi. Walk straight across onto Vodina Caddesi, and continue roughly 200 yards, to the Tahta Minare Hamamı (bath). Stay on Vodina as the street bends to the right, for another 200 yards. At #45 on the right, behind the massive stone wall, is the...*

Church of St. George (Aya Yorgi)

This Orthodox church has had a long connection with the Patriarchate of Jerusalem. Every year, on April 23, the patriarch of Jerusalem and the Ecumenical Greek Orthodox patriarch hold a special joint service here, conducted in three languages: Arabic, Greek, and Turkish.

If you're here outside the visiting hours, the caretaker may unlock the main gate into the large garden, with ancient earthenware jars lined up along the side (open to visitors Sat-Sun 14:00-17:00, donation expected).

• *Walk roughly three blocks to the end of Vodina, turn left and then right onto Yıldırım Caddesi. Walk another block to reach the...*

Greek Orthodox Patriarchate

This unassuming complex holds the modern offices of the head of the Greek Orthodox Church and its roughly 300 million followers worldwide. The Patriarchate in Istanbul is as important to followers of the Orthodox faith as the Vatican in Rome is to Catholics. The current patriarch, who has the status of "first among equals" among the various branches of the Orthodox Church, is Bartholomew I (270th archbishop of the historic throne of Constantinople), a Turkish-born Greek. Because of his work on behalf of environmental causes, he is known as the "Green Patriarch."

Hagia Sophia was the seat of the patriarch until the Ottoman conquest in 1453. After that, the Patriarchate moved to several different locations before finally finding a permanent home here in the Fener neighborhood in the early 1600s, making this the center of Greek Orthodox life in the city. The name "Fener" is often used as a nickname for the Patriarchate, just as the name "Vatican" is used as shorthand for the leaders of the Catholic Church.

You'll see three gates at the entrance to the complex. The main gate (at the center) was welded shut in honor of Patriarch Gregory V, who in 1821 was hung here by Sultan Mahmud II for supporting the Greek uprising against Ottoman rule in the Peloponnese. The three crosses on the gate symbolize the patriarch and the two *metropolitans* (similar to archbishops) who were killed with him. The gate on the right opens to the administrative side of the complex.

That leaves the gate on the left—you can use it to enter the courtyard. Straight ahead is the **Church of St. George** (which is different from the other Church of St. George described earlier), where services are held and holy relics are kept. On the facade, above the church's main door, you can spot a double-headed eagle relief, the symbol of the Byzantine Empire. The buildings on the right are the administrative offices and patriarchal residence. To your left, the single-story narrow building is where myrrh, the holy ointment for baptism, is prepared for the Greek Orthodox world.

The Patriarchate and the Church of St. George are open to visitors daily from 8:30 to 16:30. You're welcome to attend services at 16:30 (print out a church tour at www.patriarchate.org).

• *Our walk is finished. From here, you can take a cab or a bus to Taksim (#55T) or Eminönü (several lines) from the nearby Fener bus stop.*

BOSPHORUS CRUISE

From Eminönü in Downtown Istanbul to Anadolu Kavağı

In addition to separating two continents, the Bosphorus Strait serves as Istanbul's main highway. A never-ending stream of vessels—from little fishing dinghies to gigantic rusted oil tankers to luxury cruise ships—sails up and down this strategic corridor, day in and day out. The Bosphorus is one of the busiest waterways in the world; churning ship engines and clanging horns are Istanbul's constant soundtrack. This carnival of commerce is the only outlet to the Mediterranean for Russia, and the only route to any sea for the other countries on the Black Sea: Romania, Bulgaria, Ukraine, and Georgia.

Cruising the Bosphorus—a ▲▲▲ experience—is the best way to appreciate the massive size and scale of 15-million-strong Istanbul, and a convenient way to see many of its outlying landmarks. And since virtually all of Istanbul's key attractions are on the European side, a cruise may be your easiest opportunity to set foot in Asia (the last stop on the cruise is the fishing village of Anadolu Kavağı, on the Asian side).

In Turkish, the Bosphorus is Boğaziçi (boh-ahz-ee-chee), which means "pass" or "strait." This 19-mile-long waterway curves like a snake as it connects the Black Sea in the north with the Sea of Marmara and—eventually—the Mediterranean in the south. Istanbul's various districts line up along the bays, and the coastline is peppered with cute neighborhoods. Many of these areas, once separate communities, have been incorporated into Istanbul as the town has sprawled from north to south over the past several decades. Today Istanbul extends pretty much all the way up to the Black Sea. But a few neighborhoods in the north retain a village-like quality, where men still fish for a living.

The Turks view the Bosphorus as much more than just a body of water—to them, it's a sacred inheritance. Locals take joy in it,

Bosphorus Strait Cruise

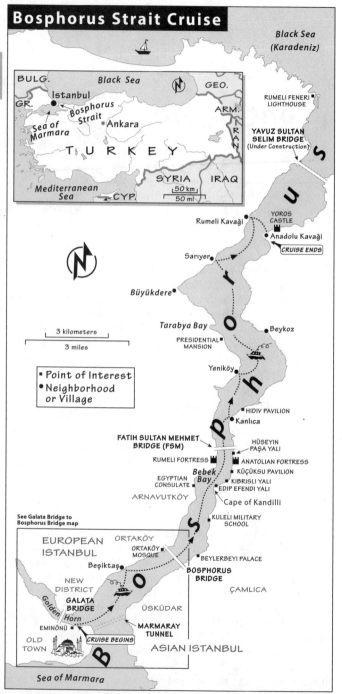

Black Sea
(Karadeniz)

BULG.
Black Sea
GEO.
GR.
Istanbul
Bosphorus
Strait
ARM.
Ankara
Sea of
Marmara
T U R K E Y
Mediterranean
Sea
SYRIA
IRAQ
CYP.

50 km
50 mi

RUMELI FENERI
LIGHTHOUSE

YAVUZ SULTAN
SELIM BRIDGE
(Under Construction)

B o s p h o r u s

YOROS
CASTLE

Rumeli Kavağı

Anadolu Kavağı
CRUISE ENDS

Sarıyer

Büyükdere

Beykoz

Tarabya Bay

PRESIDENTIAL
MANSION

Yeniköy

HIDIV PAVILION

Kanlıca

FATIH SULTAN MEHMET
BRIDGE (FSM)

HÜSEYIN
PAŞA YALI

RUMELI FORTRESS

ANATOLIAN FORTRESS

KÜÇÜKSU PAVILION

Bebek
Bay

KIBRISLI YALI

EGYPTIAN
CONSULATE

EDIP EFENDI YALI

ARNAVUTKÖY

Cape of Kandilli

KULELI MILITARY
SCHOOL

3 kilometers

3 miles

■ Point of Interest
● Neighborhood
  or Village

See Galata Bridge to
Bosphorus Bridge map

EUROPEAN
ISTANBUL

ORTAKÖY

ORTAKÖY
MOSQUE

Beşiktaş

BEYLERBEYI PALACE

NEW
DISTRICT

GALATA
BRIDGE

BOSPHORUS
BRIDGE

ÇAMLICA

Golden
Horn

ÜSKÜDAR

EMINÖNÜ

MARMARAY
TUNNEL

CRUISE BEGINS

OLD
TOWN

ASIAN ISTANBUL

Sea of Marmara

The Bosphorus Tunnel

Istanbul's Asian districts are mostly residential. That means millions of people commute to work across the strait using the bridges and ferries (which don't run in bad weather—making the commute a nightmare over the jammed-up bridges). Seeking to solve crowded Istanbul's never-ending traffic mess, a third bridge is already under construction and likely to be completed in 2016.

Another new option for transiting between continents is a rail tunnel beneath the Bosphorus—constructed as part of the ongoing, $2.5 billion Marmaray (a.k.a. Marmara Rail) project. The Marmaray incorporates a new commuter light-rail system into existing public transit, eventually extending the system roughly 50 miles across both continents and carrying about 150,000 passengers per hour. The mile-long, rail-only Bosphorus Tunnel connects the Old Town to the busy Üsküdar district across the Bosphorus. A second tunnel is under construction for motor vehicles.

and can sit for hours on a bench by the Bosphorus just watching the beautiful scenery as a United Nations of boats drifts past.

Orientation

Public Ferry: We recommend taking a day-long cruise on the public ferry, which leaves from the Old Town side of the Golden Horn. For a shorter cruise, consider a private tour operator (described later, under "Private Tours").

Ferry Cost: 15 TL one-way, 25 TL round-trip. Get the round-trip ticket. There's little sense in taking the cruise one-way; options for coming back overland from Anadolu Kavağı are limited and expensive. With the round-trip ticket you can return directly to Eminönü, or hop off early to see outlying sights on your way back to town (described later under "Sarıyer Shortcut").

Ferry Schedule: The ferry leaves at 10:35 and 13:35 April-Oct (additional departures possible in peak season); from Nov-March, 10:35 departure only. Schedules can change, so confirm these times before you set out (ask your hotelier, drop by the dock, or check online at www.sehirhatlari.com.tr/en—select "Bosphorus Tours," then click on "Full Bosphorus Cruise").

When to Go: The 10:35 departure puts you in Anadolu Kavağı just in time for lunch, and gets you back to Istanbul early enough for a little evening sightseeing. If you're in Istanbul for several days, check the forecast and plan your cruise during good weather.

Crowd-Beating Tips: Weekdays are best—the ferry can be miserably crowded on weekends, especially from late spring through early fall. Arrive at least 30 minutes before your scheduled departure time, as the best seats fill fast (on a busy day—such as a sunny weekend—show up even earlier). As you board, you'll have to choose: Have your own seat, which means you're stuck in one place the entire trip (and therefore can't see the other side of the Bosphorus very well); or stand up, giving you maximum flexibility for moving around and taking photos, but leaving you without a guaranteed seat for the entire trip (seats may free up as people move around or disembark at later stops on the route).

Getting There: The public ferry leaves from the Bosphorus Cruise Pier ferry terminal in the Old Town's Eminönü district (near the mouth of the Golden Horn, along the embankment next to the Galata Bridge). For details, see 📖 the Golden Horn Walk chapter, and consider combining that walk with this cruise.

To reach the ferry landing from the Old Town, take the tram toward Kabataş and get off at Eminönü. When you emerge from the pedestrian underpass, look for the ferry-terminal building marked *Bosphorus Cruise Pier.*

To reach the ferry from Taksim Square in the New District, you can either walk or take the Nostalgic Tram down İstiklal Street to Tünel, then take the Tünel funicular down to Karaköy at the Galata Bridge. Walk across the bridge and turn left along the embankment to find the terminal labeled *Bosphorus Cruise Pier.* Alternatively, you can ride the funicular down the hill from Taksim Square to Kabataş, and take the tram from there to Eminönü.

Ferry Route: The ferry goes from Eminönü in downtown Istanbul to the Black Sea end of the Bosphorus, where it takes a break in the Asian fishing village of Anadolu Kavağı before returning to Eminönü. It makes several other stops along the way, but only docks long enough to pick up or drop off passengers.

Length of Ferry Cruise: A round-trip Bosphorus cruise by ferry takes about 5.5-7 hours, depending on wind, weather, and traffic conditions on the Bosphorus, as well as how long your boat lingers in Anadolu Kavağı (expect about 3 hours of actual sailing time, plus a 2- to 3-hour break in Anadolu Kavağı).

Here are the approximate durations of the various legs of

the trip. Heading north, from Eminönü to: Beşiktaş (15 minutes), Kanlıca (40 minutes), Yeniköy (55 minutes), Sarıyer (70 minutes), Rumeli Kavağı (80 minutes), Anadolu Kavağı (90 minutes). Heading south, from Anadolu Kavağı to: Rumeli Kavağı (10 minutes), Sarıyer (20 minutes), Yeniköy (35 minutes), Kanlıca (50 minutes), Beşiktaş (75 minutes), Eminönü (90 minutes).

Sarıyer Shortcut: If you'd rather not go all the way to the end, consider getting off about 1.25 hours into the trip at the Sarıyer stop and taking the bus back (see sidebar on page 294). This gives you the option of visiting the Rumeli Fortress, Sakıp Sabancı Museum, Sadberk Hanım Museum, and Dolmabahçe Palace, all described in the Sights chapter. Or, get off at Sarıyer on the return trip to see some of these sights on your way back.

Services: WCs and snack bar on board.

Private Tours: For a shorter Bosphorus cruise, consider a private excursion. Various companies sell 12-TL cruise tickets on either side of the Galata Bridge (behind bus stops to the west side, and next to Bosphorus cruise pier on the east—look for *Bosphorus Tours* sign). These boats will take you as far as the second bridge (Fatih Sultan Mehmet Bridge) and back in 1.5 hours, with no stops. **Turyol**—on the west side of the bridge, next to fish-sandwich boats and behind the bus stops—is one of many options (mid-June-mid-Sept Mon-Fri cruises generally run hourly 10:00-21:00, Sat every half hour 12:00-19:00, Sun hourly 11:00-18:45; less frequent off-season, tel. 0212/527-9952, ask for Mr. İhsan).

There's no set schedule for these private boats (at least, not one that's strictly adhered to). Boats depart as soon as they have enough people. Just buy your ticket and hop on. These cruises are a good option if you're short on time or not interested in visiting Asia. But keep in mind that they only go up to the second bridge, so you'll see less of the Bosphorus and won't get a glimpse of the Black Sea. In general, the cruises stick closer to the European side on the way north and the Asian side on the way back south. Most of the information in this chapter (except for the places the ferry docks) is also relevant on these smaller cruises.

A private, day-long cruise goes all the way to the Black Sea (see page 29).

Starring: Bridges between the continents, fancy waterfront mansions, fortresses, castles, and the fishing village of Anadolu Kavağı.

The Bosphorus Strait: A Critical Location

The Bosphorus Strait—17 nautical miles long—connects the Black Sea with the Sea of Marmara (which, at its western end, flows through the Dardanelles to the

Aegean Sea, and then out to the Mediterranean Sea). The great commercial and strategic importance of the Bosphorus was a factor in the establishment of the city of Constantinople here in A.D. 330. Today, private boats and passenger ferries make more than 2,000 runs a day, carrying 2.5 million people between the two continents. Add in the hundreds of commercial vessels each day—you'll see many at anchor just offshore in the Sea of Marmara—plus fishing boats out for the daily catch, and you've got a lot of traffic.

Navigation through the strait can be extremely difficult due to its narrow width (just a half-mile across at its narrowest, between the Anatolian and Rumeli fortresses), sharp turns (there are 12 course-changing bends), tricky currents, and the immense size of the tankers and cruise ships that ply its waters. Powerful currents funnel through this narrow north-south strait. Less salty water flowing south from the Black Sea creates a strong surface current, which is generally strengthened by prevailing northerly winds. Note the fishing boats off the Old Town peninsula, straining to stay in place with their bows pointed toward the Bosphorus—evidence of that strong surface current flowing south through the strait.

Making things even more complicated, another, saltier current flows beneath the surface in the opposite direction, toward the Black Sea (because of the difference in salinity between the Black Sea and the Sea of Marmara). Clever ancient mariners fig-

GETTING STARTED

Buy your ticket at the windows facing the busy street, then go through the turnstile to reach the ferry. Hang on to your ticket—the ticket-taker will check it again on your return journey.

If you arrive at least 30 minutes early, there will usually be some seats left (but show up even earlier if you want to snag a seat on a sunny weekend). On the way up the Bosphorus, most of the attractions are on the left (European) side of the boat, so pick your spot accordingly. Ideally you'd like a clear look at both sides, though because of the width of the boat and the crowds on board, this often isn't possible. The lower deck has unobstructed view seats along the water. If you don't mind seeing only one side, grab one of

ured this out; they lowered weighted baskets on lines down into the water to catch the lower current in order to pull their boats northward.

In 1936, Turkey signed the Montreux Convention, which regulates boat traffic through the Bosphorus and the Dardanelles. In case of war, Turkey has the right to close these critically located straits to any vessel; even during times of peace, military vessels must inform authorities long in advance of their passage.

When the Montreux Convention was signed, ships were smaller and weren't required to use a local pilot to negotiate the

dangerous Bosphorus; an oversight that proved disastrous. The location of the Bosphorus, flanking populous Istanbul, magnified the consequences of shipboard accidents as the number and size of boats traveling the strait steadily increased. Boats collided in fiery explosions, tankers leaked thousands of gallons of crude oil into the fragile waters, and more than one disabled ship ran aground—smacking right into waterfront houses. An Istanbul resident reported: "I heard an unusual sound getting louder and louder, and all of a sudden, I saw the bow of the ship going right into the room!"

Now local pilots are required, and boat traffic is more strictly controlled, managed by a radar network (look for the radar towers along the Bosphorus). In addition, oil pipelines from the eastern Black Sea, the Caucasus region, and the Caspian Sea are providing an alternative way of transporting oil, which is helping to alleviate the bottleneck of tanker traffic through the strait.

these seats on the left. The open upper decks in the front and back of the boat are ideal for avid photographers. If all the good seats are taken, consider staking out a standing spot on the left near the back of the boat. Realize that people will constantly be jostling for position for the prettiest photos—so no matter where you sit or stand, you may not have the place to yourself.

Coming back, the sunlight is better for taking photos of the Asian side (during the afternoon, the sun is in your eyes looking at the European side). So a smart plan is to always sit on the left side (views of the European side on the way there and the Asian side on the way back).

On the upper deck is a snack bar where you can get a *simit* (see-meet—a sesame bread ring, like a Turkish bagel), candy bar, sandwich, or beverage. Attendants also walk around the ferry selling tea, coffee, fresh-squeezed orange juice, and water. The WCs are on the lower deck, on the sides, toward the front (past the stairs to the second deck).

For the first half-hour or so, the boat moves fast and there's a lot to see. Consider reading ahead so you're ready for the attractions as you pass them.

The Tour Begins

• *Anchors aweigh!*

EMINÖNÜ TO BEŞIKTAŞ
• *The first few sights are on the right side of the boat.*

As the boat pulls away, you're treated to a fine panorama of the Old Town peninsula—made even more dramatic by the boats scurrying around the harbor and the embankments and streets teeming with people. You see **Hagia Sophia** first, with its dome and minarets. Sirkeci train station is right behind the car ferry dock. As you move along the peninsula, the gardens of **Topkapı Palace** come into view—including Divan Tower, with the buildings of the Harem complex to its left.

On the waterfront, past the car ferry port, is the **Sepetçiler Pavilion** (seh-peht-chee-lehr; "basket weavers"), today a fine restaurant used mostly for banquets.

Within a few minutes, you reach Seraglio Point, the tip of the Old Town peninsula. This is where the Golden Horn ends and the Bosphorus begins. As you get farther from the Old Town, behind Hagia Sophia you'll notice the minarets, and later the dome, of the **Blue Mosque.** Soon the skyline of old Istanbul will be dominated by domes, minarets, and towers. Add a layer of haze, and you have a magical, mystical-looking silhouette.

Just off Seraglio Point, you can see the end of the Bosphorus—where it joins the **Sea of Marmara.** Around the base of the Old Town peninsula are intact portions of the Byzantine wall that fortified the city until the Ottomans conquered it in the 15th century. As the boat turns left, you'll begin to get some good views on the right side of Asian Istanbul, across the Bosphorus. The cranes mark the main commercial port of the city. From this angle, the Princes' Islands appear to the south in the Sea of Marmara, usually

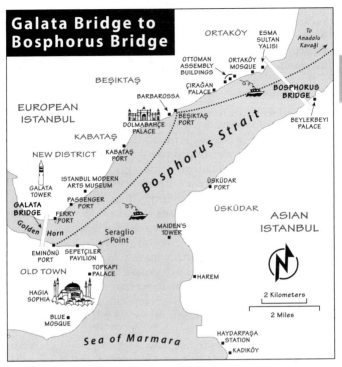

Galata Bridge to Bosphorus Bridge

ORTAKÖY
ESMA SULTAN YALISI
To Anadolu Kavaği
OTTOMAN ASSEMBLY BUILDINGS
ORTAKÖY MOSQUE
BEŞIKTAŞ
ÇIRAĞAN PALACE
BARBAROSSA
BOSPHORUS BRIDGE
EUROPEAN ISTANBUL
BEŞIKTAŞ PORT
DOLMABAHÇE PALACE
BEYLERBEYI PALACE
KABATAŞ
Bosphorus Strait
KABATAŞ PORT
NEW DISTRICT
ISTANBUL MODERN ARTS MUSEUM
ÜSKÜDAR PORT
GALATA TOWER
PASSENGER PORT
ÜSKÜDAR
GALATA BRIDGE
FERRY PORT
ASIAN ISTANBUL
Golden Horn
Seraglio Point
MAIDEN'S TOWER
EMINÖNÜ PORT
SEPETÇILER PAVILION
TOPKAPI PALACE
OLD TOWN
HAREM
HAGIA SOPHIA
2 Kilometers
2 Miles
BLUE MOSQUE
HAYDARPAŞA STATION
Sea of Marmara
KADIKÖY

as a silhouette a few miles off Asian Istanbul. On a clear day, you can even see the southern shores of Marmara.

• *Look toward Asia.*

Offshore from Asian Istanbul is one of the city's symbols, the old Byzantine tower often called the **Maiden's Tower** (just left of the harbor, but before the radar tower). Today this landmark is used as a lighthouse and a restaurant.

• *That's all for Asia for a while. The boat picks up speed—yes, it'll go this fast the whole time—and moves closer to Europe. Get settled and start reading ahead. Now focus your attention on the left, on European Istanbul.*

Just after the harbor building ends, you see the clearly marked **Istanbul Modern Arts Museum** (the gray, blocky, modern harborfront building, sometimes hidden behind parked cruise ships; described on page 51), then the Academy of Fine Arts. After that you begin to pass residential neighborhoods.

Soon you go by the Kabataş district and its seabus- and ferry-

ports. Beyond that is the **Dolmabahçe Palace** complex, the 19th-century palace of the Ottoman sultan (see page 52). The first building of the complex is the Dolmabahçe Mosque, built exclusively for the sultans and sharing the same eclectic style as the palace itself. Next door is the clock tower, built as an extravagant accessory. Right behind the tower is a soccer stadium that seats 30,000 people—but, since it's ingeniously designed to fit into its surroundings, you barely notice it. Unfortunately, the same cannot be said of the tall glass building above, the Ritz-Carlton. The other sore thumb is the Swissotel, right above the palace.

Centuries-old trees partially block your view of the monumental gate, to the right of the clock tower, leading to the palace. This also marks the start of a waterfront fence, guarded by soldiers. At the back side of the garden, just before the palace starts, you can see a second massive entryway, built for the sole use of the sultan and his guests.

The first wing of the building, including the tall middle part, was the palace's administrative section, called Selamlık.

The side gate was for officials and envoys, whom the sultan received in the front-corner rooms, each with sweeping Bosphorus views. The next wing was the Harem, the residential section, which extends behind the visible section. The building to the right, set apart from the palace, was for guests and palace employees.

Impressive as Dolmabahçe is from here, a century and a half of humidity and saltwater has taken its toll on the palace's facade. Though the palace walls facing the Bosphorus are ornate, the back is plain and dull—left undecorated when the sultan ran out of money.

The palace fence ends at an abandoned ferry port, named for **Barbarossa,** the famous pirate-turned-Ottoman admiral. When Barbarossa sailed the seas, the Ottoman armada controlled the entire Mediterranean. The park just beyond the dock, and the mosque behind the park, are also named for the beloved Barbarossa. There's a larger-than-life Barbarossa statue in the park, and his tomb is in the mosque complex. The fenced park belongs to the Naval Museum.

While you were ogling the palace, you may have noticed the ferry starting to slow down for its first stop, at **Beşiktaş** (beh-sheek-tahsh). Enjoy your last views back toward the Old Town, which is now little more than an outline. While the boat docks, look down into the water, swirling with garbage and jellyfish—two good reasons why you'll rarely see swimmers in the Bosphorus.

BEŞIKTAŞ TO KANLICA

• *Keep watching the left (European) side.*

As you leave Beşiktaş, the next building is one of the private universities *(universitesi)* of Istanbul. In front of the building, you'll see people fishing—either for sport or to catch dinner. Many local fisherfolk have favorite spots along the Bosphorus. These embankments are even more crowded on weekends, with people walking, fishing, enjoying the day with their families—sometimes even (gulp!) swimming. Keep an eye out for barbecue grills, used to cook up the fish as they're pulled from the water.

Past the university, the palatial building—formerly a state guesthouse—is a Four Seasons hotel. Next to it is the **Çırağan Palace** (chuh-rah-ahn), another late-Ottoman residence. Built two decades after Dolmabahçe Palace, in the same eclectic style by the same architect, it mysteriously burned to the ground in 1910—some say because of faulty wiring, others say arson. Only a chunk of the facade remained standing, and a local soccer team used the empty space for practice. More recently, an international hotel chain restored the palace in exchange for the right to build a hotel complex next door, the Çırağan Palace Kempinski Hotel (with the big swimming pool in front). Presidents Clinton and Bush (the Elder) have both stayed here (though not at the same time). It has theme restaurants and a ballroom, as well as a popular—and expensive—jazz bar in the basement, which moves up to the waterfront in summer.

The next building is a maritime high school (easy to recognize, thanks to the ship's mast in front). The three long buildings standing side by side, painted various shades of yellow, were the 19th-century **Ottoman Assembly.** In the late days of the Ottoman Empire, when it was becoming the "Sick Man of Europe," pressure from elsewhere in Europe—and from forces within the empire, especially the military—compelled the sultan to agree to the creation of an advisory committee. The parliament lasted only a few decades, and vanished with World War I.

Past the assembly buildings, we enter the lively **Ortaköy** (or-tah-koy) district (with the towers of Istanbul's business zone in the background). Just before the Bosphorus Bridge is the striking 19th-

century **Ortaköy Mosque**—with a Western style similar to the Dolmabahçe Mosque we passed earlier. Right next to the mosque is a 19th-century mansion, **Esma Sultan Yalısı,** which once belonged to a sultan's daughter. After the birth of the Republic, the building endured years of neglect, a fire, and use as a tobacco and coal depot. More recent owners, a hotel group, have redecorated the structure with stylish glass and metal elements, converting the mansion into a banquet hall for dinners, cultural activities, and concerts. For more on the happening Ortaköy scene, see the Entertainment chapter.

Now you are under the first bridge ever to connect two continents—the **Bosphorus Bridge.** It is the first of three suspension bridges over the Bosphorus. A Turkish-British corporation completed the span in 1973, on the 50th anniversary of the Turkish Republic. Almost two-thirds of a mile long, it carries six lanes of traffic between the continents.

• *Now look to the right (Asian) side.*

Just to the left of the bridge is **Beylerbeyi,** the late-19th-century summer palace of the sultan. The hill rising behind the palace is Çamlıca (chahm-luh-jah). Half of the city's TV and radio transmitters are on that hill: At roughly 1,200 feet, it's the highest point in greater Istanbul.

• *Look back to the left (European) side.*

Just past the bridge is a string of nightclubs—some of the most popular places in the city for the jet set. There's even a small island that belongs to a private sports club.

We've been cruising along the European coastline since leaving Beşiktaş. Now the boat will adjust its course and head for the

other side of the strait. (To follow our route from here, turn back to the overview map on page 280.) As the boat passes the center of the strait, see if you can spot any dolphins heading north on their way to the Black Sea.

• *As the boat heads for Asia, so should your gaze. Look right.*

Coming up on the Asian

side is a very wide two-story white building. Named **Kuleli** ("with towers") for the towers on either end, it was built in the early 1800s as an army barracks. Today it's a military high school.

Beyond Kuleli, the population starts to thin out. Small villages once dotted the shoreline, but today luxury yachts have replaced simple fishing boats. Especially along the Asian side, from Kuleli all the way to the second bridge, you'll see lots of impressive private waterfront **mansions** belonging to wealthy families. The generic name for these mansions is *yalı* (yah-luh). Pay attention to those made of wood—quite a few are more than a century old, although many have been renovated. Laws once prohibited the use of non-original materials in restoring historic buildings. But many historic wooden buildings mysteriously burned down, only to be quickly replaced with new, modern constructions. This led to a compromise: The core of the structure can be rebuilt according to modern specifications, but a replica of the original wooden facade must adorn the front. Regardless of their historical value, these multimillion-dollar homes on the Bosphorus are among the most expensive in the city.

Next you'll pass the **Cape of Kandilli** (kahn-dee-lee; "with candles"), named for the lamps lit to warn ships of the strong current here. The cape is marked by a hill topped with a huge electric pole, transferring high-voltage wires across to Europe. At the tip of the cape is another radar tower. Next to it is the *yalı* of **Edip Efendi,** a two-story white-and-gray wood mansion on the water.

• *Now look back to the left (European side).*

Across from the cape is the trendy Arnavutköy district (named after early Albanian settlers) and, following that, **Bebek Bay** (beh-behk; "baby"). This town on the bay is known for its almond paste, sometimes flavored with pistachios. The apartments and condos here cost a small fortune to buy or rent. Notice the many private boats anchored in the bay. To the left of the bay, the unusual-looking gray building with a French-style roof and large flag is the **Egyptian consulate.**

• *Look back to Asia (right).*

Beyond the cape, the Bosphorus makes a sharp turn into a bay. Watch for more impressive homes, especially the terra-cotta-colored one with three antique columns in its garden (it belongs to one of the wealthiest families in Turkey) and the very wide single-story 18th-century **Kıbrıslı** *yalı* with the fancy second-floor balcony.

Deeper into the bay, you'll notice the Western-looking 19th-century hunting pavilion of the sultans, named after the nearby freshwater creek, **Küçüksu** (kew-chewk-soo). It was a remote getaway for the royals, who were hunting peace and quiet more than anything.

Less than half a mile from the pavilion, past the pink building (a teachers' social club), notice the round and square towers of an old fortress rising among the

houses. This is the **Anatolian Fortress** (Anadolu Hisarı), built by the Ottoman Sultan Beyazıt at the end of the 14th century. Known as "Thunderbolt" for his speed on the battlefield, Beyazıt built this fortress at one of the narrowest points of the Bosphorus to cut off aid to Constantinople during a siege. Fifty years later, Beyazıt's grandson, Mehmet II, conquered Constantinople by following his grandpa's example across the strait....

• *Now look across to the European side (left).*

Here you see the much bigger **Rumeli Fortress** (Rumeli Hisarı), built by Sultan Mehmet II a year before the conquest of

Constantinople in 1453. Construction was completed in a record time of 80 days. Once the Ottomans had fortresses on both banks of the Bosphorus, it was virtually impossible for a ship to pass without permission. This one-two punch of mighty fortresses was a key component of Mehmet II's ultimately successful siege of Constantinople. (Read more about the Rumeli Fortress on page 57.)

• *Look back to Asia (right).*

As you near the second bridge, look for the oldest surviving *yalı* on the banks of the Bosphorus: the mansion of **Hüseyin Paşa.** Run-down but currently under renovation, this terra-cotta-painted *yalı* was built by the Ottoman Grand Vizier around 1700. It's taller than you'd expect for a single-story building, because it rises up on wood supports above a stone retaining wall.

Next up is the **Fatih Sultan Mehmet Bridge** (locals call it

FSM for short). Newer than the Bosphorus Bridge, it was built in 1988 by a Turkish-Japanese corporation and is longer (almost a mile) and wider (eight lanes) than the Bosphorus Bridge. While the first bridge is used mostly for local city traffic, the FSM sees more intercity and international travel (trucks are required to use the FSM).

As we approach **Kanlıca,** enjoy the view of impressive *yalıs,* many with drive-in "garages" for private boats. Kanlıca is a popular weekend spot, with many cafeterias and eateries along the water for locals to enjoy a cup of tea while soaking up the beautiful scenery. Kanlıca is also famous for its yogurt, served in small plastic containers and sprinkled with powdered sugar. As you leave the port, servers will scamper around the boat selling fresh yogurt just picked up here.

KANLICA TO YENIKÖY

• *Keep watching Asia.*

After cruising less than a mile, look up the hill and into the woods at the fancy tower of the renowned **Hidiv Pavilion.** It was

built in the Art Nouveau style at the end of the 19th century for the Ottoman governor of Egypt. Hidiv means just that in Turkish—"Governor of Egypt." You'll get a better

view of the building as the boat slides away from the Asian shore.

• *The next stop is on the European side (left).*

Now the boat heads back across the Bosphorus to dock at **Yeniköy** (yeh-nee-koy; "new village"). This trendy, high-end district has some of the most elaborate houses on the Bosphorus. Some are traditional wood constructions, but quite a few newer ones have a distinctly modern style. American travelers often compare these with the mansions along the Mississippi River.

YENIKÖY TO SARIYER

• *Keep watching the European side (left).*

About five minutes after you leave Yeniköy, you'll see the **Presidential Mansion.** Built in the 19th century, this has been the summer mansion for the president of Turkey since 1985. The mansion's two three-story pavilions rise behind a long, tall stone wall running along the coastal road. The closest pavilion has a steep tile roof and a decoration that looks like a little onion dome at the front-left corner.

The small **Tarabya Bay** is marked by the multistory hotel complex at its right end. Here is where you'll start to feel a cool breeze

Returning Overland from Sarıyer

If you have the time, you can get off the ferry at Sarıyer and use the bus to visit some interesting sights on the way home (or to cut your Bosphorus cruise short). The southbound bus (#25E to Kabataş or #25T to Taksim) back to central Istanbul can take between 45 and 60 minutes, depending on the time of day and traffic. The bus stop is one block from the Sarıyer port: With the port behind you, walk right along the park and look for the bus stop across the street, where the street makes a sharp curve. Bus numbers are marked on a sign at the stop. Once on board, tell your driver (or fellow passengers) where you'd like to get off so they can help you find the right stop.

Here are your options:

Bus #25E: For a pleasant ride back to the city, take southbound bus #25E (Sarıyer-Kabataş). This bus takes a scenic route along the Bosphorus (runs 6:30-22:15, less frequently after 21:00). It connects easily with the Old Town tram and the Kabataş-Taksim funicular.

Bus #25E also provides a convenient connection to the Sadberk Hanım Museum, Sakıp Sabancı Museum, and Rumeli Fortress (see page 57), as well as the ever-popular Ortaköy district by the Bosphorus Bridge. To reach the **Sadberk Hanım Museum,** walk (south) from the Sarıyer ferry stop for about 10 easy minutes. Or take southbound bus #25E and get off at the Sefaret (seh-fah-reht) stop, then walk a few blocks south along the coastal road (with the Bosphorus on your left). After you visit the museum, walk back to the same stop to catch the same bus to Kabataş. Or, if you enjoy strolling near the water, keep heading

---

from the north. It's the prevailing wind all year long, cooling Bosphorus temperatures quite a bit in the summer.

• *Turn back to Asia (right).*

Half a mile past Tarabya Bay, from the right side of the boat, you'll get your first glimpse of the **Black Sea.**

• *And then turn back to Europe again (left).*

Our next stop, **Sarıyer** (sah-ruh-yehr), is at the far end of the large bay. Transit-pass holders can consider getting off at Sarıyer—either now, or on the way home—to return to downtown Istanbul overland by bus, stopping to see some sights en route (see sidebar).

SARIYER TO RUMELI KAVAĞI

• *Watch the European side (left).*

As you leave Sarıyer, you'll cruise very close to the bank for one more stop on the European side before the boat heads to its last stop on the Asian side. Beyond this point, the wind gets stronger. Locals call this wind Poyraz (poy-rahz), after Boreas, the Greek god of wind.

south until you get tired, then catch a bus.

For the **Sakıp Sabancı Museum,** get off bus #25E at the Çınaraltı stop. After your visit, catch another bus at the same stop to return to Istanbul.

For the Rumeli Fortress, get off bus #25E at the Rumeli Hisarı (roo-meh-lee hee-sah-ruh) stop. To return to Istanbul, catch another bus where you got off, or walk to the next stop, Aşiyan, on the hillside just past the cemetery (next to the fortress).

For the **Ortaköy district,** get off bus #25E at the Ortaköy (ohr-tah-koy) stop and enjoy one of Istanbul's most picturesque pedestrian areas. Popular among the younger generation, Ortaköy is crowded on weekends, sunny days, and all summer long. It's also full of eateries: seafood restaurants, fast-food joints, cafés, and tea shops. Students and artists display their handicrafts for sale—usually souvenirs and simple jewelry.

Bus #25T: This is the quickest way to get from Sarıyer to **Taksim Square** in the New District, but what you make up in time you lose in scenery, since it takes the inland freeway. Bus #25T runs every 15-60 minutes 6:30-23:40 (less frequently after 21:00). Take this only if you want to make a beeline back to Taksim Square.

At Sarıyer: If you have time to spare before catching a bus, detour to the Sarıyer fish market. With the port behind you, follow the road to the right, and take the first right, soon after the street curves left. The fish market is a couple of blocks down on the right, behind the little square. Try the specialty: deep-fried mussels.

Cruising along fishing communities and narrow marinas where fishing boats are tied up, you'll soon come to the village of **Rumeli Kavağı** (roo-meh-lee kah-vah-uh). Then the ferry heads for its last stop: the fishing village of Anadolu Kavağı on the Asian side, right across from Rumeli Kavağı.

RUMELI KAVAĞI TO ANADOLU KAVAĞI
• *Keep watching the European side (left).*

As the boat turns toward Asia, from the left side you can enjoy a great view of the Bosphorus opening into the **Black Sea.** You may catch a glimpse of the third Bosphorus bridge, the Yavuz Sultan Selim Bridge, the world's widest suspension bridge, scheduled to open in 2016. Even the casual tourist senses the dark, foreboding

aura of this zone, where wind and rainstorms can gather within minutes, even in the middle of summer.

Up the shore on the European side are some extremely dangerous hidden rocks that have long plagued navigators. If you know the tale of Jason and the Argonauts, you may remember the **Clashing Rocks** (or Symplegades) the crew encountered as they sailed into the Black Sea. These rocks of legend are believed by some to be based on this stretch of the Bosphorus. In Jason's time, the rocks would dangerously lunge toward one another, demolishing any boats that tried to pass. To make it through, the Argonauts let loose a dove, which was guided by the goddess Athena and led them to safety. After this, the rocks stopped clashing, but remained a potentially destructive obstacle. Byzantine emperors erected a huge column here to warn passing ships. It worked...except when thick fog made this part of the Bosphorus nearly impossible to navigate. It's still difficult today, even with state-of-the-art electronic equipment.

• *Turn toward Asia (right) as we near our final stop...*

Anadolu Kavağı

Welcome to Asia: the small fishing village of Anadolu Kavağı (ah-nah-doh-loo kah-vah-uh). *Anadolu* comes from the Greek word *anatoli*, meaning "the land to the East," while *kavak* means "controlled pass." From Byzantine times to the present, this has been a strategic checkpoint for vessels going through the Bosphorus. As you approach the Asian side, watch for the Byzantine **Yoros Castle** that dominates the hilltop above the village. Below that, notice the modern military installations: The area between here and the Black Sea is a restricted-access zone.

The ferry takes a break here in Anadolu Kavağı, usually for two to three hours. Look for the scheduled departure time posted near the dock, or ask the attendant what time to be back. Be sure to arrive back at the boat at least 10 minutes before the departure time—or earlier, if you want to secure a prime seat for the return trip.

Planning Your Time: Anadolu Kavağı has two main activities—eating lunch or hiking up to Yoros Castle (although the castle is under renovation and may be closed throughout 2016). If you're speedy or have a longer break, you'll probably be able to squeeze in both; if you'd like a more leisurely experience, choose one. (Both options are described later.)

Overland Return to Istanbul: Don't miss the boat. But if you do, you can either take a taxi back to Istanbul (figure 90 TL), or use the bus (see page 294). You can catch the bus at the town center, a block straight ahead from the ferry port. Begin by taking bus #15A (Anadolu Kavağı-Kavacık) to the Körfez (Beykoz) stop. From there you can take bus #15P and #15T to Üsküdar or #15F to Kadıköy (both on the Asian side), where you can catch a ferry back to Eminönü in the Old Town.

EATING IN ANADOLU KAVAĞI

Anadolu Kavağı is made-to-order for enjoying a leisurely lunch. The town is packed with down-to-earth restaurants that cater to Bosphorus cruise passengers—both international tourists and Istanbul residents who come here for a nice meal on the weekends. As you step off the boat, the streets just ahead of you and for two blocks to the left are filled with nothing but restaurants. (The path leading up to the castle is also lined with eateries, but their quality isn't as reliable.)

The specialty is seafood, of course. You can find a wide range of fish straight out of the strait. Most eateries advertise *midye tava* (meed-yeh tah-vah)—deep-fried mussels. Popular all over Istanbul, these are mussels dipped in batter, deep-fried, and served with *tarator* (tah-rah-tohr) sauce—made from bread, crushed fresh garlic, lemon juice, yogurt, olive oil, salt, and vinegar. Upscale restaurants sometimes add crushed walnuts to the mix. Fried calamari is also common, but beware: It's not native to Istanbul and is usually frozen, not fresh.

Before settling in, ignore the hawkers and stroll around to find the place that looks best. Most of the cheaper eateries sell a fixed-price meal for 30-35 TL that includes grilled fish, fried mussels, French fries, salad, bread, and a drink. Fancier restaurants have a wider (and more expensive) menu. If you opt to go à la carte, one portion of *midye tava* can be a light meal. For about 45 TL, two people can get two portions of *midye tava*, two drinks, and split a fresh fish fillet.

Other options include sandwiches, salads, *pide* (pee-deh; Turkish pizza), kebabs, and even waffles, although your options may be limited in the off-season (late Oct-late April). For dessert, try the *lokma* (lohk-mah) advertised by stalls and restaurants. This is a crispier version of a doughnut hole, made by dipping wheat dumplings into hot syrup. Locals love it and have been known to travel to Anadolu Kavağı just for fresh-cooked *lokma*. **Yosun Restaurant,** to your immediate left as you stand with the ferry dock at your back, has a *lokma* stand at the corner.

The grocery store and the bakery are good places to pick up supplies for a people-watching picnic on a bench in the square, or to munch up at the castle. To find them, follow the narrow street straight ahead from the port. The bakery is on the other side of the intersecting street, just before the parking lot, and the grocery

The Fish of the Bosphorus Strait and the Sea of Marmara

Fish is an essential part of Istanbul's cuisine, offering a flavorful alternative to kebabs. Many locals can tell at a glance just how many hours a fish has been out of the water. But with Istanbul's population now nearly 15 million, the once-abundant native fish are becoming scarcer, and prospects for the future are uncertain. Fishing stocks have been depleted by the use of large fishing boats, which consequently are now banned from June to September. However, fishing for sport is still allowed, and many people fish along the Bosphorus. Fishermen yell at passing boats that get too close and scare away their potential catch.

While perusing Istanbul's menus, keep an eye out for the following fish. In some cases, we've listed the months when they're most abundant, but you may also find them at other times.

Barbun (bahr-boon): This little red mullet, which lives along the muddy seabed, can be caught year-round. A local delicacy, it's delicious when deep-fried and is often served as a side dish or hot appetizer. No need to remove the bones—just crunch them down.

Çinekop (chee-neh-kohp): This young bluefish is popular when grilled, and is available from early October through the

store is past the parking lot. The bakery's specialty is anchovy bread (*hamsili ekmek;* hahm-see-lee ehk-mehk)—a Black Sea delicacy made with corn flour, leeks, tomatoes, fresh peppers, and fresh anchovies.

YOROS CASTLE (YOROS KALESI)

Aside from having a meal and wandering the town, the only other activity in Anadolu Kavağı is to hike up to Yoros Castle, on the hilltop above town. The castle is undergoing renovation and may remain closed through 2016. Check its status with the ferry staff or with locals when you arrive at Anadolu Kavağı.

While this run-down castle ruin hardly reflects the glory of its past, it

end of November.

Hamsi (hahm-see): A delicacy from the Black Sea, this anchovy is in season from November to March. Natives cook this small fish in dozens of ways—including fried, steamed, and grilled, as well as mixed in casseroles and even added to cornbread. Hamsi are especially good when steamed in large trays with onions, tomatoes, green peppers, and lemons—creating a traditional dish called *hamsi buğulama* (hahm-see boo-oo-lah-mah).

Istavrit (ees-tahv-reet): This mackerel, generally served fried, is available throughout the year.

Kalkan (kahl-kahn): Best when pan-fried, this delicious turbot lives in the Sea of Marmara and is usually in the markets from December to April. As it's becoming rarer, you may find it only in upscale restaurants. It has round bones that locals call "buttons"; the female fish have fewer bones than the males.

Levrek (lehv-rehk): While its tastier wild cousins are expensive, farm-raised sea bass is cheap and available year-round. Although it's not wild, it's still worth a try—especially grilled.

Lüfer (lew-fehr): Its lack of a "fishy" taste makes this type of bluefish extremely popular in Istanbul. It's becoming rare—and expensive—and is usually available from late September to January.

Mezgit (mehz-geet): Fish-sellers hawk this whiting throughout the year. It's best either pan-fried or steamed with vegetables, though natives of Istanbul have never developed a real taste for its chicken-like flavor.

does afford fine views over the Bosphorus and to the Black Sea. You can combine a castle hike with a picnic from the grocery store in town. Public WCs are en route. You'll notice lots of litter, as well as friendly but hungry stray dogs eyeing you, hoping for your leftovers.

The moderately strenuous hike takes about 20 minutes each way. Most of the way up, you'll be passing through a military-controlled zone, so put your camera away. Once at the castle, feel free to take photos. Our hike goes up the south side of the hill where there are fewer breezes, so it may feel a little warmer than you'd expect.

Castle Hike: Standing with your back to the ferry port, walk straight ahead toward the large, square street fountain (with the gold Arabic script). After the fountain, take the street to your left, and walk about 100 yards (bearing left at the fork) until you reach the corner of the yellow, 16th-century Ali Reis Mosque (you'll see a sign to *Yoros Kalesi*—that's Yoros Castle—across the street). Turn right and walk with the mosque on your right-hand side. Soon you'll see the Navy station fence on your left. After about 100 yards, you'll come to a fork—keep to the left.

The road gets steeper and bears right as you continue up and up. After passing a stand of cypress trees, the road makes a sharp curve to the left, offering glances of the Bosphorus beyond the parking lot. Up ahead, you also see part of the lower wall of Yoros Castle. Keep walking.

Past the wall fragments, there's another fork—keep right (the left fork goes to a military checkpoint). Less than 100 yards later, after the road curves left, you'll see a large aerial photo of the castle on the wall to your left (with a sign reading *To Castle/Ceneviz Kalesi*). Follow the steps next to the sign, up past the café tables. Keep to the right as the path, punctuated with simple steps, leads you through more humble eateries on its way to the castle entrance. You'll soon see the castle wall to your left, as well as public WCs, picnic tables, and hammocks.

Reaching the end of the path, take the stairs to your left, through Yoros Café (ignore the plaster lion statues and menus—the steps are public, not part of the restaurant). These steps lead all the way up, straight to the gate of Yoros Castle. After passing through the gate (free, always open), you're in an open courtyard with several rough paths and the graffiti-marred remains of the former military fortress. Head up to the top of the courtyard for your reward: spectacular views of the Bosphorus and the Black Sea—and the cool northerly breeze. Yoros Castle is quite popular on weekends in good weather, when it's packed with locals.

• *Enjoy the view and the town below, then head back to the ferry for the cruise back to Europe, and Istanbul.*

SLEEPING IN ISTANBUL

Istanbul has an abundance of comfortable, well-located hotels. We've focused our recommendations on two safe, handy, and colorful neighborhoods: the historic Old Town (the Sultanahmet and Sirkeci districts); and the New District (İstiklal Street, a.k.a. İstiklal Caddesi). Prices aren't cheap, but there are a few deals to be found. In each neighborhood, we list good hotels and offer tourist and transit tips. These districts also have a selection of restaurants listed in the Eating in Istanbul chapter.

Staying on the banks of Bosphorus Strait gives you the chance to enjoy views not only of the sea, but also of another continent across the water. However, these views come with hefty price tags. Near the end of this chapter, we've listed two hotels which have prime locations that don't break the bank. Keep in mind that websites for some Istanbul hotels can overpromise—for example, a "sea view" may require some neck-craning, or may only be visible from the hotel's rooftop terrace.

Note that prices may vary from those listed here, and that discounts offered in this book are valid only when you book directly through a hotel's website, not through third-party booking sites. You must have the latest (seventh) edition of the guidebook to be guaranteed these deals. Discounts might also be available if you offer to pay cash.

For information and tips on pricing, getting deals, types of rooms, making reservations, and more, see page 396. To find options beyond those in this book, www.boutiquesmallhotels.com is ideal for locating small, charming hotels in Istanbul and the rest of Turkey.

In the Old Town

The Old Town, Istanbul's 3,000-year-old Byzantine core, is a welcoming, visitor-friendly area where hotels surround the city's most famous sights. Proximity to the sights is a mixed blessing: Many traditional old Ottoman houses in this area have been converted into hotels and pensions, and few locals can afford to live here anymore. So even though the buildings are in the genuine Istanbul style, the people aren't. Many of the Turks you encounter here are trying to sell you something—an inaccurate and unfortunate first impression of a kind and generous people. For tips on dealing with aggressive salespeople, see page 196.

Most of the accommodations we recommend are in a compact central district called Sultanahmet, but a few lovely gems are a bit further north in the bustling Sirkeci neighborhood.

The **Sultanahmet** district is named for the Blue Mosque (officially called the Sultan Ahmet Mosque, after its namesake), and the neighborhood is also home to some of Istanbul's other big sights—Hagia Sophia and the Grand Bazaar. Our recommended hotels are located within a 10-minute walk of these historic buildings. Daylight hours here are lively—the neighborhood is full of cafés and shops tucked into narrow streets originally built for horse-drawn carriages. In the evenings, many locals who work nearby go home, leaving the restaurants and cafés to tourists. But a few gems still frequented by locals are listed in the Eating chapter.

Busy **Sirkeci** is just a bit north of Sultanahmet, down the hill towards the Golden Horn. You'll find a commercial potpourri of tech stores, market shops, historic bazaars, restaurants, and fine, small hotels. It is also the home of Sirkeci train station (Istanbul Gar), the last stop of the famous Orient Express. Staying here gives you easy access to Taksim, Eminönü, and ferry ports on the Golden Horn.

Tourist Information: The Sultanahmet TI is at the bottom of the square called the Hippodrome, across from Hagia Sophia (generally daily 9:00-17:00). The Sirkeci TI is in the Sirkeci train station.

Transit Connections: The very convenient Sultanahmet tram stop on the main tram line is on Divan Yolu, about 200 yards up from Hagia Sophia. The Sirkeci and Gülhane tram stops are convenient to our recommended Sirkeci hotels. The tram connects you to Eminönü (a hub for public buses and ferries) and can also take you north of the Golden Horn to the New District. For more on getting around Istanbul, see page 22.

Sleep Code

Abbreviations (€1=about $1.10, 1 TL=about $0.33, country code: 90)
S=Single, **D**=Double/Twin, **T**=Triple, **Q**=Quad, **b**=bathroom, *=Turkish hotel rating system, SC=Special Class (renovated historic building).

Price Rankings
 $$$ **Higher Priced**—Most rooms €160 or more.
  $$ **Moderately Priced**—Most rooms €90-160.
   $ **Lower Priced**—Most rooms €90 or less.

Prices are listed in euros in this chapter and at most Istanbul hotels, because the euro is a more stable currency than the Turkish Lira (TL). Hotels will take cash payment in TL, euros, or US dollars.

Unless otherwise noted, credit cards are accepted, room tax and breakfast are included, free Wi-Fi and/or a guest computer is generally available, and English is spoken. Prices change; verify current rates online or by email.

IN SULTANAHMET

$$$ Hotel Sultanhan SC is an elegant hotel just off Divan Yolu, close to the Grand Bazaar and within walking distance of the Blue Mosque and Hagia Sophia. Its 40 rooms—larger than the norm for most Old Town hotels—have been restored with considerable care, and the staff is especially attentive (Sb-€200-240, Db-€240-280, Tb-€280-330, room rates can vary—check website for specials, 10 percent off best Internet rate if you mention this book when you reserve and show it at check-in, air-con, elevator, Piyer Loti Caddesi 7, tel. 0212/516-3232, www.hotelsultanhan.com, info@hotelsultanhan.com, manager Enis Akça).

$$$ Blue House SC has 26 smartly decorated rooms with bold color schemes. Some rooms have views of the nearby Blue Mosque. The terrace restaurant is wonderfully peaceful and offers great views of the Blue Mosque, the Sea of Marmara, and a bit of Hagia Sophia (Sb-€140, Db-€180, Tb-€215, lower prices off-season, 10 percent off best Internet rate if you mention this book when you reserve and show it at check-in, air-con, elevator, Dalbastı Sokak 14, tel. 0212/638-9010, www.bluehouse.com.tr, info@bluehouse.com.tr).

$$$ Hotel Golden Horn Sultanahmet**,** behind the Turkish and Islamic Arts Museum, is very close to Divan Yolu and the Sultanahmet tram stop. Recently renovated, its 75 rooms have been redecorated with new, stylish furniture and textiles. All rooms have air-conditioning, and some have views of the sea and the Blue Mosque (Sb-€165, Db-€175, Tb-€235, lower prices off-season, check website for specials, 10 percent off best Internet rate if you mention this book when you reserve and show it at check-in,

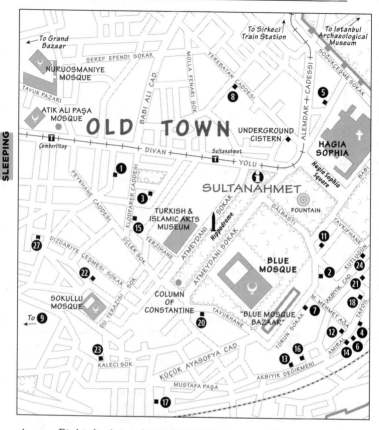

air-con, Binbirdirek 1, tel. 0212/518-1717, www.goldenhornhotel. com, info@goldenhornhotel.com).

$$$ Azade Hotel SC, about three blocks down the hill from the Blue Mosque, was converted from an old Ottoman house. Its 33 rooms manage an old-fashioned charm, and the breakfast terrace has sweeping views of the Bosphorus, Sea of Marmara, and the Blue Mosque (standard Sb-€169, standard Db-€199, Tb-€229, family room-€279, seaview rooms-€30 more, 10 percent off best Internet rate if you mention this book when you reserve and show it at check-in, free airport pickup with 3-night stay, air-con, elevator plus some stairs, Mimar Mehmet Ağa 17, tel. 0212/517-7173, www.azadehotel.com, info@azadehotel.com, helpful staff includes manager Ömer Sümengen, receptionist Sinan, and reservations supervisor İbrahim).

$$$ Azade Premier is Azade Hotel's new and slightly more expensive sister hotel, sharing the same courtyard. "Oriental" rooms are larger and tastefully decorated (prices are €20-50 more than Azade's, 10 percent off best Internet rate if you mention this

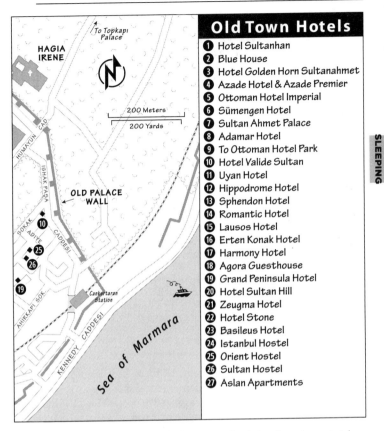

Old Town Hotels

1. Hotel Sultanhan
2. Blue House
3. Hotel Golden Horn Sultanahmet
4. Azade Hotel & Azade Premier
5. Ottoman Hotel Imperial
6. Sümengen Hotel
7. Sultan Ahmet Palace
8. Adamar Hotel
9. To Ottoman Hotel Park
10. Hotel Valide Sultan
11. Uyan Hotel
12. Hippodrome Hotel
13. Sphendon Hotel
14. Romantic Hotel
15. Lausos Hotel
16. Erten Konak Hotel
17. Harmony Hotel
18. Agora Guesthouse
19. Grand Peninsula Hotel
20. Hotel Sultan Hill
21. Zeugma Hotel
22. Hotel Stone
23. Basileus Hotel
24. Istanbul Hostel
25. Orient Hostel
26. Sultan Hostel
27. Aslan Apartments

SLEEPING

book when you reserve and show it at check-in, free airport pickup with 3-night stay, Mimar Mehmet Ağa Caddesi, Amiral Tafdil Sokak 7, tel. 0212/458-1230, www.azadepremier.com, info@azadepremier.com).

$$$ Ottoman Hotel Imperial SC is a freshly renovated former Ottoman school and hospital right across the street from Hagia Sophia. Its 27 rooms—plus 25 more in an annex building—are comfortable and plush. Managers Serdar Balta and Kenan Özkan cherish Rick Steves readers (Sb-€159, Db-€169, "premium" rooms with Hagia Sophia view-€40-60 extra, 15 percent off best Internet rate if you use the discount code "RCKSTV15" when you reserve and show the book at check-in, plus 10 percent discount at the Matbah Restaurant, free airport pickup with 3-night stay, air-con, elevator to premium rooms, laundry service, Caferiye Sokak 6/1, tel. 0212/513-6151, www.ottomanhotelimperial.com, info@ottomanhotelimperial.com).

$$$ Sümengen Hotel is one of the older small hotels in this area, with a cozy feel and reliable staff. Its rooms are larger than

---

Old Town Versus New District: Where to Sleep?

The character of your stay in Istanbul can be determined to a great extent by where your hotel is located.

If you prefer romantic and classic old Istanbul—calls to prayer, graceful minarets outside your hotel, rough cobbled lanes, and must-see sights (mosques, bazaars, and palaces) within an easy walk—go for the Old Town's Sultanahmet or Sirkeci districts. Most of the hotels listed here are in a zone that's very tourist-friendly, where foreigners can feel comfortable amid traditional surroundings.

But if you'd prefer to experience the tempo of today's Istanbul—stylish shoppers and office workers strolling down big noisy streets, filling the main pedestrian boulevard with high energy until late each night—make the New District your home base. Your New District hotel serves more businesspeople than tourists, and the neighborhood offers a diverse selection of restaurants and nightlife. Karaköy, the New District's historic banking center, was neglected for decades. Now it's becoming trendy, with small boutique hotels, fine restaurants, and inviting shops opening one after another. It may be an ideal place to stay, for its proximity to the Old Town and easy access to both parts of the city.

---

average in the Old Town, and some of them have large Jacuzzis with views of the Sea of Marmara and islands. The top-floor breakfast room also has great views (Sb-€219, Db-€229, Tb-€259, elevator, 10 percent off best Internet rate if you mention this book when you reserve and show it at check-in, Mimar Mehmet Ağa Caddesi 7, tel. 0212/517-6869, www.sumengenhotel.com, info@sumengenhotel.com).

$$$ Sultan Ahmet Palace SC, with 45 clean, classy rooms across the street below the Blue Mosque, will have you feeling like a guest of the sultan. From the deserted-feeling street, you'll pass through a lush garden, then an elegant lobby, to reach the reception desk—and in your bathroom, you'll find faux-Turkish bath fixtures. This place is likely to have space when others are full (standard Sb-€150, standard Db-€170, air-con, no elevator, Torun Sokak 19, tel. 0212/458-0460, www.sultanahmetpalace.com, saray@sultanahmetpalace.com).

$$ Adamar Hotel SC has an uninspired lobby, but its terrace has a panoramic view of the Old Town and the New District, and some of its 25 minimalist rooms also have exceptional views. It's on the same street as the Underground Cistern (Sb-€109-125, Db-€119-139, Tb-€155-181, Qb-€185-201, lower prices off-season, 5 percent off best Internet rate if you mention this book when you reserve and show it at check-in, free airport pickup with 3-night stay, air-con, elevator, laundry service, Yerebatan Caddesi 37, tel. 0212/511-1936, www.adamarhotel.com, info@adamarhotel.com, manager Serkan Doğan).

$$ Ottoman Hotel Park SC, about a 10-minute walk from the heart of the Old Town, is a new place, finely decorated in a modernized Ottoman style. The three categories of rooms differ only in size—all have the same amenities. Managers Serdar Balta and Kenan Özkan are hospitable and eager to please (standard Sb-€139, Db-€149, Tb-€179, 15 percent off best Internet rate if you use the discount code "RCKSTV15" when you reserve and show the book at check-in, lower rates off-season, check website for best prices, air-con, elevator, tel. 0212/516-0211, Kumkapı, Kadırga Limanı Caddesi 85, www.ottomanhotelpark.com, info@ottomanhotelpark.com).

$$ Hotel Valide Sultan SC ("Sultan's Mother") is 100 yards down the busy street from the Topkapı Palace's Imperial Gate. This 19th-century Ottoman mansion has 17 neat rooms, friendly staff, and an imperial lobby with elegant furnishings, though it's a bit past its prime (Sb-€95, Db-€120, Tb-€140, lower rates off-season, 10 percent off best Internet rate if you mention this book when you reserve and show it at check-in, free airport pickup with 3-night stay, some rooms have sea views, air-con, elevator, İshak Paşa Caddesi, Kutlugün Sokak 1, tel. 0212/517-6558, www.hotelvalidesultan.com, vsultan@hotelvalidesultan.com).

$$ Uyan Hotel SC is family-run and convenient—it's a very short walk to the Blue Mosque, Hagia Sophia, and Topkapı Palace—and offers sweet views from its terrace. The 29 tidy rooms are as advertised: Single rooms are true singles, and "small doubles" are compact, with no views. The basement family suite is a good value if you're traveling with two or three kids (Sb/Db-€75-99, deluxe Db-€95-130, 5 percent off best Internet rate if you mention this book when you reserve and show it at check-in, free airport pickup with 3-night stay, air-con, elevator, Utangaç Sokak 25, tel. 0212/516-4892 or 0212/518-9255, www.uyanhotel.com, info@uyanhotel.com, manager Humeyra Masanovic).

$$ Hippodrome Hotel SC is owned by the nearby Azade Hotel (listed earlier). Its recently renovated rooms, while small, are comfortably decorated with new furniture. In the building across the street, they also have two three-bedroom apartments with room for six, and a two-bedroom apartment with room for four—ideal for families (S-€99, Db-€109, Tb-€135, family room for four-€160, 10 percent off best Internet rate if you mention this book when you reserve and show it at check-in, check website for other special deals, free one-way airport transfer with 4-night stay, breakfast at Azade Hotel, air-con, elevator in main building only, Mimar

Mehmet Ağa 22, tel. 0212/517-6889, www.hippodromehotel.com, hippodrome@hippodromehotel.com).

$$ Sphendon Hotel SC is a cute place with a tiny seaview terrace and a delightful patio out back where breakfast is served in the summer. Its 12 rooms are within walking distance of the heart of the Old Town (Sb-€80, Db-€90, Tb-€100, lower prices off-season; check website for specials, 5 percent off best Internet rate if you mention this book when you reserve and show it at check-in, air-con, Akbıyık Değirmeni Sokak 50, tel. 0212/518-5820, www.hotelsphendon.com, owner Erdal Demirli).

$$ Romantic Hotel SC's nine smallish rooms are warm and woodsy, tucked inside a converted old mansion only three blocks down from the Blue Mosque. Some rooms have great views and balconies, and breakfast is served on a teeny terrace with a magnificent view of the Sea of Marmara (Sb-€75-90, Db-€85-100, Tb-€105-135; free airport pickup with 3-night stay in high season and 5-night stay in low season; air-con, Amiral Tafdil Sokak 17, tel. 0212/638-9635, www.romantichotelistanbul.com, info@romantichotelistanbul.com, friendly Atilla and Erdal).

$ Lausos Hotel SC, with 30 rooms, is a couple of blocks from the Hippodrome. Some rooms have views of the Blue Mosque and/or the Sea of Marmara and Princes' Islands (Sb/economy Db-€70-90, standard Db-€80-90, Tb-€115-125, seaview rooms-€45-65 more, air-con, elevator, Klodfarer Caddesi 33, tel. 0212/638-0707, www.hotellausos.com, manager Mustafa Özduman).

$ Erten Konak Hotel SC is set in two renovated Ottoman houses on a quiet street, a few blocks down from the Blue Mosque (reception is in the smaller house). The decor is lively, with antique paintings on glass and swirling, gold designs on white walls. Breakfast is served in the greenhouse-like structure in the pleasant garden (Sb/Db-€58-65, rates vary with demand and season, larger deluxe rooms have more frills, air-con, no elevator, Akbıyık Değirmeni Sokak 8-10, at intersection with Akbıyık Caddesi, Sultanahmet, tel. 0212/458-5000, www.ertenkonak.com, info@ertenkonak.com, owner Atahan Erten).

$ Harmony Hotel is a newly restored budget hotel with 22 small rooms and a family room for four. Like most other hotels in this part of the city, the terrace has a nice view of the Sea of Marmara. Breakfast is served in the well-lit basement (Sb-€55-60, Db-€65-70, Tb-€75-80, Qb-€85-90, 5 percent off best Internet rate if you mention this book when you reserve and show it at check-in, free one-way airport transfer, Küçük Ayasofya Mahallesi, Aksakal Caddesi 26, tel. 0212/518-8700, www.istanbulharmony.com, info@istanbulharmony.com).

$ Agora Guesthouse has doubles, triples, and dorm rooms (bunk in dorm room-€17-25, Sb/Db-€80, Tb-€120, cheaper prices in off-season, check website for specials, air-con, Akbıyık Caddesi, Amiral Tafdil Sokak 6, tel. 0212/458-5547, www.agoraguesthouse. com, info@agoraguesthouse.com).

$ Grand Peninsula Hotel SC is, despite its name, a petite place with 18 fresh, tidy rooms. The breakfast terrace has a pleasant view of the sea (Sb-€40-60, Db-€60-80 depending on size, Tb-€70-90, family room-€80-100, air-con, Akbıyık Caddesi, Çetinkaya Sokak 3, tel. 0212/458-7710, www.grandpeninsulahotel. com, info@grandpeninsulahotel.com, friendly Ramazan).

$ Hotel Sultan Hill SC, immediately behind the Blue Mosque and a few steps off the Hippodrome, has 17 clean, comfortable rooms on three floors of an old Ottoman house. Straightforward managers Nilgün and Sedat enjoy helping American travelers (Sb-€60, Db-€80, Tb-€120, family room-€140, 15 percent off best Internet rate if you mention this book when you reserve and show it at check-in, air-con, Tavukhane Sokak 15, tel. 0212/518-3293, www. hotelsultanhill.com, info@hotelsultanhill.com).

$ Zeugma Hotel, located amid hostels on backpacker-friendly Akbıyık Caddesi, offers simple, well-kept, budget rooms (Sb/Db/Tb-€50-80, suite-€80-100; air-con, Akbıyık Caddesi 35, tel. 0212/517-4040, www.zeugmahotel.com, info@zeugmahotel.com, manager Melih Taşdemir). A plethora of cafés and restaurants are just out the front door.

$ Hotel Stone SC, two long blocks from the Hippodrome (across from the Sokullu Mosque), is a suitable budget option with some of the area's lowest prices. It's located in a quiet, mostly residential neighborhood, has a relaxing stone garden out back, and was recently renovated (Sb-€69, Db-€79, Tb-€99, less off-season, 10 percent off best Internet rate if you mention this book when you reserve and show it at check-in, discount for longer stays, free airport pickup with 5-night stay, air-con, elevator, Binbirdirek Mahallesi, Şehit Mehmet Paşa Yokuşu 34, tel. 0212/638-1554, www. stonehotelistanbul.com, info@stonehotelistanbul.com).

$ Basileus Hotel is a small, well-maintained budget hotel on a relatively quiet street southwest of the Blue Mosque and a short walk from the Hippodrome and Akbıyık Caddesi. Its 20 rooms come with basic furnishings, but some have French doors and small balconies—the natural light makes them seem grander. Guests rave about the friendly staff and warm hospitality (Sb-€55-80, Db-€70-95, Tb-€80-120, family room-€95-135; 10 percent off if you mention this book when you reserve, show it at check-in, and pay cash; air-con, Küçük Ayasofya Mahallesi Şehit Mehmet Paşa Sokak 1, tel. 0212/517-7878, www.basileushotel.com, info@basileushotel.com).

SLEEPING

Sirkeci Hotels & Restaurants

GALATA BRIDGE
RAGIP GÜMÜŞPALA
Golden Horn
Eminönü
NEW MOSQUE
REŞADIYE
SPICE MARKET
KENNEDY CADDESI
HAMIDIYE CAD.
Sirkeci
SIRKECI TRAIN STATION
BÜYÜK
POSTANE CAD.
VASIF ÇINAR
AŞIR EFENDI
ANKARA
HÜDAVENDIGAR
200 Meters
200 Yards
Gülhane Park
TOPKAPI PALACE
EBUSSUUT
Gülhane
To Hagia Sophia & Blue Mosque
ISTANBUL ARCHAEOLOGICAL MUSEUM

1 Sirkeci Mansion
2 Lalahan Hotel
3 Elanaz Hotel
4 Can Oba Restaurant & Şehzade Erzurum Çağ Kebabı
5 Hocapaşa Pidecisi

IN SIRKECI

$$$ Sirkeci Mansion, tucked on a silent street between the outer wall of Topkapı Palace and Sirkeci train station, is famous for its exceptional hospitality. It is a "large" small hotel with 52 rooms, and a complimentary sauna, spa, and small indoor pool. The bright, spacious deluxe rooms on the top floor, with private terraces overlooking historic Gülhane Park, are ideal for families and longer stays (Sb-€130, Db-€184, superior Tb-€232, deluxe Tb with view terrace-€284, elevator, complimentary refreshments in the lobby, 5 percent off best Internet rate if you mention this book when you reserve and show it at check-in, check website for other promotions, Taya Hatun Caddesi 5, tel. 0212/528-4344, www.sirkecimansion. com).

$$$ Lalahan Hotel, on the busy main street midway between the Sirkeci and Gülhane tram stations, is crisp and tiny. The third bed in the triple rooms is not a fold-out or a bunk bed, but an orthopedic bed disguised as a couch (Db-€171, Tb-€212, elevator, 5 percent off best Internet rate if you mention this book when you reserve and show it at check-in, check website for other promotions, Hüdavendigar Caddesi 26, tel. 0212/512-1301, www.lalahanhotel. com, geniune Zerrin and Meriç).

$$ Elanaz Hotel, a short walk to the Sirkeci train and tram stations—and surrounded by restaurants and cafés—is family-owned with decent-size, modern rooms (economy Db-€109, standard Db-€144, view room-€15 more, elevator, Orhaniye Caddesi 34, tel. 0212/528-2426, www.elanaz.com).

HOSTELS

These three hostels are among others located on or near the bustling-with-backpackers Akbıyık Caddesi ("White Moustache Street"), a couple of blocks below the Blue Mosque (toward the Sea of Marmara). Each offers dorm beds and some double rooms, and includes a simple Turkish breakfast. If you're trying to avoid American backpackers and other international travelers, give this street a miss. The Agora Guesthouse (listed earlier) also offers hostel-type accommodations.

$ **Istanbul Hostel,** just up the street from the Four Seasons, is nicely located and well-run. Its 70 beds are filled with travelers who enjoy hanging out in the basement bar or rooftop terrace (bunk in dorm room-€15-17, D-€45, Kutlu Gün Sokak 35, tel. 0212/516-9380, www.istanbulhostel.net, istanbulhostel@yahoo.com).

$ **Orient Hostel** is an official HI hostel and a backpacker mecca. The 152 beds in more than 35 rooms are a bit institutional, but a steady stream of Australian and Kiwi backpackers keeps the place lively (bunk in dorm room-€15-17, Sb-€65, Db-€70, Tb/Qb-€90, 10 percent off best Internet rate if you mention this book when you reserve and show it at check-in, check website for specials and off-season deals, Akbıyık Caddesi 9, tel. 0212/518-0789, www.orienthostel.com, info@orienthostel.com).

$ **Sultan Hostel** is another HI hostel, but feels less institutional than the Orient Hostel (bunk in dorm room-€13-17, Sb-€46-60, Db-€52-66, Tb-€66-75, 5 percent off best Internet rate if you mention this book when you reserve and show it at check-in, check website for specials and off-season deals, Akbıyık Caddesi 21, tel. 0212/516-9260, www.sultanhostel.com, sultan@sultanhostel.com).

APARTMENTS

$ **Aslan Apartments** have four 1- to 3-bedroom contemporary units in a residential neighborhood within walking distance of the Old Town sights. Because units have a well-equipped kitchen and other homey amenities, they're a nice alternative to hotels. Most have views, and all have balconies or patios (€115-135 seaview apartments for 4-5 people, €179-275 duplex garden apartments for 8-10 people, 2-night minimum, air-con, kitchen, laundry facilities, courtyard garden, 5 percent off best Internet rate if you mention this book when you reserve and show it at check-in—10 percent discount if paying cash; near the Çemberlitaş tram stop, Piyer Loti Caddesi Satır Sokak 5, Emin Sinan Mahallesi, Sultanahmet, tel.

0212/251-8530, mobile 0553-221-4224 or 0533-273-3042, www.aslanapartments.com, info@aslanapartments.com).

In the New District

Staying near İstiklal Street (İstiklal Caddesi) puts you right at the center of the living city. This hip part of town never sleeps. From restaurants, cafés, theaters, and art galleries to bookstores, fashion boutiques, rock bars, and jazz clubs, there's something here for locals and visitors of all ages. In the New District, you can melt right in and become part of the colorful scene.

Recently, the municipal government has undertaken projects to upgrade Taksim's infrastructure and preserve its Art Nouveau buildings. Due to the New District's popularity, prices here are higher than in the Old Town. Private apartments may be a good budget alternative (see the end of this chapter).

Tourist Information: The neighborhood TI is a short walk from Taksim Square (generally daily 9:00-17:00, Mete Caddesi 6, tel. 0212/233-0592).

Transit Connections: Since Taksim Square is one of Istanbul's primary transit hubs, the New District is well-connected to the Old Town (and other parts of the city). Two options are the most convenient for reaching the Old Town sights. From Taksim Square (near the first group of hotels listed next), take the funicular down to Kabataş, where you can catch the tram that zips into the historic core (get off at Sultanahmet for Hagia Sophia, the Blue Mosque, and other Old Town attractions). Or, from the opposite end of İstiklal Street (near the Galata Tower listings, later), take the old-fashioned funicular from Tünel down to Karaköy, where you can catch the same tram mentioned previously (to reach the Old Town, take this tram to Sultanahmet). The convenient Nostalgic Tram runs down the center of İstiklal Street, between Taksim Square and Tünel. The Metro connects Taksim Square and the Galata Tower neighborhood to the light-rail line serving Atatürk Airport.

NEAR TAKSIM SQUARE, AT THE TOP OF İSTIKLAL STREET

$$$ **Germir Palas Hotel SC,** on a busy street near Taksim Square, comes with an old-fashioned but tastefully plush lobby and 49 heavily perfumed rooms. Comfortable and classy, in a sophisticated Art Nouveau shell and with a smartly uniformed staff, it's a winner (Sb-€140, Db-€160, Tb-€190, air-con, elevator, Cumhuriyet Caddesi 7, tel. 0212/361-1110, www.germirpalas.com, hotel@germirpalas.com). From Taksim Square, with İstiklal Street behind you, walk

up the busy street (Cumhuriyet) that runs alongside a big park; the hotel is on the left after two blocks, across from the park.

$$ Triada Residence SC is just below Taksim Square, facing Aya Triada Church a half-block off İstiklal Street. This small, friendly place offers 10 good-size, no-nonsense, recently renovated apartments with new furniture. Its reasonable rates and excellent location make it popular—book ahead (Sb/Db-€90-130, Tb-€145, 10 percent discount off best Internet rate if you mention this book when you reserve and show it at check-in, air-con, elevator, İstiklal Caddesi, Meşelik Sokak 4, tel. 0212/251-0101, www.triada.com.tr, info@triada.com.tr).

$ Inntel Hotel, a new place located a short walk from Taksim Square, is simple and focused on client satisfaction. It's in the pedestrian-friendly "hotels' district" popular with international business travelers and convention-goers due to its proximity to Lütfi Kırdar Congress Center (Sb-€55-85, Db-€65-95, Tb-€120-140, 10 percent discount off best Internet rate if you mention this book when you reserve and show it at check-in, air-con, elevator, Kocatepe Mah. Dolapdere Caddesi 49, Taksim, tel. 0212/361-9292, www.inntelhotelistanbul.com).

ON OR NEAR İSTIKLAL STREET

$$$ Tomtom Suites SC, located just off İstiklal Street, has 20 suites in a historic building that was once a Franciscan convent. All suites have custom furniture and plush accessories. Guests can enjoy a small library with comfy sofas, books on Istanbul, an extensive DVD collection, and jazz and classical music CDs. The terrace has a nice view of the Old Town (Sb-Db-€249-299, Tb-€329-370, more for bigger suites and additional beds, 5 percent off best Internet rate if you mention this book when you reserve and show it at check-in, laundry service, Boğazkesen Caddesi, Tomtom Kaptan Sokak 18, Beyoğlu, tel. 0212/292-4949, www.tomtomsuites.com, info@tomtomsuites.com).

$$ Richmond Hotel has 103 small, business-class rooms without any personality—it's all about the location (just a few steps up İstiklal Street from the Tünel funicular station). The rooms were recently renovated (Sb-€109-125, Db-€125-170, rates can be soft—check website for specials, air-con, elevator, İstiklal Caddesi 227, tel. 0212/252-5460, www.richmondint.com.tr, info.istanbul@richmondint.com.tr).

$$ Stories Hotels is a small local chain of four boutique hotels near İstiklal Street. Each one is charming—set in beautiful, neatly furnished historic buildings with high ceilings. Most of their rooms have kitchenettes (5 percent discount off best Internet rate if you mention this book when you reserve and show it at check-in, breakfast not included, tel. 0212/292-2980, www.storieshotel.

SLEEPING

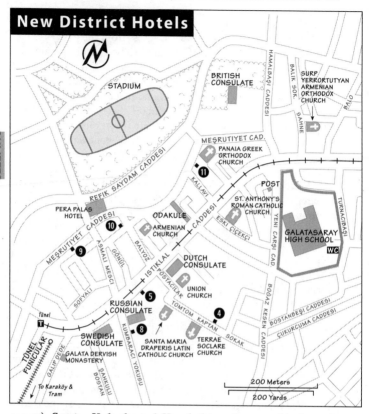

New District Hotels

com.tr). **Stories Kuloglu** and **Karakol**, on the same block, each offer well-equipped rooms and a 24-hour front desk (Db-€76-106, extra person-€30, elevator, Kuloglu: Ayhan Işık Sokak 30, Karakol: Sadri Alışık Sokak 26). **Stories Kumbaracı** is larger, with 24 rooms and a pleasant lobby. The popular restaurant next door, Yeni Lokanta, offers a special €10 breakfast deal for hotel guests. Some rooms have Bosphorus views (Db-€76-156, extra person-€30, elevator, Kumbaracı Yokuşu 66). **Stories Galata,** also called the **Rezidans,** is an apart-hotel with units available for longer-term rental. Reception is staffed during the day and there is a common lounge and kitchen in the well-lit basement (Db-€130-150, apartments-€150-€180, extra sofa bed-€30, breakfast-€10, Kumbaracı Yokuşu 37, see map on page 318).

ON MEŞRUTIYET CADDESI, NEAR İSTIKLAL STREET

$$ Pera Tulip Hotel** is large and modern, with 85 clean and spacious rooms on seven floors (some windows open onto a ventilation shaft). Top-floor "executive balcony" rooms have Golden Horn

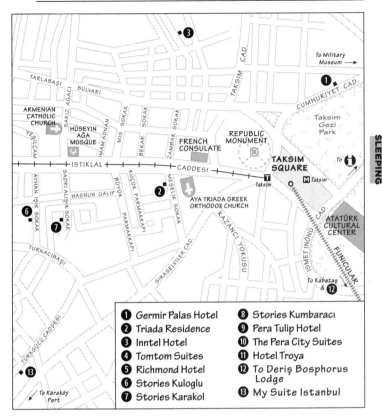

❶ Germir Palas Hotel	❽ Stories Kumbaracı
❷ Triada Residence	❾ Pera Tulip Hotel
❸ Inntel Hotel	❿ The Pera City Suites
❹ Tomtom Suites	⓫ Hotel Troya
❺ Richmond Hotel	⓬ To Deriş Bosphorus
❻ Stories Kuloglu	Lodge
❼ Stories Karakol	⓭ My Suite Istanbul

views. Renowned Turkish jazz musicians sometimes perform in their lounge (Sb/Db-€99-109, Tb-€129-139, rates vary by season, air-con, elevator, Meşrutiyet Caddesi 103, Tepebaşı, tel. 0212/243-8500, www.peratulip.com, sales@peratulip.com).

$$ The Pera City Suites SC is conveniently located and has a friendly staff, with 13 rooms that come in four categories: standard, junior, executive, and penthouse (standard Sb/Db-€89-159, Tb-€110-190, more for suites and additional beds, rates vary by season, air-con, elevator, Meşrutiyet Caddesi, Orhan Adli Apaydın Sokak 17, Tepebaşı, tel. 0212/292-4400, www.peracitysuites.com, info@peracitysuites.com).

$$ Hotel Troya SC is a newly renovated hotel just a short walk from İstiklal Street. Ask for a room with a real window—some of its 77 rooms face a ventilation shaft (Sb-€99, Db-€109, Tb-€119, rates vary by season, air-con, elevator, Meşrutiyet Caddesi 45, tel. 0212/251-8206, www.hoteltroya.com, troya@hoteltroya.com).

NEAR THE GALATA TOWER, AT
THE BOTTOM OF İSTIKLAL STREET

For the location of the following hotels, please see the map on page 318.

$$ Anemon Galata SC is next door to the Galata Tower. This historic building has been converted into a classy boutique hotel with 28 small, Old World-plush rooms and six suites, some with impressive Bosphorus or Golden Horn views (Sb-€90, Db-€112-135, lower rates off-season, air-con, elevator, breakfast terrace with spectacular view, Bereketzade Mahallesi, Büyükhendek Caddesi 5, tel. 0212/293-2343, www.anemonhotels.com, galata@ancmonhotels.com).

$$ Noble House Galata, on a dingy little alley near the Galata Tower, has eight rooms, each with its own theme, and all brimming with Old World-meets-contemporary style (Sb-€110, Db-€115, prices vary by room and season, 10 percent off best Internet rate if you mention this book when you reserve and show it at check-in, air-con, no elevator and lots of stairs, gay-friendly, late breakfast available, Şahkulu Mahallesi, Serdar-ı Ekrem Sokak 4, tel. 0212/243-7446, www.eklektikgalata.com, info@eklektikgalata.com).

$$ Galata Antique Hotel SC offers you the chance to stay in a 122-year-old Ottoman-French mansion designed by the same architect who did the Pera Palas Hotel. This family-owned boutique hotel, located close to Tünel, has lots of personality, with 22 rooms all differing in size and decor (standard Sb/Db-€115-144, superior Db-€144-174, 10 percent off best Internet rate if you mention this book when you reserve and show it at check-in, air-con, "historic" elevator, Meşrutiyet Caddesi 119, Tünel, tel. 0212/245-5944, www.galataantiquehotel.com, info@galataantiquehotel.com).

IN THE KARAKÖY NEIGHBORHOOD,
CLOSE TO THE PORT

$$$ Karaköy Rooms, in an elaborate early-20th-century building, offers nine simple, designer-decorated rooms with hardwood floors, plain white walls, and striking copper pipes. Some rooms have Bosphorus views (Sb/Db-€130-190, breakfast-€10, discounted nonrefundable rates available, Necatibey Caddesi, Galata Şarap İskelesi Sokak 10, Karaköy, tel. 0212/252-5422, www.karakoyrooms.com, info@karakoyrooms.com).

$$ Sub Hotel Karaköy is small and charming, with modern, minimalist rooms and breakfast served in its popular café. It is located on the main artery of Karaköy district (Sb/Db-€90-120, discounted nonrefundable rates available, 5 percent off best Internet rate if you mention this book when you reserve and show it at check-in, Necatibey Caddesi 91, Karaköy, tel. 0212/243-0005, http://subkarakoy.com, stay@subkarakoy.com).

$$ Karaköy Port Hotel is a little tacky, with inexpensive, gold-gilded furniture, but the gasp-inducing terrace view—including the Bosphorus, Old Town, and Golden Horn—makes up for it. Its location, with many nearby eateries, comes with noise (Sb-€119, Db-€139, partial-view Db-€159, excellent-value Db with full Bosphorus views-€169-179, Tb-€159, Tophane İskele Caddesi 10, Beyoğlu, tel. 0212/243-9868, www.karakoyporthotel.com).

$$ Portus House, a 10-room place with cheerful colors and simple decor, is one short block from the Bosphorus, and close to several fine eateries and public transportation. Family rooms and connecting rooms are available (D-€70, Db-€90, Tb-€95, Qb-€120-130, rates can be soft—check website for specials, discounted nonrefundable rates available, 5 percent off best Internet rate if you mention this book when you reserve and show it at check-in, Kemankeş Mahallesi, Mumhane Caddesi 31, Karaköy, tel. 0212/292-3850, www.portushouse.com, info@portushotel.com).

HOSTELS

$ Bada Bing Hostel, near the Karaköy port, is a short walk from the Golden Horn and ferry ports, and a quick tram ride from Sultanahmet. All bathrooms are shared (bunk in dorm room-€12-14, S/D-€40-50, breakfast not included, 10 percent off best Internet rate if you mention this book when you reserve and show it at check-in, includes sheets, no air-con, street noise when windows are open, tel. 0212/249-4111, Kemeraltı Caddesi, Serçe Sokağı 6, Karaköy, www.badabinghostel.com, info@badabinghostel.com, manager Volkan).

Elsewhere in Istanbul

ON THE BOSPHORUS

$$$ Radisson Blu Bosphorus Hotel is located right on the Bosphorus in the famous Ortaköy district, known for its busy party scene. While we don't typically list international chains, this hotel is an exception due to its location and decent prices compared to competitors on the Bosphorus. Its smallish rooms are uniform but comfortable, and some have spectacular views of the water. A generous breakfast buffet is served in the hotel restaurant, which has a terrace literally on the water (Sb-€240, Db-€220-250, €20-50 more for seaview rooms, Çırağan Caddesi 46, Ortaköy, tel. 0212/310-1500, www.radissonblu.com).

$$$ House Hotel Bosphorus belongs to a hip local chain better known for its trendy cafés and restaurants. The small, 26-room hotel is cheerful, tastefully decorated, and sits on the

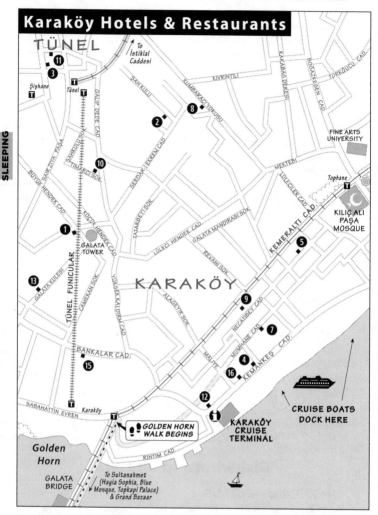

Karaköy Hotels & Restaurants

Bosphorus right at the center of Ortaköy. Breakfast is served in the first-floor café overlooking the strait. Though the rooms are soundproofed, street noise may be a problem for light sleepers. The top-floor seaview rooms with balconies and terraces match super-expensive competitors (Sb-€170-210, Db-€180-220, superior view rooms-€100 more, Salhane Sokak 1, Ortaköy, tel. 0212/327-7787, www.thehousehotel.com).

APARTMENTS

Renting an apartment can be a fun and cost-effective way to delve into Istanbul. Consider the following options; other rental resources are listed in the Practicalities chapter (page 404).

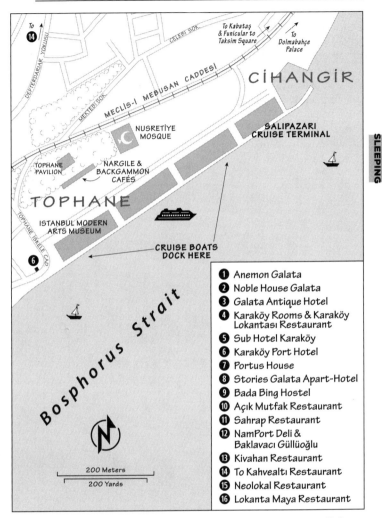

To 14

To Kabataş & Funicular to Taksim Square

To Dolmabahçe Palace

CELEBI SOK.

DEFTERDARLAR YOKUŞU

MECLİS-İ MEBUSAN CADDESİ

CİHANGİR

MEKTEBİ SOK.

NUSRETİYE MOSQUE

SALIPAZARI CRUISE TERMINAL

TOPHANE PAVILION

NARGİLE & BACKGAMMON CAFÉS

TOPHANE

ISTANBUL MODERN ARTS MUSEUM

TOPHANE İSKELE CAD.

6

CRUISE BOATS DOCK HERE

Bosphorus Strait

200 Meters
200 Yards

SLEEPING

❶ Anemon Galata
❷ Noble House Galata
❸ Galata Antique Hotel
❹ Karaköy Rooms & Karaköy Lokantası Restaurant
❺ Sub Hotel Karaköy
❻ Karaköy Port Hotel
❼ Portus House
❽ Stories Galata Apart-Hotel
❾ Bada Bing Hostel
❿ Açık Mutfak Restaurant
⓫ Sahrap Restaurant
⓬ NamPort Deli & Baklavacı Güllüoğlu
⓭ Kivahan Restaurant
⓮ To Kahvaltı Restaurant
⓯ Neolokal Restaurant
⓰ Lokanta Maya Restaurant

$$ Deriş Bosphorus Lodge, up the Bosphorus in Kabataş (close to Dolmabahçe), rents seven apartments. It's conveniently located near tram and funicular stations and the commuter ferry port. Some units have Bosphorus views, and all come with modern furniture, kitchens, and washing machines, making them ideal for families and long stays (Db/Tb-€100-150, panorama apartment that sleeps 5-€325-500, 3-night minimum, reception desk daily 8:00-23:00, overnight security staff, İnebolu Sokak 5/A, Kabataş Setüstü, tel. 0212/252-7913, www.derisbosphoruslodge.com, reservation@derisbosphoruslodge.com).

$ My Suite Istanbul is in the Cihangir neighborhood, the SoHo of Istanbul—just a few minutes' walk from İstiklal Street and full of little shops, restaurants, and cafés, none of them touristy. They offer two inviting hotel rooms and seven apartments, all decorated with warm and cheerful colors. Their central office is open 8:00-20:00; management is available by cell phone 24/7 (Sb-€75, Db-€85, Tb-€125, apartment for 4 people-€165-225 depending on view, 5 percent off best Internet rate if you mention this book when you reserve and show it at check-in, Firuzağa Mahallesi, Türkgücü Caddesi 74/A, Cihangir, tel. 0212/243-6889, www.mysuiteistanbul.com).

EATING IN ISTANBUL

Turkey's cuisine, with its roots in the Imperial Ottoman kitchen, reflects the rich cultural interaction of its ethnic ancestry: Turkish, Arab, Persian, and Greek. Indeed, what qualifies as Turkish food—and what doesn't—can be a bit ambiguous. You'll find many similar foods in the countries that neighbor Turkey. Given the immense and diverse territories that once made up the Ottoman Empire, it's no surprise that modern Turkish cuisine is multiethnic. The cuisine is further enriched by Turkey's fertile land—the varied geography and climates produce a great array of crops, vegetables, and fruits.

Turkish diners usually sit down to eat between 20:00 and 21:00, but most restaurants are ready to serve dinner much earlier. Be aware that restaurants are likely to be empty or even closed in daylight hours but busy after sunset during the religious festival of Ramadan (June 6-July 4 in 2016, May 27-June 25 in 2017). For more on Ramadan, see page 64.

A 10 percent tip is customary at sit-down cafés and restaurants; you can leave it on the table or hand it to your server when you sign the credit-card slip. While a tip isn't expected at self-service, cafeteria-style places, bussers appreciate an extra lira or two.

For more details on tipping, as well as other aspects of dining in Istanbul—including types of restaurants, advice on eating during Ramadan and navigating self-service eateries, and a rundown of Turkish cuisine and street food—see the "Eating" section in the Practicalities chapter (page 404).

When restaurant-hunting, choose a spot filled with locals, not the place with the big neon signs boasting, "We Speak English and Accept Credit Cards." Also consider Turkish street food, which is cheap, filling, and easy to find, especially in high-traffic areas such as İstiklal Street. Avoid drinking tap water in Istanbul: Restaurants

Restaurant Price Code

To help you choose among these listings, we've divided the restaurants into three categories, based on the price for a typical main course without wine (1 TL=about $0.33).

$$$ Higher Priced—Most main courses 35 TL or more
$$ Moderately Priced—Most main courses 25-35 TL
$ Lower Priced—Most main courses 25 TL or less

often serve water in plastic cups with peel-off tops, and bottled water is easy to find.

IN THE OLD TOWN'S SULTANAHMET AREA

These restaurants—along with most of our recommended hotels and much of Istanbul's best sightseeing—are concentrated in the Sultanahmet area.

$$$ Matbah Restaurant—where the manager and chef share their nearly two decades of research into imperial Ottoman cuisine—has a seasonal menu using fresh ingredients. Try the lamb neck with apricots and plums served alongside saffron rice with grape molasses; lamb shanks served with smoked eggplant puree; or *nergis kalyesi,* a vegetarian stew with mixed vegetables, walnuts, dill, and sour grapes (18-TL soups and salads, 15-20-TL starters, 35-40-TL main courses, 15-TL desserts, daily 11:30-23:30, next to Hagia Sophia in Ottoman Imperial Hotel, Caferiye Sokak 6/1, Sultanahmet, tel. 0212/514-6151).

$$$ Blue House Restaurant, located in the Blue House Hotel near the city's most important sights, boasts an outdoor terrace with amazing views of Blue Mosque and the Sea of Marmara. The atmosphere is peaceful and relaxed, and there is something for every taste on the simple menu. The staff is attentive and friendly (11-TL soups, 20-30-TL starters, 30-45-TL main courses, 11-TL desserts, Dalbastı Sokak 14, Sultanahmet, daily 12:00-23:00, tel. 0212/638-9010).

$$$ Deraliye Ottoman Palace Cuisine is a successful example of a restaurant re-creating the Sultan's food—the date of the original recipe is even listed on the menu. Though it feels somewhat upscale with its decor and attentive staff, most clients are everyday visitors looking for unrushed, well-prepared Ottoman cuisine (12-20-TL salads, soups, and starters; 25-60-TL main courses; 15-20-TL desserts; Ticarethane Sokak 10, Sultanahmet; tel. 0212/520-7778, www.deraliyerestaurant.com).

$$$ Albura Kathisma, on eatery-lined Akbıyık Street, is a versatile restaurant, where caring staff busily serve from 10:00 until midnight. It's built over the remnants of a great Byzantine palace—don't leave without peeking into the "cistern" in the basement. You have three seating options: outdoors on the front patio, in the casual and cozy interior, and on the elegant covered terrace. If you have a seating preference, consider making a reservation (10-25-TL soups, salads, mezes, pasta, pizzas, and desserts; 35-45-TL kebabs and main courses; Akbıyık Caddesi 36, Sultanahmet, tel. 0212/517-9031, www.alburakathisma.com).

$ Yıldız Restaurant started as a coffee shop run by Erol Taş, a popular 1970s Turkish actor who always played the bad guy. Locals often call it by its old name, "Erol Taş Kıraathanesi" (Erol Taş coffee shop). Today, hardworking İsmet Yıldız runs the place as a simple restaurant and neighborhood café. Inside, the walls are covered with photos of famous Turkish actors and actresses; many were personal friends and clients of the iconic villain. There's a real neighborhood vibe here, with people reading newspapers, playing backgammon, and occasionally smoking water pipes. The staff, accustomed to serving local regulars, provide mediocre service by American standards—it's not intentional. From time to time, famous Turkish actors drop in, and sometimes extras gather here for film-industry gossip (6-8-TL vegetable *mezes*, 15-TL most seafood *mezes*, 5-12-TL salads, 20-25-TL main courses, daily 9:00-24:00, Cankurtaran Meydanı 25, Sultanahmet, a few blocks toward the Sea of Marmara by the train tracks, tel. 0212/518-1334).

$ Cankurtaran Sosyal Tesisleri is a spacious, family-friendly restaurant, located within the Byzantine city walls south of Cankurtaran Meydanı. You can eat inside or out. The tables outdoors have a great view of the Bosphorus, Sea of Marmara, and Asian side of Istanbul (the downside is the noise from the four-lane road on the other side of the wall). The food is remarkably good and inexpensive. Their specialty, Topkapı Kebab, is a mix of chicken, veal, mushrooms, and tomatoes topped with cheese. They also serve delicious *künefe* (6-15-TL soups and starters, 15-25-TL kebabs, 20-25-TL seafood, 5-8-TL desserts, 15-TL breakfast plate, daily 8:30-22:00, no alcohol, Ahırkapı İskele Sokak 1, Cankurtaran, tel. 0212/458-5414). Their simple cafeteria in the garden serves only beverages.

$-$$ *On the Backpackers' Strip:* Akbıyık Caddesi ("White Moustache Street") is lined with casual restaurants serving simple food and beer to a United Nations of gregarious young travelers. Eateries usually open early in the morning to offer breakfast to youth hostelers. You'll find several small grocery stores selling basic food items and fruit on the same street (one block below the Blue Mosque, toward the Sea of Marmara).

EATING

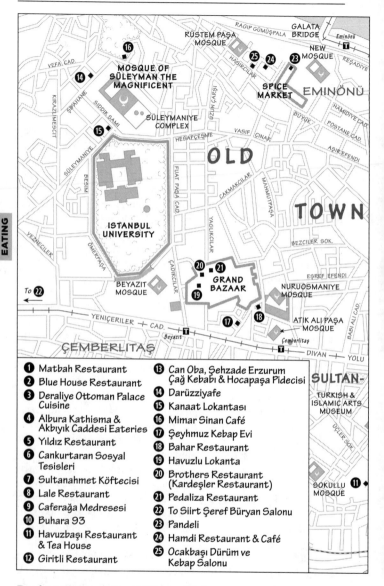

Budget Eateries on Divan Yolu, in the Heart of Sultanahmet

The first two famous—and very convenient—restaurants stand side by side along the busy street called Divan Yolu, across the tram tracks from Hagia Sophia and the Hippodrome (just downhill from the Sultanahmet tram stop).

$ Sultanahmet Köftecisi ("Sultanahmet Meatballs") is so fa-

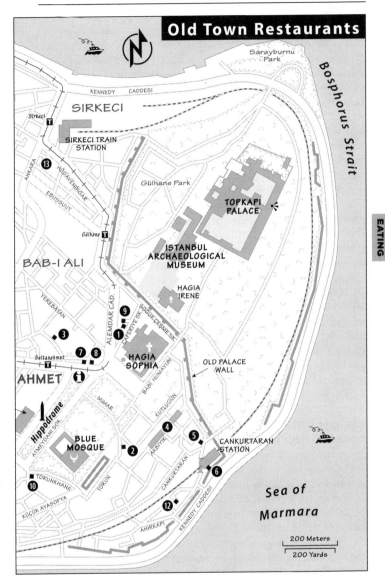

mous for its meatballs that it's inspired an epidemic of imitation joints, rolling out knockoff *köfte* throughout Turkey. The very limited menu includes just two main courses (17-TL *köfte* and 26-TL *şiş kebab*), four sides (including a tomato-and-onion salad and the local favorite, *piyaz*—a white-bean salad in olive oil for 6 TL), and two desserts. You can't come to Istanbul without sampling these *köfte* (daily 11:00-23:30, Divan Yolu 12, tel. 0212/520-0566).

$ Lale Restaurant is the **"Pudding Shop,"** where a generation of vagabond hippies started their long journey east on the "Freak Road" to Kathmandu in the 1960s. (Enjoy the hippie history shared on its wall full of clippings.) Today, this much tamer but still tourist-friendly self-service cafeteria cranks out a selection of freshly cooked, seasonal Turkish food and chicken and beef kebabs. It's a well-oiled machine, but don't expect personal attention when it's crowded. Show this book to the cashier before you pay and receive a 10 percent discount (6-TL soups, 10-12-TL salads and cold starters, 10-15-TL vegetarian dishes, 17-28-TL main courses, 8-10-TL desserts, daily 7:00-22:30, Divan Yolu 6, tel. 0212/522-2970).

$ **Caferağa Medresesi,** in an old madrassa (seminary) next to Hagia Sophia, serves basic food (mostly grilled meat and chicken) to students, amateur artists, and a handful of in-the-know locals. Drop in for a look, or stay for a cup of traditional Turkish coffee or a meal. The setting is casual and friendly, with tables in the atrium, which is filled with hundreds of tulips in the spring (7-10-TL soups, salads, sandwiches, and side dishes; 17-28-TL main courses; madrassa open 9:00-19:00, lunch served 11:00-16:00, drinks served until 19:00, Sogukkuyu Çıkmazı 5, entrance on dead end off Caferiye Sokak—the alley that runs along Hagia Sophia's outer wall, tel. 0212/513-3601). The madrassa trains students in traditional Turkish arts and crafts, including tile painting, calligraphy, gold gilding, miniature painting, and the reed flute. Email ahead of time to take part in one of their workshops (caferagamedrese@tkhv.org).

Budget Eateries Behind the Blue Mosque, near the Top of the Hippodrome

These two popular budget options—friendly rivals facing each other across the street—are a few steps off the top of the Hippodrome and tucked behind the Blue Mosque. They distinguish themselves by remaining humble, affordable, and local-feeling, despite their prime locations. To get here from the Hippodrome, face the Column of Constantine with the Blue Mosque on your left, then leave the Hippodrome on the street to the left, and hook downhill to the right...following the sounds of happy al fresco diners.

$ **Buhara 93'**s affordable, down-to-earth food tastes like Grandma just cooked it: simple and tasty. Their *lavaş* (flat bread) is baked after you order and served right out of the wood-fired oven. This is also a good place to sample *pide* (10-16-TL main dishes, daily 8:00-22:30, can be crowded at lunch and early dinner but no reservations needed, no alcohol, Nakilbend Caddesi 15, tel. 0212/516-9657).

$ **Havuzbaşı Restaurant and Tea House,** situated on a relaxed, idyllic outdoor patio just beyond the tourist crush below the

Hippodrome, is a fine place to enjoy a late evening. Stop by after dinner for dessert or coffee accompanied by live music, hookahs (20-30 TL per group, free extra mouthpieces), backgammon, and non-alcoholic drinks—it's near a mosque (Küçük Ayasofya Mahallesi, Nakilbent Sokak 2, tel. 0212/638-8819).

Seafood Splurge near the Sea of Marmara

$$$ Giritli Restaurant, a short hike from the Blue Mosque action, is a splurge, serving a single multicourse feast with booze. On cold evenings you'll dine in a two-story 19th-century mansion with a dressy white-tablecloth ambience. When it's hot, food is served across the lane in a walled, poolside garden with a Greek-island feel (its owners emigrated from Crete; *giritli* means "Cretan"). The restaurant is also the home of the Şensılay family, who owns and operates it. The mother-daughter team of İpek and Ayşe will treat you like a personal guest. The menu ranges from Aegean- and Mediterranean-style seafood to Cretan-style *mezes* and raw fish. The 165-TL (150-TL with this book) fixed-price meal includes rice, salad, your choice of 16 varieties of cold *mezes* and three kinds of hot *mezes* (octopus, calamari, or *pide*), a fish main course, and a bottomless local beverage—including *rakı*, beer, and wine. While expensive, it's a fine value if you enjoy seafood and wine. To get the discount, show this book before you pay (daily 12:00-24:00, reservations smart, several blocks south of the Blue Mosque at Keresteci Hakkı Sokak 8, tel. 0212/458-2270).

ELSEWHERE IN THE OLD TOWN

We've arranged these eateries by neighborhood, handy to the Old Town's various sights.

Sirkeci Area, near the Train Station

$$$ Can Oba looks and feels like any other restaurant in the Old Town, but its owner, Chef Can Oba, was trained by a Michelin-star chef in Germany. The regular menu is also similar to other area restaurants, so ask for the special seasonal menu, revised weekly (6-24-TL salads and soups, 15-20-TL kebabs, 40-45-TL special main courses, daily 11:00-22:00, a few blocks south of the train station at Hocapaşa Sokak 10, tel. 0212/522-1215).

$ Şehzade Erzurum Çağ Kebabı, a carnivore's fantasy, specializes in *yatık döner,* meat rotated over an Eastern-style horizontal coal or wood-fire grill until tender but crisp, then finely cut and served on skewers with *lavaş* bread (9-12 TL/skewer, Mon-Sat 11:30-21:30, closed Sun, Hocapaşa Sokak 4/6, tel. 0212/520-3361).

$ Hocapaşa Pidecisi is an unpretentious little eatery, with communal tables filled with locals, plus a few tourists who seem to have dropped in accidentally. Third-generation owner Yusuf Bey seems to do all the work, including preparing and baking the *pide*. Try the excellent *kavurmalı pide*, topped with dried meat—an uncommon menu item (12-18 TL for most *pides*, no alcohol, daily 11:00-20:00—or until food is gone, Hocapaşa Sokak 19, tel. 0212/512-0990).

Near the Mosque of Süleyman the Magnificent

$$ Darüzziyafe, near the main entrance of the Mosque of Süleyman the Magnificent (by the inner courtyard), was once the mosque's soup kitchen. Today, it's a traditional restaurant, well-regarded for its Ottoman-Turkish cuisine. In summer, sit in the tranquil courtyard; in winter, take shelter in the gorgeously decorated, multidomed dining hall. The meatballs—prepared with crushed pistachios—are particularly good, and the "Süleymaniye soup," with potatoes, carrots, and tiny meatballs, will warm you up on cool days. This is also a good opportunity to sample some unusual Ottoman drinks such as *şerbet* and *ayran* (10-20-TL starters, 20-40-TL main dishes, 10 percent discount with this book, daily 11:00-23:00, good selection of herbal drinks, no alcohol, reservations smart, Şifahane Sokak 6, tel. 0212/511-8414, www.daruzziyafe.com.tr).

$ Kanaat Lokantası, in the mosque's former madrassa (seminary), has been Istanbul's favorite bean restaurant since 1939. *Kuru fasulye* (koo-roo fah-sool-yeh) is a staple that's eaten at home at least once a week by every Turkish family. The bean soup (7 TL) is made with dried white beans and chunks of beef or pastrami and served with a side of rice pilaf (4 TL). After the meal, try the 8-TL pumpkin dessert. As this restaurant is popular with Istanbul University students and neighborhood businesspeople, don't bother calling for a reservation—the staff is so busy they may not pick up the phone (daily 8:00-21:00, Prof. Sıddık Sami Onar Caddesi 1/3, next to fountain and just across from entrance to mosque's outer courtyard, tel. 0212/520-7655). Other bean joints—not as famous or established, but fine in a pinch—populate the rest of the madrassa.

$ Mimar Sinan Café, a simple coffee shop on the large terrace of the historic Mimar Sinan Inn, offers great views of the Old Town. While the food (cheese rolls and meatballs) is basic, the hospitality and view more than make up for it (3.50-TL tea, 7-TL coffee, 8-12-TL pizza, 15-18-TL meatballs, daily 8:00-until late, Demirtaş Mahallesi, Fetva Yokuşu, Süleymaniye, Mimar Sinan Hanı 34, next to Istanbul Müftülüğü—the Directorate of Religious Affairs of Istanbul, tel. 0212/514-4414).

In or near the Grand Bazaar

$ Eating at **Şeyhmuz Kebap Evi** is like taking a trip to the Syrian border. Its owners cook traditional kebabs just the way they do it in their hometown of Mardin, in southeast Turkey. You can hear the knives chopping meat in the open kitchen even from the street. Try the *lahmacun* (*pide* topped with meat, onions, and parsley). Their specialty, *Şeyhmuz kebap,* is also good: a mix of lamb and veal served with vegetables, cheese, or pistachios (4-TL *lahmacun*, 10-TL grilled chicken, 20-30-TL kebabs, Mon-Sat 11:30-18:30, closed Sun, Atik Ali Paşa Sokak 2, Çemberlitaş, tel. 0212/526-1613 or 0212/512-4102). Walk downhill from the Çemberlitaş tram stop toward the Nuruosmaniye Mosque, turn left just past the parking lot, walk a block, and take the first left.

$ **Bahar Restaurant,** in Yağcı Han just outside the Grand Bazaar, is another well-known workers' restaurant. They're famous for their *abant kebab,* a mix of beef and chicken with onions, tomatoes, and green peppers, as well as their *begendili kebab,* made with lamb and eggplant (9-14-TL soups and salads, 10-18-TL main courses, Mon-Sat 11:00-16:00, closed Sun, cash only, no alcohol, Nuruosmaniye, Yağcı Han 13, tel. 0212/512-7439). As you face the Grand Bazaar's Nuruosmaniye Gate, walk to your left, and then take the first right to Yağcı Han.

$ **Havuzlu Lokanta,** inside the Grand Bazaar, serves a sped-up version of traditional Ottoman cuisine, with a continually changing menu. Look for the *beykoz kebab,* prepared with eggplant, veal, mushrooms, and sweet peas. The vast interior can accommodate an army of tourists (it's in all the guidebooks), but the quaint fountainside seating out front keeps you in the midst of the Grand Bazaar action (9-TL salads, 15-TL vegetarian dishes, 25-30-TL grilled meats, 20-TL main courses, 1 TL extra for water and bread, Mon-Sat 12:00-17:30, closed Sun, look for sign near Şark Kahvesi café, Gani Çelebi Sokak 3, tel. 0212/527-3346).

$ **Brothers Restaurant (Kardeşler Restaurant),** also inside the Grand Bazaar, sits in a cozy courtyard away from the swirl of shoppers and merchants. Serving up meat and vegetable dishes from southeast Turkey, this place is known for its *kaburga* dolma (kah-buhr-gah dohl-mah, lamb ribs big enough for two), *güveç* (gew-vehch, stewed vegetables and veal or lamb in an earthenware pot), and *bağırsak dolması* (bah-ur-sahk dohl-mah-suh; stuffed intestines—an eastern Turkish specialty). Since the menu changes daily, Muzaffer or one of the other waiters can tell you about their specialty of the day. You're welcome to poke into the kitchen to see what's cooking (12-15-TL main courses, 15-20-TL specialty dishes, Mon-Sat 8:00-17:00, closed Sun, Astarcı Han Yağlıkçılar 1/9, tel. 0212/519-3006).

$ **Pedaliza Restaurant,** with typical local cuisine, decent service, and high turnaround, is popular among business owners in the Grand Bazaar. It's a little more upscale than other workers' restaurants, with tablecloths and pleasant outdoor seating, and it's open only until the food's gone—get there early (5-10-TL salads and soups, 10-20-TL main courses, open Mon-Sat roughly 12:00-16:00, closed Sun, Yağlıkçılar Caddesi, Cebeci Han 55, tel. 0212/522-5903).

Near the Aqueduct (Bozdoğan Kemeri)

$ Siirt Şeref Büryan Salonu is a local favorite for its signature dish of succulent, juicy *büryan kebab*—marinated whole lamb cooked in a pit for over two hours, served with *pide*—and *perde pilavı*, a thin pastry shell filled with rice pilaf, almonds, pistachios, black pepper, and currants. *Ayran* is served in large copper cups. Located in a big historic house in a conservative neighborhood, it's an easy 10-minute walk from the Mosque of Süleyman the Magnificent (daily 11:00-22:00, later in summer, 15-TL *büryan kebab*, 15-TL *perde pilavı*, 2.50-TL *ayran* and salad, Zeyrek Mahallesi, İtfaiye Caddesi 4, Fatih Kadınlar Pazarı, tel. 0212/635-8085 or mobile 0535-345-3603).

In or near the Spice Market

$$$ Pandeli, on the Spice Market's second floor, is open for lunch only. Started by Chef Pandeli in the 1930s, it still serves a mouthwatering traditional Turkish-Ottoman menu, including an especially good eggplant *börek*. Although the restaurant always appears to be overcrowded with businesspeople, they eat quickly, so you won't wait long for a table (20-45-TL starters, 30-50-TL main dishes, daily 11:30-19:00, go up tiled staircase just inside Spice Market's main entrance at Eminönü Mısır Çarşısı 1, tel. 0212/527-3909).

$$ Hamdi Restaurant is a dressy, white-tablecloth place with vested waiters, a bright glassed-in roof terrace, and great views of the city and over the water—push for third-floor seating. They serve a variety of traditional kebabs from southeast Turkey (upper Mesopotamia), such as pistachio lamb, grilled eggplant, plum lamb, and grilled garlic lamb. The delicious *beyti* (behy-tee) *kebab*—a mix of barbecued beef and lamb wrapped in thin phyllo bread—takes longer to make. The wheat pilaf, called *firik* (fee-reek), is also good. For dessert, try the pistachio *katmer* or the baklava (25-35-TL kebabs, 8-15-TL desserts, daily 11:30-23:30, next to Spice Market, Kalçın Sokak 11, tel. 0212/528-0390). Take the elevator to the crowded third-floor terrace—the views are best from the narrow balcony (if there's an empty table here, grab it).

$ Hamdi Café, next door to the Hamdi Restaurant, offers simpler meals (meatballs, *döner kebab*, and grilled meat) in a casual, less-crowded setting. The first floor is a pastry shop with a few tables for a quick bite, while the upper floor has a large seating area overlooking the Galata Bridge and the square. Try the *kahke* cookies, made with St. Lucie cherries (16-TL meatballs, 14-TL *döner kebab*, 18-25-TL grilled meat dishes, 8-10-TL desserts, daily 9:00-20:00).

$ Ocakbaşı Dürüm ve Kebap Salonu is exactly what its name suggests: *Ocakbaşı* means "by the grill." Grab a chair by the grill, or join a communal table indoors or out. Specialties include the Adana kebab (spicy hot ground beef on skewer), Urfa kebab (similar to Adana but less spicy), and chicken *şiş*—all are succulent and juicy (most kebabs are 10-15 TL, Mon-Sat 11:00-19:00, closed Sun, Hasırcılar Caddesi 61, tel. 0212/526-3229).

IN THE NEW DISTRICT, ON AND NEAR İSTIKLAL STREET

All of these eateries are on or within a short stroll of İstiklal Street.

$$$ Hacı Abdullah, near İstiklal Street, is favored by locals and can be very busy. The specialty is Özel Hacı Abdullah Tabağı ("Abdullah's Special Hacı Platter"), loaded down with eggplant kebab, lamb shanks, and two other kebabs—enough food for two (50 TL). Also good are the quince desserts with honey and bananas topped with water-buffalo cream, and the fresh pomegranate juice from eastern Turkey (10-TL soups and salads, 6 different fixed-price meals—70-120 TL, 10-25-TL desserts, daily 11:00-22:30, closed until sundown during Ramadan, no alcohol, extra charge for water and bread, 10 percent service charge for groups of 4 or more, near the Hüseyin Ağa Mosque at Atıf Yılmaz Caddesi 9/A, tel. 0212/293-8561).

$$$ 360 is a hip restaurant with a 360-degree view of the city, located on the terrace atop an Art Nouveau building on İstiklal Street. After hours, the restaurant becomes a club with a diverse clientele (20-TL beers, 40-TL cocktails, cover charge). The jet set, consulate employees, and businesspeople are among the regulars who enjoy the international cuisine. Reservations are required (40-75-TL plates, Tue-Sun lunch starts at 12:00, dinner served in two seatings: 20:00-22:00 & 22:00-24:00, closed Mon; nightclub open from 24:00 Thu-Sat in summer, Fri-Sat in winter; İstiklal Caddesi, Mısırlı Apartmanı 163, 8th floor, Beyoğlu, tel. 0212/251-1042, www.360istanbul.com).

$$$ Bilsak 5. Kat ("Bilsak 5th Floor"), decorated with dramatic flair, is a fine restaurant with sweeping views of Istanbul. It's owned and operated by theater director/producer Yasemin Alkaya, with help from her mom. The gay-friendly Bilsak is a key player in Istanbul's evening scene, with a faithful clientele. The menu has something for every taste. Reservations are smart (25-40-TL starters and salads, 40-65-TL main courses, 20-TL desserts, 110-170-

EATING

The New Istanbul Style

Istanbul's new wave of restaurants and chefs are adapting to the tastes of its elite, educated young people, who want traditional-but-innovative food and classy-but-unpretentious decor. These places, clustered in the New District, tend to be well-lit, with a refined, elevated ambience where chefs interact with diners. Many offer tasting *menus* for a set price.

$$$ Yeni Lokanta has a somewhat experimental menu based on traditional Turkish food. Owner Civan Er, a famous chef and columnist who enjoys talking to guests, creates delicious dishes with unusual combinations, such as ravioli stuffed with dried eggplant. The place has a smart bistro feel with geometric floor tiles, traditional İznik tiles on the bar, and bread served in copper pots. Reservations are a good idea for weekend dinners (15-20-TL *mezes*, 20-30-TL salads, 40-50-TL main courses, 15-20-TL desserts, 260-TL tasting *menu* for two, prices a bit higher for dinner, Mon-Sat 12:00-until late, closed Sun, just off İstiklal Street at Kumbaracı Yokuşu 66, Beyoğlu, tel. 0212/292-2550, www.lokantayeni.com).

$$$ Meze by Lemon Tree, fronted by wall-to-wall windows, is small, simple, and friendly. It's the kind of place where locals casually chat between tables and owner/chef Gencay visits diners to explain the food. His culinary creations evolve with the seasons, featuring whatever's freshest at the market (18–28-TL salads, mezes and desserts, 35–50-TL main courses, 196-TL tasting *menu* for two, near historic Pera Palas Hotel at Meşrutiyet Caddesi 83/B, Beyoğlu, tel. 0212/252-8302, www.mezze.com.tr).

$$$ Neolokal, the trendy restaurant of renowned Chef

TL fixed-price meals, daily, bar from 17:00, dinner 19:00-24:00, close to Taksim Square at Soğancı Sokak 7, 5th floor, Cihangir, tel. 0212/293-3774, www.5kat.com).

$$$ Changa serves a wide range of fusion cuisine to trendy expats and local yuppies from fall through spring. The bar by the entrance is lively on Friday and Saturday evenings, when dinner reservations are recommended (Mon-Sat 18:00-24:00, closed Sun and June-mid-Oct, a short walk from Taksim Square and İstiklal Street at Siraselviler Caddesi 47, tel. 0212/249-1348, www.changa-istanbul.com). In summer, this main location closes down, and they open an outdoor restaurant called **Müzedechanga** ("Changa at the Museum") on the grounds of the Sakıp Sabancı Museum, overlooking the Bosphorus (not worth the long trek unless you're visiting the museum).

$$$ *In the Flower Passage (Çiçek Pasajı):* The Flower Passage is not one restaurant, but a row of seafood places with six-seat tables (you'll share) in a historic, beautifully restored passage on İstiklal

Maksut Aşkur, boasts a well-educated team of cooks who prepare delicious, innovative international and local dishes, always with the best ingredients. It is located on the top floor of SALT Galata, a cultural center and modern art gallery. The structure is a historical landmark built by the famous 19th-century architect Alexandre Vallaury. The dining area is elegant, and the floor-to-ceiling window offers amazing views of the domes and minarets of the Old Town (25-35-TL starters and salads, 35-55-TL main courses, 20-25-TL desserts, Mon-Sat 8:00-24:00, Sun 8:00-12:00, Salt Galata, Bankalar Caddesi, Karaköy, tel. 0212/244-0016, www.neolokal.com, see map on page 318).

$$$ Lokanta Maya is owned and operated by chef Didem Şenol, who was educated at the French Culinary Institute in New York and uses the finest Turkish ingredients. Located right across from the Karaköy cruise port, the restaurant's decor is casual-chic (25-35-TL starters, 40-60-TL main courses, 15-20-TL desserts, Mon-Sat 12:00-17:00 & 19:00-23:00, closed Sun, Kemankaş Caddesi 35 A, Karaköy, tel. 0212/252-6884, www.lokantamaya.com, see map on page 318).

$$ Gram Pera looks like a pastry shop from the outside, but feels like a simple, casual family home within. Featuring a self-service buffet on weekdays and lots of vegetarian options, it's a favorite among the yuppies who work nearby (20-30-TL buffet, 25-40-TL main courses, Mon-Fri 8:30-18:00, Sat 10:30-18:00, closed Sun, closes one hour earlier in winter, Asmalı Mescit, Meşrutiyet Caddesi 107D, Beyoğlu, tel. 0212/243-1048).

Street. The 10 restaurants are mostly interchangeable, with similar value, quality, and a genteel late-19th-century atmosphere. In the evening, some have live music, usually traditional Istanbul songs. But the area is grotesquely touristy and overpriced, and because many menus include unlimited alcohol, drunkenness crescendos as the night wears on (most Flower Passage restaurants have 10-25-TL salads and *mezes*, 25-80-TL fish dishes, daily 12:00-24:00, İstiklal Caddesi). For more on the history of the passage, see page 237.

$$$ House Café, part of a trendy, gay-friendly chain, makes up for its slow service with good ambience and a wide variety of eclectic food (20-40-TL salads, 20-30-TL starters, 40-50-TL main courses). In addition to the İstiklal Street location (in the Mısırlı Apartmanı building at #163, Mon-Thu 9:00-2:00 in the morning, Fri-Sat until 4:00 in the morning, Sun until 24:00, tel. 0212/251-7991), you'll find branches at Tünel (Asmalımescit Sokak 9), and literally right on the Bosphorus in the Ortaköy district (on Salhane Sokak 1).

New District Restaurants

STADIUM

BRITISH CONSULATE

SÜRP YERRORTUTYAN ARMENIAN ORTHODOX CHURCH

8

HAMALBAŞI CADDESI

BALIK SOK.

ŞAHNE

BALO

MEŞRUTIYET CAD.

BEYOĞLU

4 ■ **10**

PANAIA GREEK ORTHODOX CHURCH

TEPEBAŞI

REFIK SAYDAM CADDESI

KALLAVI

◆ **9**

2 ◆ **15**

ST. ANTHONY'S ROMAN CATHOLIC CHURCH

12

ESKI ÇIÇEKÇI

YENI ÇARŞI CAD.

GALATASARAY HIGH SCHOOL

WC

TURNACIBAŞI

PERA PALAS HOTEL

MEŞRUTIYET CADDESI

ODAKULE

CADDESI

ARMENIAN CHURCH

BALYOZ

7

18

16

AŞMALI MESCI

GÖNÜL

SOFYALI

İSTIKLAL

POSTACILAR

DUTCH CONSULATE

UNION CHURCH

19

TÜNEL

TOMTOM KAPTAN

GALATASARAY

BOĞAZ KESEN CADDESI

6

5

RUSSIAN CONSULATE

Tünel **T**

TÜNEL FUNICULAR

GALIP DEDE

SWEDISH CONSULATE

KUMBARACI

17

ŞAHKULU BOSTAN

STA. MARIA DRAPERIS LATIN CATHOLIC CHURCH

TERRAE SOCLARE CHURCH

SOKAK

GALATA DERVISH MONASTERY

To Karaköy & Tram

200 Meters

200 Yards

To Karaköy Port

EATING

$$$ Münferit is a contemporary, gay-friendly *meyhane*, deftly mixing traditional and modern cuisines. Open evenings only, they serve an unusual, Mediterranean-influenced menu, with lots of fresh herbs and veggies. They have an especially good selection of starters: asparagus with *tarator* (cucumber) dressing, Circassian chicken salad (actually made with duck), stuffed artichoke with mussels, and monkfish. Service is slow, and reservations are wise (15-20-TL cheese starters, 25-40-TL *mezes*, 30-50-TL main courses, open for dinner only 19:30-1:00 in the morning, closed Sun, Firuzağa Mahallesi, Yeni Çarşı Caddesi 19, down the hill from Galatasaray High School, tel. 0212/252-5067).

$$ Pera Thai, a small, modest restaurant close to the Şişhane metro stop, serves up delicious Thai food, including vegetarian options. The food does not contain MSG, and spice levels can be customized. Head waiter İsmail Saydır is eager to please. Reserve ahead on weekends, especially in fall and winter (20-30-TL soups, starters, and salads, 30–45-TL main courses and noodle dishes; Mon-Sat 12:00-23:00, closed Sun; Meşrutiyet Caddesi 74/A, Tünel, tel. 0212/245-5725).

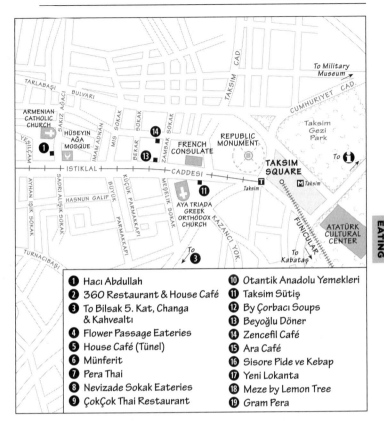

1 Hacı Abdullah
2 360 Restaurant & House Café
3 To Bilsak 5. Kat, Changa & Kahvaltı
4 Flower Passage Eateries
5 House Café (Tünel)
6 Münferit
7 Pera Thai
8 Nevizade Sokak Eateries
9 ÇokÇok Thai Restaurant
10 Otantik Anadolu Yemekleri
11 Taksim Sütiş
12 By Çorbacı Soups
13 Beyoğlu Döner
14 Zencefil Café
15 Ara Café
16 Sisore Pide ve Kebap
17 Yeni Lokanta
18 Meze by Lemon Tree
19 Gram Pera

$$ **On Nevizade Sokak:** This lane is home to several reliably good restaurants. Just a block off İstiklal Street, past the fish market, it's where trendy locals head for a seafood dinner. Bars and restaurants line up one after the other on either side of the street. In spring and summer, they set tables out front, making the place seem even more crowded, fun, and noisy. Restaurants take pride in their *mezes* and compete to serve the widest variety. Try the casual pubs if all you want is a glass of beer and simple seafood *meze* (e.g., a platter of calamari or deep-fried mussels). Restaurants here are also casual, but they'll serve you a full meal with all the frills. The prices and variety of food are similar to those in the Flower Passage, listed earlier.

$$ **ÇokÇok Thai Restaurant** is a good choice if you want a break from Turkish food—they even import organic ingredients from Thailand. You'll choose from a menu created by a chef who has cooked for the Thai royal family, and dine in an interior designed by an award-winning architect (15-40-TL salads, soups, and des-

serts; 30-45-TL main courses; daily 12:00-24:00, Meşrutiyet Caddesi 51, Tepebaşı, Beyoğlu, tel. 0212/292-6496).

$ Otantik Anadolu Yemekleri is so successful that it quickly became a chain. It serves traditional Anatolian food, representing different ethnic groups living within Turkey. It's a great opportunity to sample affordable cuisine from around the country. Watch as the costumed cooks prepare the *gözleme* bread (7-10 TL, the filled versions are big enough for a light meal). The restaurant has the ambiance of a practical diner, with a handy photo menu that makes ordering easy, and four floors of seating that ensure that there's plenty of space (25-45-TL meat dishes, 9-11-TL traditional dishes, daily 9:00-24:00, next to entrance to Flower Passage at İstiklal Caddesi 80/A, tel. 0212/293-8451).

$ Taksim Sütiş, while technically a "pudding shop," is a time-warp cafeteria serving everything from puddings to omelets to *döner kebabs.* Among its famous puddings, *tavuk göğüsü* (tahvook gooh-sew) stands out. It's made with finely shredded chicken breast, but doesn't taste like chicken at all. Locals love the rice pilaf with chicken and the baklava. Consider the *su böreği* (soo bohreh-ee), a layered pastry. On a cold day, try the *sahlep* (sah-lehp), a warm, creamy sweet drink made with the powdered roots of wild Taurus mountain orchids and served with cinnamon. The photo menu is convenient, but you can also step up to the display case and point to what you want (8-10-TL puddings, 13-18-TL meat dishes, daily 6:00-24:00, İstiklal Caddesi 7, tel. 0212/251-3270).

$ By Çorbacı offers 30 inexpensive, healthy soups from its repertoire of 600, with even cheaper to-go cups (6-10-TL, daily 8:00-24:00, no alcohol, Yeniçarşı Caddesi 8-A, tel. 0212/244 5169).

$ Beyoğlu Döner is a budget, cafeteria-style eatery right on İstiklal Street. It's bright, modern, fast, clean, and a fine value. Choose your meal from the fresh food displayed on the buffet at the entrance, and take advantage of the spacious seating areas on three floors (5-7-TL salads and soups, 11-14-TL main courses, daily 10:30-24:00, İstiklal Caddesi 10, Beyoğlu, tel. 0212/243-6759).

$ Zencefil Café is a vegetarian restaurant with a relaxing interior and a lovely garden a block away from the crowded main drag. It's also frequented by carnivores for its appetizing and healthy food and great prices. The menu of freshly grown products changes with the season. It also offers pomegranate, blueberry, and cherry fruit wines (7-18-TL soups and salads, 12-20-TL main courses, Mon-Sat 10:00-23:30, closed Sun, at #8A on Kurabiye Sokak—a lane that runs parallel to İstiklal Street, tel. 0212/243-8234).

$ Ara Café, undergoing renovation but should reopen by the time of your visit, is owned by Ara Güler, the renowned Turkish-Armenian photojournalist. A popular place to see and be seen, the café attracts intellectuals, yuppies, and models. Grab a table outdoors in nice weather, or opt for a spot in the cozy split-level interior (daily 7:30-24:00, between post office and İstiklal Street at Tosbağa Sokak 2, tel. 0212/245-4105).

$ Sisore Pide ve Kebap is a simple restaurant that serves mainly *pides* from the Black Sea, along with a variety of dishes and soups prepared fresh each day. Try *kavurmalı* (roasted meat) or *pastırmalı* (pastrami) on *pide* (4-8-TL soups and salads, 8-20-TL *pides* and main courses, 5-7-TL desserts, soup only daily 7:00-12:00, lunch and dinner daily 12:00-24:00, Oteller Sokak 6, Asmalı Mescit Mahallesi, Beyoğlu, tel. 0212/245-4900).

IN KARAKÖY, BY THE CRUISE PORT

These restaurants, along with Lokanta Maya and Neolokal (described in sidebar, earlier), are located near the main cruise port in Karaköy. See the map on page 318 for locations.

$$ Karaköy Lokantası, with a down-to-earth ambience and flashy blue tiles, is a well-known landmark famous for its *mezes* and main courses, such as sea bass baked in foil. Rushed service hasn't hurt its popularity (8-12-TL vegetarian *mezes*, 15-20-TL seafood *mezes*; Mon-Sat lunch served 12:00-16:00, tavern-style dinner served 18:00-24:00; Sun dinner only; Kemankeş Caddesi 37A, tel. 0212/292-4455).

$$ Açık Mutfak serves up plain Turkish food created from chef-owner Esra Şener's family recipes in a tiny, cozy place stuffed with quirky bric-a-brac. A center island displays daily *mezes*, and specials are posted on a chalkboard (8-10-TL starters, 25-35-TL main courses, 10-TL desserts, Mon-Sat 18:00-24:00, kitchen closes at 22:20, cash only, a few outdoor tables, Galip Dede Caddesi, Tımarcı Sokak 6B, Galata, tel. 0212/293-7433).

$$ Sahrap Restaurant is a new eatery owned by a famous food writer named Sahrap. Frequented by smartly dressed locals and expats, it is brightly lit and spotlessly clean. But the feel is still warm and welcoming, thanks to old-style floor tiles, turquoise wall decorations resembling traditional Seljuk ceramics, and wooden furniture. Well-trained waiters literally wait on you, keeping a comfortable distance (12-16-TL salads, *mezes*, and soups; 25-35-TL main courses; 9-13-TL desserts; off of the Meşrutiyet Caddesi and close to İstiklal Street at General Yazgan Sokak 13, Asmalı Mescit, tel. 0212/243-1616, www.sahraprestaurant.com, see map on page 318).

$ NamPort (Namlı Şarküteri) is a deli with a huge selection of cheeses, sausages, and *mezes* from all over Turkey—all so delicious you'll "eat your fingers," as the Turkish saying goes (see page 406 for a more detailed description). Dine at a full-service table, or get it to go. On weekends, they serve an all-day buffet brunch for 44 TL per person (15.50 TL/pound vegetarian *mezes*, 9-12-TL grilled meat and chicken dishes, daily 7:00-22:00; the restaurant is undergoing renovation—price increases likely; Rıhtım Caddesi 7, tel. 0212/251-1541).

$ At **Kivahan,** your taste buds will never get bored: The restaurant has about 5,000 dishes in its repertoire. The chefs are dedicated to the diversity of Turkish cuisine, preparing 30-35 different dishes each day with regional ingredients direct from the farm. It's a festive place; if a customer has tried more than 30 specialties, he may get a free meal, or a round of applause from the staff. It's hard to interpret and explain the always-changing selections; to avoid confusion you might want to try the daily buffet—it's ready at 12:00 (8-10-TL salads, *mezes,* and soups; 15-TL stews; 18-28-TL main courses; daily 7:30-23:00, by the Galata Tower at Galata Kulesi Meydanı 4, Beyoğlu, tel. 0212/292-9898). To sample a variety of food and wine, ask about their Chef's Table, offered on Tuesday evenings outside of summer (80 TL/person including wine). You'll join about a dozen people at a table laden with the most special delicacies the chef has to offer.

For Dessert: $ **Baklavacı Güllüoğlu** is the most recognized name in quality baklava. Their main shop is right across the cruise port at Rıhtım Caddesi, Katlı Otopark Altı 3-4, Karaköy (tel. 0212/293-0910, www.karakoygulluoglu.com). You'll spot other Baklavacı Güllüoğlu shops around the city—they're owned and operated by rival brothers and cousins, vying for the right to use the popular brand name. All serve fine baklava (for more on this honey-infused treat, see the sidebar on page 411).

Between Karaköy and the New District: $ **Kahvealtı,** near the Firuzağa Mosque in Cihangir, is a popular, gay-friendly restaurant and café serving tasty organic and natural food (6-7-TL tea/coffee, 15-20-TL salads and sandwiches, 13-24-TL main courses, daily 9:30-21:30, Akarsu Caddesi, Anahtar Sokak 13/A, tel. 0212/293-0849).

BEYOND THE NEW DISTRICT

"Kumpir" Stands in Ortaköy: At the entrance of the popular pedestrian area on the Bosphorus, a row of stands serve *kumpir* (kuhm-peer): baked potatoes topped with your choice of ingredients. Often, you'll find additional options, such as stuffed or deep-fried mussels. Buy your food, follow the local crowd toward the water, and look for an empty bench (or sit at a waterfront coffee-shop table and get a drink) and enjoy the view of Asian Istanbul and the Old Town's silhouette. Weekends are crowded, especially in nice weather (daily 10:00-1:00 in the morning, Mecidiye Köprüsü Sokak, Ortaköy).

IN ASIAN ISTANBUL

For locations of the first two restaurants, see the map on page 54.

\$\$ Kadı Nimet Balıkçısı, at the heart of Kadıköy market area, provides seating indoors surrounded by photos of Atatürk and early national leaders, or at outdoor tables amidst the hubbub. The food is great (try the hard-to-find nettle salad), but the service is not. You may see a pet goose—like the one on the restaurant's logo (daily 12:00-23:00, 10-15-TL *mezes*, 10-14 TL/portion of small fish like anchovies and sardines, other fish priced daily, Serasker Caddesi 10/A, Kadıköy, tel. 0216/348-7389).

\$ Kebapçı İskender has no menu. Your waiter will ask if you want one or one-and-a-half portions of "İskender" kebab—basically *döner kebab* served on crusty *pide* bread, dressed with tomato sauce and sizzling butter. Vegetarians can substitute eggplant for meat (daily 12:00-21:00, 23.50 TL/portion, Rıhtım Caddesi 3/A, Kadıköy, tel. 0216/336-0777).

\$\$\$ Lacivert, a classy seafood restaurant with magnificent views and tables right on the water, has a boat that will pick you up from anywhere along the Bosphorus. It's best when it's warm enough for outdoor seating. Reservations are suggested (20-45-TL starters, soups, and salads, 45-60-TL main courses, 25-TL desserts, daily 12:00-17:00 & 18:00-24:00, Körfez Caddesi 57/A Anadolu Hisari, Beykoz, on the Asian bank of Bosphorus, just under the Fatih Sultan Mehmet Bridge, tel. 0216/413-4224, www.lacivertrestaurant.com).

EATING

SHOPPING IN ISTANBUL

Shopping can provide a good break from Istanbul's mosques, museums, and monuments. And diving into the city's bustling, colorful marketplaces can be a culturally enlightening experience. In this chapter, you'll find information on shopping for textiles, ceramics and tiles, gold and silver, carpets, spices, souvenirs, and bargains.

İndirim (een-dee-reem) is Turkish for "sale." July, August, January, and February are the big months for sales; in January, sales start right after the shopping frenzy for New Year's Day is over (most Turks don't celebrate Christmas, but they do buy gifts for New Year's).

Istanbul's merchants, especially at the Grand Bazaar and other touristy areas in the Old Town, can be aggressive, and may try to engage you in casual conversation as an entrée to offering products for sale. It's OK to say, "No, thanks"—firmly—and walk on by. (For more tips, see the sidebar on page 196.)

For information on VAT refunds and customs, see page 393.

WHERE TO SHOP

Shopping in the Grand Bazaar and at other Old Town merchants (such as the Arasta Bazaar craft market tucked behind the Blue Mosque) is lively, memorable, and fun, and prices can be low— but the quality is often questionable. Though it's also touristy, you won't want to miss the colorful, aromatic Spice Market.

Istanbul's residents prefer shopping at the more expensive but reliably good-quality stores on and near İstiklal Street in the

New District. This area is less colorful—it feels like a shopping street in any big European city—but you won't feel preyed upon by vendors.

This book includes self-guided tours of most of these areas (see the Grand Bazaar Tour, New District Walk, and Old Town Back Street Walk chapters); you could combine your shopping with one of those tours.

WHAT TO BUY
Textiles, Silk, and Leather

Turkish textiles—known around the world—are the country's biggest industry and a source of local pride. While Turkey was once a major manufacturer for Victoria's Secret and other international clothing labels, competition from China has forced local clothing-makers to change tactics: Turkey now focuses on producing its own labels, in the hope of competing in the world market. These new **clothing** brands, such as Mavi Jeans, are well-made and affordable. To get the best merchandise, go beyond the Old Town to the New District and other uptown neighborhoods; İstiklal Street and the Taksim Square area are your best bets. The cotton T-shirts you'll see around the Old Town and in the Grand Bazaar make decent souvenirs or gifts, but are usually low-quality—they'll likely fade and shrink after a few washes.

Many people associate Turkey with **pashminas**—high-quality shawls traditionally made with Himalayan goat wool. And, in fact, the Old Town is a pashmina paradise, with every color of the rainbow. But Turkey doesn't produce pashmina wool, so the ones you see here are either imports or fakes. Still, they're practical and fun, and cheaper than the fakes sold in the US.

Cashmere House, in the Grand Bazaar, carries a wide array of shawls and scarfs in materials ranging from synthetic to high-end cashmere and pashmina wool. Items have price tags, but there is still a little wiggle room for bargaining. Owner İlyas and his brother Yusuf take time to give you accurate information about their products. Shop anonymously, then—after you have bargained and agreed on prices—show this book for an added discount of up to 5 percent (enter Grand Bazaar at the Nuru Osmaniye gate, walk straight and turn right at the fourth street, keep walking down the hill until you see the fountain, then find Cashmere House on the right corner at Keseciler Caddesi 49).

A *peştemal* (pehsh-teh-mahl) is a large, thin, cotton **bath towel** that Turks wrap around themselves at the baths; nowadays they're also used as curtains or tablecloths. Bathing Turks scrub away dead skin and dirt with *kese* (keh-seh)—simple rectangular **mittens** made out of raw silk or synthetic fabric. Look for these two authentically Turkish items at the **Eğin Tekstil** and other shops on Yağlıkçılar Caddesi in the Grand Bazaar (see page 201).

The **Sivaslı Yazmacı** shop carries a wide collection of handmade textiles, including the traditional gauzy cotton *yazma* (yahz-mah), the head-covering worn by rural Turkish women (on the same street as Eğin Tekstil, Yağlıkçılar Caddesi 57, Grand Bazaar).

Jennifer's Hamam, run by a Canadian expat, sells bath towels, bathrobes, *keses,* and tablecloths at set prices. They're made by a small group of **fine weavers** from throughout Turkey, using organic fibers on old-style shuttle looms (Arasta Bazaar 135 & 43, tel. 0212/518-0548).

Ahmet owns two eclectic stores in the Arasta Bazaar, by the Blue Mosque. **Sufi,** at #27, offers fine **felt** works, a wide spectrum of **pashminas** from cheap synthetics to expensive originals, handmade olive oil soaps, and dresses. All items carry price tags, but there is room for bargaining. **Art East,** at #46, sells collectibles, semi-precious **jewelry,** art, and **handicrafts.** After shopping and haggling anonymously, flash your book to get an added discount of up to 10 percent.

Turkey produces wonderful **silk,** but be careful: In the Grand Bazaar and other Old Town shops, scarves and other items billed as silk are often made of polyester or, at best, low-grade silk. For real silk scarves and shawls, go to the New District. **İpek Silk Shop,** near St. Anthony's Church on İstiklal Street, has knowledgeable employees and reliable, quality silk-wear. Isaac and his helpful staff speak English and are happy to demonstrate the latest in scarf fashion (İstiklal Caddesi 120, tel. 0212/249-8207).

Most **leather** goods are a better deal in the US than in Turkey. Shoes and bags are the exception: If you're into Italian-style leather shoes, you're in the right place. For shoes, head to İstiklal Street in the New District. **Tuğra,** in the Spice Market, carries quality leather goods and bags. Prices are negotiable. Browse and haggle anonymously, then show this book for an added discount of up to 10 percent. If staff is unsure about the added discount, ask them to check it with owner Mehmet Gülçek or senior staffer Mehmet Akif (Spice Market 70, tel. 0212/527-6701).

Carpets and Kilims

If you want to buy a Turkish carpet, it's worth knowing a bit about what you're looking for—if only to avoid advertising your inexperience. For example, folding a carpet to check the knots will not only

give you away as a novice, but can actually ruin the carpet if it's silk. Rubbing a carpet with a piece of wet tissue to test its colorfastness is akin to licking a shirt before you buy it. And beware of shopkeepers who stress "authenticity" over quality. Authenticity is an important consideration when shopping for traditional wool-on-wool carpets. But for wool-on-cotton or silk-on-silk, it can actually be better to get a piece made with newer techniques, which produce tighter weaves, brighter and more durable colors, and more intricate patterns.

Carpets can range in price from several hundred dollars to several thousand or more, depending on the age, size, quality, and uniqueness. Merchants will ship them home for you, though many tourists find it cheaper and more foolproof to carry them back (the carpets can be folded and tied tightly into a squarish bundle).

Wool-on-wool carpets, which are made of wool pile on a wool skeleton (formed by vertical warp and horizontal weft threads), are the most traditional kind of Turkish carpet. Although becoming less common, these are still woven in countryside villages. Each region has its own distinctive, centuries-old design-and-color combination. In general, wool-on-wool carpets cost less than other Turkish rugs. The best way to gauge the authenticity of a wool-on-wool carpet is to look for the natural, less-vibrant colors that come from vegetable dyes made from local plants. Density—the number of knots per inch—is less important to the quality of a wool-on-wool carpet. Fewer knots don't signify a lower-quality wool rug, but they do mean that the rug is more likely to stretch over time.

Newer carpet styles, such as **wool-on-cotton** (wool pile on a cotton skeleton) and **silk-on-silk,** first appeared in the 19th century. The new materials allowed weavers to create more intricate floral and geometric patterns than those found in traditional designs. (A weaver can fit more knots onto a cotton skeleton than onto a wool one.) Professional designers make these patterns with the exact thickness of the yarn in mind—so irregular hand-spun wool won't work. Wool-on-cotton and silk-on-silk carpets are colored with chemical dyes, which can be as good, or even better, than natural dyes. If someone tries to sell you a wool-on-cotton carpet by advertising that it's "made with hand-spun wool," "dyed with vegetable colors," or that it "features a traditional design, passed from mother to daughter," walk away. Unlike wool-on-wool carpets, density is important in assessing quality for wool-on-cotton and silk-on-silk carpets.

The towns of Hereke and Kayseri are famous for their carpets. **Hereke** (heh-reh-keh) carpets are denser, require much more

How to Get the Best Bargain

Many visitors to Istanbul are surprised to find that bargaining for a lower price is no longer common in much of the city. At modern stores or shopping malls, the posted prices are final. But in the tourist zones—such as the Grand Bazaar, Spice Market, and other shops around the Old Town—merchants know you're expecting to haggle...and they're happy to play along. (Local shoppers have less patience for this game. Notice that even in the Grand Bazaar, locals don't often haggle—if they think something is overpriced, they either ask for a discount or simply walk away.)

In the Old Town market areas where bargaining is common, you'll constantly be bombarded by sales pitches. If you aren't interested in what they're selling, try not to establish eye contact. Although this may feel rude, it's the best way to avoid unnecessary conversations and save your time and energy for the items you do want.

If you are interested in an item, don't make it obvious. Take your time, browse around, and pretend you might just wander off at any moment—feigned disinterest is part of the game. You're better off keeping a low profile—this isn't the time to show off your nicest clothes, jewelry, and wads of cash.

Merchandise often doesn't have price tags, because shop owners want you to ask—giving them an opening to launch into a sales pitch. Don't suggest a number; let them be the first to mention a price. When they do, assume it's elevated. Even if you counter with only half their original offer, you may find your price easily accepted—meaning you've already offered too much.

More likely, a spirited haggling war will ensue. If you don't like to bargain, you'll pay more than you should. Play along to get a lower price and a fun cultural interaction. These haggling sessions can drag on for some time, as you sip tea (usually apple-flavored) offered by shopkeepers who want to keep you around. When you start to walk away, that last price they call out is often the best price you'll get.

There's room for bargaining even on fixed-price commodities, such as gold and silver, where you're being charged not only for the precious metal but also for the workmanship.

If you're haggling over something unique, be prepared to pay a premium. Shopkeepers already know that you won't be able to find it elsewhere.

workmanship, and are more expensive. Authentic Hereke carpets are becoming rare, and cheap imported knockoffs are in the market nowadays, so watch out. **Kayseri** (kay-seh-ree) wool-on-cotton and silk-on-silk carpets generally have floral designs. Their wool-on-wool carpets are favored for their unique patterns and lively colors.

Kilims (kee-leem) feature a flat weave without the pile, similar to a Navajo rug. These also have traditional designs and natural colors. Used in the past as blankets and bedspreads, they're mainly popular now as decorative items (and can be used as wall hangings). Kilims are generally inexpensive, but old and rare pieces can cost several thousand dollars. For a wearable, affordable kilim, consider a vest made out of the material; you'll see these at the Grand Bazaar and elsewhere.

Osman's Carpet Shop, in Zincirli Han in the Grand Bazaar, is regarded as *the* place to go for expert advice—and high-quality (expensive) carpets. Osman, who's often assisted by son Nurullah or nephew Bilgin, won't hustle you. Instead, he educates customers so they can select just the right carpet.

Punto of Istanbul, a couple of blocks away from the Grand Bazaar's Nuruosmaniye Gate, carries a wide variety of carpets—from simple kilims to fancy silk carpets—and has down-to-earth prices compared to most. Shop anonymously as you haggle, then, before you pay, show this book for an additional 10 percent discount from manager Metin (Nuru Osmaniye, Gazi Sinan Paşa Sokak, Vezirhan 17, tel. 0212/511-0854).

Tiles and Ceramics

A Turkish ceramic specialty is *çini* (chee-nee), which is usually translated in English as "**tile**" (or "quartz tile"). The word *çini* can describe flat tiles used for architectural decoration or functional items such as bowls, vases, and cups. The clay in *çini* products has a high quartz content and is difficult to work with. High-quality glazed *çini* tiles were at their peak in the 16th and 17th centuries, and the style is considered very traditional in Turkey. Other ceramics (*seramik;* seh-rah-meek) don't have much of a history here—though you will find them sold in markets. You'll also see **pottery** (*çömlek;* chom-lehk): simple, fired earthenware objects shaped on a wheel, usually without any design or glaze.

Many stores sell copies of old, authentic tiles as well as new designs. When comparing tiles for quality, keep these tips in mind: Recycled clay has a creamy, darker look and

costs much less than higher-quality white clay. To check the clay and glaze for cracks, balance the item on your fingertips (or your hand, if it's heavy) and flick the edge with your finger. If the sound is clear and the piece rings like a bell, it's free of cracks. The value is determined by the quality of the workmanship, combined with the chemical formula of the glaze, clay, and dyes. Superior-quality tile or ceramic has quartz (or kaolin) in the clay, little or no lead in the glaze, and metal oxide dyes. Also check whether colors have smeared over one another. Intricate, multicolored, and hand-drawn designs are the most prized.

High-quality items are often too costly for regular stores to carry. If you are seriously interested in the best ceramics and tile, try the **İznik Foundation,** which carries on Turkey's long-established tile tradition. Their main store is in the Kuruçeşme neighborhood, north of the New District, by the Bosphorus Bridge at Öksüz Çocuk Sokak.

If you're looking for something simple, you'll find plenty of inexpensive, pretty pieces at souvenir stores all around the Old Town and Grand Bazaar.

Traditional Arts: *Hat, Tezhip, Ebru,* and *Minyatür*

Hat (pronounced "hot") is artful Arabic calligraphy. To make written words appear more beautiful, the calligrapher (*hattat;* hot-taht) bends grammatical rules and often takes liberties with the forms of letters. Over the centuries, this decorative art has reached a very sophisticated level of expression, almost like a painting. Turks are proud of *hat,* saying "The Quran was revealed in Mecca and Medina, recited in Egypt, and written in Istanbul."

Tezhip (tehz-heep) is the illumination and embellishment of manuscripts, scrolls, and books with geometric or floral patterns. The Arabic word *tezhip* literally means "gilding," and designs often incorporate gold. Gold is crushed into powder, and then mixed with a solution of gelatin before being used as a paint.

Hat and *tezhip* artists work closely together. When a *hattat* finishes a piece of work, it's passed on to the *tezhip* artist for further decoration. Artists generally work with a magnifying glass and use a very fine brush, traditionally made with a few hairs from the neck of a kitten.

Ebru (ehb-roo) is the art of transferring colored designs from water to paper, and is better known as "marbling" for the designs it sometimes produces. Paper colored in this way was traditionally used for *hat* and *tezhip,* as well as for official documentation and contracts (as a fraud deterrent; if someone tried to change a document's wording, the designed paper would be damaged). Today it is considered an independent art, much like abstract painting.

Minyatür (miniature) was the dominant form of painting in

SHOPPING

Turkey from the 13th through 19th century. Traditionally called *nakış* (nah-kush), *minyatür* artists drew or painted illustrations related to a text. Unlike Western paintings of this time, artists of Turkish miniatures ignored lighting, perspective, and realistic colors, instead turning scenes into abstract or decorative motifs.

For the highest-quality crafts, visit **Ebristan,** on the Asian side of the city (near the Üsküdar pier). This is the studio and home of the colorful, world-famous *ebru* artist Hikmet Barutçugil and his hospitable wife, Füsun, a *tezhip* artist. If you happen to visit while Hikmet is teaching, you're welcome to watch him or his students at work. The gallery shows *ebru* pieces, along with multidisciplinary works that combine calligraphy, illumination, paper marbling, and miniature painting (Mon-Sat 9:30-18:00, closed Sun, Hafız Mehmet Bey Sokak 8, Salacak, Üsküdar, tel. 0216/334-5934, www.ebristan.com).

Near Ebristan, the **Klasik Türk Sanatları Vakfı** (Foundation of Classical Turkish Art) is dedicated to continuing Turkey's classical arts. Here Turkey's most respected artists pass their skills onto students of their crafts (crash a class when you visit). Art by resident teachers is shown in the center's gallery (daily 9:30-18:00, a short walk from the Üsküdar pier, Doğancılar Caddesi 82, Üsküdar, tel. 0216/391-1122).

If you're just curious, the **Turkish Handicrafts Center** is a good place to visit. The center offers courses in traditional arts ranging from bookbinding to lacemaking, and a small gallery displays works for sale. You're welcome to watch amateur artists learning the techniques of *ebru*, *tezhip*, and *hat*, and musicians practicing classical music on the *ney* (reed flute), *kanun* (zither), and *ud* (lute). The center is in the historic and lovely Caferağa Medresesi, built in 1599 by the imperial architect Sinan. Each room around the madrassa's peaceful courtyard is assigned to a particular art form (Tue-Sun 8:30-19:00, closed Mon; kitchen serves basic meals, snacks, tea, and coffee; Caferiye Sokak, Soğukkuyu Çıkmazı 1, next door to Yeşil Ev Hotel on a dead end along Hagia Sophia's outer wall in Sultanahmet, tel. 0212/513-3601).

For traditional dolls, visit the **doll shop** in the handicrafts center by the Blue Mosque at Kabasakal Caddesi 5. The folk dolls made by Lütfiye Bakutan and Selma Yurtlu are masterpieces you can't find anywhere else. Look for Selma's unique wall-hangings featuring dolls playing flutes, praying, and more (daily April-Oct 9:00-18:00, until 17:00 in winter, Sultanahmet).

Gold Jewelry

Gold is a good buy in Turkey. Prices change with the daily rate of gold; when you ask the price of a piece, the shopkeeper will weigh it for you. The Grand Bazaar's many displays of 22-carat gold bracelets reflect Turkey's distrust of banks—many people literally wear their life's savings on their sleeves in the form of these bracelets. These simple bangles often cost little more than the gold itself.

Most mass-produced jewelry is made from molds with 14-carat gold, as it is harder and cheaper. Handmade items are the most expensive; in some pieces, the fine workmanship is more valuable than the gold itself. While the cheaper items (14-18 carat) cost around $25-40 per gram, the price can go as high as $50-75 per gram for finely crafted pieces. Precious and semiprecious stones are generally paired with 18-carat gold.

Like several other **jewelry masters** in the Grand Bazaar, **Sevan Bıçakcı** (a.k.a. Lord of the Rings) is Turkish Armenian. His unique style of ring-making gained him his nickname. He carves intricate forms in precious stones, colors them with special techniques, turns them upside down, and mounts them on gold rings in unusual shapes: a gladiator helmet, the dome of Hagia Sophia, a whirling dervish. Difficult to make and very expensive, they are somewhat like a snow globe on a ring—but without the snow. If you want to see more than what's on display, Herman (Sevan's cousin), Natali, or İda will gladly comply (Sevan Bıçakcı, Nuruosmaniye Caddesi, Gazi Sinanpaşa Sokak 16 Cağaloğlu, www.sevanbicakci.com).

Viktor Öcal, another Armenian master, produces similarly inspiring jewelry at more reasonable prices (Çatalçeşme Sokak Kılıç Han 18 Kat:2 Sultanahmet, tel. 0212/520-5281).

Silver Jewelry and Collectibles

Silver jewelry, with or without semiprecious stones, is a good and affordable alternative to fancy gold pieces. As with gold, silver items usually are sold by weight and won't have a price tag. Look around a bit in the Grand Bazaar to get an idea of what's available and the range of prices. **Kalcılar Han** in the Grand Bazaar (see page 197) is a production center for silver items, with shops on its lower and upper levels. Most of the silver you see in the Grand Bazaar shops is handcrafted on site.

In Kalcılar Han, silver master **Aruş Taş** and his son **Dikran,** an inlayer, make and sell decorative and functional silver objects (Barocco Silver, Kalcılar Han, main floor 37, upper floor 31).

At **Art East,** whose owner Ahmet also runs Sufi (listed under "Textiles, Silk, and Leather," earlier), you'll find **collectibles,** semiprecious **jewelry, art,** and **handicrafts.** Prices are marked, but feel free to haggle—then show this book to get an added discount (Arasta Bazaar 46).

Designer **Emel Toktaş** makes interesting, basic jewelry at reasonable prices. She sells her crafts in a small shop managed by friendly Nur Atınç (off İstiklal Street at Şehir Muhtar Caddesi 33A, Taksim, mobile 0535-896-4779, www.emeltoktas.com).

You can also find beads to make your own jewelry. A few shops in the Grand Bazaar (in and near Cevahir Bedesten, see page 202) carry silver jewelry and semiprecious stone beads.

Spices, Coffee, and Tea

A short walk through the Spice Market can be a great learning and shopping experience. But too often travelers leave this wonderful market with a pack of powdered "apple tea" and a strip of mysterious little spice bags. Armed with a little knowledge, you can bring home authentic Turkish items.

For Turks, real apple tea is made by boiling dried apple skin or adding some dried apple skin to regular black tea, or simmering dried apple skin with cinnamon. (Meanwhile, the apple tea sold to tourists is a mix of sugar, citric acid, ascorbic acid, tricalcium phosphate, apple flavoring, and caramel coloring.) Go for the real deal; several shops in the Spice Market carry dried apple skin.

Dried fruits and vegetables, nuts, and spices are irreplaceable ingredients in Turkish cuisine. But contrary to what many believe, Turkish cuisine is not really all that spicy. Turkish cooks use just enough spices to enhance the taste (the exception being cuisine from the southeastern part of the country, largely because of the ethnic backgrounds of the people who live in that region).

If you would like to cook a true Turkish meal at home, here are the top 10 spices and food items to look for in the Spice Market (or elsewhere in Istanbul):

Sumak (sumac) looks like pepper with a dark red/burgundy color, but in fact it is a berry, dried and crushed. It has a sour lime taste. *Sumak* is mainly used with kebabs and salads, especially those containing onions, as it suppresses the strong flavor and scent.

Çam fıstığı (pine nuts) is a luxury item that is grown in the mountains of the Aegean coastline. It adds a matchless taste to rice pilaf, dolma, and desserts.

Nar ekşisi (pomegranate molasses) is a thick syrup that can be used anywhere in place of lemon, mostly in salads.

Çörek otu (nigella seeds, a.k.a. black cumin) is known for its healing properties, and is traditionally believed to help with the digestive system. Turks generously sprinkle it over savory pastries and salads.

Kimyon (cumin) is used in meatballs, meat dishes, and in making the local spicy sausage, *sucuk*.

Wild **safran** (saffron) is said to be the best, but local varieties of this spice are comparable in quality—and relatively inexpensive. For good saffron, look for a bright red color and fine strands. It may cost as much as 25 TL for a gram (shopkeepers treat *safran* like diamonds and handle it using fine tweezers), which sounds expensive, but it's still a good deal compared with what this spice costs in the States.

Kekik (oregano) is the most common spice used in grilled and barbecued meat dishes. It is a natural antiseptic as well. *Kekik* oil is effective in treating upper-respiratory-system diseases.

İsot (Urfa pepper) is a sun-dried red pepper with a dark red/ purple color and a smoky taste. It is used extensively in southeastern cuisine, especially in regional kebabs.

Pul biber (flaked red pepper) is a staple in Turkey, and takes its place alongside salt and pepper in most restaurants and kitchens. It's the go-to spice for just about any food.

Nane (dried mint) is mostly used in soups and salads, and is also added to lamb and mutton dishes. *Nane*, when boiled with lemon, is often used for treating nausea.

While you're at the Spice Market, be sure to visit **Ucuzcular Baharat,** a 200-year-old spice business. Bilge Kadıoğlu, who studied in the US, is the fifth-generation owner of the shop. She and her brother Ahmet conduct spice-tasting sessions for interested visitors, and teach about spices and how they're used. Bilge also willingly shares recipes she's tried and tested herself. In addition to spices, they carry essential oils and rose oil. Show this book for a discount of up to 5 percent (Spice Market 51, tel. 0212/528-2895, www.ucuzcular.com.tr).

Another Spice Market standby is Topkapı, where you can sample and buy Turkish Delights, spices, and a housemade pomegranate infusion. Managers Murat Onur and Metin Çiftçi are eager to serve Rick Steves readers—show this book for up to a 5 percent discount (Spice Market 13, tel. 0212/514-3500).

Also near the Spice Market entrance is **Kurukahveci Mehmet Efendi Mahdumları,** a locally famous spot to buy high-quality ground coffee.

Souvenirs and Trinkets

The Grand Bazaar is filled with stalls hawking endless mountains of junk, most of it imported. This stuff sells well, as it's cheap and looks "Oriental." Those hats with tiny circular mirrors are common not because they're crafted by local artisans (they're made outside of Turkey), but because the merchants know tourists will buy them. Fortu-

nately, the bazaar is also filled with plenty of affordable, authentically Turkish trinkets that make wonderful gifts.

You can't miss the **"evil eyes"** (*nazarlık;* nah-zahr-luhk)—
blue-and-white glass beads that look like eyes. Traditionally
thought to ward off negative energy from jealous eyes, these are a
kind of good-luck charm popular among Turks. You'll see them on
doorways, hanging down from rearview mirrors, or anywhere else
people want protection. Babies wear them, adults wear them, and
teenage girls braid them in their hair. *Nazarlık*s are authentically
and uniquely Turkish, which makes them good gifts. They come in
various sizes—some with a metal frame, others on a hooked pin,
still others embedded in tiles.

Small Turkish **tea glasses,** made of clear glass and shaped
like a tulip blossom, are easy to find. Buy them toward the end of
your trip to minimize the risk of breaking them as you carry them
around.

Machine-made textiles with traditional designs make good
tablecloths, pillowcases, bedspreads, and sofa throws. Some are
velvet, with silky-looking, colorful embroideries.

Coffee and pepper grinders don't break easily, since they're
made of brass or wood.

The same goes for **backgammon sets** and **inlaid wooden
boxes.** The best are inlaid with mother-of-pearl, while the cheapest
are inlaid with plastic.

If you decide to buy a glass **water pipe** (*nargile;* nahr-gee-leh),
get the kind that separates into parts and is easily reassembled. For
more on water pipes, see page 66.

Mined in central Turkey, **onyx** is plentiful, affordable, and
popular in decorative objects such as vases and bowls, as well as
chess sets (but not so common in jewelry).

Gifts for children are more limited. Consider Halloween **costumes.** You'll find tiny, colorful Turkish princess outfits for girls,
with coins adorning the sleeves and trousers. Cheap knockoffs of
soccer jerseys also abound.

SHOPPING

ENTERTAINMENT IN ISTANBUL

Lively Istanbul is a happening place, with thousands of nightclubs and bars, regular stage performances, and several annual world-class festivals. But if you're expecting nightlife full of shimmying belly dancers, you may be disappointed. Belly dancing in Istanbul is as popular as square dancing is in New York City. Until very recently, belly dancing was looked down upon by modern Turks, though its presence on TV and in competitions is growing.

So rather than seeking out cultural clichés, spend your Istanbul evenings enjoying modern-day, international activities...with a Turkish flair, of course.

Concerts and Performances

WHIRLING DERVISHES

Touristy, fake "Whirling Dervish" performances spin through many of Istanbul's theaters and restaurants. But to see the authentic two-hour religious ritual (called Sema) performed by the Mevlevi, followers of the Muslim mystic Rumi, visit the Galata Dervish Monastery or the Foundation of Universal Lovers of Mevlana, both described next (for more on Rumi and the whirling dervishes, see the sidebar on the next page).

Galata Dervish Monastery (Galata Mevlevihanesi)

This *mevlevihane* (mehv-leh-vee-hah-neh) or monastery is easy to reach (at the southern end of İstiklal Street at Galip Dede Caddesi 15). Knockoff dervish performances are a dime a dozen in Istanbul—this is a rare opportunity to witness one enacted by real worshippers, rather than performers. The lackluster museum is skippable (see page 49).

Seeing a Service: Services are generally held on Sundays at

Rumi and the Whirling Dervishes

In the 13th century, a Muslim mystic named Rumi (better known to Turks as Mevlana, meaning "master" in Persian) began to incorporate whirling meditation into his teachings. He believed that a dervish, spinning in a circle, becomes part of the universal harmony. A *mevlevihane* is a gathering place or residence for dervishes—similar to a monastery in Christian Europe.

If you get a chance to watch dervishes whirl, consider the theology behind this unusual ceremony (called Sema). Rumi believed that the purpose of life was to purify oneself, to become free of the material desires of the flesh that entrap the soul, such as greed, rage, and jealousy. When rid of negative influences, a person's soul can attain eternal happiness. To accomplish this, one must "die before death"—so the dervish ritual symbolizes finding enlightenment through the death of one's self (unchaining the soul from worldly desires). Even the costume worn by dervishes evokes death: a tall camel-felt hat, resembling a tombstone, and a black cloak that represents earthly attachments. As the ritual begins, the black cloak is removed, revealing a long, white dress—similar to the shroud that deceased Muslims are wrapped in when they are buried.

Everything in the universe whirls, from the smallest to the largest particle. By whirling, the dervish becomes one with the created and the Creator.

17:00; extra services may be held on Saturdays as well (about 50 TL, confirm schedule by dropping by the monastery or calling 0212/245-4141). Tickets are available at the monastery on the day of the performance; show up no later than 16:00 to be sure you get a ticket. Ticket sales usually start around 11:00 on the day of the performance, but if you pass by earlier in the day, go ahead and ask. For advance tickets, try contacting Tebit Çakmut (mobile 0536-607-4163).

Once inside, it's open seating, so try to get a seat as close as you can to the center of the hall. As this is a prayer service rather than a show, it's pensive and very slow-paced (about two hours total)—not ideal for impatient camcorder-toting tourists who wish those guys would just start spinning already. To slow down your pulse, ponder what a dervish told me: "As I spin around, my hand above receives the love from our Creator, and my hand below showers it onto all of his creation."

Foundation of Universal Lovers of Mevlana

Whirling dervishes can also be seen at the service held by this nonprofit organization (EMAV), which was established to spread Rumi's philosophy. On certain evenings they hold a Sema ceremony, which begins with a sermon at 19:30, followed by the whirling ceremony around 21:00 (lasts about an hour). This is one of the rare events in which you can see both male and female *semazen* whirl together. If you visit, dress modestly and remove your shoes before entering (and keep them with you). There's a 40-TL charge to attend, and donations may be requested for the maintenance of the facility (Yeni Tavanlı Çeşme Sokak 6, Mevlanakapı Mahallesi, Silivrikapı, near the outer city walls, about 10 minutes and 30 TL by taxi from Sultanahmet; tel. 0212/588-5780, www.emav.org). If you can't get your questions answered at one of the official numbers, call helpful Mete Edman (mobile 0542-422-1544) or Sevtap Demirtaş (mobile 0505-498-9923, fluent in English).

Hodjapasha Cultural Center

Dervishes also whirl in the Old Town in this converted 15th-century Turkish bath, with hour-long performances taking place most nights at 19:00. Reserve seats in person or online (60 TL, children 7-12-40 TL, no children under 7; Ankara Caddesi Hocapaşa Hamamı Sokak 3B, Sirkeci, tel. 0212/511-4626, www.hodjapasha.com).

OPERA, BALLET, AND SYMPHONY

The Atatürk Cultural Center (AKM) at Taksim Square hosts top-notch performances by the Istanbul State Opera, State Ballet, and State Symphony Orchestra. Unfortunately, the venue is closed for renovation until further notice.

In the meantime, programs and tickets for performances in alternative venues (such as Hagia Irene in the Topkapı Palace grounds, the Fulya Show Center, or the Süreyya Opera House in Kadıköy) are available online and at the Atatürk Cultural Center ticket office (as you face the building, the ticket office is at the right-front corner). The state-subsidized tickets are dirt cheap; front-row tickets can cost as little as 20-30 TL. The dress code is casual, but steer clear of shorts and sandals. Opera and ballet tickets are available 30 days in advance; symphony tickets are available a week in advance. Performance times vary (for details and online tickets for ballet and opera, see www.dobgm.gov.tr and choose Istanbul on the menu; see www.idso.gov.tr for details on symphony performances).

TURKISH "RIVERDANCE"

The Fire of Anatolia is a well-promoted, high-energy show with beautiful sets. Many visitors interested in a Turkish folk show may

Buying Tickets

To avoid an unnecessary trek out to a venue's box office, consider buying tickets online. Biletix (www.biletix.com) sells tickets for most events, including movies and soccer games. Buy your ticket online, and then pick it up at the ticket office on the day of the performance—just show the credit card you used for the online purchase. The deadline to pick up your ticket is usually an hour before the start of the event.

TicketTurk (www.ticketturk.com) concentrates on theater tickets, but also provides tickets to alternative events not available through Biletix.

For popular events, tickets can sell out fast. Even if a performance is sold out online, try going to the ticket office the day of the show to see if there have been any returns—your chances of scoring a ticket are fairly decent.

be tempted to choose this over a touristy restaurant show. But while advertised as a "folk show," it's really a Turkish "Riverdance," painfully similar to the Irish stomper with recorded music. For venues and details, see www.fireofanatolia.com.

FESTIVALS

The Istanbul Foundation of Culture and Arts organizes several city-wide festivals every year, including the International Music Festival (June), the International Jazz Festival (early to mid-July), and the International Film Week (mid-Oct). Every other year in the fall, Istanbul also hosts Turkey's largest contemporary art show, the International Istanbul Biennial. Schedules for these festivals vary from year to year, and tickets can go fast, so it's worth checking the foundation's site at www.iksv.org.

The music and jazz festivals are worthwhile, partly for their venues. The jazz concerts take place in lively music clubs and on outdoor stages, while music events are often held at historic monuments. Past festival performers have included members of Milan's La Scala Opera House and the New York Philharmonic.

Nightlife

LOW-KEY EVENINGS ON THE GOLDEN HORN AND THE BOSPHORUS

Warm, clear evenings in Istanbul are perhaps best enjoyed with a short walk across the **Galata Bridge** to watch the sun go down. Take in the Old Town's magnificent skyline, dominated by floodlit domes and minarets. After sunset, head to the lower level of the Galata Bridge, where you'll find sev-

eral moderately priced tavern-style eateries (*meyhane;* mehy-hah-neh) and seafood restaurants.

Restaurants, bars, and clubs along the Bosphorus tend to be expensive, but some areas are more affordable than others. For instance, the **Ortaköy neighborhood,** by the European side of the Bosphorus Bridge, is a pedestrian area with many bars, teahouses, and restaurants. In nice weather, especially on weekends, the area is packed with hundreds of people strolling its streets and alleys. Even on the warmest evenings, you'll want to bring along a sweater or shawl, as a cool breeze blows along the Bosphorus at night (in bad weather, the area is often empty). If you're on a tight budget, get a baked potato or a sandwich from one of the numerous summertime food stalls. Grab a drink from a grocery store, and enjoy your evening picnic on a bench by the Bosphorus, watching the boats pass by, with the bridge lit up like a pearl necklace and the Ortaköy Mosque as its backdrop. A couple of teahouses with good views of the Bosphorus are usually packed with Turks playing backgammon or a tile game called OK. To get to Ortaköy from Taksim Square in the New District, catch bus #40 or #40T (from the transit tunnels below Taksim Square).

PARTYING ON İSTIKLAL STREET, IN THE NEW DISTRICT

In the evenings, the neighborhood surrounding İstiklal Street is transformed into a vast entertainment center. The street itself has several bars, jazz clubs, and *meyhanes* (taverns), all popular among the locals.

Fasıl Music

Many visitors enjoy *fasıl* (fah-suhl) music, often performed in the inviting ambience of a *meyhane*. *Fasıl* is a performance of live, old-time Istanbul songs or classical Turkish tunes, played by a trio of musicians. Locals sing along as they drink *rakı* (firewater) and nibble on *mezes* (appetizers; see the Eating chapter). You won't have to pay a cover charge for the music, but it's customary to tip the musicians—watch locals and imitate.

One good venue is **Şahika** (shah-hee-kah), in a narrow townhouse on Nevizade Sokak (enter the fish market by the corner of

Flower Passage/Çiçek Pasajı, then take the first right). A different style of music, including *fasıl* and contemporary, is played on each of its five floors. If you're a solo male, they may not let you in, so find a fellow traveler to bring along.

Note that some of the restaurants in the Flower Passage and others on İstiklal Street feature "Gypsy music," which is louder, faster, and more danceable than *fasıl*.

Clubs and Nightspots

If you're serious about nightlife, dip into one of the many night-spots on or near İstiklal Street. These generally get rolling late in the evening, around 23:00 or later, and hit their peak around 1:00 to 2:00 in the morning. Quite a few clubs stay open until 4:00. To get tickets in advance for big-name shows, see the "Buying Tickets" sidebar, earlier.

Babylon, near Tünel, is a popular club featuring international bands and performers. It usually has jazz and ethnic music, but it's not unusual to see reggae or percussion bands. Its box office opens at noon, although for more popular performances, you might want to buy tickets in advance (Seyhbender Sokak 3, tel. 0212/292-7368, www.babylon.com.tr).

Hayal Kahvesi is a bar and rock-music venue with daily live performances. It's an institution on the Turkish rock scene; almost all of Turkey's famous rock bands and singers have taken the Hayal Kahvesi stage at least once (just off İstiklal Street at Meşelik Sokak 10, tel. 0212/245-1048, www.hayalkahvesibeyoglu.com).

Nardis Jazz Club, hosting both local and international performers, has been called Istanbul's best live-music club. There's live jazz daily except Sunday, with programs starting at 21:30 on weekdays and 22:30 at weekends (15-TL drinks, 35-70-TL cover charge based on who's performing, Kuledibi Sokak 14, Galata, tel. 0212/244-6327, www.nardisjazz.com).

Ghetto Istanbul offers the spectrum of live music—everything from electro-swing to Gypsy. Reservations are a must for dinner. Doors open at 21:30; performances usually start at 23:00 and go until 2:00 or so in the morning (generally closed Sun-Mon and Sept; 20-50-TL cover charge, Kamer Hatun Caddesi 10, Beyoğlu, tel. 0212/251-7501, www.ghettoist.com).

The prestigious **IKSV Salon** hosts quality jazz and classical music performances. Schedules are irregular, so check their website for the latest (50-90-TL seats, 25-50-TL standing tickets, 25-50 percent student discount on standing tickets, Sadi Konuralp Caddesi 5, Şişhane, tel. 0212/334-0752, www.saloniksv.com).

Love Dance Point is a classy, predominantly gay dance club with popular DJs, special events, and occasional theme parties. Doors open on weekends at 23:30, and they party until 4:00 or 5:00 in the morning (20-25-TL cover charge, open Fri-Sat only but check website for additional days, across from Military Museum at Cumhuriyet Caddesi 349/1, Harbiye, tel. 0212/296-3358, www. lovedp.net).

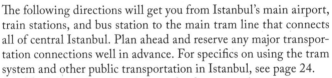

ISTANBUL CONNECTIONS

The following directions will get you from Istanbul's main airport, train stations, and bus station to the main tram line that connects all of central Istanbul. Plan ahead and reserve any major transportation connections well in advance. For specifics on using the tram system and other public transportation in Istanbul, see page 24.

The following website has good information about transportation within and from Istanbul: www.turkeytravelplanner.com/go/Istanbul/Transport.

ATATÜRK AIRPORT

Istanbul's main airport, Atatürk, is used for most international flights (except some flights from Europe, which use Sabiha Gökçen Airport—described in the sidebar). Located to the west of the city center on the European side, Atatürk Airport is a 30- to 60-minute taxi ride (depending on traffic) to either the Old Town or the New District (airport code: IST, airport info tel. 0212/463-3000, www.ataturkairport.com).

Atatürk Airport's international and domestic terminals are located across from each other and connected by an indoor corridor on the upper level. Both terminals occupy two floors, with arrivals on the ground level and departures on the upper level. The arrivals level of the international terminal has a TI desk, where you can pick up a free map and brochures. Each terminal also has an airport information desk, a pharmacy, car-rental agencies, exchange offices, and ATMs (located mainly on the arrivals level).

Arriving at Atatürk Airport

When you arrive at the international terminal, signs and airport staff direct you to passport control. Before leaving for Turkey, you'll have to buy a visa online at www.evisa.gov.tr or at a Turkish em-

Flying in Turkey

Atatürk Airport is the hub for Turkish Airlines (www. turkishairlines.com), the country's major airline. Private carriers—which fly from Atatürk Airport to other major Turkish cities, such as Ankara, İzmir, and Trabzon—include AtlasGlobal (www.atlasglb.com), Pegasus Airlines (www.flypgs.com), and Onur Air (www.onurair.com).

Istanbul's other airport, Sabiha Gökçen Airport, is on the Asian side. It's served mainly by smaller airlines such as Pegasus, AtlasGlobal, EasyJet, and Onur Air, besides AnadoluJet (the budget branch of Turkish Airlines for domestic connections). The ticket prices may seem reasonable if bought ahead of time, but the added expense of getting across the Bosphorus to your hotel might negate your savings. Bus connections and transfer services are available, or figure 95-110 TL for a taxi; it takes at least an hour and a half—depending on traffic (airport code: SAW, tel. 0216/588-8888, www.sabihagokcen. aero).

For a domestic economy flight within Turkey, estimate 90-425 TL one-way (about $30-150). You can buy your ticket in Turkey from a travel agent, or book online through the airline's website. Flights book up more quickly in high season (May-Sept) and during holidays.

bassy or consulate. Americans pay $20; Canadians pay $60 in US dollars. This visa is only valid for tourism or business purposes. For other purposes such as work or study, you'll have to apply at an embassy. (For more information, see page 387.)

From here, you have several options for getting to the Old Town or the New District: cheap public transportation (via light rail and tram, easiest for the Old Town), the airport shuttle bus (most convenient for the New District), a private transfer service, or a taxi. The last two options are the priciest, but provide door-to-door service to your hotel.

By Light Rail and Tram: Public transportation from the airport into Istanbul is inexpensive (8 TL to the Old Town, 12 TL to the New District) but involves at least one transfer. From the international terminal's arrivals level, take the escalator (located midway along the terminal) to the light-rail platform; trains leave from the airport station (called Havalimanı) every 5-15 minutes (6:00-24:00, www.istanbul-ulasim.com.tr/en). To reach the Old Town, take the light rail to Zeytinburnu, where you can catch the tram (look for signs to the tram, or ask) and take it to the Sultanahmet stop. To go all the way to the Galata area hotels in the New District, stay on the tram and take it across the Golden Horn; get off at the Karaköy stop (near Tünel funicular). For Taksim Square hotels in the New District, take the light rail to Yenikapı—the end of the line—and transfer to the Metro for Taskim. Remember that any time you change between the light rail, tram, Metro, or funicular, you'll need to pay for a new ride (for ticket details, see sidebar on page 26). For more on Istanbul's rail network, see page 24.

By Airport Shuttle Bus: Airport shuttle buses are usually white and marked with *Havataş* (hah-vah-tash) signs. As you exit the arrivals level, go past the taxi stand to the Havataş stop. Shuttles leave the airport every 30 minutes around the clock—except from 1:00 to 4:00 in the morning (13 TL, www.havatas.com). The shuttle bus is especially handy if you're heading for the New District. It takes roughly an hour to get to Taksim Square; if your hotel is located in the Galata district, or near the southern end of İstiklal Street, get off at Tepebaşı (teh-peh-bah-shuh; the stop before Taksim), which is a few minutes' walk from either location. For hotels near Taksim Square and the northern end of İstiklal Street, get off at the Taksim (tahk-seem) stop. If you're heading to the Old Town, get off at Aksaray (ahk-sah-ray), and then take a taxi or tram (described later) to the core of the Old Town.

Back to the Airport by Shuttle Bus: If you're heading from the Old Town to the airport, you'll probably notice that local travel agencies advertise shuttle-bus services for as little as €5-10 per person (get details at each agency). If you go this route, note that you may need to catch the bus at the travel agency; some buses don't pick up at hotels.

By Private Transfer Service: Several private companies offer transportation between your hotel and your arrival/departure point: at either of the two airports or the cruise-ship port. Prices are slightly above what you would pay for a taxi, but it's money well spent, as they usually have a set fee between the Old Town and the airport (about $30-35, not affected by traffic or route).

One of these companies, **Ataturk Airports Transfer Services,** has a large fleet and a staff that works around the clock (book online, pay driver, fees for each destination shown on website, 24-hour tel. 0212/638-6343, 24-hour mobile 0554-363-8512, http://ataturkairporttransfer.com, transfer@ataturkairporttransfer.com). The company is run by Efendi Travel, so if you are arriving at the airport, look for a driver holding their sign.

By Taxi: The taxi stand is right outside the arrivals (ground) level of the terminal. Airport cabs are yellow; as long as they're in the line, you know they work for the official airport-taxi service. It's a 30-60-minute ride to your hotel in the Old Town or the New District; expect to pay roughly 45-65 TL ($15-25). Up to four people can fit into a cab—share to save money. For taxi tips, see page 22.

CONNECTIONS

Departing from Atatürk Airport

To leave Turkey by air, enter the airport's international terminal after first going through a security checkpoint. Once inside, scan the screens for the check-in desk for your flight. After checking in, you'll go through passport control and a second security checkpoint to reach the gate area. If you want a VAT tax refund, the tax-free approval desks are at check-in counters A14 and C32—before security. However, these locations can change—be prepared to ask airport staff for help. For more about VAT tax refunds, see page 393.

BUSES
Arriving by Bus

Buses arrive at the city's **main bus terminal** (*otogar;* oh-toh-gar), located in the Esenler (eh-sehn-lehr) district on the European side. Some bus lines stop at other points in the city, which may be closer to your hotel—ask when you buy your ticket. Some bus companies offer a free transfer to alternate locations in the city.

From the main *otogar,* it's about a 30-minute taxi ride to either the Old Town or the New District. You can also catch the light rail from the *otogar* to Aksaray, where you can take the tram to your destination in the Old Town (Sultanahmet stop) or in the southern part of the New District (Karaköy stop for Galata district hotels). If your hotel is near Taskim Square, take the light rail to Yenikapı and transfer to the Metro for Taksim.

Traveling by Bus Within Turkey

Turkey has a good network of highways, and the bus system is easy to figure out. Every major city or town in Turkey has a bus terminal (*otogar),* usually located close to the city center and lined with small ticket offices run by competing companies. Additional, centrally located offices are linked to the *otogar* by shuttle. Service and prices are similar—just take whichever bus leaves soonest for your destination.

Bus rides cost about 20-30 TL for every 60 miles. Turkish buses are quite comfortable, and usually have WCs and tea/coffee/snack service aboard. Buses stop every two hours or so for breaks, giving passengers time to use the restroom, buy food, or stretch. Most bus lines make local stops. A few companies have nonstop express services to major destinations; these don't make local stops and usually have an attendant on board.

Certain bus companies stand out for their good service, including Ulusoy (www.ulusoy.com.tr) and Varan (www.varan.com.tr). While you'll pay up to 50 percent more to go with these companies rather than the cheaper ones, these carriers are more convenient since they have more centrally located bus terminals in the city (and may not even stop at the main *otogar*).

TRAINS

Although Turkey is now covered by Eurail Global and Select passes and Balkan rail passes, trains will not run to central Istanbul in 2016 due to ongoing renovations of train stations. Istanbul's main Asian-side train station—**Haydarpaşa Garı**—is closed for renovation with no trains arriving or departing. The **Pendik Station** in an Istanbul suburb on the Asian side of the Bosphorus is—for now—the main station serving the greater area.

One daily night train connects Istanbul's **Sirkeci Station** with Sofia and Bucharest (and points west in Europe), but due to rail construction passengers are bused to the Sirkeci train station from the Turkish border. If you do manage to arrive at Sirkeci, note that it's located on the Old Town side of the Golden Horn, just a few steps from the Galata Bridge. Go out the main entrance; across the street, you'll see the Sirkeci stop on the tram line, which you can take either to the core of the Old Town (Sultanahmet stop) or to the New District (Karaköy or Kabataş stop).

There are no trains between Turkey and Greece. For more information, see the Turkish State Railways website at www.tcdd.gov.tr.

Traveling by Train Within Turkey

Getting to **Pendik Station** in Istanbul's heavy traffic may take about two hours, so it's a good idea to travel to the Asian side by ferry from either Eminönu or Karaköy to Kadıköy. When you arrive in Kadıköy, take Metro line 4 to Kartal, the last stop, and then take a taxi to Pendik Station (takes about 15 minutes). Eventually the Metro line will extend all the way to Pendik Station.

One of the trains terminating at Pendik is the new high-speed train that connects Istanbul and Ankara in about four hours—almost half the time it used to take on regular trains (70 TL each way, 5-6/day).

See a travel agent or the Turkish Railways website (www.tcdd.gov.tr) for more information.

CRUISE SHIPS

Until renovations are completed on the main cruise port (Karaköy Limanı) at the end of 2017, cruise ships are docking at **Salıpazarı Limanı**, located in the New District, across from the Old Town.

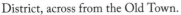

To get into town from the port complex, exit onto Meclis-i Mebusan Caddesi and head to the nearest tram stop, called Fındıklı (400 yards to the north/right and located in the middle of the street). Buy tokens (4 TL) at the automated machines on the platforms, or, if you only have big bills, walk another 500 yards north to the next stop, Kabataş, where there are staffed ticket booths (see page 26 for transit ticket details).

To reach the Sultanahmet stop in the Old Town, take the southbound tram in the direction of Bağcılar. For Taksim Square and İstiklal Street, walk or take the northbound tram to Kabataş, then take the Taksim funicular (see page 25).

If your trip includes cruising beyond Istanbul, consider my guidebook, *Rick Steves Mediterranean Cruise Ports*.

TURKISH HISTORY AND CULTURE

Anatolia is the ancient term for the geographical baklava that makes up most of modern Turkey. This fertile peninsula has nourished civilizations for thousands of years. The oldest city in the world—dating from 7500 B.C.—is thought to be Çatalhoyuk, about 300 miles southeast of Istanbul, near modern-day Konya.

Geographically, the terms "Anatolia" and "Asia Minor" both describe the Asian portion of Turkey—the part of the country east of the Bosphorus Strait. (European Turkey, west of the Bosphorus, is called "Thrace.") Istanbul itself straddles the continents; the oldest, most historic portion of the city (including most of what's covered in this book) is located west of the Bosphorus, on the European side.

Here at the crossroads of continents, Turkish history played out against a backdrop of the greatest empires of East and West. As Turkey has entered the 21st century, the empires of the past have given way to a proud democracy with a predominantly Muslim population.

Turkish History

HITTITES IN ANATOLIA, 2000-1180 B.C.

Anatolia, which quietly coasted through the Neolithic and Bronze Ages, was easily conquered in 2000 B.C. by the Hittites, an Indo-European people. The Hittites' records indicate an advanced legal system. By uniting all of Anatolia, the Hittites created a super-power that rivaled Egypt. In 1180 B.C., the Hittites' civilization abruptly—and mysteriously—fell.

AFTER THE HITTITES, 1180-334 B.C.

Anatolian unity passed with the Hittites, and the land became filled with small, unrelated, and relatively unimportant groups.

The Lycians lived in city-states fringing Anatolia's southern coast. The Phrygians (FRIJ-ee-ans), who settled in the middle of Anatolia, were known for their bravery, artistic talents, and intricately designed tombs. Their King Midas was endowed with the touch of gold (in legend only). The Lydians (not to be confused with the Lycians), known for their creativity, invented numerous musical instruments (such as the lyre and harp). More significantly, they invented coinage. During this period, Greek city-states such as Smyrna (today's İzmir) hugged Anatolia's western coast—an area the Greeks called Ionia. These cities existed as separate entities, united only by their Greek culture.

Among those city-states was one called **Byzantium**—today's Istanbul. It was founded in the seventh century B.C. by Greek colonists (led by a man named Byzas), who built a hill city surrounded by ramparts at the tip of a peninsula (today's Old Town). It had a port and a sheltered cove, and prospered due to its key geopolitical position: Byzantium not only had strategic water access, but also was located on the busy trade route to Greek colonies around the Black Sea. While Byzantium was founded within recorded history, recent excavations for the Bosphorus tunnel project uncovered artifacts from a Neolithic settlement dating between 6400 B.C. and 5800 B.C.—indicating that people lived in this area at least 5,000 years before Byzantium's birth.

Around 600 B.C., the Persians swept in from the east. Cyrus the Great conquered all of Anatolia and began a 300-year period of Persian rule. It was during this time that people first attempted to bridge the Bosphorus Strait, which is only a half-mile wide at its narrowest point. In 490 B.C., the Persian emperor Darius the Great ordered his men to build a bridge for the safe passage of his troops. Boats were tied to one another, allowing thousands of troops to cross the strait.

HELLENISTIC AND ROMAN ANATOLIA (334 B.C.-A.D. 330)

After conquering Greece in the late fourth century B.C., Alexander the Great, a Macedonian, turned his eye to the east. Alexander beat back Persia and conquered Anatolia in 334 B.C. Wherever he went, he founded new "Hellenistic" cities (patterned after the Greek city model and based on the Greek culture and language). Trade and prosperity increased.

After Alexander's death in 323 B.C., his generals fought over an empire that stretched from Italy to India. Anatolia got chopped up. The biggest chunk, called the Pergamon Kingdom, struck up

A City of Many Names

Istanbul has had several names through its history, including Byzantium, Nova Roma, Constantinople, Konstantiniye, and finally, Istanbul.

Byzantium, which means "the city of Byzas," was named for its legendary Greek founder. When Constantine proclaimed  Byzantium as the new capital of the Roman Empire, the official name was changed to Nova Roma (New Rome). However, the people of the city called it Constantinople, or "the city of Constantine." That name survived during the period of the Ottoman Empire as Konstantiniye, the Arabic rendering of Constantinople.

So, when did the city's name become Istanbul? Actually, Constantinople was always Istanbul. The word "Istanbul" comes from the Greek phrase "*(i)stinpoli(n)*," which means "to the city." So when people used this phrase, it meant that they were going into the city... that is, to Constantinople. The Turks kept using the adopted version of this phrase, and called the city Istanbul.

an alliance with Rome. Byzantium struggled to preserve its autonomy, cutting deals with the Romans over the centuries to avoid an invasion. But in A.D. 73, Roman armies under Emperor Vespasian marched through the gates of Byzantium, making the city part of the Roman Empire. Eventually Rome took over most of Anatolia, and over the next 300 years, Rome's "Province of Asia" prospered.

When Septimius Severus claimed the throne of Rome in A.D. 193, his rival, Pescennius Niger, had the support of Byzantium. Severus and his armies crushed Niger's forces and reduced Byzantium to ashes in A.D. 196. Soon realizing the city's strategic importance, Severus had Byzantium rebuilt on an even grander scale. But even Severus' walls couldn't protect the city against Goth raids during the third century.

Just a few decades later, fortune would again smile on Byzantium, when Constantine the Great became the emperor of Rome.

CONSTANTINOPLE AND THE BYZANTINE EMPIRE (A.D. 330-1453)

Constantine decided to move the capital of his far-flung empire from a declining Rome to a more strategic, powerful position in the east. After considering Troy, he instead chose Byzantium, a city

HISTORY & CULTURE

that linked Europe and Asia. In A.D. 330, Constantine declared Byzantium to be the "New Rome" (Nova Roma).

Thus began the Eastern Roman Empire, later known as the Byzantine Empire: a synthesis of Greek culture, Roman politics, and Christian religion that would survive for more than a thousand years. Constantine kicked things off by converting to Christianity, hastening the demise of traditional Roman gods and culture. Even the Roman language, Latin, was eventually abandoned (Greek became the official language when the Byzantine Empire was reorganized in A.D. 620). The word "Byzantine" comes from Byzantium, the original name of the ancient city—a reflection of the city's central role in the vast empire.

Theodosius (r. 379-395) was the last Roman emperor to rule a united Roman Empire from Constantinople. After his death, the eastern part of the empire permanently broke away from the western part. While the last western Roman emperor submitted to a barbarian king less than a century later, the Byzantines to the east continued to thrive for a millennium.

From across the sweep of a thousand years of Byzantine history, one emperor stands out: Emperor Justinian (r. 527-565). Under Justinian, the Byzantine Empire expanded its borders and reconquered some of the empire's lost Roman territories in the west, including most of Italy; his vast holdings also included the Balkans, Egypt, and North Africa. Justinian's code of law, the Codex Justinianus, regulated public and private affairs and business dealings. Also known as Corpus Juris Civilis (Body of Civil Law), it later provided a foundation for the legal system of the West. Justinian's most recognizable contribution was the construction of Hagia Sophia, the Great Church of Constantinople.

Although Justinian's 38-year reign marks the zenith of the empire, he left behind a crippled state. Ambitious building projects drained the treasury. Farms were deserted, as owners lacked the income to pay their taxes. Soon after Justinian died, Italy was lost to Germanic invaders. And so the Byzantines began their slow and steady decline (800-1453)—partly because of their own political mistakes, and partly because of an upstart religion on their doorstep: Islam.

THE SELÇUKS (1037-1243)

In the 11th century, Selçuk Turks from Central Asia rode a wave of Islam into Anatolia, where they established a Selçuk kingdom. After taking over present-day Iran and Iraq, the Selçuks fought Byzantine forces, winning control of nearly all of Anatolia but leaving Constantinople to the Christians. The Selçuks created a wealth of beautiful architecture, ornate tiles, and poetry.

In the 13th century, the Selçuks' greatest philosopher was

born. A religious leader and mystic, Rumi (a.k.a. Mevlana) inspired an Islamic sect in Konya known for its Whirling Dervishes. Rumi's words were simple and profound. He said, "Love lies out of the reach of dogma. In all mosques, temples, churches, I find one shrine alone. The lovers of God have no religion but God alone."

Meanwhile, Constantinople limped along as its rulers fought over succession. From 1202 to 1204, during the Fourth Crusade, crude Crusaders sacked the Christian city and carried off its wealth. They stuck around for 50 years as the "Latin Empire" before the Byzantines regained control. With friends like these, the Byzantines hardly needed enemies. But look out...

OTTOMAN EMPIRE (1299-1918)

The Mongols trampled through Anatolia in 1243, scattering the Turks and ending Selçuk rule. The Turks formed small principalities, or city-states, one of which was ruled by a warrior named Osman. His subjects took his name and called themselves Osmanlı. Contemporary Europeans mangled the pronunciation of "Osmanlı" into "Ottoman."

Over the years, Osman's principality grew in size and power, taking over Bursa as its capital and capturing Byzantine territories in Anatolia. However, the Byzantine presence—centered in Constantinople and nearby towns—lasted for another 200 years, as the continuing Mongolian raids from the east helped preserve the status quo.

By the mid-1400s, the Ottomans had grown strong enough to challenge Constantinople, the eastern stronghold of Christendom. Leading the charge was a young Ottoman sultan, Mehmet II (r. 1451-1481). Mehmet II became sultan when he was only 12 years old, after his father retired. A military crisis soon broke out, and Mehmet II asked his father to lead the army one last time. When his father refused, the enraged Mehmet II proclaimed, "If I am the sultan, I order thee to command the armies"...and, sure enough, his father returned to the throne. Upon his father's death, Mehmet II resumed the throne at the age of 19.

Two years later, Mehmet II laid siege to Constantinople. The Orthodox Byzantines looked for help in the Catholic West, but their pleas were in vain, due to the long-standing conflicts between these two branches of the divided Church. Giving up, the Byzantine clergy reportedly said, "We would rather be ruled by the Ottoman turban than by the Latin miter" (referring to the hat worn by Roman Catholic bishops).

The siege lasted for almost two months. Constantinople was the best-fortified city of its time, with the world's strongest city walls. The Byzantines stretched a large chain across the entrance of the Golden Horn to keep enemy fleets from sailing into the heart

Top 10 Figures in Istanbul History

Byzas (seventh century B.C.): Greek colonist who founded a namesake city on the Bosphorus: Byzantium.

Constantine the Great (r. 306-337): Roman emperor who legalized Christianity and moved the capital of his vast empire from Rome to Byzantium (which became known as Constantinople).

Justinian (r. 527-565): Byzantine emperor who expanded the empire to its greatest extent, codified law, and built Hagia Sophia.

Rumi, a.k.a. **Mevlana** (1207-1273): Great Selçuk philosopher and mystic who inspired the order of Whirling Dervishes.

Osman I (1258-1326): Founder of a small Anatolian principality that eventually grew into a 600-year-long empire, which bore a modified version of his name—"Ottoman."

Sultan Mehmet II, the Conqueror (r. 1451-1481): Successfully laid siege to Constantinople, putting the Ottoman Empire on the map as a world power.

Sultan Süleyman the Magnificent (r. 1520-1566): With his wife, Roxelana, vastly expanded Ottoman territory and financed many fine buildings. See page 208.

Mimar Sinan (1489-1588): Süleyman's magnificent architect, whose grand but tastefully restrained buildings and monuments still rank among Istanbul's best. See page 211.

Kösem (1590-1651): "Favorite" of Sultan Ahmet I, who ran the empire through her sultan sons as the most significant figure in a 150-year-long "reign of the ladies." See page 83.

Mustafa Kemal Atatürk (1881-1938): The "Grand Turk" who liberated his people from Western invasion at the end of World War I, founded the modern Turkish Republic, and enacted sweeping reforms that made Turkey more European than Asian. See page 230.

of the city. Mehmet II knew he had to gain control of this inlet if he was to conquer Constantinople. But instead of trying to break through the chain, he went around it. In just one night, his troops pulled their ships out of the Bosphorus Strait on greased logs, slid them up over the hills past the entrance of the Golden Horn, and then deposited them back into the Horn. The next morning, the Ottomans' cannons—at that time a fairly new form of weaponry—bombarded the city's western walls. Constantinople—and with it, Byzantine and Christian rule in the region—fell on May 29, 1453.

Mehmet the Conqueror made Constantinople the new capital of his Islamic empire and Turk-ified its name to "Konstantiniye." Although Mehmet was a soldier at heart, he was also a man of intellect. He spoke six languages fluently and appreciated art and science. He assembled both Christian and Muslim scholars in his court, beginning a practice of religious tolerance that was continued by succeeding sultans.

Mehmet II transformed the Ottoman state into a formidable empire. However, it was one of his descendants, Süleyman the Magnificent (r. 1520-1566), who made it into a world power. Süleyman triggered an explosion of architecture (with the help of his master architect, Sinan) and expanded his territory as far west as Hungary and as far south as North Africa. Under Süleyman, one-third of Europe's population lived within the borders of the Ottoman Empire, and Istanbul was the largest and most prosperous city in the world. (For more on Süleyman, see the sidebar on page 208.)

However, the titles of Süleyman's successors—such as Selim the Sot and İbrahim the Mad—tell a story of decay. Incompetent sultans, overtaxation, corruption, and technological advances in the West would eventually combine to bring down the mighty Ottomans.

DECLINE OF THE OTTOMANS AND WESTERNIZATION STRUGGLES (1700s-1914)

By the 1700s, sultans and state administrators agreed that the Ottoman Empire had to be reorganized in order to function effectively. The empire sought inspiration from the West.

The Ottoman Empire's first Westernization attempt was the so-called Tulip Era (1718-1730), but due to the sultan's extravagant lifestyle and increased taxes, it ended in riots (see sidebar on page 124). A century later, the 1839 Reformation Decree—which promoted social, political, and economic reform—marked the empire's first serious attempt to Westernize. The concept of citizenship entered the political jargon, and while the sultan still had authority, bureaucrats were given more power. In 1876, under pressure from within the empire as well as from Western powers, the sultan established a parliament, with representatives elected by popular vote. But shortly thereafter, the Ottoman-Russian War provided a good excuse for the sultan to abolish the parliament.

The strongest opposition to the sultan's limitless authority came from intellectuals known as the Young Turks (or New Ottomans). Agitating for civil rights, they printed papers and periodicals in Europe and distributed them in Istanbul. Their efforts came to fruition in 1908, when the sultan issued a decree limiting his executive power and reinstating the parliament. But this parliament would last only a decade; it was abolished by the Allies as they invaded Istanbul in 1918. Most of the Young Turks fled Istanbul at the close of World War I. To some Turkish people, they were heroes; to others, they were traitors. Although they didn't succeed in creating a lasting Western-style government, their contribution to democracy in Turkey was significant.

In spite of the various attempts at reform, the Ottoman Empire continued to decline. Rotten from within, and stifled by palace intrigue and infighting, by the late 1800s the Ottoman Empire had become known as the "Sick Man of Europe"...and World War I finally took it off life support.

WORLD WAR I (1914-1918)

In the early 20th century, the clueless Ottoman Empire sided with Germany. The sultan hoped the war would help the empire regain lost territories in the Balkans and the Middle East, and unify the various ethnicities of the empire. Instead, the war only hastened the empire's demise.

The Ottomans fought valiantly despite their limited resources. Though the bloody Gallipoli battle on the Dardanelles Strait cost heavy human losses on both sides, it ultimately triggered the process of independence for three nations: Australia, New Zealand, and the Turkish Republic.

World War I also saw a controversial chapter in Turkish history. In 1915, the Ottoman government decided to relocate its independence-minded Armenian population in the east, some of whom had staged armed uprisings. During the course of this relocation, hundreds of thousands of Armenians died. Some say this was due to interethnic fighting and disease, while others say it was a concerted government campaign of ethnic cleansing. Today, many Armenians (and many other people outside Turkey) consider it genocide. But most Turks—including the government—don't accept that it was state-sponsored, and maintain that such claims lack historical evidence.

From the ashes of that same tragic war rose the greatest hero of the Turkish people: Atatürk.

ATATÜRK AND THE TURKISH REPUBLIC (1923-PRESENT)

When Germany surrendered at the end of World War I, so did the Ottomans. The sultan signed a disarmament truce, and Allied troops marched through the streets of Istanbul. The eager vultures of Europe—France, Britain, and Italy—could hardly wait for the feast to begin. The Allies drew up a treaty that would carve up Turkey among the victors.

But even as the sultan was capitulating to Allied demands, Turkish nationalists and ex-army officers were mobilizing to fight back. One of them was Mustafa Kemal (1881-1938), a former army officer who had shown great success and bravery in Gallipoli and on other fronts during the war. Kemal—later bestowed with the honorary last name "Atatürk" ("The Grand Turk") by the Turkish parliament—led a three-year-long liberation movement to repel the invading armies. He eventually prevailed and, in 1923, established the Turkish Republic.

Atatürk enacted a series of sweeping reforms to propel Turkey into the 20th century and orient it toward the West rather than the East. State administration, education, lifestyle, dress, language—every aspect of Turkish life was affected. The new parliament abolished all of the old Ottoman institutions—the sultan was history, and the royal family was sent into exile. Constantinople was officially renamed Istanbul, but lost its capital-city status to Ankara, which was then a small town. Atatürk, who saved Turkey from dissolution, remains revered by the Turkish people. For more on Turkey's greatest visionary leader, see the sidebar on page 230.

After Atatürk's death in 1938, Turkey floundered as it searched for a leader and experimented with democracy. İsmet İnönü, the second president of the Turkish Republic, managed to keep Turkey neutral during World War II, but immense financial losses due to the war led to friction and new political movements.

Ongoing political clashes resulted in three military interventions, the last one in 1980. Each time, the military returned control of the country to the people. In 1982, a new constitution abolished the Senate and made the National Assembly the sole legislative body. The current political system is based on the concept of a strong administration, rather than fractured coalitions.

ISTANBUL TODAY

Today, Turkey is a member of NATO and is negotiating to join the European Union. Although Istanbul is no longer the capital, it remains the financial and cultural center of Turkey. With nearly 15 million people, Istanbul is also the biggest city in Turkey (one out of every five citizens lives here) and one of the largest metropolitan areas in the world.

Several issues power Turkey's politics today: the tension between secular and Islamic parties, and the ongoing regional conflicts in the east (such as the civil war in Syria). Visitors to today's Turkey will encounter several hot-button issues.

Turkey has applied to join the EU. But the idea of admitting this Texas-size country (with 74 million people, 98 percent of whom are Muslims) presents the EU with some challenges. The inability of white Europe and its Muslim minorities (10 percent of the Continent's population) to assimilate comfortably is a serious problem that won't just disappear. The EU remains split on whether Turkish membership is in its best interest, and some Turkish politicians are now questioning the move as well.

The issues with the EU are further complicated by efforts of the ruling party, AKP, to adopt more conservative social policies at home. In May 2013, Turkey saw nationwide demonstrations against the AKP regime. Pro-secular crowds took to the streets in what many believe was the largest anti-government uprising in the history of the republic (see page 228).

There is also the issue of the hundreds of thousands of Armenians who died in Turkey during World War I. Was it genocide—or the "collateral damage" so common in war? Most Turks would prefer if this question were debated by historians, rather than politicians. But outside observers see it as a formidable obstacle in Turkey's bid to join the EU. Around Europe, parliaments have debated whether or not to recognize it as genocide. The now independent country of Armenia lies just northeast of Turkey, yet many historic Armenian treasures lie ruined and desolate in eastern Turkey. But the two countries are making progress: In 2009 they reestablished diplomatic relations and opened the previously sealed border.

In addition, Turkey has a huge Kurdish population of about 10 million people, located mostly in the southeast. (The Kurdish people also occupy land in Syria, Iraq, and Iran.) While Turkey's persistent Kurdish insurgency was pretty much quelled in the last decade, the prospect of Iraq or Syria falling apart—and its Kurds forming an autonomous nation—reignites this prickly issue. One thing is for sure: Turkey doesn't want to share a border with an independent Kurdistan.

The civil war in Syria has caused a refugee crisis along the border, and a few military incidents have increased tensions. Prime Minister Recep Tayyip Erdogan was one of the first world leaders to advocate the overthrow of Syrian President Bashar al-Assad.

Despite these challenges, Turkey is enjoying a period of unprecedented wealth at the beginning of the 21st century (it weathered the recent economic downturn much better than its neighbors). With its grand tradition of East meets West, it's a great time to visit one of Europe's most dynamic cities, Istanbul...and make your own history.

Turkish Language

Most urban Turks speak at least a little English—certainly a lot more English than Americans speak Turkish. The younger generation is particularly fluent, and most learn a foreign language (usually English, German, or French) at school. Even if they don't speak English, most Turks will do their best to communicate with you. Still, it helps to know a few words of the local language. The Turkish people love visitors, and a friendly greeting in their language is an easy icebreaker. Give it your best shot. The locals will appreciate your efforts.

To hurdle the language barrier, bring a phrase book (or use the Turkish Survival Phrases on page 433), a small English/Turkish dictionary, and a good supply of patience. In transactions, a small notepad and pen minimize misunderstandings about prices: Have vendors write down the price.

Since Turkish is pronounced exactly as it's spelled, it's easy to sound things out—once you know a few key rules. Most notably, some letters are pronounced differently than in English, and Turkish includes a few diacritics—little markings below and above the letters that change their sound:

Vowels
A / a sounds like "ah" as in "call"
E / e sounds like "eh" as in "egg"
I / ı (with no dot) sounds like "uh" as in "the"
İ / i (with a dot) sounds like "ee" as in "bee"
O / o sounds like "oh" as in "old"
Ö / ö sounds like "uhr" as in "urn" (the same as the German Ö / ö)
U / u sounds like "oo" as in "ooze"
Ü / ü sounds like "ew" as in "dew" (the same as the German Ü / ü)

Consonants
Most consonants are pronounced just as they are in English. Here are the exceptions:
C / c sounds like "j" as in "jet"
Ç / ç sounds like "ch" as in "church"
G / g sounds like a hard "g" as in "good"
Ğ / ğ is almost silent, and makes the preceding vowel longer (so the word *Ağa* is pronounced "aah-ah")
J / j sounds like "zh" as in "leisure"
Ş / ş sounds like "sh" as in "shoe"
V / v usually sounds like "v" as in "viper," but sometimes like "w" as in "wiper"

The letters q, x, and w don't currently exist in the Turkish alphabet. The "q" sound isn't used. The letter x in borrowed words is spelled as "ks," as in the Turkish word for taxi, *taksi*. And, with the increase in foreign words entering Turkish, the Turks are now considering adding w to the alphabet...but only if it behaves itself.

Turkish is usually pronounced rather flatly, without much emphasis on certain syllables—unless you're asking a question. If you

It's All Turkish to Me

The Turkish language—a distant relative of Hungarian, Finnish, and Mongolian—is very unfamiliar to American ears. Yet Turkish is spoken by more than 200 million people worldwide and is also the native language of some areas of Asia and the Balkans.

For a millennium, the people of today's Turkey spoke a confusing mix of languages—Turkish, Persian, and Arabic—depending on the subject and the speaker. Turkish was written in the Arabic alphabet. But in 1928, when modern-day Turkey was founded, the reforms that swept the country included an overhaul of the language. The Arabic script was abandoned in favor of the Latin alphabet. Not only did this nudge the country further toward Europe, but it was also more effective for conveying Turkish sounds than Arabic had been. As a result, more and more Turks became comfortable with their written language; today, the nation's illiteracy rate is less than 3 percent.

want to invite someone to coffee *(kahve)*, you'd say, "kah-VEH?" (accent on the second syllable).

Also note that the word order in Turkish can be different from English. For instance, to ask for a beer, you'd say, *"Bira lütfen"* (bee-rah lewt-fehn; "Beer, please"). But to ask where the toilet is, you'd say, *"Tuvalet nerede?"* (too-vah-leht neh-reh-deh; literally "Toilet where is?").

Adding *-lar* or *-ler* to the end of a word makes it plural (which one you add depends on which vowel comes last). Words in Turkish don't have a gender, and the language doesn't use articles (such as "the" or "a").

If you master only four phrases, learn and use these: To say hello, say *merhaba* (mehr-hah-bah). Please is *lütfen* (lewt-fehn). Thank you is *teşekkür* (teh-sheh-kewr). For good-bye, say *hoşçakal* (hohsh-chah-kahl).

A few common phrases you may hear: *inşallah* (een-shah-lah; God willing), *maşallah* (mah-shah-lah; may God keep it so), *kolay gelsin* (koh-lay gehl-seen; may it be easy), and *rastgele* (rust-geh-leh; may you receive some).

Glossary

ablution: The ritual self-cleansing that Muslims do before entering a mosque for the five daily prayer services

aigrette: Spray of gems used on a turban

alem: Bronze or brass minaret tops (see "minaret")

Allah: Muslim name for the one God

bedesten: Commercial building, also known as a *han*

Bosphorus Strait: Waterway running through the middle of Istanbul, separating Europe from Asia

Byzantine Empire: Eastern branch of the Roman Empire (A.D. 330-1453), with its capital at Constantinople, now Istanbul

cadde/caddesi: Street

caftan: Traditional outer garment, made of silk, velvet, or wool

caliph: Muhammad's successors as head of Islam; during Ottoman times, the sultan also held this title

caliphate: Government based on Islamic law

çini: Quartz tile, or any functional ceramics (such as bowls or vases) made with a high quartz content

concubine: Female slave kept in a harem

Constantinople: Capital of the Eastern Roman, Byzantine, and Ottoman Empires; now called Istanbul

dervish: Member of the Sufi religious order; the Mevlevi sect practices whirling to reach enlightenment (Whirling Dervishes)

Divan: Chamber where the sultan's advisers (viziers) met during Ottoman times

Eastern Orthodox: Branch of Christianity established in the 11th century, after splitting from the Roman Catholic Church

eunuch: Castrated slave; often caretakers of the harem

fasıl: Traditional Turkish tunes performed live by a trio of musicians

favorite: Favored concubine (see "*haseki*")

Golden Horn: Inlet separating Istanbul's Old Town from its New District

Grand Vizier: Prime minister to the sultan in Ottoman times

hadith: Recorded works and words of the Prophet Muhammad

hajj: Once-in-a-lifetime pilgrimage to Mecca required of Muslim people (*hac* in Turkish)

hamam: Turkish bath

harem: Part of the home that was off-limits to male strangers; also refers collectively to the sultan's wives and favorites

haseki: Favorite concubine of the sultan, who, if she bore his child, became known as a "*haseki sultan*" (and was treated more like a wife)

hat: Artistic calligraphy using Arabic script, often used to decorate a mosque

hattat: Calligrapher who creates *hat* (elaborate Arabic script)

henna: Green powder commonly sold in the Spice Market, used to dye hair and to decoratively stain the palms of young brides

imam: Muslim cleric or prayer leader, like a Christian priest or Jewish rabbi

Islam: The Muslim faith (see "Muslim")

İznik tiles: The most prized of all Turkish tiles, typically with a blue-and-white pattern, most famously produced in the 16th and 17th centuries in the city of İznik

janissary: An elite professional soldier for the sultan; usually a non-Muslim who was taken from his family, converted to Islam, and raised and trained according to Muslim traditions

Kaaba: Black cube-like temple in Mecca and focal point for Islamic prayer services

kathisma: Grandstand for royals to watch chariot races

kese: Raw-silk mitten used by an attendant at a Turkish bath to scrub the skin of bathers

kilim: Reversible rug that differs from a carpet in that it features a flat weave, without a raised pile

kiosk: Turkish pavilion

kontör: Credit, as on a prepaid telephone card

Kufic script: Early form of Arabic script

kuruş: Currency sub-unit; 1/100th of one Turkish Lira

Latin Empire: Brief Roman Catholic empire (1204-1261) located in formerly Byzantine land, formed by Crusaders who sacked Constantinople in 1204

lokum: See "Turkish delight"

madrassa: School of theology, attached to a mosque

meydan/meydanı: City square or neighborhood

meyhane: Tavern-style restaurant

meze: Appetizer

mihrab: Prayer niche in a mosque, always oriented toward Mecca

mimber: Small, symbolic staircase near the front of a mosque's interior, used as a pulpit

minaret: Skinny tower adjacent to a mosque, used for call to prayer

mosque: Islamic house of worship

mother sultan: Ottoman sultan's mother, who directed the harem

muezzin: Person who announces call to prayer

muezzin *mahfili:* A mosque's elevated choir loge

Muhammad: The central figure of Islam, a sixth- and seventh-century A.D. prophet who received revelations from God (Allah), which were recorded in the Quran

Muslim: A person who follows the Islamic faith

nargile: Water pipe

nazarlık: "Evil eye"; blue-and-white beads thought to ward off bad luck

Ottoman Empire: Powerful Turkish dynasty that ruled present-day Turkey and huge swaths of the Middle East, Africa, and

HISTORY & CULTURE

Europe (lasted from 1299 to 1922; conquered Constantinople in 1453)

peştemal: Large cotton wrap used at Turkish bath

Quran: Islam's holy book, which collects God's revelations to the Prophet Muhammad

rahle: Holder for a Quran or other large book

Ramadan: One-month Islamic fasting observance (see sidebar on page 64)

Ramazan bayramı (or Seker bayramı): Breaking-of-fast celebration at end of Ramadan

satrap: Persian governor, akin to a viceroy ruling in the emperor's name

Selçuk Empire: Pre-Ottoman Turkish dynasty that ruled much of today's Turkey, Middle East, and Iran (11th-14th centuries)

sıcaklık: Hot, steamy room at the center of a Turkish bath

stele: Carved stone pillar used to mark important events

Sufi: Muslim mystic, including Whirling Dervishes

sultan: Sovereign Ottoman ruler, equivalent to an emperor; also known as Padişah or Han in Turkish

sultana: Ottoman emperor's wife, in Western languages

sultan's loge: A mosque's elevated prayer section for the sultan

sultan's paste: Herbal energy-booster and reported aphrodisiac, more recently known as "Turkish Viagra"

tuğra: Calligraphy representing the sultan's signature, often marking a building

tumulus: Ancient Phrygian burial mound

türban: Muslim woman's head covering

türbe: Mausoleum

Turkish delight: Sweet cube of gelatin dusted with powdered sugar and often embedded with nuts (*lokum* in Turkish)

vizier: High executive officer in Ottoman times

Whirling Dervish: See "dervish"

yalı: Expensive waterfront mansion along the Bosphorus

UNDERSTANDING ISLAM

Turkey offers Western visitors a unique opportunity to explore a land that's fully Muslim, moderate, and welcoming. This chapter, written by the Turkish Muslim authors of this book, explains the practice of Islam in Turkey to help travelers from the Christian West understand and respect a very rich but often misunderstood faith.

"Islam" is an Arabic word meaning "to surrender"—to submit to God's will. The word "Muslim" refers to a person who surrenders to God in all things.

Over 98 percent of Turks identify themselves as Muslims, mostly of the Sunni denomination. But the decision to practice Islam, and to what degree, is an individual choice—a freedom protected by the secular state. Turks don't talk much when it comes to religion, considering it a private matter. An old saying goes, "You never know who's got the faith, or who's got the money." There is a great diversity in the way Islam is practiced among Turkish people, with many different sects or paths tending to focus on Islam's spiritual side. Turks, who have a tradition of tolerance, accept the various sects, as long as none tries to impose its individual interpretation on others.

THE ROOTS OF ISLAM

The Prophet Muhammad (A.D. 570-632) was born in Mecca (in today's Saudi Arabia), in a community he believed was in the throes of moral decadence. Most of the Arab people at the time were pagans who worshipped idols.

Muhammad sought a new way. He retired to a cave for a whole month every year to meditate and seek truth. When Muhammad was 40 years old, the Archangel Gabriel appeared to him in the cave and said that God had chosen Muhammad to be God's prophet.

His first revelation was, "Read in the name of Allah who created you." Revelations kept coming over the next 21 years. Muhammad's followers memorized and wrote down the revelations, and they compiled them in a book called the Quran, which Muslims believe is a faithful recounting of God's word.

Muhammad didn't introduce a new religion. Rather, he invited people to return to the religion of Abraham: submitting to one God. That alone was enough to cause trouble, as Muhammad's words clashed with the personal interests of local community leaders and even Muhammad's own tribe. Early converts to Islam had a difficult time in Mecca, where they were persecuted. Seeking freedom to practice their beliefs, a group of Muhammad's followers migrated to the city of Medina in 622. This event and date mark the beginning of the Muslim calendar.

THE FIVE PILLARS OF ISLAM

Most Muslims largely accept these five essential practices, or "pillars," of Islam as the basis of their faith:

1. Say and believe, "There is no other God but Allah, and Muhammad is his Prophet." This is called *şehadet* (sheh-hah-deht) in Turkish, which means to declare, witness, or accept. A Muslim bears witness by accepting and declaring the fundamentals of the faith.

2. Pray five times a day. *Namaz* (nah-mahz) is the word for daily ritual prayers. It means to pray, to recite "Allah," and to prostrate oneself before God.

3. Give to the poor. Charity, or *zekat* (zeh-kaht), is required of Muslims who can afford a decent living for their family. They should give away one-fortieth (about 2.5 percent) of their annual income to help the needy. Their giving should be discreet—undertaken without boasting and with care not to hurt the feelings of the receiver.

4. Fast during Ramadan. Devout Muslims in good health are required to fast (*oruç*; oh-rooch) from sunrise to sunset during the month of Ramadan. If for some reason a believer cannot fast, he must instead feed the poor. Fasting is not just about staying away from food and drink all day; it is about self-discipline and becoming closer to God. (For more, see the sidebar on page 64.)

5. Make a pilgrimage to Mecca. Muslims who can afford it, and who are physically able, are required to go on a pilgrimage, called a *hac* (hahdge), to the sacred sites in Mecca and Medina at least once in their lifetime. The highlight of this journey to Islam's

An Essential Part of Prayer

Fatiha (fah-tee-hah) means "the opening"—specifically, the opening chapter of the Quran. *Fatiha* is an important part of Muslim worship: No spiritual contact, or prayer, is complete unless it is recited. On Turkish tombstones, you'll often see the phrase "*Ruhuna El Fatiha*" ("*fatiha* for the soul"). People praying with open hands at shrines recite the words of the *fatiha*:

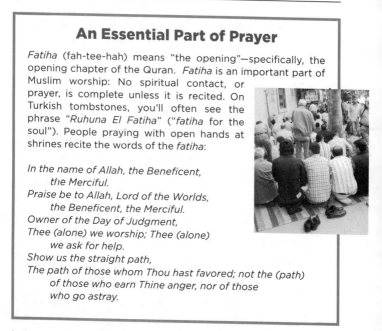

In the name of Allah, the Beneficent,
   the Merciful.
Praise be to Allah, Lord of the Worlds,
   the Beneficent, the Merciful.
Owner of the Day of Judgment,
Thee (alone) we worship; Thee (alone)
   we ask for help.
Show us the straight path,
The path of those whom Thou hast favored; not the (path)
   of those who earn Thine anger, nor of those
   who go astray.

holiest places is a visit to the Kaaba, the iconic cube-like building in Mecca. Muslims believe the Kaaba was built by the Prophet Abraham and is dedicated to the worship of the one God, Allah.

God requires more than just these five elements from those who truly "submit." To Muslim Turks, God's will is recorded in the Quran—giving believers a more extensive code of ethics governing daily conduct. Muslims also follow the Prophet Muhammad's works and life, known as the *sünnet* (sew-neht), "the path," which appear in the hadith, the recorded works and words of the prophet.

COMPONENTS OF ISLAM
Prayer

Mainstream Islam asks believers to perform *namaz* (ritual prayer) five times each day: morning, noon, afternoon, evening, and night. The exact times of prayers change each day according to the position of the sun, and are announced by the call to prayer, or *ezan* (eh-zahn). This very Eastern-sounding chant warbles across Istanbul's rooftops five times daily. However, you won't see Turks in shops, restaurants, and on the streets suddenly prostrate themselves in prayer; people pray mainly in mosques.

No matter where they are in the world, Muslims face Islam's holy city of Mecca when they pray. Muslims are not required to go to a mosque to pray, except for the Friday noon prayer, which the Quran tells believers to perform with their congregation. But

Friday is not a day of rest like the Christian or Jewish Sabbath, because the Quran says Muslims should go back to work when the service is over.

The Mosque

The English word "mosque" comes from the Arabic *masjid* (mahs-jeed), meaning "place for prostration." The Turkish word for mosque is *cami* (jah-mee), meaning "place for congregation." Turks also use the word *mescit* (mehs-jeet; from the Arabic *masjid*) for a small mosque, or a simple chamber to perform *namaz*.

The mosque grew from the need to provide a safe place for Islamic congregations to practice their religion, protected from the world and the blazing desert sun. Mosques are not described in the Quran, so there is no prescribed architectural form. A building's function is what makes it a mosque.

Even within the predominantly Muslim world, religious architecture varies according to place and time. Istanbul's older mosques, to a great extent, were built in the Ottoman style. The classical Ottoman architecture in the Old Town gives way in the New District to a more eclectic style with Western influences.

The most common form of mosque (exemplified by the Blue Mosque and the Mosque of Süleyman the Magnificent) has a central dome, with cascading semi- and quarter-domes. The concept of a massive central dome supported by pillars was first used at Hagia Sophia, built originally as an Eastern Orthodox Christian church. In the centuries since, Turkish architects have refined this traditional design, which is still reflected in many contemporary mosques.

Because early Muslims were turning away from the pagan worship and idolatry of their time, Islamic tradition prohibits portrayals of humans in places of worship. It was believed that icons could distract followers from worshipping Allah as the only God, and mainstream Islam continues this tradition today. Mosques are instead decorated with fine calligraphy and floral and geometric patterns, often displayed on colored tiles.

Minarets—the tall, skinny towers near a mosque—were originally functional: From here, the call went out five times a day to let people know it was time for prayer. Even though the call to prayer is now usually broadcast electronically, minarets remain a symbolic fixture of mosque architecture, like bell towers on Christian churches in Europe.

Prayer services in a mosque are generally segregated, with women and men in different parts of the mosque or separated by a screen. This is for practical reasons: Islamic prayer involves different body positions, such as kneeling with one's forehead on the floor, and early believers thought it could be distracting to have members of the opposite sex doing this in close proximity.

For details on the proper protocol for visiting a mosque, see page 63.

Ablution

Ablution (*abdest;* ahb-dehst) is the physical—and spiritual—cleansing prescribed for a Muslim before prayer. It involves ritual washing of certain parts of the body: hands and arms to the elbows, feet and lower legs, face, nose, ears, and so on. The fountains and water taps you'll see outside of every mosque are for ablution.

The Imam

In Turkey, the imam (ee-mahm) is the Muslim counterpart of a Christian priest or Jewish rabbi. His primary role is to lead the service in a mosque, five times a day. In the past, the imam was more active in Turkish society, in both religious and social matters. Though the imams' influence has waned in urban areas, villagers in rural Turkey usually go to their imam when they need advice.

The imam is usually responsible for calling the congregation to prayer, but at large mosques, this duty is delegated to a second person, called a muezzin (muh-ehz-zeen). The muezzin is chosen for his talent in correctly voicing the call to prayer.

Although Turkey is a secular country, both imams and muezzins in Turkey are civil servants, appointed and paid by the state's Religious Affairs Directorate. To become an imam, you must complete a four-year university degree in theology (studying Islam as well as other religions) and pass a rigorous final exam. The government regulates the rotation of imams, but there is no hierarchy among them (such as with the bishops and cardinals in the Catholic Church).

ISLAM, CHRISTIANITY, AND JUDAISM

The Quran refers to Muslims, Christians, and Jews as "People of the Book" and to people in general as either "believers" or "nonbelievers." Just as the word "catholic" can mean "universal," the words "Islam" and "Muslim" can have a wider meaning in the verses: "Muslim" can be taken to mean all those who have faith in the one God and "Islam" as all those who submit to God's will. For instance, in a verse related to "People of the Book," the Quran says, "There are good Muslims among them."

The Quran recognizes 28 prophets by their names, including Abraham, Noah, Moses, Jesus, and Muhammad. According to the Quran, Allah sent hundreds of prophets to take his message to humankind.

The Quran speaks of an afterlife (heaven and hell), but no

UNDERSTANDING ISLAM

eternal punishment and no original sin. There is no confession in Islam—faith and repentance are strictly between God and the believer.

MUSLIM WOMEN: SCARF OR NO?

Islam advises modesty for both men and women in attire and attitude. Some Muslims interpret this as an order for women to

cover their bodies from head to toe. Veils or black coverings are not traditionally a part of Turkish culture, but in Turkey you'll sometimes see these trends borrowed from Arab Muslim cultures farther east.

The majority of Turkish Muslims prefer a more liberal interpretation of modesty; in fact, the way a woman dresses is left to individual choice. On the streets of Istanbul, you'll mostly see women dressed in contemporary styles, ranging from conservative dresses to miniskirts. But you'll also see many women wearing headscarves, as well as some women wearing head-to-toe coverings.

How does a woman decide how to dress? Her particular community, personal beliefs, family, status, age, education, and profession all play a role. For example, wearing a head covering or scarf does not always have religious significance. Some women simply feel more comfortable in public wearing a scarf—or maybe they're just having a bad hair day.

In poorer and more rural areas, women tend to dress more conservatively. The young women generally dress however they like, as long as they are modest, but elderly women typically wear a scarf in public, often accompanied by a cloak that looks like a long raincoat. In the countryside, it's traditional for women to wear a simple white or colorful scarf—not only as part of their religion, but also as practical protection from the sun and dust.

PRACTICALITIES

This chapter covers the practical skills of European travel: how to get tourist information, pay for things, sightsee efficiently, find good-value accommodations, eat affordably but well, and use technology wisely. To study ahead and round out your knowledge, check out "Resources."

Tourist Information

Turkey's national tourist office **in the US** is a wealth of information. Before your trip, get the free general information packet, and request any specifics you may want, such as city maps and festival schedules. To contact the office directly, call 212/687-2194.

Several brochures can be downloaded from www.goturkey.com or www.tourismturkey.org. The Turkish Ministry of Culture and Tourism website at www.kultur.gov.tr is also helpful and has short movie clips on Istanbul's main sights—great for pretrip viewing.

In **Istanbul,** the city's tourist information office (abbreviated TI in this book) often misses the mark, but it's worth stopping in to pick up a free map. For branch locations, see page 14 in the Orientation to Istanbul chapter.

Travel Tips

Visa Requirement: You're required to buy a three-month visa (a document that goes along with your passport) prior to entering the country. You can get a visa at a Turkish consulate or embassy, but it is easier to purchase it online at www.evisa.gov.tr. Simply enter the required information and make your payment by credit card. The e-Visa will be emailed to you directly. You must print out your e-Visa, show it to airport officials and customs officers when you arrive, and carry it with you at all times during your stay in Turkey. American citizens pay $20, while Canadians pay $60 (also in US currency, Canadian currency not accepted). For all tourism and business-related activities, you are allowed to remain in Turkey for 90 days within a 180-day period. If you are planning to stay more than three months, you must obtain a visa in person from a Turkish embassy or consulate before entering; see www.turkishembassy.org.

Emergency and Medical Help: In Istanbul, dial 444-1212 for English-speaking medical help (for more services, see page 423). The following numbers are Turkish-language only (so require the help of a local person such as your hotelier to help communicate): 112 for medical emergencies and 155 for police.

Theft or Loss: To replace a passport, you'll need to go in person to a consulate (see page 423). If your credit and debit cards disappear, cancel and replace them (see "Damage Control for Lost Cards" on page 392). File a police report, either on the spot or within a day or two; you'll need it to submit an insurance claim for lost or stolen rail passes or travel gear, and it can help with replacing your passport or credit and debit cards. For more info, see www.ricksteves.com/help. To minimize the effects of loss, back up your digital photos and other files frequently.

Time Zones: Istanbul, which is one hour ahead of most of continental Europe, is generally seven/ten hours ahead of the East/West Coasts of the US. The exceptions are the beginning and end of Daylight Saving Time: Europe "springs forward" the last Sunday in March (two weeks after most of North America) and "falls back" the last Sunday in October (one week before North America). For a handy online time converter, try www.timeanddate.com/worldclock.

Business Hours: Most shops are open daily 9:00-19:00; on Sundays, they open a little later in the morning. On holidays, most museums and shops in tourist areas are open (and shops may stay open a little later than usual). The Grand Bazaar is closed on Sundays. On the first day of religious festivals, both the Grand Bazaar and Spice Market are closed, and museums are closed for a half-day (usually in the morning).

Most government offices and banks are open Monday-Friday

9:00-17:00; some are also open Saturday 9:00-12:00 (closed Saturday afternoon and all day Sunday and holidays). On the day before a national or religious holiday, many government offices and banks close in the afternoon.

Watt's Up? Europe's electrical system is 220 volts, instead of North America's 110 volts. Most newer electronics (such as laptops, battery chargers, and hair dryers) convert automatically, so you won't need a converter, but you will need an adapter plug with two round prongs, sold inexpensively at travel stores in the US. Avoid bringing older appliances that don't automatically convert voltage; instead, buy a cheap replacement in Europe.

Discounts: Discounts are not listed in this book. Children under 13 (with a passport for proof) can get in free to museums and sites run by the Turkish Ministry of Culture and Tourism, including Topkapı Palace, Hagia Sophia, Chora Church, Turkish and Islamic Arts Museum, and Istanbul Archaeological Museum. Other museums and sites may not follow this policy. Some discounts are available only for Turkish citizens.

Online Translation Tips: You can use Google's Chrome browser (available free at www.google.com/chrome) to instantly translate websites. With one click, the page appears in (very rough) English translation. You can also paste the URL of the site into the translation window at www.google.com/translate. The Google Translate app converts spoken English into most European languages (and vice versa) and can also translate text it "reads" with your mobile device's camera.

Money

This section offers advice on how to pay for purchases on your trip (including getting cash from ATMs and paying with plastic), dealing with lost or stolen cards, VAT (sales tax) refunds, and tipping.

WHAT TO BRING

Bring both a credit card and a debit card. You'll use the debit card at cash machines (ATMs) to withdraw local cash for most purchases, and the credit card to pay for larger items. Some travelers carry a third card, in case one gets demagnetized or eaten by a temperamental machine.

For an emergency stash, bring several hundred dollars in hard cash in $20 bills. If you need to exchange the bills, go to a bank; avoid using currency-exchange booths because of their lousy rates and/or outrageous (and often hard-to-spot) fees.

Exchange Rate

In this book, we list most prices in Turkish Liras (Türk Lirası, or TL).

1 Turkish Lira (TL) = about $0.33

Just like the dollar, one Turkish Lira (TL) is broken down into 100 cents, or *kuruş* (koo-roosh; abbreviated Kr). Coins range from 1 Kr to 1 TL, and bills from 5 TL to 200 TL.

To roughly convert prices in liras to dollars, subtract two-thirds. (Pretend everything is on a "60 percent·off sale.") So that 9-TL coffee-and-baklava break is about $3, that 45-TL shawl is about $15, and that 200-TL taxi ride is...uh-oh.

Prices are sometimes listed in either dollars or euros, especially in tourist areas. This is partly for convenience, but also to protect vendors against lira inflation. Hotels almost always list prices in euros, and we've followed suit in the Sleeping in Istanbul chapter. (Check www.oanda.com for the latest exchange rates for either lira or euros.)

1 euro (€) = about $1.10

To convert prices in euros to dollars, add about 10 percent: €20 is about $22, €50 is about $55. Just like the dollar, one euro (€) is broken down into 100 cents. Coins range from €0.01 to €2, and bills from €5 to €500 (bills over €50 are rarely used).

CASH

Cash is just as desirable in Istanbul as it is at home. Small businesses (hotels, mom-and-pop cafés, shops, etc.) prefer that you pay your bills with cash. Some vendors will charge you extra for using a credit card, some won't accept foreign credit cards, and some won't take any credit cards at all. Cash is the best—and sometimes only—way to pay for cheap food, bus fare, taxis, and local guides.

Throughout Europe, ATMs are the standard way for travelers to get cash. They work just like they do at home. ATMs in Turkey are known as a *Bankamatik*, bahn-kah-mah-teek, though some banks use different names—"24," "self-service," or *paramatik*—literally "money-matic." All of Istanbul's ATMs have instructions in English.

To withdraw money, you'll need a debit card (ideally with a Visa or MasterCard logo for maximum usability), plus a PIN code (numeric and four digits). For increased security, shield the keypad when entering your PIN code, and don't use an ATM if anything on the front of the machine looks loose or damaged (a sign that someone may have attached a "skimming" device to capture account information). Try to withdraw large sums of money to reduce the number of per-transaction bank fees you'll pay.

When possible, use ATMs located outside banks—a thief is less likely to target a cash machine near surveillance cameras, and if your card is munched by a machine, you can go inside for help. Stay away from "independent" ATMs such as Travelex, Euronet, YourCash, Cardpoint, and Cashzone, which charge huge commissions, have terrible exchange rates, and may try to trick users with "dynamic currency conversion" (described at the end of "Credit and Debit Cards," next). Although you can use a credit card to withdraw cash at an ATM, this comes with high bank fees and only makes sense in an emergency.

While traveling, if you want to monitor your accounts online to detect any unauthorized transactions, be sure to use a secure connection (see page 419).

Pickpockets target tourists. To safeguard your cash, use a money belt—a pouch with a strap that you buckle around your waist like a belt and tuck under your clothes. Keep your cash, credit cards, and passport secure in your money belt, and carry only a day's spending money in your front pocket.

CREDIT AND DEBIT CARDS

For purchases, Visa and MasterCard are more commonly accepted than American Express. Just like at home, credit and debit cards work easily at larger hotels, restaurants, and shops. We typically use our debit cards to withdraw cash to pay for most purchases. We use our credit cards sparingly: to book hotel reservations, to buy advance tickets for events or sights, to cover major expenses (such as car rentals or plane tickets), and to pay for things online or near the end of our trips (to avoid another visit to the ATM). While you could instead use a debit card for these purchases, a credit card offers a greater degree of fraud protection.

Ask Your Credit- or Debit-Card Company: Before your trip, contact the company that issued your debit or credit card.

• Confirm your **card will work overseas,** and alert them that you'll be using it in Europe; otherwise, they may deny transactions if they perceive unusual spending patterns.

• Ask for the specifics on transaction **fees.** When you use your credit or debit card—either for purchases or ATM withdrawals—you'll typically be charged additional "international transaction" fees of up to 3 percent (1 percent is normal) plus $5 per transaction. If your card's fees seem high, consider getting a different card just for your trip: Capital One (www.capitalone.com) and most credit unions have low-to-no international fees.

• Verify your daily ATM **withdrawal limit,** and if necessary, ask your bank to adjust it. We prefer a high limit that allows us to take out more cash at each ATM stop and save on bank fees; some travelers prefer to set a lower limit in case their card is stolen. Note that foreign banks also set maximum withdrawal amounts for their ATMs.

• Get your bank's emergency **phone number** in the US (but not its 800 number, which isn't accessible from overseas) to call collect if you have a problem.

• Ask for your credit card's **PIN** in case you need to make an emergency cash withdrawal or encounter Europe's chip-and-PIN system; the bank won't tell you your PIN over the phone, so allow time for it to be mailed to you.

Magnetic-Stripe versus Chip-and-PIN Credit Cards: Europeans are increasingly using chip-and-PIN credit cards embedded with an electronic security chip and requiring a four-digit PIN. In Istanbul, most machines will recognize your credit card as being foreign and generally will not ask you for a PIN number. If you have problems, try entering your card's PIN, look for a machine that takes cash, or find a clerk who can process the transaction manually.

Major US banks are beginning to offer credit cards with chips. Many of these are not true chip-and-PIN cards, but instead are chip-and-signature cards, for which your signature verifies your identity. These cards should work for live transactions and at most payment machines, but won't work for offline transactions such as at unattended baggage lockers. If you're concerned, ask if your bank offers a true chip-and-PIN card. Andrews Federal Credit Union (www.andrewsfcu.org) and the State Department Federal Credit Union (www.sdfcu.org) offer these cards and are open to all US residents.

No matter what kind of card you have, it pays to carry Turkish lira; remember, you can always use an ATM to withdraw cash with your magnetic-stripe debit card.

Dynamic Currency Conversion: If merchants or hoteliers offer to convert your purchase price into dollars (called dynamic currency conversion, or DCC), refuse this "service." You'll pay even more in fees for the expensive convenience of seeing your charge in dollars. If your receipt shows the total in dollars only, ask for the transaction to be processed in the local currency. If the clerk refuses, pay in cash—or mark the receipt "local currency not offered" and dispute the DCC charges with your bank.

Some ATMs and retailers try to confuse customers by presenting DCC in misleading terms. If an ATM offers to "lock in" or "guarantee" your conversion rate, choose "proceed without conversion." Other prompts might state, "You can be charged in dollars: Press YES for dollars, NO for Turkish lira." Always choose the local currency in these situations.

Damage Control for Lost Cards

If you lose your credit, debit, or ATM card, you can stop people from using your card by reporting the loss immediately to the respective global customer-assistance center. Call these 24-hour US numbers collect: Visa (tel. 303/967-1096), MasterCard (tel. 636/722-7111), or American Express (tel. 336/393-1111). In Turkey, to make a collect call to the US, dial 0-811-288-0001. Press zero or stay on the line for an English-speaking operator. European toll-free numbers (listed by country) can be found at the websites for Visa and MasterCard.

Try to have this information ready: full card number, whether you are the primary or secondary cardholder, the cardholder's name exactly as printed on the card, billing address, home phone number, circumstances of the loss or theft, and identification verification (your birth date, your mother's maiden name, or your Social Security number—memorize this, don't carry a copy). If you are the secondary cardholder, you'll also need to provide the primary cardholder's identification-verification details. You can generally receive a temporary card within two or three business days in Europe (see www.ricksteves.com/help for more).

If you report your loss within two days, you typically won't be responsible for any unauthorized transactions on your account, although many banks charge a liability fee of $50.

TIPPING

Tipping in Turkey is as automatic as it is in the US—for special service, tips are appreciated, if not expected. As in the US, the proper amount depends on your resources, tipping philosophy, and the circumstances, but some general guidelines apply. A 10 percent tip is average.

Restaurants: In restaurants with table service, tip 10 percent for good service, even if your bill includes a service charge. For details, see page 404.

Taxis: For a typical ride, round up your fare to the next lira (for instance, if the fare is 14 TL, pay 15 TL); for a long ride, round to the nearest 5 TL (for a 47-TL fare, pay 50 TL). If the cabbie hauls your bags and zips you to the airport to help you catch your flight, you might want to toss in a little more. But if you feel like you're being driven in circles or otherwise ripped off, skip the tip.

Services: In general, if someone in the service industry does a super job for you, a small tip of a few liras is appropriate...but not required. If you're not sure whether (or how much) to tip for a service, ask your hotelier or the TI.

GETTING A VAT REFUND

Wrapped into the purchase price of your Turkish souvenirs is a Value-Added Tax (VAT) of 18 percent. You're entitled to get most of that tax back if you purchase more than 100 TL (about $33) worth of goods at a store that participates in the VAT-refund scheme. Typically, you must ring up the minimum at a single retailer—you can't add up your purchases from various shops to reach the required amount.

Getting your refund is straightforward and, if you buy a substantial amount of souvenirs, well worth the hassle. (Note that if the store ships the goods to your US home, VAT is not assessed on your purchase.) You'll need to:

Get the paperwork. Have the merchant completely fill out the necessary refund document, called a "Tax-Free Shopping Cheque." You'll have to present your passport at the store. Get the paperwork done before you leave the store to ensure you'll have everything you need (including your original sales receipt).

Get your stamp at the border or airport. Process your VAT document at your last stop in Turkey (such as at the airport) with the customs agent who deals with VAT refunds. Arrive an additional hour before you need to check in for your flight to allow time to find the local customs office—and to stand in line (VAT refund desks at Istanbul's Atatürk Airport are at check-in counters A14 and C32, but be aware that the locations could change). It's best to keep your purchases in your carry-on. If they're too large or dangerous to carry on (such as knives), pack them in your checked bags and alert the check-in agent. You'll be sent (with your tagged bag) to a customs desk outside security; someone will examine your bag, stamp your paperwork, and put your bag on the belt. You're not supposed to use your purchased goods before you leave. If you show up at customs wearing your new belly-dancing costume from the Grand Bazaar, officials might look the other way—or deny you a refund.

Collect your refund. You'll need to return your stamped document to the retailer or its representative. Many merchants work with services, such as Global Blue or Premier Tax Free, that have offices at major airports, ports, or border crossings (either before or after security, probably strategically located near a duty-free shop). These services, which extract a 4 percent fee, can refund your money immediately in cash or credit your card (within two billing cycles). If the retailer handles VAT refunds directly, it's up to you to contact the merchant for your refund. You can mail the documents from home, or more quickly, from your point of departure (using an envelope you've prepared in advance or one that's been provided by the merchant). You'll then have to wait—it can take months.

CUSTOMS FOR AMERICAN SHOPPERS

You are allowed to take home $800 worth of items per person duty-free, once every 31 days. You can take home many processed and packaged foods: vacuum-packed cheeses, dried herbs, jams, baked goods, candy, chocolate, oil, vinegar, mustard, and honey. Fresh fruits and vegetables and most meats are not allowed, with exceptions for some canned items. You can bring in one liter of alcohol duty-free (it can be packed securely in your checked luggage, along with any other liquid-containing items).

To bring alcohol or liquid-packed foods in your carry-on bag on your flight home, buy it at a duty-free shop at the airport. You'll increase your odds of getting it onto a connecting flight if it's packaged in a "STEB"—a secure, tamper-evident bag. But stay away from liquids in opaque, ceramic, or metallic containers, which usually cannot be successfully screened (STEB or no STEB).

For details on allowable goods, customs rules, and duty rates, visit http://help.cbp.gov.

Sightseeing

Sightseeing can be hard work. Use these tips to make your visits to Istanbul's finest sights meaningful, fun, efficient, and painless.

PLAN AHEAD

Set up an itinerary that allows you to fit in all your must-see sights. For a one-stop look at opening hours, see "Istanbul at a Glance" (page 38); also see the "Daily Reminder" on page 15. Most sights keep stable hours, but you can easily confirm the latest by checking with the TI or visiting museum websites.

Don't put off visiting a must-see sight—you never know when a place will close unexpectedly for a holiday, strike, or restoration. Many museums are closed or have reduced hours at least a few days a year, especially on religious holidays, New Year's Day, and Republic Day (Oct 29). A list of holidays is on page 424; check online for possible museum closures during your trip. Off-season, many museums have shorter hours; in summer, some sights may stay open late.

Going at the right time helps avoid crowds. This book offers tips on the best times to see specific sights. Try visiting popular sights very early or very late. Evening visits are usually peaceful, with fewer crowds. If you plan on visiting many sights, consider getting a Museum Pass (see page 31).

Study up. To get the most out of the self-guided tours and

sight descriptions in this book, read them before you visit. Hagia Sophia is much more fascinating if you've been busy learning about Byzantine architecture.

AT SIGHTS

Here's what you can typically expect:

Entering: Be warned that you may not be allowed to enter if you arrive 30 to 60 minutes before closing time. And guards start ushering people out well before the actual closing time, so don't save the best for last.

Some important sights have a security check, where you must open your bag or send it through a metal detector. Some sights require you to check daypacks and coats. (If you'd rather not check your daypack, try carrying it tucked under your arm like a purse as you enter.)

At mosques, respect the dress code (covered knees and shoulders, and head scarves for women). For more information, see "Visiting a Mosque" on page 63.

Photography: If the museum's photo policy isn't clearly posted, ask a guard. Generally, taking photos without a flash or tripod is allowed. Some sights ban photos altogether.

Temporary Exhibits: Museums may show special exhibits in addition to their permanent collection. Some exhibits are included in the entry price, while others come at an extra cost (which you may have to pay even if you don't want to see the exhibit).

Expect Changes: Items can be on tour, on loan, out sick, or shifted at the whim of the curator. Pick up a floor plan as you enter, and ask museum staff if you can't find a particular item. Point to the photograph in this book and ask, *"Nerede?"* (neh-reh-deh; "Where is?").

Audioguides and Apps: Some sights in Istanbul rent audioguides, which generally offer recorded descriptions in English; unfortunately, the commentary is likely to be dry. While most readers will find this book's tours more interesting, eager students take advantage of both types of tours and learn even more. If you bring your own earbuds, you can enjoy better sound and avoid holding the device to your ear. To save money, bring a Y-jack and share one audioguide with your travel partner. Increasingly, museums and other sights offer apps—often free—that you can download to your mobile device (check their websites).

Services: Important sights may have an on-site café or cafeteria (usually a handy place to rejuvenate during a long visit). The WCs at sights are free and generally clean.

Before Leaving: At the gift shop, scan the postcard rack or thumb through a guidebook to be sure that you haven't overlooked something that you'd like to see.

Every sight or museum offers more than what is covered in this book. Use the information in this book as an introduction—not the final word.

Sleeping

We favor hotels and restaurants that are handy to your sightseeing activities. Rather than list hotels scattered throughout a city, we choose hotels in our favorite neighborhoods. Our recommendations run the gamut, from dorm beds to fancy rooms with all of the comforts.

A major feature of the Sleeping chapter in this book is its extensive and opinionated listing of good-value rooms. We like places that are clean, central, relatively quiet at night, reasonably priced, friendly, small enough to have a hands-on owner and stable staff, run with a respect for Turkish traditions, and not listed in other guidebooks. (In Istanbul, six out of these eight criteria mean it's a keeper.) We're more impressed by a convenient location and a fun-loving philosophy than flat-screen TVs and a pricey laundry service.

Book your accommodations well in advance if you want to stay at one of our top listings or if you'll be traveling during busy times. Popular places are even busier on weekends...and can be inundated on three-day weekends. Hotels are crowded in May, June, September, and October. See page 424 for a list of major holidays and festivals in Istanbul; for tips on making reservations, see page 398.

Surprisingly, major Christian holidays (Easter and Christmas, including the weeks before and after) can cause prices and demand to spike in Muslim Turkey, because Europeans flock here when they have time off. Conversely, Muslim holidays do not generally affect Istanbul hotel prices, as many Turks travel away from the city during those times. Most hotel rates go down from mid-November through mid-March (except around New Year's, when they charge peak rates). Some places also offer small discounts in July and August, when the city is hotter and quieter.

RATES AND DEALS

We've described our recommended accommodations using a Sleep Code (see the sidebar on page 303). The prices we list are for one-night stays in peak season.

Our recommended hotels each have a website (often with a built-in booking form) and an email address; you can expect a response in English within a day (and often sooner). If you're on a budget, it's smart to email several hotels to ask for their best price.

As you look over the listings in this chapter, you'll notice that some places promise special prices or other bonuses (such as free

Types of Rooms and Beds

Study the price list on the hotel's website or posted at the desk, so you know your options. Receptionists often don't mention the cheaper rooms (they assume you want a private bathroom or a bigger room). Here are the types of rooms and beds:

"**French bed**"
   Double bed (queen size or smaller)
"**King bed**"
   King-size bed
İki ayrı yatak (ee-kee eye-ruh yah-tahk)
   Twin beds
Çift kişilik oda (cheeft kee-shee-leek oh-dah)
   Double room; indicate whether you want a French bed, king-size bed, or twin beds
Geniş yataklı oda (geh-neesh yah-tahk-luh oh-dah)
   Single or double room with one large bed (usually queen size or smaller)
Tek kişilik oda (tehk kee-shee-leek oh-dah)
   Room for two used by a single person; may be a double bed or two twin beds
Üç kişilik oda (ewch kee-shee-leek oh-dah)
   Triple room (double bed and a twin, or three twin beds)
"**Promotion room**"
   Smaller room, often with toilet and shower down the hall

airport transfers) to Rick Steves readers. To get these rates, you must book direct (that is, not through a booking site like TripAdvisor or Booking.com), mention this book when you reserve, and then show the book upon arrival—discounts are only good with the seventh edition of this book. Rick Steves discounts apply to readers with a seventh-edition ebook as well. "Best Internet rate" refers to the hotel's best published offer on its own website.

Some Istanbul hotels use "dynamic pricing," which enables room rates to change depending on demand. These flexible rates may not be published on hotels' websites (which tend to be fairly static), but may be available through websites such as Booking.com or TripAdvisor. When you're ready to reserve, check first to see who has the best price: the hotel or a booking site.

Even if you don't qualify for a free airport transfer, hotels can arrange an airport shuttle. However, it might not be the cheapest—a €25 hotel shuttle to the airport is no deal given that it's easy to arrange a €5-10 shuttle through many Old Town travel agencies (though you may need to catch the bus at the travel agency, rather than at your hotel).

Making Hotel Reservations

Reserve your rooms several weeks in advance—or as soon as you've pinned down your travel dates—particularly if you'll be traveling during peak times. Note that some national holidays jam things up and merit your making reservations far in advance (see page 424).

Requesting a Reservation: It's usually easiest to book your room through the hotel's website. Many have a reservation-request form built right in. (To ensure you're getting the best price, also check a booking agency's website.) Simpler websites will generate an email to the hotelier with your request. If there's no reservation form, or for complicated requests, send an email (see next page for a sample request). Most recommended hotels are accustomed to guests who speak only English.

The hotelier wants to know:
- the number and type of rooms you need
- the number of nights you'll stay
- your date of arrival
- your date of departure
- any special needs (such as bathroom in the room or down the hall, cheapest room, twin beds vs. double bed, crib, air-conditioning, quiet, view, ground floor or no stairs, and so on)

If you request a room by email, use the European style for writing dates: day/month/year. For example, for a two-night stay in July of 2017, ask for "1 double room for 2 nights, arrive 16/07/17, depart 18/07/17." Make sure you mention any discounts—for Rick Steves readers or otherwise—when you make the reservation.

Confirming a Reservation: Most places will request a credit-card number to hold your room. If they don't have a secure online reservation form—look for the *https*—you can email it, but it's

TYPES OF ACCOMMODATIONS
Hotels

Like most European hotels, Istanbul hotel rooms are smaller than comparable hotel rooms in the US. In this book, the price for a double room ranges from $50 (very simple—toilet and shower down the hall) to more than $300 (grand lobbies, maximum plumbing, the works), with most clustering around $140-170. When we've listed seasonal prices, "summer" refers to mid-March through mid-November, and "winter" (or "low season") refers to mid-November through mid-March.

Turkey has a simple hotel rating system that's based on amenities (one through five stars, indicated in this book by * through *****). Hotels with one star (or no stars) are simple and can be bar-

PRACTICALITIES

From:	rick@ricksteves.com
Sent:	Today
To:	info@hotelcentral.com
Subject:	Reservation request for 19-22 July

Dear Hotel Central,

I would like to reserve a room for 2 people for 3 nights, arriving 19 July and departing 22 July. If possible, I would like a quiet room with a double bed and private bathroom inside the room.

Please let me know if you have a room available and the price.

Thank you!
Rick Steves

safer to share that confidential info via a phone call or two emails (splitting your number between them).

Canceling a Reservation: If you must cancel your reservation, it's courteous—and smart—to do so with as much notice as possible, especially for smaller family-run places. Be warned that cancellation policies can be strict; read the fine print or ask about these before you book. Internet deals may require prepayment, with no refunds for cancellations.

Reconfirming a Reservation: Always call or email to reconfirm your room reservation a few days in advance. For very small hotels, we call again on our day of arrival to tell our host what time we expect to get there (especially important if arriving late—after 17:00).

Phoning: For tips on calling hotels overseas, see page 416.

gains—or depressing dumps. Two stars offer basic facilities but little charm. Three stars have most of the comforts, and four is generally just a three-star with a fancier lobby and more elaborately designed rooms. Five stars offer more luxury than you'll have time to appreciate.

Generally, the number of stars does not reflect room size or guarantee quality. Some two-star hotels are better than many three-star hotels. One- and two-star hotels are inexpensive, but some three-star (and even a few four-star hotels) offer good value, justifying the extra cost.

A separate designation called "Special Class" (which we've marked with this symbol: **SC**) indicates the hotel is either a historic building or a residential building converted to lodging—in other words, it has a unique character. There are no subcategories among

The Good and Bad of Online Reviews

User-generated travel review websites—such as TripAdvisor, Booking.com, and Yelp—have quickly become a huge player in the travel industry. These sites give you access to actual reports—good and bad—from travelers who have experienced the hotel, restaurant, tour, or attraction.

Our hotelier friends in Europe are in awe of these sites' influence. Small hoteliers who want to stay in business have no choice but to work with review sites—which often charge fees for good placement or photos, and tack on commissions if users book through the site instead of directly with the hotel.

While these sites work hard to weed out bogus users, our hunch is that a significant percentage of reviews are posted by friends or enemies of the business being reviewed. I've even seen hotels "bribe" guests (for example, offer a free breakfast) in exchange for a positive review. Also, review sites are uncurated and can become an echo chamber, with one or two flashy businesses camped out atop the ratings, while better, more affordable, and more authentic alternatives sit ignored farther down the list. (For example, we find review sites' restaurant recommendations skew to very touristy, obvious options.) And you can't always give credence to the negative reviews: Different people have different expectations.

Remember that a user-generated review is based on the experience of one person. That person likely stayed at one hotel and ate at a few restaurants, and doesn't have much of a basis for comparison. A guidebook is the work of a trained researcher who has exhaustively visited many alternatives to assess their relative value. We recently checked out some top-rated TripAdvisor listings in various towns; when stacked up against their competitors, some are gems, while just as many are duds.

Both types of information have their place, and in many ways, they're complementary. If a hotel or restaurant is well-reviewed in a guidebook or two, and also gets good ratings on one of these sites, it's likely a winner.

Special Class hotels. Some are upscale; others are run-down. While the rooms can be quite comfortable, most don't have Western-style amenities such as saunas, pools, multiple restaurants, or parking. Many of the Old Town's Special Class hotels are equivalent to two- or three-star hotels.

Most hotels have lots of doubles and a few singles and triples. Quads are rare. Traveling alone can be expensive, as singles are mostly doubles used by one person—at about two-thirds the price of a double room. Room prices vary within each hotel depending on size, views, whether the room has a bath or shower, and the size of the beds (tubs and twins cost more than showers and double beds—called "French beds" in Turkey). Rooms with king-size beds may be pricier than rooms with double beds. A triple is generally a double bed with a cot, and is generally cheaper than the cost of a double and a single. Hotels cannot legally allow more people to stay in a room than what's shown on their price list. Some hotels may have family-friendly connecting rooms.

Most hotel rooms have a sink, toilet, and bath or shower en suite, while hostels offer the option of rooms without showers and toilets. There's a reason many bathrooms in Old Town hotels have a small wastebasket next to the toilet: bad plumbing. Many places prefer that you don't flush toilet paper; use the wastebasket instead. Hotel elevators, while becoming more common, are often very small—pack light, or you may need to take your bags up one at a time.

All of the hotels listed in this book have English-speaking staff. Still, it can be helpful to use the correct hotel jargon to get the right size room and bed (see sidebar on page 397). A "double room" isn't necessarily a room with one big bed for two. It can also mean a twin room, with two separate beds. Ask for what you want. You can save money by asking for a smaller room, often called a "promotion room." At some hotels, these rooms may share a bathroom down the hall.

Most hotels include VAT in their posted rates; others add it to your bill. Unless we've noted otherwise, you can assume tax is included in these rates.

If you're arriving early in the morning, your room probably won't be ready. You should be able to safely check your bag at the hotel and dive right into sightseeing.

Hoteliers can be a great help and source of advice. Most know their city well, and can assist you with everything from public transit and airport connections to finding a good restaurant or a bookstore.

Even at the best places, mechanical breakdowns occur: Air-conditioning malfunctions, sinks leak, hot water turns cold, and toilets gurgle and smell. Report your concerns clearly and calmly at the front desk. For more complicated problems, don't expect instant results.

If you suspect night noise will be a problem (for instance, your room is over a noisy bar), ask for a quiet room in the back or on an upper floor. To guard against theft in your room, keep valuables out of sight. Some rooms come with a safe, and other hotels have safes at the front desk. We've never bothered using one.

If you're planning to visit Istanbul in the summer, it's worthwhile to choose an air-conditioned hotel. When using the air-conditioner in your room, remember that 20°C is a comfortable 68°F (see the temperature conversion chart in the appendix). When

Sleep Code

(€1=about $1.10, 1 TL=about $0.33, country code: 90)

Price Rankings

To help you sort easily through these listings, we've divided the accommodations into three categories based on the price for a basic double room with bath:

$$$ Higher Priced—Most rooms €160 or more.
  $$ Moderately Priced—Most rooms €90-160.
    $ Lower Priced—Most rooms €90 or less.

We always rate hostels as $, whether or not they have double rooms, because they have the cheapest beds in town.

Many hotels have a wide range of official rates, so we've based our rankings on the predominant rate during busy times. Prices are listed in euros in the Sleeping chapter and at most Istanbul hotels, because the euro is a more stable currency than the Turkish Lira (TL). Hotels will take cash payment in TL, euros, or US dollars. All of our listings accept credit cards.

Prices can change without notice; verify the hotel's current rates online or by email.

Abbreviations

To pack maximum information into minimum of space, we use the following code to describe the accommodations. Prices listed are per room, not per person. When a price range is given for a type of room (such as double rooms listing for €110-160), it means the price fluctuates with the season, size of room, or length of stay; expect to pay the upper end for peak-season stays.

  S = Single room (or price for one person in a double).
  D = Double or Twin room. "Double beds" can be two twins sheeted together and are usually big enough for nonromantic couples.
  T = Triple (a double bed with a single, or three twin beds).
  Q = Quad (usually two double beds; adding an extra child's bed to a T is usually cheaper).
  b = Private bathroom with toilet and shower or tub.
  * = Turkey's star system for rating hotels.
  SC = "Special Class" (renovated historic building).

According to this code, a couple staying at a "Db-€140" hotel would pay a total of €140 ($154) for a double room with a private bathroom. Unless otherwise noted, prices include room tax and breakfast (if breakfast isn't included, it's usually optional), hotel staff speak basic English, and credit cards are accepted.

There's almost always Wi-Fi and/or a guest computer available, either free or for a fee.

you leave your room for the day, turning off the air-conditioning is good form. Extra pillows and blankets are sometimes in the closet or available on request. To get a pillow, ask for *"Yastık, lütfen"* (yahs-tuhk lewt-fehn).

If you need to do laundry, it's best to have your hotel do it or send it out—self-service launderettes are rare.

Checkout can pose problems if surprise charges pop up on your bill. If you settle your bill the night before you leave, you'll have time to discuss and address any points of contention (before 19:00, when the night shift usually arrives).

Above all, don't expect things to be the same as back home. Keep a positive attitude. Remember, you're on vacation. If your hotel is a disappointment, spend more time out enjoying the city you came to see.

Breakfast: Turkish hotels see a good breakfast as a badge of honor, and they are quite competitive—so unless you're sleeping at a dive, you can expect a decent breakfast. (Breakfast is almost always included in the room rate, except at a few international chain hotels.) A Turkish hotel breakfast often consists of cheese, olives, bread, jam or honey, butter, tomatoes, cucumbers, eggs (usually hard-boiled), Turkish tea, and instant coffee. Don't expect the thick "Turkish coffee" for breakfast—Turks drink this not as a side beverage, but as a digestive after meals (see page 63). Fresh-squeezed fruit juice may be available for an additional charge.

Hostels

A hostel provides cheap beds where you sleep alongside strangers for about €14-18 per night. Hostels are concentrated in the Old Town, especially on or near the street called Akbıyık. Travelers of any age are welcome if they don't mind dorm-style accommodations and meeting other travelers. Hostel membership is not required. Cheap meals may be available, and most hostels offer kitchen facilities, guest computers, Wi-Fi, and a self-service laundry. Nowadays, concerned about bedbugs, hostels are likely to provide all bedding, including sheets. Family and private rooms may be available on request.

Independent hostels tend to be easygoing, colorful, and informal (no membership required); www.hostelworld.com is the standard way backpackers search and book hostels, but also try www.hostelz.com and www.hostels.com.

Official hostels are part of Hostelling International (HI) and share an online booking site (www.hihostels.com). HI hostels typically require that you either have a membership card or pay extra per night.

Other Options

Short-term rental apartments are hard to find in Istanbul. We've listed several apartments worth considering if you're traveling with your family or staying for a week or more on page 311. Websites such as Booking.com, Airbnb, VRBO, and FlipKey let you browse properties and correspond directly with European property owners or managers. Istanbul listings range from a B&B room for two for €50 per night to a two-bedroom apartment sleeping five for €115 per night. Minimum stays vary from one to seven nights.

Airbnb and Roomorama also list rooms in private homes. Beds range from air-mattress-in-living-room basic to plush-B&B-suite posh. If you want a place to sleep that's free, Couchsurfing.org is a vagabond's alternative to Airbnb. It lists millions of outgoing members, who host fellow "surfers" in their homes.

Eating

Turkish eating habits vary by location and lifestyle. Traditionally, the evening dinner is the big meal of the day. As in other Mediterranean countries, dinner is eaten late in Turkey (generally between 20:00 and 21:00), and it can last for hours. But most restaurants are ready to serve dinner much earlier, and you can make your meal as long or as short as you like. Except for high-end, international places, restaurants in Turkey generally have a single menu and price list for both lunch and dinner. For the most part, once a restaurant is open, it serves meals nonstop until closing time.

The American custom of asking for separate checks is uncommon in Turkey. Instead, usually one member of the group gets the bill and pays, and the group repays him afterward.

Tipping is an issue only at restaurants that have table service. If you order your food at a counter, don't tip (though it's nice to leave a lira or two on the table for the busser). At cafés and restaurants that have a waitstaff, tip 10 percent for good service. If you're not satisfied, tip less—or not at all. Some upscale restaurants may include a service charge in the bill; this fee goes to the restaurant, not the servers, so it's still appropriate to round up your bill about 10 percent. If you're not sure whether your bill includes the tip, just ask.

Some restaurants don't serve alcohol, as noted in the listings in the Eating chapter. Alcohol permits are expensive, and some restaurants are located too close to a place of worship or a school to qualify for a permit.

Restaurants (indoor spaces) are now non-smoking. Water pipes (a.k.a. hookahs, or *nargile* in Turkish) are available at many restaurants. For more information on this pastime, see page 66.

A number of the recommended restaurants in the New District are gay-friendly and described as such in the listings. Their clientele is not solely gay, but gay people would feel welcome.

During the religious festival of Ramadan (June 6-July 4 in 2016, May 27-June 24 in 2017), Muslims fast during the day, then gorge themselves at sunset. This means that restaurants are likely to be empty during the day, and a few actually close altogether. But as the sun sets, you might see long lines in front of fast-food-type places. For more on Ramadan, see page 64.

TYPES OF RESTAURANTS

A *kebab lokantası* or *kebabçı* (keh-bahb-chuh) is a restaurant that serves the traditional Turkish meat dish: the kebab (described later). Kebab restaurants usually start serving around 11:00 and stay open until about 23:00.

A *meyhane* (mehy-hah-neh) is a tavern-style restaurant. While these places may be open during the day, they do most of their busi-

ness during dinner and later. People usually go to a *meyhane* to enjoy *rakı* and *mezes* (appetizers; described later). A *meyhane* is judged not by its main courses, but by the quality and the variety of its *mezes*. A *meyhane* usually offers live music for entertainment.

A *balık lokantası* or *balıkçı* (bah-luhk-chuh) is a fish and seafood restaurant, often offering a variety of *mezes* and salads as well. Most of the *mezes* are made with seafood—such as calamari, octopus, shrimp, or mussels—or with seaweed. Waiters usually bring out a tray of cold *mezes* to choose from. *Rakı*, the classic Turkish alcoholic drink, is commonly served with seafood, but almost all seafood restaurants also sell wine and soft drinks. When selecting a fish dish, ask how big the portions are: One portion may be enough for two or three eaters to share. Often fish is priced daily and by weight. (This means you might pay two different prices for the same fish in the same restaurant on two different nights.) Ask your server to explain the pricing if it's not outlined in the menu. Beware—ambiguity here can lead to tourist gouging.

"**Self-servis**" restaurants function like cafeterias, but with restaurant-quality food. These are some of the best-value and most atmospheric places to eat in town. Don't be put off by the absence of menus—simply survey the scene, and point to what looks good. For tips on navigating self-service restaurants, see the sidebar on page 408.

An *esnaf lokantası* ("workers' restaurant") offers a real "Back Door" eating experience. These simple eateries, usually hiding out on back streets in low-rent areas and business districts, serve up inexpensive, wholesome food for local workers. They're usually only open for lunch (standard hours are 11:00-16:00) and don't accept credit cards. Most *esnaf lokantası* (ehs-nahf loh-kahn-tah-suh) don't have menus—customers choose from the cooked food that's on display. You'll usually find at least one type of stew, a few vegetable and meat dishes, and side dishes such as rice, bulgur pilaf, pasta, or potatoes. Go early—the best dishes go fast.

Turkish Cuisine

Understanding the basics of typical Turkish food will help you better enjoy the cuisine. This section focuses on lunch and dinner. For information on a typical Turkish breakfast (almost always provided by your hotel), see page 403.

LUNCH AND DINNER

Meze (meh-zeh) is the general term for any appetizer served in small portions, usually eaten before the main course. There are two kinds of *mezes:* cold and hot. **Cold *mezes*** (*soğuk mezes;* soh-ook meh-zeh) are usually cooked in olive oil and can include cheese, stuffed grape leaves, eggplant salad, and *cacık* (jah-juhk; a thick mix of yogurt, cucumbers, and garlic with olive oil—like Greek *tzatziki*). **Hot *mezes*** (*sıcak mezes;* suh-jahk meh-zeh) are traditionally served after the cold *mezes,* and can include tiny meatballs, grilled or deep-fried calamari or shrimp, or *börek* (boh-rehk; pastry—described later). *Mezes* can be a meal in themselves, so save some room if you're ordering a main course. In seafood restaurants, you usually choose *mezes* from a tray presented at your table.

The prices we've given in this book for *mezes* are for one portion. When ordering, keep in mind that waiters are not used to the American custom of sharing appetizers. If you ask for a *meze* you plan to share, your waiter will likely think you want portions for every person at your table, so make sure the waiter understands that you want only a single portion. Or you can avoid any confusion by having each person at the table order one appetizer, then share after the *mezes* arrive.

Soup (*çorba;* chor-bah) is often served at the beginning of the meal. *Mercimek* (mehr-jee-mehk) *çorba* is made with mashed lentils, and *yoğurt çorbası* is made with yogurt and served hot.

Zeytinyağlı (zey-teen-yah-luh; "in olive oil") is a common term for vegetables cooked in olive oil. Vegetables can be a main course or—if they're deep-fried, chilled, and served with yogurt—an appetizer.

Seafood is an essential part of Istanbul cuisine. For details on the local varieties of fish, see the sidebar on page 298.

Kebabs (keh-bahbz) are the primary means of preparing and

serving meats—generally marinated, skewered, and grilled. Kebabs have different names based on how they're cooked. *Şiş* (shish) means "skewer," and *şiş kebab* means any type of meat cut into small pieces and grilled on a skewer. A *döner* (doh-nehr; "to spin") *kebab* is a big chunk of meat that cooks as it rotates in front of a vertical grill; the chef cuts off thin slices that are served either wrapped in pita bread or sandwich bread, or with a side of rice pilaf. *Döner kebabs* were traditionally veal or a mix of lamb and veal, but more recently chicken (*tavuk;* tah-vook) and fish have become popular.

Dolma (dohl-mah) means "stuffed" and typically refers to stuffed vegetables such as bell peppers, tomatoes, eggplants, zucchinis, or grape leaves. When stuffed with rice, raisins, or onions—and cooked in olive oil—dolma is a vegetarian dish served as a cold *meze*. When stuffed with rice and meat, dolma is a main course, often accompanied by yogurt (not to be confused with *dolmus*—a minibus stuffed with people).

Börek (boh-rehk) is a savory pastry made of phyllo dough with various ingredients nestled between the layers. *Su böreği* (soo boh-reh-ee) is prepared with thick sheets of dough that are briefly dipped in boiling water before they're layered over the stuffing. *Sigara böreği* (see-gah-rah boh-reh-ee), a deep-fried cheese roll served cold, is a popular *meze*.

Pide (pee-deh) is Turkish-style pita bread (sans pocket) usually topped with vegetables and cheese. Take a thin, flat *pide*, top it with meat, onions, and parsley, and you have *lahmacun*. Or try *lavaş* (lah-vahsh), a flat bread that, when baked fresh, arrives on your table looking like an inflated pillow. **Gözleme** (gohz-leh-meh) is flat bread cooked on a convex steel sheet.

DRINKS

Ayran (eye-rahn) is a popular, everyday beverage made of yogurt diluted with water and seasoned with a pinch of salt. This refreshing drink pairs well with many local dishes. You'll even see it on the menu at McDonald's and Burger King. Most eateries serve bottled

Self-Service Survival Guide

Self-service, cafeteria-style restaurants are common in the city, especially along the street with the tram tracks (Divan Yolu) in the center of the Old Town, and on İstiklal Street in the New District. They serve freshly cooked, typical Turkish food at good prices, and are perfect for travelers who are short on time—simply choose your food, pay for it, eat it, and leave.

Before you get in line for food, survey the counter to see what's available. Bread, water, yogurt, salads, desserts, and beverages may be placed before or after the main courses. Most eateries won't label the dishes in English, so if you need advice, ask a cook or the person next to you. Keep an eye out for what others are ordering; locals know what's good. Make up your mind quickly—busy lunchtime eaters aren't too tolerant of dilly-dallying.

Point to what you'd like, and the staff will hand it to you. Prices are set and for a full portion. Even if you ask for smaller portions to be served on one plate (like a sampler plate), you'll still pay the full price per item. If you're with a companion and want to sample several items, it's easiest if you both order full portions at the counter and then split your order later when you sit down at your table.

Keep things moving by having your cash ready at the end of the line (most places also accept credit cards). Once you're done, don't bus your dishes, but do leave a lira or two for the staff.

Here are some of the dishes you'll likely find in a self-service restaurant:

Soup (Çorba): Most places will have at least one kind of soup on hand. Most common are *yayla çorbası* (yay-lah chohr-bah-suh), a light, delicious soup made with yogurt, rice, flour, and egg; *mercimek* (mehr-jee-mehk) *çorbası*, lentil soup; *ezogelin* (eh-zoh-geh-leen) *çorbası*, a slightly spicy soup with rice or bulgur, lentils, tomato-and-pepper paste, garlic, and a few spices; and *domates* (doh-mah-tehs) *çorbası*, tomato soup.

Side Dishes: Try *pirinç pilavı* (pee-reench pee-lah-vuh; rice pilaf), *hıngal* (huhn-gahl; potato-filled steamed dumplings), *patates* (pah-tah-tehs; potatoes served mashed, steamed, or deep-fried), and *bulgur pilavı* (bool-goor pee-lah-vuh; pilaf made with cracked wheat and fresh tomatoes and/or tomato paste).

Pasta (Makarna): While not that common, you might see spaghetti with house-specialty dressings, or dishes such as *fırında makarna* (fuh-ruhn-dah mah-kahr-nah): macaroni and cheese.

Vegetables: Seasonal veggies are usually stewed, boiled, fried, or deep-fried. Peas, carrots, zucchini, and out-of-season vegetables may be canned.

Vegetarian Dishes: Most common are green string beans (*yeşil fasulye*; yeh-sheel fah-sool-yeh) and different types of dolma (stuffed vegetables) cooked in olive oil.

Meat Dishes: Most main courses have meat, even vegetable dishes. For example, *karnıyarık* (kahr-nuh yah-ruhk; "split tummy") is made by cutting an eggplant open and stuffing it with minced veal, onions, and tomatoes. When cooked in olive oil and made without meat, it's called *imam bayıldı* (ee-mum bah-yuhl-duh, "the imam loved it"). *Musakka* (moo-sahk-kah) is also similar to *karnıyarık*, but with the eggplant chopped into slices or rings.

Veal (*dana*; dah-nah) is common (usually cooked with tomatoes, onions, green pepper, and/or potatoes), but you'll generally also find **chicken** (*tavuk*; tah-vook)—steamed, cooked with vegetables, or grilled. **Lamb** (*kuzu*), particularly the shank (*kuzu haşlama*; koo-zoo hush-lah-mah), is a local favorite. Lamb is often cooked and served with carrots, potatoes, and onions. Never hard to find are **meatballs** (*köfte*; kohf-teh), which are usually made of minced veal or lamb. *Köfte*, which come in all kinds of shapes, are grilled or cooked with vegetables and often accompanied by French fries, fresh tomatoes and peppers, or rice. *İçli köfte* (eech-lee kohf-teh) is a bulgur pouch filled with meat, onions, and spices.

Salad: You can count on at least two kinds of salads being available at most restaurants: *Çoban salatası* (choh-bahn sah-lah-tah-suh; "shepherds' salad"), made with small chopped tomatoes, cucumbers, onions, and peppers; and green salad (*yeşil salata*; yeh-sheel sah-lah-tah), which usually has iceberg or green lettuce, tomatoes, onions, and/or shredded carrots.

Yogurt: Turks eat a lot of yogurt. Usually made from cow's milk, it comes in disposable containers or steel bowls. *Cacık* (jah-juhk), a thick, savory yogurt, is popular. *Ayran* (eye-rahn), a white, slightly salted yogurt drink, is usually on the beverage list.

Dessert: *Sütlaç* (sewt-lahch; rice pudding) is the most common pudding; others include *fırın* (fuh-ruhn) *sütlaç*, rice pudding with a burned top; and *keşkül* (kash-kuhl), milk pudding with coconuts, vanilla, and eggs. You'll also want to sample Turkish baklava, served with cream or crushed nuts; *kadayıf* (kah-dah-yuhf), shredded wheat served with crushed nuts, or *künefe* (koo-nef-ay), shredded wheat with unsalted cheese. *Ekmak kadayıfı* (ehk-mehk kah-dah-yuh-fuh) is bread pudding served with *kaymak* (kahy-mahk), the thick cream of water buffalo milk. *Ayva tatlısı* (ahy-vah that-luh-suh) is a quince dessert topped with *kaymak* and/or crushed nuts, and *şekerpare* (sheh-kehr-pah-reh) are cookies in honey syrup.

ayran made from pasteurized milk and safe drinking water. If yours isn't served from a bottle (or in a sealed plastic cup), ask whether it was made with bottled water, or ask for bottled *ayran*.

Turkish coffee (*kahve*; kah-veh) is unfiltered coffee, with the grounds mixed right in. It's typically drunk as a digestive after dinner, and sometimes after lunch—but never at breakfast (for more details, see page 63).

Tea (*çay*; pronounced "chai") is actually a more common drink among Turks than coffee. Tea is grown locally along the Black Sea coastline. Regular Turkish tea generally tastes like English breakfast tea, although some varieties are closer to Earl Grey. Turks never put milk in their tea. Herbal tea and similar drinks are quite common in Turkey. *Adaçayı* (ah-dah-chah-yuh; sage), *ıhlamur* (uh-lah-moor; linden), and *kuşburnu* (koosh-boor-noo; rosehip) are popular flavors. When you ask for herbal tea, unless you're in a specialty café, you'll be given a teabag and a cup of hot water. In the Old Town, you'll likely be offered apple tea made with granulated apple and sugar. The real thing is made from dried and boiled apple skin. You can find dried apple skin in the Spice Market (see page 42). Make it tastier by adding honey or cinnamon.

Rakı (rah-kuh) is the quintessentially Turkish firewater you'll see anywhere alcohol is allowed. It's made of distilled grape juice and anise—giving it a strong licorice taste. Turks dilute it with water or ice, which turns the drink a cloudy white color. *Rakı*—like its licorice-flavored Greek equivalent, ouzo—is an acquired taste. It's particularly good with a light meal, meat, fish, or some *mezes*. If you drink a lot of *rakı*, watch out—too much *rakı* with too much bread, pasta, or dessert will give you a mega-headache the next morning.

Şerbet (shehr-beht) is boiled fruit juice with sugar added (with various fruit flavors, depending on the season). During meals, sultans didn't drink water, but *şerbet*.

Fresh-squeezed juice (*suyu*, soo-yoo) is widely available at cafés, restaurants, and street stands, and usually quite cheap (1-3 TL at stands). The most popular squeezable fruits are orange (*portakal*, por-tah-kahl) and pomegranate (*nar*, which is very tart—try it mixed with OJ), but stands usually sell a wide range of choices.

Turkish Baklava

For centuries, baklava has reigned as the queen of desserts. At its most basic, it consists of several very thin layers of phyllo dough, baked and soaked in syrup. Of the countless variations, Turks tend to favor baklava with pistachios.

When you visit a *baklavacı* (bahk-lah-vah-cuh) specialty shop, use all five senses to tell good baklava from bad. First, it must be crisp—neither hard nor spongy—with no excess syrup visible, and should smell deliciously of butter and nuts. Poke it with a fork; if it has been baked just right, you'll hear a crunch. And as you take that first heavenly bite, the fine layers of dough should melt in your mouth. In Istanbul, **Baklavacı Güllüoğlu** is the go-to place for the best baklava, see page 338.

Remember, don't drink the **tap water** in Istanbul. Bottled or canned drinks, like those sold in restaurants, are, of course, perfectly fine. Most restaurants serve little plastic cups of water, with peel-off tops, that are fine to drink. Fresh fruit juices are generally also safe to drink.

STREET-VENDOR FARE

Common street-vendor fare includes *döner kebabs,* sandwiches, bagel-like *simit,* mussels, and sheep intestines...which taste better than you might expect.

Döner kebabs, described earlier, are the most popular type of Turkish fast food.

For **sandwiches,** locals usually use white bread. Ordering *yarım ekmek* (yah-ruhm ehk-mehk; "half bread") will get you half a sandwich. For a smaller snack, request a quarter-sandwich: *çeyrek ekmek* (chehy-rehk ehk-mehk).

Simit (see-meet) is made by dipping a ring of dough in grape molasses and sesame seeds before baking. You can buy it from street vendors, or from the growing number of *simit* chains, such as Simit Sarayı (see-meet sah-rah-yuh). Besides plain *simit,* they carry a range of flavors (similar to what you'd find in a bagel shop). For a cheap picnic, buy a crunchy, freshly baked *simit,* and top it with tomatoes, cucumbers, and some *beyaz peynir* (beh-yahz pehy-neer; white cheese made from cow's or sheep's milk) from a grocery.

Midye tava (meed-yeh tah-vah), deep-fried mussels, are served either in a sandwich or on a plate, and usually come with *tarator* (tah-rah-tohr), a dip made of breadcrumbs, yogurt, garlic, vinegar, and sometimes walnuts as well. *Midye dolma* (stuffed mussel shells) is a local delicacy. The shell is stuffed with olive-oil-soaked rice, raisins, and herbs.

May It Please the Sultan

Cooks in royal kitchens concocted quite a few creative dishes to please the sultan. Who else would have thought of cooking stuffed melon, mixing rice with almonds and apricots, or stewing eggplant jam? At restaurants that serve traditional cuisine, you may come across dishes listed as *hünkar beğendi* ("the sultan liked it"), *imam bayıldı* ("the imam loved it"), or *dilber dudağı* ("belle's lips"). These names show the close link between food, people, and the palace.

Standing by the Galata Bridge on the Golden Horn, you'll smell the **balık ekmek** (bah-luhk ehk-mehk; fish sandwiches), even from a distance. Usually grilled mackerel sandwiched in bread, these are served with onions and lettuce. Small boats tied by the ferry docks in Eminönü serve *balık ekmek* to go, as do a few stands, pubs, and restaurants along the bridge (lower level, pedestrian area).

A big favorite among Turks is **kokoreç** (koh-koh-retch)—sheep intestines that are chopped up, grilled, seasoned, and served with tomatoes and peppers. (If this sounds inedible, remember that sausages are traditionally packed in sheep intestines.) If you want to give this a try, ask for a small *çeyrek ekmek* (chey-rehk ehk-mehk; "quarter-portion"). A popular place for this local treat is Şampiyon Kokoreç (described on page 237).

Staying Connected

Staying connected in Europe gets easier and cheaper every year. The simplest solution is to bring your own device—mobile phone, tablet, or laptop—and use it just as you would at home (following the tips below, such as connecting to free Wi-Fi whenever possible). Another option is to buy a European SIM card for your mobile phone—either your US phone or one you buy in Europe. Or you can travel without a mobile device and use European landlines and computers to connect. Each of these options is described below, and you'll find even more details at www.ricksteves.com/phoning.

USING YOUR OWN MOBILE DEVICE IN EUROPE

Without an international plan, typical rates from major service providers (AT&T, Verizon, etc.) for using your device abroad are about $1.50/minute for voice calls, 50 cents to send text messages, 5 cents to receive them, and $20 to download one megabyte of data. But at these rates, costs can add up quickly. Here are some budget tips and options.

Use free Wi-Fi whenever possible. Unless you have an unlimited-data plan, you're best off saving most of your online tasks for Wi-Fi (sometimes called WLAN). You can access the Internet, send texts, and even make voice calls over Wi-Fi.

Many cafés (including Starbucks and McDonald's) have hotspots for customers; look for signs offering it and ask for the Wi-Fi password when you buy something. You'll also often find Wi-Fi at TIs, city squares, major museums, public-transit hubs, airports, and aboard trains and buses.

Sign up for an international plan. Most providers offer a global calling plan that cuts the per-minute cost of phone calls and texts, and a flat-fee data plan that includes a certain amount of megabytes. Your normal plan may already include international coverage (T-Mobile's does).

Before your trip, call your provider or check online to confirm that your phone will work in Europe, and research your provider's international rates. A day or two before you leave, activate the plan by calling your provider or logging on to your mobile phone account. Remember to cancel your plan (if necessary) when your trip's over.

Minimize the use of your cellular network. When you can't find Wi-Fi, you can use your cellular network—convenient but slower and potentially expensive—to connect to the Internet, text, or make voice calls. When you're done, avoid further charges by manually switching off "data roaming" or "cellular data" (in your device's Settings menu; if you don't know how to switch it off, ask your service provider or Google it). Another way to make sure you're not accidentally using data roaming is to put your device in "airplane" or "flight" mode (which also disables phone calls and texts, as well as data), and then turn on Wi-Fi as needed.

Don't use your cellular network for bandwidth-gobbling tasks, such as Skyping, downloading apps, and watching YouTube—save these for when you're on Wi-Fi. Using a navigation app such as Google Maps can take lots of data, so use this sparingly.

Limit automatic updates. By default, your device is constantly checking for a data connection and updating apps. It's smart to disable these features so they'll only update when you're on Wi-Fi, and to change your device's email settings from "auto-retrieve" to "manual" (or from "push" to "fetch").

It's also a good idea to keep track of your data usage. On your device's menu, look for "cellular data usage" or "mobile data" and reset the counter at the start of your trip.

Hurdling the Language Barrier

The language barrier in Istanbul is no bigger than in Western Europe. In fact, visitors often find that it's even easier to communicate in Istanbul than it is in Madrid. Most people in the tourist industry, and quite a few young people, speak English.

The Turkish are among the friendliest people in the world. The locals you meet will often invite you to have tea with them. You'll likely be able to communicate with them in English, but it's fun to know some key Turkish words (see "Turkish Survival Phrases" on page 447). In this hospitable country, you'll find that doors will open to you regardless, but you'll get more smiles when you can speak a few words of the language.

Use Skype or other calling/messaging apps for cheaper calls and texts. Certain apps let you make voice or video calls or send texts over the Internet for free or cheap. If you're bringing a tablet or laptop, you can also use them for voice calls and texts. All you have to do is log on to a Wi-Fi network, then contact any of your friends or family members who are also online and signed into the same service. You can make voice and video calls using Skype, Viber, FaceTime, and Google+ Hangouts. If the connection is bad, try making an audio-only call.

You can also make voice calls from your device to telephones worldwide for just a few cents per minute using Skype, Viber, or Hangouts, if you prebuy credit.

To text for free over Wi-Fi, try apps like Google+ Hangouts, What's App, Viber, and Facebook Messenger. Apple's iMessage connects with other Apple users, but make sure you're on Wi-Fi to avoid data charges.

USING A EUROPEAN SIM CARD IN A MOBILE PHONE

This option works well for those who want to make a lot of voice calls at cheap local rates. Either buy a phone in Turkey, or bring an "unlocked" US phone (check with your carrier about unlocking it). With an unlocked phone, you can replace the original SIM card (the microchip that stores info about the phone) with one that will work with a Turkish provider. Inserted into your phone, this card gives you a Turkish phone number—and Turkish rates. And you can still use your phone's Wi-Fi function to get online. You can also ask for a SIM card that includes data costs (including roaming). This can be cheaper than data roaming through your home provider.

The main providers in Turkey—with stores everywhere—are Turkcell (www.turkcell.com.tr), Vodafone (www.vodafone.com.tr), and Avea (www.avea.com.tr). Ask the clerk to help you insert your SIM card, set it up, and show you how to use it. When you run out of credit, you can top it up at newsstands, tobacco shops, mobile-phone stores, or many other businesses (look for your SIM card's logo in the window), or online.

If you plan to use your mobile phone with a Turkish SIM card for more than 60 days, you may have to register your phone with the Turkish service provider. It's probably simplest to do this all at once: Buy your Turkish SIM card at one of the service-provider's shops, have your passport handy, and ask if you need to register your phone (look for a shop at the airport's arrival terminal).

It's also possible to buy a mobile phone in Turkey that already comes with a SIM card. These are usually quite expensive to buy ($80 and up) and work affordably only in Turkey. The Turkish word for a mobile phone is *cep* (jehp; meaning "pocket phone"). Within Turkey, domestic calls are reasonable, and incoming calls are free. You'll pay more if you're roaming in another country. If your Turkish phone is "unlocked," you can swap out its SIM card for a new one when you travel to other countries.

USING LANDLINES AND COMPUTERS IN EUROPE

It's easy to travel in Europe without a mobile device. You can check email or browse websites using public computers and Internet cafés, and make calls from your hotel room and/or public phones.

Phones in your **hotel room** can be inexpensive for local calls and calls made with cheap international phone cards (TT Kart [teh-teh kart]) sold at many post offices, Türk Telekom shops, mobile-phone dealers (that also sell tram and bus tickets), most newsstands, and at food kiosks near phone booths. Cards come in three denominations: 5, 10, and 25 TL. Buy a lower denomination in case the card is a dud. Some shops also sell cardless codes, printed right on the receipt. The cards can also be used to make local calls, and they work from any type of phone, including your hotel-room phone or a mobile phone with a European SIM card. To use the card, dial a toll-free access number, then enter your scratch-to-reveal PIN code.

Most hotels charge a fee for placing local and "toll-free" calls, as well as long-distance or international calls—ask for the rates before you dial. Since you're never charged for receiving calls, it's better to have someone from the US call you in your room.

You'll see **public pay phones** in post offices and train stations. The phones generally come with multilingual instructions, and most work with insertable phone cards (TT Smart Cards or Smart Telefon Kartı [teh-leh-fohn kar-tuh] sold at post of-

How to Dial

Many Americans are intimidated by dialing European phone numbers. You needn't be. It's simple, once you break the code.

Dialing Rules

Here are the rules for dialing, along with examples of how to call one of our recommended hotels in the European part of Istanbul (tel. 0212/517-7173). The 0212 is European Istanbul's area code. (Asian Istanbul's area code is 0216).

Dialing Internationally to Turkey

Whether you're phoning from a US landline, your own mobile phone, a Skype account, or a number in another European country (e.g., Greece to Turkey), you're making an international call. Here's how to do it:

1. Dial the **international access code** (011 if calling from a US or Canadian phone; 00 if calling from any European phone number outside of Turkey). If dialing from a mobile phone, you can enter a + in place of the international access code (press and hold the 0 key).
2. Dial the **country code** (90 for Turkey).
3. Dial the **phone number** (drop the initial 0).

Examples:

- To call our recommended hotel from a **US or Canadian phone,** dial 011, then 90, then 212/517-7173.
- To call from **any European phone number** (outside of Turkey), dial 00, then 90, then 212/517-7173.
- To call from any **mobile phone** (except a Turkish one), dial +, then 90, then 212/517-7173.

Dialing Within Turkey

To make a domestic call (either from a Turkish mobile phone or landline), you'll generally dial both the area code (including the

---

fices, newsstands, etc.). These cards can only be used at public pay phones. The cards come in three denominations of units *(kontörs):* 100 units (5 TL), 200 units (10 TL), and 350 units (25 TL). Be aware that *kontörs* are not equivalent to minutes; ask how many units a call will take. To use the card, find a public phone with a display screen, which you'll use to pick your language, then insert the card into a slot in the phone. While you can use these cards to call anywhere in the world, they're only a good deal for making quick local calls from a phone booth. With the exception of Great Britain, each European country has its own insertable phone card—so your Turkish card won't work in a Greek phone.

Cheap **call shops,** often located in train-station neighbor-

initial 0) and the local number. If you're calling within the same area code on a landline, you could drop the area code and just dial the local number. So if you're calling within European Istanbul on a landline (area code 0212), you need only dial the seven-digit number. But if you're using a mobile phone, dial the full phone number, including the area code.

Example: To call our recommended hotel from any Turkish landline or mobile phone, including from Asian Istanbul, dial 0212/517-7173. If dialing from within the same 0212 area code, you can just enter 517-7173.

Calling from any European Country to the US

To call the US or Canada from Europe (either from a mobile phone or landline), dial 00 (Europe's international access code), 1 (US/Canada country code), and the phone number, including area code. If calling from a mobile phone, you can enter a + instead of 00.

Example: To call Rick Steves' office in Edmonds, Washington, from anywhere in Europe, we dial 00-1-425-771-8303; or, from a mobile phone, +-1-425-771-8303.

More Dialing Tips

Turkish Phone Numbers: Mobile phone numbers generally start with 05. To call special numbers in Istanbul that start with 444 (such as 444-3777, the American Hospital), there's no need to dial an area code, whether you're on the European or Asian side.

Toll Calls: Some numbers are premium toll calls and cost more than a regular landline call. The per-minute charge should be listed in small print next to the phone number.

More Resources: The "Phoning Cheat Sheet" on the next page shows how to dial per country, or you can check www.countrycallingcodes.com or www.howtocallabroad.com.

hoods, advertise low international rates. Before making your call, be completely clear on the rates (e.g., if there's a charge per unit, find out how long a unit is).

It's always possible to find **public computers:** at your hotel (many have one in their lobby for guests to use), or at an Internet café or library (ask your hotelier or the TI for the nearest location). Turkish keyboards include many unfamiliar letters. Most of these are on the right part of the keyboard (where you'd find the punctuation keys on an English keyboard). To type an "@" symbol, press two keys at the same time: "Alt Gr" (a special shift key to the right of the space bar) + Q. When typing passwords or addresses, be careful to select the right version of the two Turkish letters equivalent to the English "i (I)." One is undotted: ı (I). The other

PRACTICALITIES

Phoning Cheat Sheet

Just smile and dial, using these rules.

Calling a European number

- **From a mobile phone** (whether you're in the US or in Europe):
  Dial + (press and hold 0), then country code and number*
- **From a US/Canadian number:** Dial 011, then country code and number*
- **From a different European country** (e.g., German number to French
  number): Dial 00, then country code and number*
- **Within the same European country** (e.g., German number to another
  German number): Dial the number as printed, including initial 0 if there
  is one

  * Drop initial 0 (if present) from phone number
  in all countries except Italy

Calling the US or Canada from Europe

Dial 00, then 1 (country code for US/Canada), then area code and number;
on mobile phones, enter + in place of 00

Country	Country Code	Country	Country Code
Austria	43	Italy	39 [2]
Belgium	32	Latvia	371
Bosnia-Herzegovina	387	Montenegro	382
Croatia	385	Morocco	212
Czech Republic	420	Netherlands	31
Denmark	45	Norway	47
Estonia	372	Poland	48
Finland	358	Portugal	351
France	33	Russia	7 [3]
Germany	49	Slovakia	421
Gibraltar	350	Slovenia	386
Great Britain & N. Ireland	44	Spain	34
Greece	30	Sweden	46
Hungary	36 [1]	Switzerland	41
Ireland	353	Turkey	90

[1] For long-distance calls within Hungary, dial 06, then the area code and number.
[2] When making international calls to Italy, do not drop the initial 0 from the
phone number.
[3] For long-distance calls within Russia, dial 8, then the area code and number.
To call the US or Canada from Russia, dial 8, then 10, then 1, then the area
code and number.

Tips on Internet Security

Using the Internet while traveling brings added security risks, whether you're getting online with your own device or at a public terminal using a shared network.

First, make sure that your device is running the latest version of its operating system and security software. Next, ensure that your device is password- or passcode-protected so thieves can't access your information if your device is stolen. For extra security, set passwords on apps that access key info (such as email or Facebook).

On the road, use only legitimate Wi-Fi hotspots. Ask the hotel or café staff for the specific name of their Wi-Fi network, and make sure you log on to that exact one. Hackers sometimes create a bogus hotspot with a similar or vague name (such as "Hotel Europa Free Wi-Fi"). The best Wi-Fi networks require entering a password.

Be especially cautious when checking your online banking, credit-card statements, or other personal-finance accounts. Internet security experts advise against accessing these sites while traveling. Even if you're using your own mobile device at a password-protected hotspot, any hacker who's logged on to the same network may be able see what you're doing. If you do need to log on to a banking website, use a hard-wired connection (such as an Ethernet cable in your hotel room) or a cellular network, which is safer than Wi-Fi.

Never share your credit-card number (or any other sensitive information) online unless you know that the site is secure. A secure site displays a little padlock icon, and the URL begins with *https* (instead of the usual *http*).

is dotted: i (İ). This means that an English capital *I* and lowercase *i* are actually on different keys. If you can't locate a special character (such as @), simply copy it from a Web page and paste it into your email message.

MAIL

You can buy stamps only at Turkish post offices, which are usually marked with yellow *PTT* signs (for "Post, Telephone, and Telegraph"). Most are open Monday-Friday 9:00-17:00 and are closed on weekends. It costs about 2.50 TL to mail a postcard to the US.

You can mail one package per day to yourself worth up to $200 duty-free from Europe to the US (mark it "personal purchases"). If you're sending a gift to someone, mark it "unsolicited gift." For details, visit www.cbp.gov and search for "Know Before You Go."

The Turkish postal service works fine, but for quick transatlantic delivery (in either direction), consider services such as DHL (www.dhl.com).

Resources

RESOURCES FROM RICK STEVES

Rick Steves Istanbul is one of many books in Rick's series on European travel, which includes country guidebooks, city guidebooks (Rome, Florence, Paris, London, etc.), Snapshot guides (excerpted chapters from Rick's country guides), Pocket Guides (full-color little books on big cities), and a budget-travel skills handbook, *Rick Steves Europe Through the Back Door.* Most of these titles are available as ebooks. Rick's phrase books—for German, French, Italian, Spanish, and Portuguese—are practical and budget-oriented. Rick's other books include *Europe 101* (a crash course on art and history designed for travelers); *Mediterranean Cruise Ports* and *Northern European Cruise Ports* (how to make the most of your time in port); and *Travel as a Political Act* (a travelogue sprinkled with tips for bringing home a global perspective). A more complete list of Rick's titles appears near the end of this book.

Video: Rick's public television series, *Rick Steves' Europe,* covers European destinations from top to bottom with more than 100 half-hour episodes, with five episodes on Turkey. To watch full episodes online for free, see www.ricksteves.com/tv. Or to raise your travel I.Q. with video versions of our popular classes (including Rick's talks on travel skills, packing smart, European art for travelers, travel as a political act, and individual talks covering most European countries), see www.ricksteves.com/travel-talks.

Audio: Rick's weekly public radio show, *Travel with Rick Steves,* features interviews with travel experts from around the world, including the co-writers of this book, Tankut and Lale, and other Turkish friends. A complete archive of 10 years of programs (over 400 in all) is available in the radio section of www.ricksteves.com/radio. Most of this audio content is available for free through the **Rick Steves Audio Europe** app (see page 8).

Begin Your Trip at
www.ricksteves.com

Rick's mobile-friendly **website** is *the* place to explore Europe. You'll find thousands of fun articles, videos, photos, and radio interviews organized by country; a wealth of money-saving tips for planning your dream trip; monthly travel news dispatches; his travel talks and travel blog; his latest guidebook updates (www.ricksteves.com/update); and his free Rick Steves Audio Europe app. You can also follow Rick on Facebook and Twitter.

Our **Travel Forum** is an immense, yet well-groomed collection of message boards, where our travel-savvy community answers questions and shares their personal travel experiences—and our well-traveled staff chimes in when they can be helpful (www.ricksteves.com/forums).

Our **online Travel Store** offers travel bags and accessories that we've designed specifically to help you travel smarter and lighter. These include Rick's popular bags (rolling carry-on and backpack versions, which he helped design...and lives out of four months a year), money belts, totes, toiletries kits, adapters, other accessories, and a wide selection of guidebooks and planning maps.

Choosing the right **rail pass** for your trip—amid hundreds of options—can drive you nutty. Our website will help you find the perfect fit for your itinerary and your budget: We offer easy, one-stop shopping for rail passes, seat reservations, and point-to-point tickets.

Want to travel with greater efficiency and less stress? We organize **tours** with more than three dozen itineraries and more than 900 departures reaching the best destinations in this book...and beyond. Rick offers a seven-day tour of Istanbul and a 13-day Best of Turkey tour (beginning in Istanbul and ending in seaside Kuşadası). You'll enjoy great guides, a fun bunch of travel partners (with small groups of 24 to 28 travelers), and plenty of room to spread out in a big, comfy bus when touring between towns. You'll find European adventures to fit every vacation length. For all the details, and to get our Tour Catalog and a free Rick Steves Tour Experience DVD (filmed on location during an actual tour), visit www.ricksteves.com or call us at 425/608-4217.

MAPS

The black-and-white maps in this book are concise and simple, designed to help you locate recommended places and get to local TIs, where you can pick up more in-depth maps of cities and regions (usually free). Better maps are sold at newsstands and bookstores. Before you buy a map, look at it to be sure it has the level of detail you want.

If you use Google Maps or Apple Maps on your mobile device, pulling up maps on the fly or looking up turn-by-turn walking directions requires you to go online—so it's smart to get an international data plan (see page 412). In either app, it's possible to download a map while on Wi-Fi, then navigate with it all day long without incurring data-roaming charges—though you can't search for an address or get directions. A number of well-designed apps, including City Maps 2Go, OffMaps, and Navfree, allow you much of the convenience of online maps without any costly data demands.

APPENDIX

Useful Contacts

For the phone numbers answered in Turkish, ask a local person (such as your hotelier) to make the call for you.

Emergency Needs
Police (Turkish-language only): Tel. 155
Fire (Turkish-language only): Tel. 110
Emergency Medical Assistance in English: Tel. 444-1212 (Medline Ambulance)
Emergency Medical Assistance (Turkish-language only): Tel. 112
American Hospital: In the New District at Güzelbahçe Sokak 20, Nişantaşı, tel. 444-3777
International Hospital: Close to Atatürk Airport at İstanbul Caddesi 82, Yeşilköy, hospital tel. 0212/468-4444, ambulance service tel. 444-9724

Consulates
US Consulate: Üç Şehitler Sokak 2, İstinye Mahallesi, 30-minute cab ride from downtown Istanbul, passport services Mon-Fri 7:45-16:30, closed Sat-Sun and on Turkish and American holidays,

24-hour emergency assistance tel. 0212/335-9000, http://istanbul.usconsulate.gov

Canadian Consulate: Buyukdere Caddesi 209, passport services Mon-Fri 9:00-12:00, closed Sat-Sun, general info tel. 0212/385-9700, www.turkey.gc.ca

Dialing Assistance
Directory Assistance for Istanbul (Turkish-language only): Tel. 11811

Holidays and Festivals

This list includes selected festivals in Istanbul, plus national holidays observed throughout Turkey. Many sights and banks close on national holidays—keep this in mind when planning your itinerary. Dates for Muslim holidays are set according to a lunar calendar, so the specific dates vary from year to year. Even though Christian holidays (such as Easter, Ascension, and Christmas) are not celebrated in Istanbul, the city is especially crowded with visiting Europeans during these times.

Before planning a trip around a festival, make sure you verify its dates by checking the festival's website or www.goturkey.com.

Jan 1	New Year's Day (Yılbaşı, national holiday)
Late March	Istanbul Film Festival (http://film.iksv.org)
March 27	Easter 2016 for Western denominations
April 16	Easter 2017 for all Christian denominations
April 23	National Sovereignty and Children's Day (national holiday)
May 1	Easter 2016 for Orthodox denominations
May 1	Labor and Solidarity Day (national holiday)
May 5	Ascension 2016 for Western denominations
May 19	Atatürk Commemoration and Youth Day (national holiday)
May 25	Ascension 2017 for all Christian denominations
May 27-June 24	Ramadan 2017 (Muslim holy month)
June	Istanbul Music Festival (http://muzik.iksv.org)
Early July	Istanbul Jazz Festival (http://caz.iksv.org)
June 6-July 4	Ramadan 2016 (Muslim holy month)
June 9	Ascension 2016 for Orthodox denominations

June-July	Ramadan Bayramı (Seker Bayramı, Muslim festival): July 5-7, 2016; June 25-27, 2017
Aug 30	Victory Day (national holiday)
Sept	International Istanbul Biennial (four weeks, next held in 2017, www.iksv.org/bienal/english)
Sept	Kurban Bayramı (Muslim festival): Sept 12-15 in 2016; Sept 1-4 in 2017
Mid-Oct	October Film Week (www.iksv.org)
Oct 29	Republic Day (national holiday)
Dec 24-Jan 1	Christmas Week

APPENDIX

Recommended Books and Films

To learn more about Istanbul and Turkey past and present, check out a few of these books and films.

Nonfiction

Atatürk: The Biography of the Founder of Modern Turkey (Andrew Mango, 1999). This is the most comprehensive biography of Atatürk since Lord Kinross's 1967 *Atatürk: A Biography of Mustafa Kemal.*

Crescent & Star (Stephen Kinzer, 2001). Kinzer sheds light on Turkey's culture and reports on its fraught political landscape.

Eat Smart in Turkey (Joan Peterson, 2004). Peterson describes the fascinating history and culture of Turkish cuisine and includes delicious recipes.

The Drop That Became the Sea (Yunus Emre, 1999). A compilation of Sufi poetry introduces readers to the spirit of Islamic mysticism.

Istanbul: The Imperial City (John Freely, 1996). Freely's book serves as both a brief history and a travel guide.

Istanbul: Memories and the City (Orhan Pamuk, 2005). Pamuk's portrait of Istanbul is also a portrait of his own life within the city.

Memoirs of an Exile (Aziz Nesin, 1957) The famous Turkish satirist tells of his forced banishment to Bursa.

Osman's Dream: The History of the Ottoman Empire (Caroline Finkel, 2005). Finkel traces the empire from medieval times to modernity.

The Pleasantries of the Incredible Mullah Nasrudin (Idries Shah, 1968). Shah gives the mysterious 13th-century Sufi Mullah Nasrudin a voice by collecting stories told by other mystics.

Sailing from Byzantium (Colin Wells, 2006). The story of Byzantium is full of high drama and exciting adventure.

A Short History of Byzantium (John Julius Norwich, 1997). Norwich's history is a good way to learn about the rise and fall of Constantinople.

Suleiman the Magnificent (André Clot, 1992). This history chronicles the life of the most celebrated of Ottoman sultans.

Tales from the Expat Harem (Anastasia M. Ashman and Jennifer Eaton Gökmen, 2006). This anthology compiles 29 personal stories from foreign women living in Turkey.

Turkish Odyssey (Serif Yenen, 1998). This handy guide to Turkish society and culture is comprehensive and beautifully illustrated.

Turkish Reflections (Mary Lee Settle, 1991). Mary Lee Settle recounts two visits to Turkey, 15 years apart.

The Turks Today (Andrew Mango, 2004). This sequel to *Atatürk* showcases a portrait of Turkey's recent development.

Fiction

The Bastard of Istanbul (Elif Shafak, 2006). A young Armenian girl living in Arizona secretly travels to Istanbul to find out more about her identity and cultural heritage.

Birds Without Wings (Louis de Bernières, 2004). Bernières depicts a village tragedy amid the fall of the Ottoman Empire.

The Black Book (Orhan Pamuk, 1990). After an Istanbul lawyer's wife disappears, he begins assuming the identity of her ex-husband.

Bliss (O. Z. Livaneli, 2002). After intense trauma, a young Turkish girl begins a journey of transformation in Istanbul.

Human Landscapes from My Country (Nazim Hikmet, 1966). This novel, written in verse, describes Hikmet's time in a Turkish prison during World War II.

Memed, My Hawk (Yashar Kemal, 1955). This is a dramatic tale of a bandit hero seeking justice in the Turkish countryside.

My Name is Red (Orhan Pamuk, 1998). A group of artists in 16th-century Istanbul are commissioned with a dangerous task resulting in a frightening mystery.

One for Sorrow (Mary Reed and Eric Mayer, 1999). The first of six mysteries set in a vividly Byzantine Constantinople follows the Lord Chamberlain of Emperor Justinian.

Portrait of a Turkish Family (Irfan Orga, 1950). A wealthy Ottoman family disintegrates at the end of the Ottoman Empire.

Snow (Orhan Pamuk, 2002). An exiled poet returns to Turkey and faces suspicion after making a controversial report.

Film

The Accidental Spy (2001). Parts of this Jackie Chan film take place in Istanbul, featuring many Turkish artists, actors, models, and stuntmen.

Crossing the Bridge: The Sound of Istanbul (2005). This documentary stands out for its fascinating musical portrait of modern Istanbul.

Distant (2002). A photographer and his unemployed cousin try to connect in snow-covered Istanbul in this award-winning film.

From Russia with Love (1963). Sean Connery sneaks around Istanbul as James Bond, with a great scene filmed inside the Underground Cistern.

Gallipoli (1981). Two Australian soldiers (including a very young Mel Gibson) fight in the Gallipoli campaign during World War I.

Hamam (Steam: The Turkish Bath) (1997). An Italian inherits a traditional public bath in Istanbul.

Istanbul (1957). Errol Flynn stars as a suspected diamond smuggler who returns to Istanbul and finds a woman he thought long dead.

Tinker Tailor Soldier Spy (2011). Parts of this Cold War drama take place in the heart of Istanbul.

Topkapi (1964). Peter Ustinov won an Oscar for his supporting role in this crime caper, worth seeing for its grand tour of 1960s Istanbul.

A Touch of Spice (2003). A Greek boy growing up in Istanbul learns about both food and life from his grandfather.

The Water Diviner (2014). An Australian man goes to Turkey after the Battle of Gallipoli in order to find his three missing sons.

The World Is Not Enough (1999). In this James Bond film, M is imprisoned in Istanbul's Maiden's Tower.

Yol (1982). Five political prisoners in Turkey struggle with readjusting to the outside world when they are given a week's home leave.

Books for Kids

Delilah Dirk and the Turkish Lieutenant (Tony Cliff, 2011). The first book in the Delilah Dirk series of graphic novels finds the Indiana Jones-esque heroine causing trouble in Constantinople.

Istanbul for Kids (Burçak Gürün Muraben, 2014). Adults and children alike can enjoy the stories and histories presented in this easy-to-read book.

The Road from Home: The Story of an Armenian Girl (David Kherdian, 1979). This non-fiction book chronicles the life of Kherdian's mother, who survived the Armenian Genocide as a girl.

The Stone of Destiny: Tales from Turkey (Elspeth Tavaci, 2012). A poor stonecutter journeys to Istanbul and must tell stories to stay alive.

T Is for Turkey (Nilufer Topaloglu Pyper, 2010). Turkey is showcased in each letter of the alphabet, illustrated by colorful photographs.

Turkish Delight: A Kid's Guide to Istanbul, Turkey (Penelope Dyan, 2011). Using poetry and photographs, this guide focuses on what children might find interesting in the city.

Conversions and Climate

NUMBERS AND STUMBLERS

- Europeans write a few of their numbers differently than Americans do. 1 = 1, 4 = 4, 7 = 7.
- In Europe, dates appear as day/month/year, so Christmas 2017 is 25/12/17.
- Commas are decimal points and decimals are commas. A dollar and a half is $1,50, one thousand is 1.000, and there are 5.280 feet in a mile.
- When counting with fingers, start with your thumb. If you hold up your first finger to request one item, you'll probably get two.
- What Americans call the second floor of a building is the first floor in Europe. The entrance level is generally called the *zemin* or *zemin kat* (zeh-meen kaht) in Turkey, and marked as "0" on elevators, or "L" (lobby) at hotels.
- On escalators and moving sidewalks, Europeans keep the left "lane" open for passing. Keep to the right.

METRIC CONVERSIONS

A kilogram is 2.2 pounds, and 1 liter is about a quart, or almost four liters to a gallon. A kilometer is six-tenths of a mile. We figure kilometers to miles by cutting them in half and adding back 10 percent of the original (120 km: 60 + 12 = 72 miles, 300 km: 150 + 30 = 180 miles).

1 foot = 0.3 meter	1 square yard = 0.8 square meter
1 yard = 0.9 meter	1 square mile = 2.6 square kilometers
1 mile = 1.6 kilometers	1 ounce = 28 grams
1 centimeter = 0.4 inch	1 quart = 0.95 liter
1 meter = 39.4 inches	1 kilogram = 2.2 pounds
1 kilometer = 0.62 mile	32°F = 0°C

Clothing Sizes

When shopping for clothing, use these US-to-European comparisons as general guidelines (but note that no conversion is perfect).
- Women's dresses and blouses: Add 30
  (US size 10 = European size 40)
- Men's suits and jackets: Add 10
  (US size 40 regular = European size 50)
- Men's shirts: Multiply by 2 and add about 8
  (US size 15 collar = European size 38)
- Women's shoes: Add about 30
  (US size 8 = European size 38-39)
- Men's shoes: Add 32-34
  (US size 9 = European size 41; US size 11 = European size 45)

TURKEY'S CLIMATE

First line, average daily high; second line, average daily low; third line, average days without rain. For more detailed weather statistics for destinations in this book (as well as the rest of the world), check www.wunderground.com.

J	F	M	A	M	J	J	A	S	O	N	D
48°	49°	53°	63°	70°	79°	82°	82°	77°	68°	60°	52°
35°	36°	39°	45°	53°	60°	65°	66°	60°	53°	45°	39°
13	14	17	21	23	24	27	27	23	20	16	13

APPENDIX

FAHRENHEIT AND CELSIUS CONVERSION

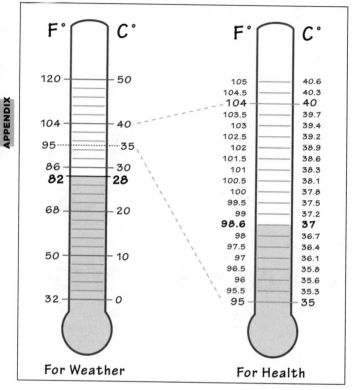

APPENDIX

Turkey takes its temperature using the Celsius scale, while we opt for Fahrenheit. For a rough conversion from Celsius to Fahrenheit, double the number and add 30. For weather, remember that 28°C is 82°F— perfect. For health, 37°C is just right. At a launderette, 30°C is cold, 40°C is warm (usually the default setting), 60°C is hot, and 95°C is boiling.

Packing Checklist

Whether you're traveling for five days or five weeks, you won't need more than this. Pack light to enjoy the sweet freedom of true mobility.

Clothing

- ❑ 5 shirts: long- & short-sleeve
- ❑ 2 pairs pants or skirt
- ❑ 1 pair shorts or capris
- ❑ 5 pairs underwear & socks
- ❑ 1 pair walking shoes
- ❑ Sweater or fleece top
- ❑ Rainproof jacket with hood
- ❑ Tie or scarf
- ❑ Swimsuit
- ❑ Sleepwear

Money

- ❑ Debit card
- ❑ Credit card(s)
- ❑ Hard cash ($20 bills)
- ❑ Money belt or neck wallet

Documents & Travel Info

- ❑ Passport
- ❑ Airline reservations
- ❑ Rail pass/train reservations
- ❑ Car-rental voucher
- ❑ Driver's license
- ❑ Student ID, hostel card, etc.
- ❑ Photocopies of all the above
- ❑ Hotel confirmations
- ❑ Insurance details
- ❑ Guidebooks & maps
- ❑ Notepad & pen
- ❑ Journal

Toiletries Kit

- ❑ Toiletries
- ❑ Medicines & vitamins
- ❑ First-aid kit
- ❑ Glasses/contacts/sunglasses (with prescriptions)
- ❑ Earplugs
- ❑ Packet of tissues (for WC)

Miscellaneous

- ❑ Daypack
- ❑ Sealable plastic baggies
- ❑ Laundry soap
- ❑ Spot remover
- ❑ Clothesline
- ❑ Sewing kit
- ❑ Travel alarm/watch

Electronics

- ❑ Smartphone or mobile phone
- ❑ Camera & related gear
- ❑ Tablet/ereader/media player
- ❑ Laptop & flash drive
- ❑ Earbuds or headphones
- ❑ Chargers
- ❑ Plug adapters

Optional Extras

- ❑ Flipflops or slippers
- ❑ Mini-umbrella or poncho
- ❑ Travel hairdryer
- ❑ Belt
- ❑ Hat (for sun or cold)
- ❑ Picnic supplies
- ❑ Water bottle
- ❑ Fold-up tote bag
- ❑ Small flashlight
- ❑ Small binoculars
- ❑ Insect repellent
- ❑ Small towel or washcloth
- ❑ Inflatable pillow
- ❑ Some duct tape (for repairs)
- ❑ Tiny lock
- ❑ Address list (to mail postcards)
- ❑ Postcards/photos from home
- ❑ Extra passport photos
- ❑ Good book

Turkish Survival Phrases

When using the phonetics, pronounce "ī" as the long "i" sound in "light"; "ew" as "oo" (with your lips pursed); and "g" as the hard "g" in "go."

English	Turkish	Pronunciation
Hello.	Merhaba.	mehr-hah-bah
Good day.	İyi günler.	ee-yee gewn-lehr
Good morning.	Günaydın.	gew-nī-duhn
Good evening.	İyi akşamlar.	ee-yee ahk-shahm-lahr
How are you?*	Nasılsınız?	nah-suhl-suh-nuhz
Do you speak English?	İngilizce biliyormusunuz?	een-gee-leez-jeh bee-lee-yohr-moo-soo-nooz
Yes. / No.	Evet. / Hayır.	eh-veht / hah-yur
I understand.	Anlıyorum.	ahn-luh-yoh-room
I don't understand.	Anlamıyorum.	ahn-lah-muh-yoh-room
Please.	Lütfen.	lewt-fehn
Thank you (very much).	Teşekkür (ederim).	teh-shehk-kewr (eh-deh-reem)
I'm sorry.	Üzgünüm.	ewz-gew-newm
Excuse me. (to pass)	Afedersiniz. / Pardon.	ah-feh-dehr-see-neez / pahr-dohn
No problem.	Sorun yok.	soh-roon yohk
There is a problem.	Sorun var.	soh-roon vahr
Good.	İyi.	ee-yee
Goodbye. (said by person leaving)	Hoşçakal.	hohsh-chah-kahl
Goodbye. (said by person staying)	Güle güle.	gew-leh gew-leh
one / two	bir / iki	beer / ee-kee
three / four	üç / dört	ewch / dirt
five / six	beş / altı	behsh / ahl-tuh
seven / eight	yedi / sekiz	yeh-dee / seh-keez
nine / ten	dokuz / on	doh-kooz / ohn
How much is it?	Ne kadar?	neh kah-dahr
Write it?	Yazarmısınız?	yah-zahr-muh-suh-nuhz
Is it free?	Ücretsizmi?	ewj-reht-seez-mee
Is it included?	Dahilmi?	dah-heel-mee
Where can I find...?	Nerede bulurum...?	neh-reh-deh boo-loo-room
Where can I buy...?	Nereden alabilirim...?	neh-reh-dehn ah-lah-bee-lee-reem
I'd like / We'd like...	İstiyorum / İstiyoruz...	ees-tee-yoh-room / ees-tee-yoh-rooz
...a room.	...oda.	oh-dah
...a ticket to ___.	...___'ya bilet.	___ yah bee-leht
Is it possible?	Olasımı?	oh-lah-suh-muh
Where is...?	...nerede?	neh-reh-deh
...the train station	Tren istasyonu...	trehn ees-tahs-yoh-noo
...the bus station	Otobüs durağı...	oh-toh-bews doo-rah-uh
...the tourist information office	Turizm enformasyon bürosu...	too-reezm ehn-fohr-mahs-yohn bew-roh-soo
...the toilet	Tuvalet...	too-vah-leht
men / women	bay / bayan	bī / bah-yahn
left / right	sol / sağ	sohl / saah
straight	doğru	doh-roo
What time does this open / close?	Ne zaman açılıyor / kapanıyor?	neh zah-mahn ah-chuh-luh-yohr / kah-pah-nuh-yohr
At what time?	Ne zaman?	neh zah-mahn
Just a moment.	Bir saniye.	beer sah-nee-yeh
now / soon / later	şimdi / birazdan / sonra	sheem-dee / bee-rahz-dahn / sohn-rah
today / tomorrow	bugün / yarın	boo-gewn / yah-ruhn

*People will answer you by saying, *"Teşekkür ederim"* (Thank you very much).

In a Turkish Restaurant

English	Turkish	Pronunciation
restaurant	lokanta / restaurant	loh-kahn-tah / rehs-toh-rahnt
I'd like / We'd like to make a reservation.	Rezervasyon yapmak istiyorum / istiyoruz.	reh-zehr-vahs-yohn yahp-mahk ee-stee-yoh-room / ees-tee-yoh-rooz
One / Two persons.	Bir / İki kişilik.	beer / ee-kee kee-shee-leek
Non-smoking.	Sigarasız.	see-gah-rah-suhz
Is this table free?	Bu masa boşmu?	boo mah-sah bohsh-moo
The menu (in English), please.	(İngilizce) menü lütfen.	een-ghee-leez-jeh meh-new lewt-fehn
tax included	KDV hariç	kah-deh-veh hah-reech
tax not included	KDV değil	kah-deh-veh deh-eel
service included	servis hariç	sehr-vees hah-reech
service not included	servis değil	sehr-vees deh-eel
"to go"	Paket	pah-keht
and / or	ve / veya	veh / veh-yah
menu	menü	meh-new
daily menu / meal of the day	günün menüsü / günün yemeği	gew-newn meh-new-sew / gew-newn yeh-meh-ee
portion / half-portion	porsiyon / yarım porsiyon	pohr-see-yohn / yah-ruhm pohr-see-yohn
daily special	günün spesyali	gew-newn spehs-yah-lee
appetizers	meze	meh-zeh
bread	ekmek	ehk-mehk
cheese	peynir	peh-neer
sandwich	sandöviç	sahn-doh-veech
soup	çorba	chohr-bah
salad	salata	sah-lah-tah
meat	et	eht
poultry	tavuk	tah-vook
fish	balık	bah-luhk
seafood	deniz ürünleri	deh-neez ew-rewn-leh-ree
fruit	meyve	mey-veh
vegetables	sebze	sehb-zeh
dessert	tatlı	taht-luh
water	su	soo
milk	süt	sewt
orange juice	portakal suyu	pohr-tah-kahl soo-yoo
coffee	kahve	kahh-veh
tea	çay	chī
wine	şarap	shah-rahp
red / white	kırmızı / beyaz	kuhr-muh-zuh / beh-yahz
beer	bira	bee-rah
glass / bottle	bardak / şişe	bahr-dahk / shee-sheh
big / small	büyük / küçük	bew-yewk / kew-chewk
Cheers!	Şerefe!	sheh-reh-feh
more / another	biraz daha / bir tane daha	bee-rahz dah-hah / beer tah-neh dah-hah
The same.	Aynısından.	ī-nuh-suhn-dahn
Bill, please.	Hesap, lütfen.	heh-sahp lewt-fehn
tip	bahşiş	bah-sheesh
Delicious!	Nefis!	neh-fees

INDEX

INDEX

MAP INDEX

Start your trip at

Our website enhances this book and turns

Explore Europe

At ricksteves.com you can browse through thousands of articles, videos, photos and radio interviews, plus find a wealth of money-saving travel tips for planning your dream trip. And with our mobile-friendly website, you can easily access all this great travel information anywhere you go.

TV Shows

Preview the places you'll visit by watching entire half-hour episodes of Rick Steves' Europe (choose from all 100 shows) on-demand, for free.

ricksteves.com

your travel dreams into affordable reality

Radio Interviews

Enjoy ready access to Rick's vast library of radio interviews covering travel

tips and cultural insights that relate specifically to your Europe travel plans.

Travel Forums

Learn, ask, share! Our online community of savvy travelers is a great resource for first-time travelers to Europe, as well as seasoned pros. You'll find forums on each country, plus travel tips and restaurant/hotel reviews. You can even ask one of our well-traveled staff to chime in with an opinion.

Travel News

Subscribe to our free Travel News e-newsletter, and get monthly updates from Rick on what's happening in Europe.

Audio Europe™

Rick's Free Travel App

Get your FREE **Rick Steves Audio Europe**™ app to enjoy…

- Dozens of self-guided tours of Europe's top museums, sights and historic walks

- Hundreds of tracks filled with cultural insights and sightseeing tips from Rick's radio interviews

- All organized into handy geographic playlists

- For iPhone, iPad, iPod Touch, Android

With Rick whispering in your ear, Europe gets even better.

Find out more at ricksteves.com

Pack Light and Right

Gear up for your next adventure at ricksteves.com

Light Luggage

Pack light and right with Rick Steves' affordable, custom-designed rolling carry-on bags, backpacks, day packs and shoulder bags.

Accessories

From packing cubes to moneybelts and beyond, Rick has personally selected the travel goodies that will help your trip go smoother.

Shop at ricksteves.com

Rick Steves has

Experience maximum Europe

Save time and energy

This guidebook is your independent-travel toolkit. But for all it delivers, it's still up to you to devote the time and energy it takes to manage the preparation and logistics that are essential for a happy trip. If that's a hassle, there's a solution.

Rick Steves Tours

A Rick Steves tour takes you to Europe's most interesting places with great

great tours, too!

with minimum stress

guides and small groups of 28 or less. We follow Rick's favorite itineraries, ride in comfy buses, stay in family-run hotels, and bring you intimately close to the Europe you've traveled so far to see. Most importantly, we take away the logistical headaches so you can focus on the fun.

customers—along with us on 40 different itineraries, from Ireland to Italy to Istanbul. Is a Rick Steves tour the right fit for your travel dreams? Find out at ricksteves.com, where you can also get Rick's latest tour catalog and free Tour Experience DVD.

Join the fun

This year we'll take 18,000 free-spirited travelers—nearly half of them repeat

Europe is best experienced with happy travel partners. We hope you can join us.

See our itineraries at ricksteves.com

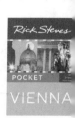

Maximize your travel skills with a good guidebook.

TRAVEL CULTURE

Europe 101
European Christmas
Postcards from Europe
Travel as a Political Act

eBOOKS

Nearly all Rick Steves guides are available as ebooks. Check with your favorite bookseller.

RICK STEVES' EUROPE DVDs

12 New Shows 2015-2016
Austria & the Alps
The Complete Collection 2000-2016
Eastern Europe
England & Wales
European Christmas
European Travel Skills & Specials
France
Germany, BeNeLux & More
Greece, Turkey & Portugal
The Holy Land: Israelis & Palestinians Today
Iran
Ireland & Scotland
Italy's Cities
Italy's Countryside
Scandinavia
Spain
Travel Extras

PHRASE BOOKS & DICTIONARIES

French
French, Italian & German
German
Italian
Portuguese
Spanish

PLANNING MAPS

Britain, Ireland & London
Europe
France & Paris
Germany, Austria & Switzerland
Ireland
Italy
Spain & Portugal

Photo © Patricia Feaster

RickSteves.com ⓕ ⓨ **@RickSteves**

Rick Steves books are available at bookstores
and through online booksellers.

Credits

CONTRIBUTOR
Cameron Hewitt

Cameron was born in Denver and grew up in central Ohio. The Polish nursery rhymes and gentle spirit of his grandfather, Jan Paweł Dąbrowski, instilled in him a deep affection for the Slavic world. After college, a backpacking trip reignited Cameron's interest in Eastern (ahem, "Central") Europe, and he's enjoyed annual trips to the region ever since. Since moving to Seattle and joining Rick Steves' Europe (where he serves as content manager) in 2000, Cameron has traveled to more than 35 European countries, contributing to guidebooks, tours, radio and television shows, and other media. Cameron married his high school sweetheart (and favorite travel partner), Shawna, and enjoys taking pictures, trying new restaurants, and planning his next trip.

Avalon Travel
a member of the Perseus Books Group
1700 Fourth Street
Berkeley, CA 94710

Text © 2016 by Rick Steves
Cover © 2016 by Avalon Travel. All rights reserved.
Maps © 2016 by Tankut Aran and Rick Steves' Europe
Printed in Canada by Friesens.
Seventh edition. First printing April 2016.

For the latest on Rick's lectures, guidebooks, tours, public radio show, and public
television series, contact Rick Steves' Europe, 130 Fourth Avenue North, Edmonds,
WA 98020, 425/771-8303, www.ricksteves.com, rick@ricksteves.com.

ISBN 978-1-63121-305-2
Seventh Edition
ISSN 1936-7112

Rick Steves' Europe
Special Publications Manager: Risa Laib
Managing Editor: Jennifer Madison Davis
Editors: Glenn Eriksen, Tom Griffin, Katherine Gustafson, Suzanne Kotz, Cathy Lu,
   Carrie Shepherd
Editorial & Production Assistant: Jessica Shaw
Editorial Intern: Chelsea Wing
Contributor: Cameron Hewitt
Maps & Graphics: David C. Hoerlein, Sandra Hundacker, Lauren Mills, Mary Rostad

Avalon Travel
Senior Editor and Series Manager: Madhu Prasher
Editor: Jamie Andrade
Associate Editor: Sierra Machado
Copy Editor: Patrick Collins
Proofreader: Patty Mon
Indexer: Beatrice Wikander
Production & Typesetting: Tabitha Lahr
Cover Design: Kimberly Glyder Design
Maps & Graphics: Kat Bennett, Mike Morgenfeld

Photo Credits
Front Cover Photo: Inner courtyard of Blue Mosque (Sultan Ahmet Camii) © Tim
   Gerard Barker
Title Page: Visiting Hagia Sophia © Dominic Arizona Bonuccelli
Additional Photography: Lale Surmen Aran, Tankut Aran, Dominic Arizona
   Bonuccelli, Cameron Hewitt, Rudi Nisargand, Rhonda Pelikan, Carol Ries, Rick
   Steves, Gretchen Strauch, Laura VanDeventer, Wikimedia Commons (PD-Art/
   PD-US). Photos are used by permission and are the property of the original copy-
   right owners.

More for your trip!
Maximize the experience with Rick Steves as your guide